Poverty in the Theology
of John Calvin

Princeton Theological Monograph Series

K. C. Hanson, Series Editor

Recent volumes in the series

Anette Ejsing
*Theology of Anticipation:
A Constructive Study of C. S. Peirce*

Michael G. Cartwright
*Practices, Politics, and Performance:
Toward a Communal Hermeneutic for Christian Ethics*

Stephen Finlan and Vladimir Kharlamov, editors
Theōsis: Deification in Christian Theology

John A. Vissers
The Neo-Orthodox Theology of W. W. Bryden

Sam Hamstra, editor
The Reformed Pastor by John Williamson Nevin

Byron C. Bangert
*Consenting to God and Nature:
Toward a Theocentric, Naturalistic, Theological Ethics*

Richard Valantasis et al., editors
The Subjective Eye: Essays in Honor of Margaret Miles

Caryn Riswold
Coram Deo: Human Life in the Vision of God

Paul O. Ingram, editor
Constructing a Relational Cosmology

Poverty in the Theology of John Calvin

Bonnie L. Pattison

Pickwick *Publications*
An imprint of *Wipf and Stock Publishers*
199 West 8th Avenue • Eugene OR 97401

POVERTY IN THE THEOLOGY OF JOHN CALVIN
Princeton Theological Monograph Series 69

Copyright © 2006 Bonnie Pattison. All rights reserved. Except for brief quotations in critical publications or reviews, no part of this book may be reproduced in any manner without prior written permission from the publisher. Write: Permissions, Wipf & Stock, 199 W. 8th Ave., Eugene, OR 97401.

Revised Standard Version of the Bible, copyright 1952 [2nd edition, 1971] by the Division of Christian Education of the National Council of the Churches of Christ in the United States of America. Used by permission. All rights reserved.

ISBN 10: 1-59752-691-6
ISBN 13: 978-1-59752-691-3

Cataloging-in-Publication data:

Pattison, Bonnie L.
    Poverty in the theology of John Calvin / Bonnie L. Pattison.

Princeton Theological Monograph Series 69

xii + 380 p. ; 23 cm.

Includes bibliography

ISBN 10: 1-59752-691-6
ISBN 13: 978-1-59752-691-3

1. Calvin, Jean, 1509–1564. 2. Poverty—History. 3. Poverty—Religious aspects—Christianity—History of doctrines. 4. Theology, Doctrinal History Early church, ca. 30–600. 5. Theology, Doctrinal History Middle Ages, 600–1500. I. Title. II. Series.

BX9418 P375 2006

Manufactured in the U.S.A.

*To Stewart,
Julia, Brandon, and William*

Contents

Acknowledgements / ix
Abbreviations / xi
Introduction / 1

PART I
Spiritual and Physical Poverty in the Theology
of the Church from the Patristics to the Reformation

1 Introduction to Part I / 11

2 Poverty in the Thought of the Church Fathers / 17

3 Poverty in the Thought of the Middle Ages / 39

4 Poverty in the Thought of the Reformers / 81

5 Religious Poverty and Stewardship in
the Thought of John Calvin / 123

PART II
Spiritual and Physical Poverty in Calvin's Theology

6 Introduction to Part II / 145

7 Poverty and Calvin's Christology / 151

8 Poverty in Calvin's Doctrine of the Christian Life / 189

9 Poverty and Affliction in Calvin's Ecclesiology / 225

10 Poverty and Wealth in Calvin's Ecclesiology / 283

Summary and Conclusion / 347
Bibliography / 355

Acknowledgements

BECAUSE this book began as my doctoral dissertation at Princeton Theological Seminary in 1997, I owe a very great debt of gratitude to my faculty advisor, Dr. David Willis, who led me to research Calvin's theological understanding of poverty. I am grateful for his inspiration, direction, and advice along the way. Due to his guidance, this topic has given me a profound understanding of the cross and respect for the thought of John Calvin. There are a number of people to whom I owe my thanks who were involved many years ago during the dissertation phase. I am grateful to Dr. Elsie McKee for her careful reading of my drafts, numerous suggestions for its improvements, and attentive editing of my Old French translations. She has been and continues to be an inspiration as a person and scholar. I extend a special thanks to the Henry H. Meeter Center for Calvin Studies at Calvin College for its Student Research Scholarship, and to Dr. Richard Gamble, Paul Fields, and Susan Schmurr for all their support and willingness to accommodate my schedule. I am appreciative of Lavone Holt who faithfully read and edited early drafts of this work and for the suggestions of Jane Prugh.

In the course of preparing this research for publication, I have made numerous revisions and have written an additional chapter. As a result, there are many people here at Wheaton that I owe my deep appreciation. I am especially indebted to Emily Welch, who tirelessly edited my final drafts. I owe Jim Crile, my graduate T. A., and his wife, Rachelle, my full gratitude for all their late nights and careful proofreading. Emily, Jim, and Rachelle all went the extra mile. In addition, I wish to extend a special note of thanks to Charlie Collier at Wipf and Stock Publishers, who has spent endless hours preparing this manuscript for publication. He brought this whole project to completion.

The burden of this book, however, has been shouldered by those who are closest to me. The words "thank you" seem inadequate for the personal sacrifice of my family members. My mother, Arlene Goding, and mother-in-law, Myrna Pattison, provided care for my children when I could not.

Acknowledgements

This project would never have been completed without their generosity and selflessness. I thank my children Julia, Brandon, and William for the joy they bring me every day. Finally, I am above all grateful to my husband, Stewart, who, in addition to maintaining the demanding duties of a senior pastor, always supported and encouraged me without complaint. Without his continual personal sacrifices and servant-hood, this work would never have been completed.

Abbreviations

BOL Bucer, *Martini Bvceri Opera Latina*
CO   Calvin, *Opera quae supersunt omnia*
CR   *Corpus Reformatorum*
LW   Luther, *Luther's Works*
OS   Calvin, *Opera Selecta*
PG   Migne, *Patrologia graeca* [=*Patrologiae cursus completus: Series graeca*]
PL   Migne, *Patrologia latina* [=*Patrologiae cursus completus: Series latina*]
RSV *Revised Standard Version of the Holy Bible*
WA   Luther, *D. Martin Luthers Werke*, Weimar Ausgabe
ZW   Zwingli, *Huldreich Zwingli's Werke*

Introduction

JOHN Calvin was one of several Reformers who challenged the Roman Church's understanding of poverty. During the Reformation, the practice of taking clerical and monastic vows was rejected, able-bodied vagrants were exhorted to work, and the poor were no longer seen as virtuous or to be indulged by the rich in order to gain eternal security. As one historian states, "Poverty or rather the poor were not despised," yet most importantly, they "were no longer idealized."[1] As a leader of the Protestant Reformation, John Calvin shared this view which separated poverty from the virtue attached to it. This change of attitude prompted some, like Philip Mulhern, to conclude:

> Religious poverty received relatively little direct and immediate attention from the leaders of the Protestant Reformation. While the religious life itself was the object of their concern and interest and was the subject of some reformation writings, poverty was given minimal consideration.[2]

Mulhern's statement immediately precedes his discussion of Luther and Calvin's positions on religious poverty. It is true that Calvin and Luther rejected the practice of "religious poverty,"[3] and this is probably why they gave it minimal consideration in their writings. But does this mean that the reformers neglected the *topic* of poverty, both spiritual and physical, altogether in their writings? More significantly for this study, did Calvin

---

[1] Heller, *Conquest of Poverty*, 138.
[2] Mulhern, *Dedicated Poverty*, 133.
[3] In 1521, Luther wrote the treatise entitled *De votis monasticis Martini Lutheri juicium* attacking monastic vows. See Biot, *Rise of Protestant Monasticism*, 12. Calvin never wrote a treatise like Luther's *De votis monasticis*, and early editions of the *Institutes* failed to discuss the nature of religious life altogether. However, by the third Latin edition of 1543, Calvin wrote a significant passage on the subject of religious life by addressing the topic of vows in *Institutes* 4.13.1–21 (Battles 1254–76); *OS* 5, 238.1–258.32. See also Steinmetz, "Calvin and the Monastic Ideal," 605–16; and Yule, "Luther and the Ascetic Life," 229–39.

devote "minimal consideration" to these matters? Is it true that Calvin gave the topic, in Mulhern's words, "little direct . . . attention"?

It is important to remember that Calvin was born a French Catholic who became interested in the reform of the Church. Parker states:

> [Calvin's] early training never deserted him; always he was to think within the framework of the ideas of the school men, and though it was to the Fathers that he turned for an exposition of the faith, the Middle Ages are always present, only just hidden in the *Institutes*. But, for the rest, when time came, he was to educate himself in theology.[4]

Applying Parker's statement to the subject of poverty, a prominent feature of Roman doctrine from the Patristics through the medieval period of the Church, it is reasonable to question whether Calvin's thought and writings are devoid of a theological perspective on poverty. It is true that Calvin rejected the Roman Catholic teachings surrounding the practice of religious poverty which had become the primary interpretation of living a devout Christian life. But did he also negate the theological significance of poverty? If not, what part do poverty and the poor have in Calvin's theology? Does he relate this issue to his Christology, the nature of the Christian life, and the Church?

Research on Calvin and Poverty

In recent years, a growing number of historical and theological studies on Calvin's social and economic thought have been written, as well as numerous studies on the ministry of the Genevan Church to the poor.[5] Most of these inquiries have approached the topic of Calvin, Geneva, and the poor from the standpoints of history, Calvin's ethics, or his practical theology. Despite the necessity and quality of these works, a void remains regarding Calvin's *theological* understanding of the concept of poverty. This lack is

[4] Parker, *Portrait of Calvin*, 16.

[5] A good representative selection of some of the works in this area are as follows: Biéler, *Pensée Économique*; Biéler, *Social Humanism*; Douglass, "Calvin's Relation"; Graham, *Constructive Revolutionary*; Gilbreath, "Luther and Calvin on Property"; Innes, *Social Concern*; Henderson, "Sixteenth Century Community Benevolence"; Kingdon, "Social Welfare in Calvin's Geneva"; Kingdon, "Deacons of the Reformed Church"; Kingdon, "Calvin's Ideas about the Diaconate"; Kramer, "Calvins Einstellung zur Armut," in *Umgang mit der Armut*, 32–34; Olson, *Calvin and Social Welfare*; McKee, *Calvin on the Diaconate*; Scholl, "Church and the Poor"; Schulze, *Calvin and 'Social Ethics'*; Schulze, "Calvin on Interest and Property"; Stone, "Reformed Economic Ethics"; Wallace, *Calvin, Geneva*; Woudstra, "Calvin's Concern."

Introduction

not limited to Calvin studies. The void characterizes much of Reformation studies. The scarcity of *theological* research on the Reformers' understandings of poverty is notable. The majority of the existing studies are historical and/or ethical studies pertaining to various Reformers' views of ministering to the needs of the poor.[6] Outside Calvin, the Reformation figure that has received the most attention in this area is Luther.[7] Lee Brummel has investigated Luther's exegetical treatment of the biblical language and theology of poverty,[8] and a few others have examined the views of Luther and Calvin on monasticism.[9] This demonstrates that most of the scholarship done on Reformation views of poverty center around historical and logistical issues of poor relief, a city's social welfare plan, or a particular Reformer's ethical stance towards these things. Very little research has been undertaken to learn how particular Reformers' theological beliefs concerning poverty and the poor engaged their Christology, doctrine of the Christian life, and ecclesiology.

On the other hand, Catholic scholarship has proved the most prolific where the topic of poverty is concerned, and these studies are far too numerous to list here. From the Apostolic Fathers through the Middle Ages, a theological understanding of poverty was well integrated into Catholic doctrine. This may be one reason why a theological examination of poverty has been a neglected locus of Reformation research. Nevertheless, due to the studies already done on Calvin's ethics of wealth, the Genevan church's ministry to the refugees fleeing religious persecution, and its exemplary care for the poor, it is time to examine the notion of spiritual and physical poverty in Calvin's theology.

There is one additional point that needs further clarification concerning a theology of poverty. When speaking of poverty in the theology of the church, it is important to understand that Scripture and the writings of the Church are inclusive of the two kinds of poverty. The first kind of

---

[6] Wandel, *Always Among Us*; Nottingham, "Social Ethics"; Scholl, "Church and the Poor"; Kramer, "Zwinglis Stellung zur Armut," in *Umgang mit der Armut*, 34–37.

[7] There are numerous studies by Carter Lindberg and others on Luther's ethic in regards to the poor: See Lindberg, "Luther on Property and Poverty;" Lindberg, "Reformation Initiatives"; Lindberg, "There Should be no Beggars"; Lindberg, "Through a Glass Darkly"; Lindberg, *Beyond Charity*; Hordern, "Luther's Attitude Towards Poverty"; Gilbreath, "Luther and Calvin on Property"; and Kramer, "Luthers Stellung zur Armutsfrage," in *Umgang mit der Armut*, 25–32.

[8] See Brummel, "Biblical Language of Poverty"; and Brummel, "Luther on Poverty and the Poor."

[9] Steinmetz, "Monastic Ideal"; Biot, *Rise of Protestant Monasticism*; Yule, "Luther and the Acetic life."

3

poverty is a poverty of a spiritual nature, and the second is physical poverty or affliction. Since spiritual and physical poverty do not always appear as distinct concepts easily distinguished in Scripture, Christian thought on this subject has also manifested a great deal of ambiguity. Therefore, when approaching Calvin's theological understanding of poverty, it is important to note that both spiritual and physical poverty[10] hold theological significance in Calvin's thought. Thus, the phrase "concept of poverty" is meant to function as an overarching category that includes these two types of poverty.

Thesis

Just because theological reflection on poverty has been a neglected topic in Reformation research does not mean that scholars like Calvin lacked a profound doctrinal understanding of it. Calvin saw himself as a reformer of the *Catholic* faith. He knew the Fathers, the Church's tradition, and the witness of Scripture well. This study will show that an understanding of poverty, both spiritual and physical, is essential for grasping how Calvin understood the gospel. Examining Calvin's thought on poverty will also reveal how thoroughly Luther's theology of the cross affected Calvin's thought. It is the thesis of this study that in Calvin's theology, poverty and affliction—not splendor and glory—mark and manifest the kingdom of God on earth. Poverty makes the kingdom visible to the eyes and therefore recognizable as divine. Poverty acts to reveal or disclose that which is spiritual, or that which is "of God" in the Christian faith. This does not mean that Calvin sees the condition of physical poverty as revelatory in and of itself. Rather, poverty and affliction function as agents of divine revelation. They are a condition or a chosen instrument God uses to disclose to humanity the nature of true spirituality, godliness, and poverty of spirit. How this is demonstrated in Calvin's thought depends upon the specific doctrine under examination. This study explores three particular areas in Calvin's theology where his theological understanding of spiritual poverty and physical poverty (or affliction) intersect; these are his Christology, his doctrine of the Christian life, and his ecclesiology.

This study will demonstrate that there is a logical progression in Calvin's thought on poverty. Calvin's Christology is fundamental to his thought on poverty. The manner in which poverty and affliction reveal that which is spiritual are fundamentally rooted in Calvin's Christology. He recognizes that physical and spiritual poverty intersect in Christ. This

[10] See Minnema, "Calvin's Interpretation."

notion lays the groundwork for not only the character of the kingdom but also that of the Christian life and life of the Church.

Outline of this Study

This study will be divided into two parts. The purpose of Part I is to create a sense of the significance poverty had for the Church in the centuries preceding Calvin. The objective of these opening chapters is two-fold: First, to show that there is no single authoritative position that dominates the Church's history of the interpretation of poverty from the time of the patristic writers and on through the Middle Ages as well as in the Reformation. Second, to demonstrate that the diverse range of historical opinion on poverty is strongly connected to how well the Church was open to reform and living an authentic spirituality. It will be shown that the multifarious interpretations of the poverty of Christ and its significance for the Christian life and the Church is largely delineated by the way the Scriptures were (or were not) brought to bear on the ever shifting cultural, social, and historical circumstances of the Church.

Part I consists of five chapters that sketch an historical context for Calvin's theological ideas on poverty. Chapter 1 introduces Part I and addresses some of the scholarly challenges in the study of poverty. Chapter 2 will briefly survey select writings of four Church Fathers and their interpretation of poverty: those of Clement of Alexandria, Cyprian, Chrysostom, and Augustine. Because Calvin regularly cites the "ancient Fathers of the Church" when arguing particular points of historical theology, and since he integrates Patristic writings into his theological thought as no other reformer of his day,[11] this chapter will be devoted to a select group of Fathers who wrote on poverty and whom Calvin read. Chapter 3 will focus on the cultural and theological development of poverty throughout the Middle Ages. It will examine Western thought on poverty from the standpoints of vocabulary, major thinkers, conflicts, and movements. This chapter will demonstrate how a theological understanding of the poor and poverty was embedded in Rome's ecclesiology, soteriology, and doctrine of the Christian life. Chapter 4 looks at the shift in thinking regarding the poor and poverty during the Reformation and how Luther, Zwingli, Melanchthon, and Bucer theologically approached it. Being a second generation reformer, Calvin had the privilege of benefiting from the work of these men. Chapter 5 examines Calvin's thought on the right use of this world. It will demonstrate that Calvin's ecclesiology guides his critique of

---

[11] See Todd, "Function of the Patristic Writings," 170.

monasticism and his view of stewardship. It will show that stewardship, for Calvin, is a significant component of worship which finds its purpose in meeting the needs of the poor.

Part II is the core of this project. Its five chapters examine Calvin's understanding of poverty in light of specific doctrines. Though Calvin's theological interpretation of poverty is highly nuanced, at a fundamental level it is straightforward in the way that it always proceeds from his Christology. Because physical and spiritual poverty are joined in Christ, for Calvin, they are almost always associated with each other in his understanding of the Christian life and the Church. Chapter 6 introduces Part II and highlights a number of key distinctions in Calvin's theology. Chapter 7 will show that wherever Calvin speaks about Christ's affliction, or his lack of pomp, wealth, and display, he also discusses the nature of Christ's kingship. For Calvin, Christ's poverty and affliction always emphasize that Christ's kingship is spiritual and thus becomes a distinguishing mark of his kingdom. Furthermore, the reality of Christ's physical poverty is inextricably bound up with his poverty of spirit. Because Calvin's doctrine of the Christian life and ecclesiology are rooted in his Christology, the significance of this observation has numerous ramifications that can be traced throughout these doctrines.

In Chapter 8, it will be shown that Christ's poverty most noticeably impacts Calvin's understanding of the Christian life when he discusses what it means for the believer to "bear the cross." To "bear the cross" in the Christian life specifically pertains to the way in which a believer endures the experience of poverty and affliction. This idea is synonymous with what Calvin calls the "mortification of the outward man." The thesis of chapter 8 is that Calvin regards the experience of poverty and affliction as having been consecrated in the life and death of Christ in such a way that it can become an instrument of divine grace and blessing for the believer. This is made possible because hardships create opportunities for a knowledge of God's glory to be revealed to the believer. Adversity reveals God's glory in a way that is otherwise concealed when poverty and affliction are absent. In addition to occasioning a knowledge of God's glory, the experience of affliction, or "bearing the cross," also brings a knowledge of one's own spiritual poverty, which should foster humility in the believer. Furthermore, Calvin also teaches that when poverty and affliction are viewed with eyes of faith, the experience reveals a knowledge of God. The parallels between affliction in the believer's life and Calvin's understanding of the way the law functions in the Christian life will also become apparent. As one will see, the reason for these parallels stems from a deep theological connection

Introduction

between Christ's relationship to the law and the notion of poverty, in addition to the way that the cross functions in Calvin's theology.

The thesis that poverty and affliction disclose that which is spiritual is also manifest in Calvin's ecclesiology. Chapter 9 demonstrates this thesis in several ways. First, it shows that the affliction of the Church reveals the judgments of God. Through poverty and suffering, the people of God become awakened to their sin and upon repentance find renewal in their spiritual life. Affliction results in the purification of the Church, which in turn brings the Church to testify to God's power and thus mark herself as the true Church of God. This chapter proves that Calvin's understanding of a poor and suffering Church is no small part of his ecclesiology: he believes that as the Church follows Christ, suffering, poverty, and affliction are at the heart of its divinely ordained purpose as long as it continues in this world. Finally, this chapter examines Calvin's understanding of the nature of the Church. He establishes poverty and affliction as a primary expression of the true nature of the Church.

Chapter 10 examines what Calvin says about wealth and poverty in relationship to the worship of the Church. Calvin upholds the revelatory quality of poverty regarding true spirituality by maintaining that the Church and its worship need to be simple. When Calvin speaks of simplicity, he means that worship must be void of pomp, lacking in display of wealth and magnificent ceremony so that the spiritual nature of the gospel is not obscured but is instead revealed. Furthermore, because the worship of the Church is spiritual, her true splendor consists in being spiritual and not in elaborate physical ornamentation. Because Calvin understands the spiritual nature of the Church's worship, he advocates for a kind of simplicity of life, or what he calls "moderation," which Christ and the ancient Church Fathers modeled to be practiced among the clergy. In this way, the resources of the Church can be used for true spiritual worship of the Church, which is expressed in caring for the needs of the physically impoverished.

Part I

Spiritual and Physical Poverty in the Theology of the Church from the Patristics to the Reformation

1

Introduction to Part I

Clarifications in the Study of Poverty

A number of clarifications must be made at the outset of this study. First, this section will not focus upon the reality or the experience of physical poverty in the patristic or Middle Ages as judged by the economic, social, and historical tools of the twentieth century. Rather, it will focus upon the perception of physical poverty and its impact on poverty of spirit during the patristic or Middle Ages and how these concepts functioned culturally, religiously, and theologically. Second, these chapters will present information on the reality or experience of physical poverty only as it influences the basic components and ambiguities of the perception and understanding of the notion of poverty at a particular time. Since every major city in Europe had numerous beggars and poor, Calvin indeed encountered the reality or experience of physical poverty in his day. Yet it is through reading that Calvin experienced the range of perceptions toward physical and spiritual poverty throughout the centuries as they were articulated in the writings of the Church, especially as they were expressed by the Fathers. Therefore, perception of poverty as a whole, particularly the theological significance attached to the development of the perception of physical and spiritual poverty over the centuries is of primary importance for understanding and appreciating Calvin's range of thought on this issue.

Historical Problems Facing the Study of Poverty

Historians face a number of unique problems when trying to analyze the question of poverty. Because some of these problems influence this study, they need to be delineated. The first problem is the overwhelming number of sources on the topic of religious or voluntary poverty throughout the history of the Church. These have dominated the pages of history and most scholars' understanding of poverty in the patristic and Middle Ages. Those who took vows of poverty voluntarily were, by definition, not impoverished involuntarily. These individuals were usually the landless sons of noblemen who could retain their social location by serving the Church. Because these men did not come from the struggling classes, their literary legacy and practice of voluntary poverty are hardly representative of the masses who were physically and involuntarily impoverished. This abundance of literature affected the perception of poverty for centuries throughout the Middle Ages.

The Lack of Sources on Involuntary Poverty

The second problem is the paucity of sources, records, and documents concerning those who were involuntarily poor in the patristic or Middle Ages.[1] Mollat laments that no specific sources on physical poverty in the Middle Ages exist. This is because "the poor have never had a say; they have always played a minor role, [and] they have left no records."[2] To put this scarcity of sources into perspective, Carter Lindberg turns to a 1986 article in the Boston Globe which discusses the difficulty of obtaining an accurate census count of the homeless in the city of Boston, not to mention the reports of the politically influenced and controversial statistics on the poor in America.[3] This observation raises an important question: If it is so difficult to get hard data on the poor in our day, then how much more difficult is it for the historian to obtain information on this social group 500 to 1800 years ago? This realization is significant for this study on Calvin. It suggests that any good understanding of involuntary poverty or its social or political causes in the Middle Ages or during the times of the Church Fathers was historically inaccessible to Calvin except in its broader outlines.[4] This statement, of course, is not entirely true for the

---

[1] See Murray's comments in "Religion Among the Poor," 285; especially notes 1–4.

[2] Mollat, "Poor in the Middle Ages," 29. Though Mollat's work does not take into consideration the patristic age, it is probably safe to assume that the amount of sources available on the poor in the Church's early centuries is as scarce or more scarce than they are in the Middle Ages.

[3] See Lindberg, "Reformation Initiatives," 85, for Boston Globe citation.

[4] For example, Todd relates that though Calvin's understanding of the patristic writings was exceptional for his day, there is little evidence for his knowledge of the social and political forces, which were at work in the ancient Church. This observation would be especially true concerning the topic of economic forces and poverty. See Todd, "Function

sixteenth century into which Calvin was born. Calvin was no doubt an eyewitness to the impoverished class in Paris as a student. Furthermore, he experienced the displacement of thousands of French who fled persecution in their homeland for Geneva and Strasbourg.

The Relative Nature of Poverty

The third problem is the relative nature of the notion of poverty, which exists in varying degrees and has particular thresholds at various times in history. "One is always more or less poor than someone else."[5] Its relative nature introduces a great deal of latitude in the use of the term.[6] The state of poverty could be applied to someone who has crossed one of several thresholds: economic, biological, or social, and these thresholds were only vaguely understood at the end of the Middle Ages.[7]

Biologically speaking, people could be afflicted by disease, injury, age, or handicap, causing them to be dependent on others and unable to work. Economically, they could be afflicted with the inability to obtain or provide enough resources (food, clothing, and shelter) for themselves or their family's existence. The social dimension of poverty is described as either being deprived of one's instruments of labor or social position, or suffering of a loss of status. This result occurs when a person lacks the ability to obtain the necessary capital to function and support himself or herself. For a merchant, this is the loss of his shop; a young girl—her dowry; a farmer—his plow, animals, or seed; for a scholar—his books; or a nobleman—the loss of his armor or horse. Though all these are economic losses, Mollat argues that they are social impoverishments as well. Such losses prevent people from participating in their social existence and hence exclude them from participating in their community.[8]

The biological, economic, and social thresholds of poverty generally apply to those who are involuntarily impoverished. But the relative nature of poverty applies to the dimension of spiritual poverty and voluntarily poor as well. Through the centuries, the interpretation of poverty by Fathers like Chrysostom and Augustine, as well as by the Merovingian bishops, the ninth-century monastic movement, the eleventh-century hermits, and the thirteenth-century friars, not to mention the majority of

---

of the Patristic Writings," 172.

[5] Mollat, "Poor in the Middle Ages," 32.

[6] Murray, "Religion Among the Poor," 291.

[7] Mollat, "Poor in the Middle Ages," 32–33; Mollat, *Poor in the Middle Ages*, 5.

[8] Mollat, *Poor in the Middle Ages*, 5–6.

heretical movements, all differed in the way they understood the practice of religious poverty and interpreted its impact on the poverty of spirit. The conditional and relative nature of their ideas depended on the particular configuration of the current society and the need for reform in the Church. It will be shown that Calvin himself cannot escape the relative nature of poverty. The Church and society in his day had different needs than they had in the fourth, ninth, eleventh, or thirteenth centuries. Hence, Calvin's perception of poverty and his assessment of its ecclesiastical value look different than they did in preceding centuries.

The Ambiguity of Poverty

Finally, a problem that is especially germane to this study is the high degree of ambiguity connected with the meaning, use, and application of the word "poverty."[9] This problem is related to the problems of historical scholarship mentioned above. First, there is a significant degree of ambiguity for scholars due to the overwhelming number of sources on the voluntarily poor and the corresponding lack of information on the involuntarily poor. Second, much cultural and theological development occurred during and since the time of the Church Fathers and on through the Middle Ages. This development included variations in the understanding of physical and spiritual poverty as well. Many who would not have been considered physically "poor" in the tenth-century were considered "poor" by the fourteenth. Third, at times the variations in the meaning and application of poverty appear conflicting and even contradictory. With the huge wave of impoverished masses that swept Europe at the ends of the eleventh, twelfth, thirteenth, and fourteenth centuries, people asked whether physical poverty was a blessing or a curse. Was it sanctifying or sinful? Was it a state of virtue to be honored and revered and a means toward a life of spiritual perfection? Or was it a scourge and result of divine judgment?[10] These conflicting evaluations and variations in interpretation did not always fall neatly along the lines of voluntary *versus* involuntary poverty. The most notable conflicts over a religious understanding of poverty occurred in the late thirteenth to early fourteenth century, commonly known as the Mendicant Controversy and the controversy over *usus pauper*.[11] Yet

---

[9] Ibid., 8–9. Many of the following points are made also by Lindberg in *Beyond Charity*, 17–22.

[10] Mollat, "En guise de Préface," 13; See also Mollat, *Poor in the Middle Ages*, 9.

[11] See Burr, *Olivi and Franciscan Poverty*, and his essay "Poverty as a Constituent Element," 71–78.

the reason why physical poverty, involuntary and voluntary, has faced a good deal of confusion in its cultural and religious understanding is that Scripture is ambiguous concerning the relationship between physical poverty and poverty of spirit. After years of research Mollat concludes, "The problem of poverty is complex and ambiguous and does not lend itself to simplification."[12] Therefore, for this study, the reader must recognize the high degree of ambiguity involved in approaching the topic of poverty in the patristic and Middle Ages. Therefore it is both an historical and a theological problem.

A Definition of Poverty in the Ancient Church and Middle Ages

After the above delineation of the problems and challenges inherent in the historical and theological study of poverty, the idea of a definition of poverty seems fanciful. Nonetheless, it is a necessary step in order to aid the process of clarification. The definition of poverty offered here is not Calvin's. Rather, it is a working definition of the state or condition of poverty in the patristic or Middle Ages in its broadest use and application. An overarching definition of poverty from research on Western Europe that predates Calvin is necessary in order to set a context for a study of Calvin's ideas on the topic.

Michel Mollat describes physical poverty as "a state of weakness, dependency or humiliation" in which someone lives, either on a "temporary or permanent" basis which is "characterized by a privation of means, power, social esteem (which varies with time and place)."[13] This situation may include a lack of "money, relations, influence, power, knowledge, skill, nobility of birth, physical strength, intellectual capacity, personal freedom and dignity."[14] Mollat points out that the above definition is broad enough to include the two most important distinctions or categories of the physically "poor" in the West: Those who assumed poverty voluntarily and those who did not.

---

[12] Mollat, *Poor in the Middle Ages*, 11.

[13] Mollat, "Poverty and the Service of the Poor," 47; *Poor in the Middle Ages*, 5; "Poor in the Middle Ages," 31–32; "En guise de Préface," 12; see also Lindberg, *Beyond Charity*, 22.

[14] Mollat, *Poor in the Middle Ages*, 5; Mollat's definition comes exclusively from his study of the Middle Ages. Because of its broad nature it is the choice of this author to extend it to the patristic age as well.

Though Mollat intended the above definition to be applied to poor physical conditions in which people lived, similar language can be used to describe the other kind of poverty which the ancient Church and Middle Ages were occupied, that is, spiritual poverty. Spiritual poverty may be described as a condition of weakness, dependency, or humiliation which someone chooses to manifest in their life before God. It is a person's recognition of the spiritual condition he or she shares with all humanity and is also "characterized by a privation of means, power"[15] and ability to change an individual's spiritual situation. Though all humanity is spiritually poor in that all people are sinful and unable to change their situation, only those who recognize their spiritual lack and dependency upon God are said to have *spiritual* poverty.

The above definitions bring some clarity to the relative and ambiguous nature of poverty, voluntary and involuntary, physical and spiritual. Part I of this study will take a cursory look at three important times in Church history that set the historical background for a study of Calvin and his thought on poverty. It will pay special attention to the issue of how physical poverty, both involuntary and voluntary, was theologically and culturally joined to the idea of spiritual poverty in the centuries up to and including the time of Calvin.

---

[15] Mollat, "Poverty and the Service of the Poor," 47.

2

Poverty in the Thought of the Church Fathers

Poverty in the Ancient Church

The Importance of the Church Fathers for Understanding Calvin's Thought on Poverty

IF one takes a glance at the "Author and Source Index" at the back of the second volume of Battles' translation of the *Institutes*, it will reveal the breadth of Calvin's familiarity with the Patristics.[1] According to Todd, Calvin's "knowledge of Fathers, councils and history of antiquity was outstanding for his day."[2] He claims that there was no other Reformer who made "the Fathers a natural part of his entire theological system and of his exegetical studies" as did Calvin.[3] This means that the Fathers are an appropriate starting point for understanding the background to Calvin's thought on poverty as well as grasping the roots of the Medieval culture and interpretation on this issue.[4]

---

[1] See *Institutes*, "Author and Source Index" (Battles, 1592–1634).
[2] Todd, "Function of the Patristic Writings," 169.
[3] Ibid., 170. Todd points out that there were those humanists and Catholics who could rival Calvin in their knowledge of the Fathers, but none who incorporated them so thoroughly into their theological system as did Calvin. See 169–70.
[4] After acknowledging the monograph on Calvin and Augustine by Luchesius Smits, and the studies by Walchenbach and Meijering, David Steinmetz comments that "very little has been done to illuminate the relationship of Calvin to the exegetical tradition of the early church." See Steinmetz, "Calvin and the Patristic Exegesis of Paul," 100. Also, Smits, *Saint Augustin*; Meijering, *Calvin wider die Neugirde*; and Walchenbach, "John Calvin as Biblical Commentator."

There are a few significant patterns in Calvin's use of the Fathers that should be noted at the outset of this chapter. Calvin's works are void of any reference to the Apostolic Fathers and possess few citations from the Apologists.[5] Furthermore, Calvin was largely unacquainted with the Greek Fathers prior to Chrysostom with the exception of a few writings by Eusebius (b.263–d.339?) and Origen (b.185?–d.254?),[6] and only slightly acquainted with writings of Clement of Alexandria.[7] Calvin frequently criticizes Origen for his allegorical exegesis, the philosophical nature of his theology, and his love of the human will.[8] Instead, Calvin was most familiar with the Latin Fathers beginning with Irenaeus (b.125?–d.202?)[9] and in more depth when it came to Tertullian (b.160?–d.230?)[10] and Cyprian (b.210–d.258).[11] Todd concludes that this evidence suggests that Calvin studied all the Fathers in Latin and was familiar with Eastern Fathers like Origen and Chrysostom only to the extent that they were translated into Latin.[12] Given Calvin's familiarity with the Fathers of the ancient Church,

---

[5] It was not until 1672 that a complete edition of the Apostolic Fathers was published by the French Roman Catholic scholar Cotelerius. See Old, *Patristic Roots*, 160. Among the Apologists, Calvin was acquainted with the writings of Tertullian and St. Justin, though he did not know St. Justin in any depth. See Todd, "Function of the Patristic Writings," 170.

[6] Todd, "Function of the Patristic Writings," 170.

[7] From the *Institutes*, it is evident that Calvin was familiar with Eusebius' *Ecclesiastical History*, *Life of Constantine*, and *Prep. Gospel* (see *Institutes* [Battles, 1612]), Origen's *Against Celsus*, *Commentary on Romans*, *First Principles*, *Homilies on Exodus*, and *On Prayer* (ibid., 1622), and Clement of Alexandria's *Stromata* and *The Instructor* (ibid., 1608).

[8] Todd, "Function of the Patristic Writings," 173.

[9] Calvin most likely used the Erasmus edition of Irenaeus' works published in 1526. Old, *Patristic Roots*, 171–72.

[10] Two different editions of Tertullian's works were in circulation in Calvin's day, one published in Basel by John Froben in 1521, the other published in Basel in 1539, by Hieronymus Froben and Nicolas Episcopius. Old, *Patristic Roots*, 179.

[11] A number of editions of Cyprian's collected works were available to the Reformers. One edition was published in Rome in 1471, another published in 1477 in Memmingen, and the Erasmus edition was published in Basel in 1520. Old, *Patristic Roots*, 164–65.

[12] Todd points out that his research shows that Calvin did not study the Greek Fathers in classical Greek, but in Latin. "Function of the Patristic Writings," 76–77, 170–71. The fact that Calvin was not versed in classical Greek was not unusual for humanists in his day. Paul Kristeller writes: "The knowledge of Greek, even among humanists scholars, was never as thorough or as wide spread as was their knowledge of Latin, because the study of Greek was a new and purely scholarly pursuit that lacked the indigenous tradition and the practical usefulness which the study of Latin had inherited from the Middle Ages. As a result, a large amount of effort was dedicated by the humanists to the task of translating ancient Greek texts into Latin in order to make them available to a larger number of their contemporaries, even among the humanists." Kristeller, "Humanism," 120. The Merlin edition, Paris, 1512

it is important to provide a brief examination of how wealth and poverty were conceived in the Greco-Roman world and how the Fathers responded to it.

Poverty and Wealth in the Ancient Church

In Greco-Roman culture, the social significance of wealth and poverty was understood in a highly specific way. Those who were considered rich were those who lived off their investments and/or the labor of others. Countryman describes a wealthy man as a gentleman farmer who had slaves working the land and slave bailiffs overseeing tenants and other slaves. This was the epitome of what it meant to be rich in the ancient world.[13] The poor, on the other hand, were identified as those who lived by their own labor. Greco-Roman society had two different kinds of classifications in which they grouped the "poor." The first group of poor were referred to as the *ptochoi* or the *indigentes*. These people were completely without property, tools, or any kind of resources. Consequently, they were forced to live by begging or by obtaining day-labor. These were considered the poorest of the poor. The second type of poor were called *penetai* or *pauperes*. This group was made up of those who had to work for a living. It included shopkeepers, artisans, and farmers who obtained a consistent income from their labor. Even if a shopkeeper possessed a staff of slaves he was considered poor as long as he himself remained personally engaged in the work.[14]

In the ecclesial writings of the time, some broad outlines and patterns concerning the Church's understanding of poverty and wealth appear. First, it is important to note that the extant ecclesial literature from this period is rarely specific about wealth. Most early Christian writers express their thoughts on the topic in passing or in the context of another discussion.[15] This means that there is no document or individual to which one can turn to for a "definitive expression of the mind of the ancient church" on the matter of poverty and wealth.[16] Rebecca Weaver explains:

---

of Origen's works was well known by the Reformers and is probably what was available to Calvin. This work, bound in four volumes, contained nearly all of Calvin's references to Origen (Old, *Patristic Roots*, 178). Concerning Chrysostom's works, Calvin used the Erasmus edition, which is presently preserved in Geneva. See ibid., 173–74, for a list of Chrysostom's works that had been translated into Latin and available to the Reformers.

[13] Countryman, *Rich Christian*, 24.

[14] Ibid., 24–25.

[15] Ibid., 19, 47.

[16] Weaver, "Wealth and Poverty," 368.

The early Christians who wrote on wealth and poverty generally did so in response to a specific set of problems and questions and the arguments which an author might offer in one context were not necessarily in accord with those developed by other Christians in another context.[17]

However, she does state that there are two striking and reoccurring features contained in most patristic writings on the topic of wealth and poverty. The first is "a persistent call to almsgiving . . . coupled with the promise of divine reward," and the second is that "rich Christians were treated with considerable ambivalence . . . [and] an undertone of misgiving pervades references to the wealthy."[18]

This chapter will examine the ancient Church's ideas on poverty and wealth through the writings of four Fathers. The first figure is an early Greek father named Clement of Alexandria (b.150?–d.215). Of all the writers discussed here, Calvin was probably least knowledgeable with Clement.[19] This study will also examine some of the ancient writers more familiar to Calvin—Cyprian, an early Latin Father; Chrysostom (b.347–d.407), a later Greek Father; and finally Augustine (b.354–d.430), a later Latin Father. It is important to note that Clement of Alexandria, Chrysostom, Cyprian, and Augustine are a narrow representative selection of thinkers from patristic times on the question of poverty and have been selected for a number of reasons. First, for the way these men represent the ancient Church's thought on poverty and wealth from the Eastern or Western traditions; and second, for their influence on Calvin; and finally, for the impact of their ideas on the Western Church as a whole.

Poverty in the Writings of the Church Fathers

Clement of Alexandria

Clement of Alexandria was an early Greek Father and teacher in the city of Alexandria. Even though he was a favorite of many humanists, Calvin appears to be least knowledgeable of his writings than the other Fathers

---

[17] Ibid.

[18] Ibid.

[19] This study has included an examination of Clement of Alexandria's ideas because he was one of the first theologians to provide an extended treatment on the topic the nature of poverty and wealth and their impact on spirituality, and therefore is significant for the development of thought on this topic for the Middle Ages. See Ramsey, "Christian Attitudes," 257.

which this section will examine.[20] From the Index in Battles' edition of Calvin's *Institutes*, it is evident that Calvin read at least two of Clement's works, *Paedogogus* [*Instructor*] and *Stromata* [*Miscellanies*].[21] It is not known whether Calvin was acquainted with Clement's treatise in the form of a sermon entitled "The Rich Man's Salvation," in which Clement tackles the issue of wealth and poverty in the Christian life.[22] Even though it is not known whether Calvin read this work, Clement's ideas are important to examine since of all the Fathers, Clement provides one of the most comprehensive treatments on the topic of poverty and wealth in the history of the Church.[23] Though a detailed examination of this treatise is beyond the scope of this study, a few observations are needed to provide an adequate context for understanding the development of the concept of poverty in the Middle Ages.

First, Clement rejects radical asceticism and does not regard wealth as inherently evil. In fact, he refuses to tell the wealthy to give up their riches.[24] Concerning Christ's words to the rich young ruler in Matt 19:21, Clement exclaims:

> What is this? It is not what some hastily take it to be, a command to fling away the substance that belongs to him and to part with his riches, but to banish from the soul its opinions about riches, its attachment to them, its excessive desire, its morbid excitement over them, its anxious cares, the thorns of our earthly existence which choke the seed of the true life."[25]

Wealth is a neutral thing. It is neither inherently good nor evil but only an "instrument . . . [whose] nature is to minister, not to rule."[26] Clement recognizes that good or evil does not reside in wealth itself but in the

---

[20] Clement became a favorite of the humanists because of the way he was faithful to Hellenistic ideals. Campenhausen, *Fathers of the Greek Church*, 33. Calvin did not have an edition of Clement's work until after 1550, when Torrentius published the Greek text. See Old, *Patristic Roots*, 164.

[21] See *Institutes*, "Author and Source Index," (Battles, 1608).

[22] A good English translation is Clement of Alexandria, "Rich Man's Salvation," (Butterworth, 265–367); Another English translation of this sermon is Barnard, *Homily of Clement*. Todd states that, other than Chrysostom, Calvin paid little attention to most of the Greek Fathers. See Todd, "Function of the Patristic Writings," 174–81.

[23] Countryman, *Rich Christian*, 19, 47–48.

[24] Clement, "Rich Man's Salvation," pars. 11, 13 (Butterworth, 291–93, 295–97); *PG* 9, 616–17.

[25] Ibid., par. 11 (Butterworth, 291–93); *PG* 9, 616.

[26] Ibid., par. 14 (Butterworth, 299); *PG* 9, 617.

soul of the person who possesses it. Thus, Clement spiritualizes Christ's directive to the rich young ruler to 'sell all you have' and counsels, "let a man do away, not with his possessions, but rather with the passions of his soul."[27] Though he places wealth in the category of "*adiaphora*," in his works *Instructor* and *Miscellanies*, he stresses that the believer needs to practice an attitude of detachment from wealth and that this will manifest itself in the cultivation of a lifestyle of simplicity.[28] In *The Rich Man's Salvation*, he instructs that the believer must "render his soul pure of the lust for wealth" in order to make it

> poor and bare, and then only must he listen to the Savior when He says, 'Come, follow me.' For He Himself now becomes the way to the pure of heart, but to an impure soul God's grace does not penetrate. . . . [T]his is the man who is called 'blessed' by the Lord and called poor in spirit . . . .[29]

The key to a pure heart and receiving the grace of God is not in the external act of divesting oneself of one's possessions but in living a repentant life from the sin of greed and lust. This leads Clement to redefine the terms "poor" and "rich." The "nobly rich man" is "he who is rich in virtues, and able to use every fortune in a holy and faithful manner," whereas the "spurious rich man is he who is rich according to the flesh, and has changed his life into outward possessions."[30] Clement qualifies "the poor man" in a similar fashion: The "genuine poor man" is a man "poor in spirit," as one who has "inner personal poverty," whereas the "spurious . . . poor man" is a man who is "poor in worldly goods and is rich in passions."[31]

Ramsey calls Clement's sermon "the first extended argument in favour of the Christian possession of wealth," and it "became in one form or other the classic justification for the ownership of wealth by Christians."[32] In all fairness to Clement, his desire to emphasize the attitude of the heart before God over the external acts or appearances was for a specific spiritual reason, as it was for a practical reason. Clement believed that a person was incapable of spiritually knowing God without first having an interior de-

---

[27] Ibid. Martin Hengel notes the Stoic influences in Clement's remarks on this point. See Hengel, *Property and Riches*, 74–75.

[28] See Countryman, *Rich Christian*, 52–53. He reviews Clement's understanding of wealth from these writings.

[29] Clement, "Rich Man's Salvation," par. 16 (Butterworth, 301–3); *PG* 9, 620.

[30] Ibid., par. 19 (Butterworth, 309); *PG* 9, 624.

[31] Ibid.

[32] Ramsey, "Christian Attitudes," 257–58.

tachment to the things of this world. Weaver notes that this notion came from a combination of popular philosophic thought of his day, especially Stoicism, and some elements within the Christian New Testament tradition.[33] Clement's reasoning went as follows: Wealth and possessions were "gifts of God." They were to be used by those who possessed them to further "the salvation of men for God." A person needs to recognize that he "possesses them for his brother's sakes rather than his own."[34] This leads to the practical reason why Clement justifies the ownership of wealth by Christians—so that the wealthy may participate in almsgiving and acts of charity towards the poor.

Clement argues that "all possessions are by nature unrighteous, when a man possesses them for personal advantage . . . , and does not bring them into the common use for those in need."[35] When Clement speaks of those "in need" he does so in regards to the biblical concept of 'our neighbor.' His understanding of the biblical concept of 'neighbor' is "the Savior himself."[36] Because of the way he joins the concept of neighbor to that of Christ, Clement has a narrow definition of who one's neighbor is: To serve Christ means that one serves Christ's disciples or the man "who loves Christ . . . , for whatever service a man does for a disciple the Lord accepts for Himself, and reckons it all His own."[37] Winslow observes how this thinking impacts Clement's understanding of the poor: In short, the poor "are not from the ranks of the outcast, not from the collegium of the destitute, but from the family of believers,"[38] or those who are poor in spirit *as well as* physically destitute.

In good stoic fashion, it is evident that Clement is far more concerned about the condition of the soul than what condition a person's body may be in. Nonetheless he does warn believers: "Do not yourself decide who is worthy and unworthy,"[39] for a mistake can be made. It is

---

[33] Stoicism taught that an ideal life was a life detached or free from the passions, particularly attachments to possessions, which it regarded as morally neutral. Stoicism taught that things are judged as good or evil depending on how they are used. See Weaver, "Wealth and Poverty," 370.

[34] "Rich Man's Salvation," par.16 (Butterworth, 303); *PG* 9, 620.

[35] Ibid., par. 31 (Butterworth, 337); *PG* 9, 637.

[36] Ibid., par. 29 (Butterworth, 331); *PG* 9, 633. Using the parable of the Good Samaritan, Clement teaches our neighbor is the one who binds up our wounds of "fears, lusts, wraths, griefs, deceits and pleasures" (ibid.). Therefore, this must refer to Christ.

[37] Ibid., par. 30 (Butterworth, 333); *PG* 9, 636.

[38] Winslow, "Poverty and Riches," 325.

[39] "Rich Man's Salvation," par. 33 (Butterworth, 339–41); *PG* 9, 637–40.

far better to widen one's charity and let some fall on those who may be unworthy than to "neglect some who are beloved to God."[40] To be generous with one's possessions brings eternal reward—and to withhold charity brings the "penalty for which is eternal punishment by fire."[41] Clement offers his readers a warning: Hidden within the poor "dwells the Father, and His Son, who died for us and rose with us."[42]

Clement was not alone in arguing that the alms and charity of the Church should be directed toward the needy believer. A generation earlier, both Justin Martyr and Tertullian state that only believers are to be supported by the Church's common fund.[43] Nonetheless, what is evident is that by the end of the second century, one influential thinker in the Eastern Church made significant delineations concerning the meaning and redemptive value of wealth and poverty for the Christian life.

Cyprian

The Latin Father Cyprian (b.210–d.258) was born about the time that Clement of Alexandria died.[44] He was baptized and ordained to the priesthood around 246 and elected as Bishop of Carthage in North Africa around 248 or 249.[45] In the year after his election to the episcopacy, he wrote the treatise *De habitu virginum* [*On the Dress of Virgins*].[46] Not long after this, an empire wide persecution broke out under the Emperor Decius where Bishops were ordered put to death and other Christians were tortured until they recanted their faith. Cyprian withdrew to a safe place while many Christians apostatized. By 251, Cyprian returned to Carthage to deal with the apostates who wished to regain their membership in the Church. It

---

[40] Ibid., par. 33 (Butterworth, 341); *PG* 9, 640.

[41] Ibid.

[42] Ibid.

[43] Tertullian's *Apologia* mentions that monies from the common fund were to go to support "the burial of the poor, . . . and for poor orphans, aged household slaves, shipwrecked persons, and anyone in the mines . . . because of his Christian confession." Cited in Winslow, "Poverty and Riches," 325–26.

[44] A number of editions were available to Calvin and the Reformers on Cyprian's works in the sixteenth century. At Rome, in 1471 the first edition of Cyprian's collected works were published and at Basel, in 1520, Erasmus published his edition of Cyprian's works. Old, *Patristic Roots*, 164–65.

[45] Deferrari, *Treatises*, vi–ix.

[46] Weaver, "Wealth and Poverty," 372. Calvin does not cite this treatise in the *Institutes*. See *Institutes* (Battles, 1609–10).

was at this time that Cyprian wrote the treatise *De Lapsis* [*The Lapsed*].⁴⁷ Not long afterward, Christians were blamed for a terrible plague and attacks by barbarians. Emperor Valerian renewed the persecution. Cyprian was exiled to Curubis where he continued to pastor Carthage through letters and treatises for the next seven years. In 258 persecution broke out again. Pope Sixtus and four of his deacons were put to death in Rome. All bishops, priests, and deacons were ordered to be killed and any Christian officers were to become slaves. All others were to lose their wealth, be exiled, or killed. At this time, Cyprian was taken back to Carthage and was beheaded outside the city. He became the Church's first African bishop to be martyred.⁴⁸

Calvin was familiar with Cyprian from early in his life, and used him in his *Commentary on De Clementia* mostly because of his popularity among humanists. In Cyprian's day, he was considered "an expert rhetorician" and a "master of eloquence."⁴⁹ In Cyprian's early years he wrote in a similar manner to Clement on the topic of a Christian's attitude towards poverty and wealth.⁵⁰ In his treatise *On the Dress of Virgins*, Cyprian calls these women, not to strict asceticism, but to modesty while reminding them of the spiritual dangers involved with wealth.⁵¹ To encourage these virgins to "despise" the "pomps and pleasures" of the world, Cyprian provides a definition of wealth:⁵²

> But there are some women who are wealthy and rich in the abundance of their possessions, who display their riches and who argue that they ought to use the blessings that are theirs. Let them know, first of all, that she is rich who is rich in God; that she is wealthy who is wealthy in Christ; that those are blessings which are spiri-

---

⁴⁷ Calvin is familiar with this work. See *Institutes*, "Index" (Battles, 1609).

⁴⁸ Deferrari, *Treatises*, vi–ix. Countryman explains that Cyprian must have been a man of great wealth and standing before he became a Christian by the way he was treated during the persecution. The fact that he was first deported, never tortured, and in the end beheaded and not burned at the stake like others showed the kind of respect given to only the highest ranks of society. See Countryman, *Rich Christian*, 184.

⁴⁹ See Todd, "Function of the Patristic Writings," 43–44.

⁵⁰ This is the observation of both Weaver, "Wealth and Poverty," 372; and Hengel, *Property and Riches*, 79–80.

⁵¹ Cyprian, *Treatises*, "On the Dress of Virgins," chaps. 5, 9 (Deferrari, 35–36, 39); *PL* 4, 456, 460–61.

⁵² Ibid., chap. 7 (Deferrari, 37); *PL* 4, 459.

tual, divine, heavenly, which lead us to God, which remain with us in everlasting possession with God.[53]

Cyprian stresses that ornamentation belongs not on the body but on the heart.[54] Christians need to be as those who possess and use things in a manner which recognizes their transience.[55] He continues:

> You say that you are wealthy and rich and you think that you must use the things that God has wished you to possess. Use them, but for your salvation and for good works; use them for what God has ordained, for what the Lord has pointed out. Let the poor feel that you are rich; let the needy feel that you are wealthy; through your patrimony make God your debtor; feed Christ. . . . For you are offending God even in this very point, if you believe that wealth has been given to you by Him for the express purpose of enjoying it without thought of salvation.[56]

Cyprian argues that the Christian is called to live a simple life, and that a believer's wealth is a gift from God meant to be generously used for those in need.

Weaver notes that Cyprian's attitudes towards wealth underwent a marked changed after he wrote the treatise *On the Dress of Virgins* and after the persecution of 250 under the Emperor Decius.[57] The effect of the persecution on the Church at Carthage was that it produced a large number of lapses, "particularly among the rich."[58] In his treatise *On the Lapsed*, Cyprian's tone towards wealth hardens. He places the blame for the persecution of the Church squarely on the greed of its leadership and members. He refers to "all that happened" as "an examination rather than a persecution."[59] In this treatise, Cyprian describes the depravity of the Church:

> Everyone was eager to increase his estate, and forgetful of what believers in apostolic times either had done or always should have done, with the insatiable ardor of covetousness they applied themselves to increase their possessions. Among priests there was no

---

[53] Ibid., chap. 7 (Deferrari, 37); *PL* 4, 458–59.
[54] Ibid., chap. 8 (Deferrari, 38); *PL* 4, 460.
[55] Ibid., chap. 10 (Deferrari, 40); *PL* 4, 461.
[56] Ibid., chap. 11 (Deferrari, 40–41); *PL* 4, 461–62.
[57] Weaver, "Wealth and Poverty," 372–73.
[58] Countryman, 190.
[59] Cyprian, *Treatises*, "On the Lapsed," chap. 5 (Deferrari, 61); *PL* 4, 482.

devout religion; in their ministries no sound faith, in their works no mercy, in their morals no discipline. . . . Many bishops, who ought to be a source of encouragement and an example to the rest, contemning their divine charge came under the charge of secular kings; after abandoning their thrones and deserting the people, they wandered through foreign provinces and sought the market places for gainful business; while their brethren in the Church were starving, they wished to possess money in abundance; they seized estates by crafty deceits; they increased their capital by multiplying usuries.[60]

Cyprian states that God wanted "his family to be proved . . . because the long peace had corrupted the discipline divinely handed down to us," and because "a heavenly rebuke has aroused a prostrate . . . and sleeping faith."[61] Cyprian challenges his people:

How can they follow Christ who are held back by the chain of their personal property? Or how can they seek heaven, and ascend to the sublime and lofty, who are weighed down by earthly desires?[62]

Cyprian exhibits insight into the toxic element of wealth which has power to destroy faith and genuine spirituality. "Wealth is to be avoided as an enemy, as a thief to be fled, as a sword to be feared by those who possess it, and a poison."[63] Yet, there is hope for the lapsed. He instructs the believer "to confess his sin":

Let us turn to the Lord with our whole mind, and, expressing repentance for our sin with true grief, let us implore God's mercy. Let the soul prostrate itself before Him; let sorrow give satisfaction to Him; let our every hope rest upon him.[64]

Ultimately, the only way a believer might overcome the snares of wealth is by the grace and mercy of God. Cyprian exhorts his congregation that "if anyone performs prayer with his whole heart, if he groans with genuine lamentations and tears of repentance, if by continuous just works he turns to the Lord for the forgiveness of his sins, such can receive His mercy."[65]

---

[60] Ibid., chap. 6 (Deferrari, 61–62); *PL* 4, 482–83.
[61] Ibid., chap. 5 (Deferrari, 61); *PL* 4, 482.
[62] Ibid., chap. 12 (Deferrari, 67); *PL* 4, 488.
[63] Ibid., chap. 35 (Deferrari, 87); *PL* 4, 507–8.
[64] Ibid., chap. 29 (Deferrari, 82); *PL* 4, 503–4.
[65] Ibid., chap. 36 (Deferrari, 88); *PL* 4, 508.

One of the ways the wealthy demonstrated their repentance, or did penance, was to provide alms for the poor.[66] Cyprian warns the wealthy that unless they share their gains "with Christ," that is—with the poor, "the richer they become in the things of this world, the poorer they become in the sight of God."[67] If the wealthy "make Christ a partner" in their "earthly possessions," Cyprian states, Christ will make them "co-heirs of His heavenly kingdom."[68] To bestow alms upon the poor was a way that the wealthy could store up reward in heaven and could gain confidence before their God.[69] For later interpreters of his work, Cyprian's words appeared to say that almsgiving is a way a rich man could purchase his salvation. Bishop Benson assesses Cyprian's theology as "a commencement of much medieval trouble."[70]

If the poor are to receive the alms of the rich, how does Cyprian define the term "poor" here? Like Justin Martyr, Tertullian, and Clement of Alexandria, Cyprian also reasons that to offer alms to the poor is what it means to offer alms to Christ. Like the Fathers before him, he interprets the biblical concept of "poor" to be those who are needy *and* fellow believers. Cyprian offers the following challenge:

> How more could He have stimulated the works of our justice and mercy than by having said that whatever is offered to the poor and the needy is offered to Him, and by having said that He is offended unless offering is made to the needy and the poor? So that he in the Church, who is not moved by consideration of *his brother*, may indeed be moved by contemplation of Christ, and he who does not give thought to *his fellow servant* in trouble and in need may

---

[66] Ibid., chap. 35 (Deferrari, 87); *PL* 4, 507.
[67] Cyprian, *Treatises*, "On Works and Almsgiving," chap. 13 (Deferrari, 239); *PL* 4, 634.
[68] Ibid.
[69] Ibid., chap. 20 (Deferrari, 246); *PL* 4, 641.
[70] Countryman, *Rich Christian*, 197, 199. Countryman also explains that Cyprian was faced with a huge pastoral problem of what to do with the large group of rich Christians who lapsed during the persecution. He explains that Cyprian's teaching on almsgiving solved two problems for him. During the persecution the Church's coffers emptied out as masses of people fell into indigence, prisoners needed to be ransomed and mass poverty was rampant. The tithes and alms of the rich were necessary to feed, clothe and care for the large numbers of poor and sick. Cyprian taught that such gifts needed to be accompanied by a true confession of sin and were to be part of a type of penance that demonstrated the sincerity of their confession. Thus the merit system of salvation germinated in a milieu of what to do with those who fell away from the faith at a very difficult time of persecution and later repented in hopes of being restored to the Church.

indeed give thought to the Lord abiding in that very one whom he despises.⁷¹

From this text, it is clear that Cyprian believes that the charge Christ gives to the believer is to look after other believers who are in need and poor.⁷² In addition to the fact that Cyprian's interpretation is congruent with that of Justin Martyr, Tertullian, and Clement of Alexandria, it will be shown that on this point, Calvin agrees with this view.

John Chrysostom

In his preface to his proposed translation of Chrysostom's homilies, John Calvin states that Chrysostom (b.347–d.407) was the greatest exegete in the history of the Church because of the way he exhibits an outstandingly clear understanding of New Testament times.⁷³ Outside of Augustine, Chrysostom is one of Calvin's most often quoted Fathers.⁷⁴ Therefore, what Chrysostom has to say about poverty and wealth is as significant

---

⁷¹ Cyprian, *Treatises*, "On Works and Almsgiving," chap. 23 (Deferrari, 250); *PL* 4, 643. Emphasis mine.

⁷² See also Cyprian, *Treatises*, "On Works and Almsgiving," chap. 25 (Deferrari, 251); *PL* 4, 644.

⁷³ *CO* 9, 834. The date of Calvin's "Preface to Chrysostom's Homilies," is unknown. Hazlett argues for an earlier date of 1538–1540, which is also supported by Ganoczy and Müller's work, *Calvins handschriftliche Annotationen*, which suggests that Calvin used a 1536 copy of Chrysostom's works "as a means to learn how to preach sermons that are practically relevant. See Hazlett, "Calvin's Latin Preface," 133. He argues that Calvin was very familiar with the writings of the patristics from early in his career. Of all the patristics, Chrysostom was Calvin's favorite exegete even though, and by Calvin's own recognition, he taught the importance of the doctrine of free-will in his doctrine of election. Calvin writes in his Preface to Chrysostom's Homilies: "My reason for selecting Chrysostom as the most preferable needs likewise to be dealt with in passing. From the outset, the reader ought to bear in mind the kind of literary genre it is in which I prefer him to others. Although homilies are something which consist of a variety of elements, the interpretation of Scripture is, however, their priority. In this area, no one of sound judgment would deny that our Chysostom excels all the ancient writers currently extant" (Hazlett, 144). A good English translation of this "Preface" may be found in the essay by Hazlett, "Calvin's Latin Preface," 129–50. An older English translation is McIndoe, "John Calvin," 19–26. See also *CO* 9, 836. Calvin states that Chrysostom was a faithful interpreter of Scripture and follower of Christ and that he always had "the highest end in view" or "the best intentions." See Hazlett, "Calvin's Latin Preface," 144; *CO* 9, 834. See also Walchenbach, "Calvin as Biblical Commentator" 36, 42–43; Todd, "Function of the Patristic Writings," 74, 172. Another reason Calvin may have liked Chrysostom is that he preached through whole books of the Bible. See Campenhausen, *Fathers of the Greek Church*, 133.

⁷⁴ Todd, "Function of the Patristic Writings," 74–75.

to understanding Calvin's thought as it is to understanding the Middle Ages.

John Chrysostom was born in Antioch of Syria and educated in the tradition of the Stoics, Cynics, and the New Testament by his teacher Libanius. He became ordained as a priest in Antioch around 386 and was assigned to the task of preaching. In time, his popularity as a preacher earned him the name "golden mouthed."[75] John's priestly service came to an abrupt end in 397 with the death of the patriarch of Constantinople, St. Nectarius. Out of fear of an uprising by the people, John was kidnapped from Antioch and brought to the capital city for his consecration as bishop in 398. However, in a few years, empress Eudoxia took offense at Chrysostom's preaching against luxury and license and sent John into exile (404), where he died in 407, "still giving glory to God."[76] However, while he was a priest in Antioch, John preached a series of seven sermons on the parable of Lazarus and the rich man (around 388 or 389). These sermons embody Chrysostom's thought on poverty and wealth and it is to these sermons that this brief study will now turn.[77]

In exegeting the parable, Chrysostom understands that the biblical text offers a more nuanced definition of who is to be considered rich and poor. He explains that Christ tells the hearer about the final fate of the rich man and Lazarus "to keep you from thinking that wealth is worth anything without virtue," as well as "to keep you from thinking that poverty is any evil."[78] Chrysostom continues:

> Let us learn from this man not to call the rich lucky nor the poor unfortunate. Rather, if we are to tell the truth, the rich man is not the one who has collected many possessions but the one who has few possessions; and the poor man is not the one who has no possessions but the one who has many desires. We ought to consider this the definition of poverty and wealth. So if you see someone

---

[75] The name "Chrysostom" means "golden-mouthed" and was not bestowed upon him until the sixth century. Nevertheless John Chrysostom was widely admired in his own day for being the most popular preacher in Antioch. See Campenhausen, *Fathers of the Greek Church*, 133.

[76] Roth, *Wealth and Poverty*, 9–10. For a more details on his life and death, see Campenhausen, *Fathers of the Greek Church*, 133–44.

[77] Roth, *Wealth and Poverty*, 7–10, 18. Battles' Index shows that Calvin quotes from this series of sermons in the *Institutes*, and therefore it is evident that Calvin was acquainted with the ideas presented in them. See *Institutes*, "Index" (Battles, 1607). Also, the fifth sermon of the series is the only sermon out of the seven, which is not directly relevant to the subject of poverty and wealth and therefore will be left aside.

[78] Chrysostom, *Wealth and Poverty* (Roth, 39); *PG* 48, 981.

greedy for many things, you should consider him the poorest of all, even if he has acquired everyone's money. If on the other hand, you see someone with few needs, you should count him richest of all, even if he has acquired nothing.[79]

Chrysostom defines poverty and wealth according to the measure of virtue a person exhibits and not according to their physical circumstances. In order to illustrate this point, he likens the poor and the rich to actors in a play. Chrysostom reasons:

> If you are sitting in the theater and see one of the actors wearing the mask of a king, you do not call him fortunate or think that he is a king. . . . In the same way even here, sitting in this world as if in a theater and looking at the players on the stage, when you see many rich, but that they are wearing the masks of rich people. Just as that man who acts the part of a king or general on the stage often turns out to be a household servant or somebody who sells figs or grapes in the market, so also the rich man often turns out to be the poorest of all. If you take off his mask, open up his conscience, and enter into his mind, you will often find there a great poverty of virtue: you will find that he belongs to the lowest class of all. Just as in the theater, when evening falls and the audience departs, and the kings and generals go outside to remove the costumes of their roles, they are revealed to everyone thereafter appearing to be exactly what they are; so also now when death arrives and the theater is dissolved, everyone puts off the masks of wealth or poverty and departs to the other world. When all are judged by their deeds alone, some are revealed truly wealthy, others poor, some of high class, others of no account.[80]

Wealth and poverty are but masks which conceal the true identity of one's virtue. In death, as at the close of a play, the masks of poverty and wealth are stripped off to reveal the goodness of the conscience of the one who wore it. Chrysostom points out that when the rich man died, his mask was removed and was revealed to be "the poorest of all, . . . so poor indeed that he was not master even of a drop of water."[81]

Chrysostom discusses the reason why God permits some to be poor and others to be rich. Lazarus' poverty proved his righteousness by the fact that he endured it patiently.[82] Poverty and misfortune are divinely sent to

[79] Ibid., (Roth, 40); *PG* 48, 982.
[80] Ibid., (Roth, 46–47); *PG* 48, 986.
[81] Ibid., (Roth, 47); *PG* 48, 987.
[82] Ibid., (Roth, 23); *PG* 48, 972.

help purge sin and evil from the soul.[83] But the rich have no such medicine for their spiritual life.[84] Chrysostom makes a comparison:

> Suppose that there are two fornicators . . . but one rich and the other poor. Which has more hope of salvation? Obviously . . . the poor man. So you must not say, "the rich man commits fornication and is rich; therefore I call him lucky." You ought rather to call him lucky if he fornicated in poverty, if he fornicated in hunger; then he would have a forcible teacher of wisdom, his poverty. When you see a bad person faring well then weep: for there are two evils, the disease and its incurability.[85]

Poverty and misery have the ability to teach wisdom and help to lead one out of one's sins. Wealth, however, has no such advantage. Wealth only fosters the "incurability" of one's sins.

Since the rich man does not have the spiritual advantage of the experience of poverty, God sends him the poor man so that the poor might teach him virtue and love. A believer's money belongs to the Lord. What belongs to the Lord also belongs to the poor.[86] God instructs that the wealthy are God's stewards to the poor. For the rich to withhold their wealth and not bestow it on the needy is theft in Chrysostom's estimation. He warns:

> Just as in the imperial treasury, if he neglects to distribute where he is ordered, but spends instead for his own indolence, pays the penalty and is put to death, so also the rich man is a kind of steward of the money which is owed for distribution to the poor. . . . So if he spends more on himself than his need requires, he will pay the harshest penalty hereafter. For his own goods are not his own, but belong to his fellow servants.

A believer's stewardship towards the poor does not depend on how worthy or unworthy the recipient may be to receive aid. "For if you wish to show kindness, you must not require an accounting of a person's life, but merely correct his poverty and fill his need."[87] Chrysostom continues:

> Need alone is the poor man's worthiness; if anyone at all ever comes to us with this recommendation, let us not meddle any further. We

---

[83] For some practical applications of Chrysostom's ideas see Benestad, "Chrysostom on Wealth and Poverty," 201–10.
[84] Chrysostom, *Wealth and Poverty* (Roth, 102); *PG* 48, 1030–31.
[85] Ibid., (Roth, 103); *PG* 48, 1031.
[86] Ibid., (Roth, 48–49); *PG* 48, 987.
[87] Ibid., (Roth, 52); *PG* 48, 989.

do not provide for the manners but for the man. We show mercy on him not because of his virtue but because of his misfortune, in order that we ourselves may receive from the Master His great mercy, in order that we ourselves, unworthy as we are, may enjoy His philanthropy.[88]

Chrysostom believes that the language of worthiness should only be applied to those who are virtuous. It is only by "the grace and love of our Lord Jesus Christ" that one will "enjoy the bosom of the patriarch," as Lazarus, and will "feast on the immortal good things."[89] For it is only the poor in spirit who will receive the promised blessings of the kingdom.

Augustine

Luchesius Smits has done an extensive study of Calvin's use of Augustine (b.354–d.430) throughout his writings. What is evident from Smits' study is that Calvin became highly knowledgeable of Augustine's works from his days as a student,[90] which is demonstrated in the first edition of the *Institutes*, as well as in his "Prefatory Letter to King Francis of France."[91] In Calvin's unpublished "Preface to Chrysostom's Homilies," he contends that even though no Father comes closer to explaining the plain meaning of the text than Chrysostom, "Augustine does surpass everyone [including Chrysostom] in dogmatics."[92]

Of all the Fathers studied thus far, Augustine came from the most humble background. Nevertheless, he claims to have had a great drive for money and success in his youth.[93] Augustine was exposed to the value of asceticism when he became involved with the teachings of Manicheism as a young man. Yet, it was not until he converted to Christianity, through the teachings of Ambrose, that he actively took up the ascetic lifestyle,

---

[88] Ibid., (Roth, 53); *PG* 48, 990.

[89] Ibid., (Roth, 78); *PG* 48, 1006.

[90] Smits, *Saint Augustine*. See chapter 1, "Saint Augustine dans la Conversion de Calvin," 13–24, for a review of how Augustine was formative in Calvin's theological thought and conversion to the Reformation.

[91] See Smits, *Saint Augustine*, 26–30.

[92] Hazlett, "Calvin's Latin Preface," 145; *CO* 9, 385. Calvin does not bother to explain in his "Preface" how Augustine can be deficient in biblical exegetical skills and be outstanding in dogmatics. Likewise he does not explain how a man like Chrysostom can have outstanding skills in biblical exposition and yet be deficient in dogmatics (see *CO* 9, 836–37).

[93] See Augustine, *Confessions*, 2.3.5, 6.6.9, 9.2.4 (Bourke 36–37, 139–41, 230–31); *PL* 32, 677; 32, 723–24; 32, 764–65; and Weaver, "Wealth and Poverty," 378.

leaving his common law wife of more than ten years for the monastery. A little over a decade later, Augustine was appointed Bishop of Hippo.

Though Augustine took up the monastic/ascetic lifestyle, his writings do not condemn wealth or the wealthy per se. Like the writers examined above, Augustine did not exclude the rich man from the kingdom of heaven. This point is especially evident by the way he deals with certain biblical passages and characters. One good source of Augustine's thinking on this topic is found in an extensive letter he wrote to a Sicilian layman named Hilarius in 414.[94] Hilarius wrote and asked Augustine about some teachings that were circulating around Syracuse. One of these teachings concerned whether a rich man who continued to live with his riches could enter the kingdom of God, or did he need to sell all?[95] Augustine replied using a number of Old and New Testament passages and characters. He argues that Abraham, Isaac, and Jacob were all wealthy men, and notes that it was wealthy Abraham who received poor Lazarus into the kingdom. Furthermore, the rich man was condemned and tormented in Hell, not because of his riches, but because he had shown no mercy towards the poverty of Lazarus.[96] Augustine writes:

> This was intended to show us that on the one hand it was not poverty in itself that was divinely honored, nor, on the other, riches that were condemned, but that the godliness of the one and the ungodliness of the other had their own consequences . . .[97]

Augustine further explains what he means by the "ungodliness" of the rich man. The sin of the rich man was essentially his pride. The man's pride directed him to put his trust in his riches and to despise poor Lazarus.[98] For Augustine, Abraham is a model of how a rich man should "lightly hold onto his riches and think of them as having little worth in comparison with the commandments of God."[99]

Augustine also argues in a similar fashion concerning the story of the rich young ruler. He shows that Christ did not tell the young man that if he wished to enter the kingdom of God that he had to sell all he had, but rather that he had to keep all the commandments. It was only if he wanted

---

[94] Augustine, *Letters* (Parsons, 318 n. 1); *PL* 33, 678, n. b.
[95] Ibid., (Parsons, 318–19); *PL* 33, 674.
[96] Ibid., (Parsons, 340); *PL* 33, 686.
[97] Ibid., (Parsons, 340–41); *PL* 33, 686.
[98] Ibid., (Parsons, 343); *PL* 33, 687.
[99] Ibid., (Parsons, 341); *PL* 33, 686.

to be "perfect" that he needed to sell all, give to the poor, and follow Christ so that he could have treasure in heaven. Thus, Augustine concludes that "the good Master distinguished between the commandments of the Law and that higher perfection,"[100] not making poverty a requirement for entrance into the eternal life.

Nevertheless, Augustine is clear that even if the rich do not sell all they have but choose to live a generous life, clothing the naked, ransoming the prisoner and feeding the hungry, they must be willing to forsake their riches if they are forced to choose between their wealth and Christ.[101] Augustine's main concern is that the rich and the poor alike recognize that it is God that gives the grace to properly use wealth or to do good works. He does not want people to trust in their own strength or in their own abilities. To the rich man he says:

> 'What is impossible for men is easy for God,' and whether they retain riches and do their good works by means of them, or enter into the kingdom of heaven by selling them and distributing them to provide for the needs of the poor, let them attribute their good works to the grace of God, and not to their own strength.[102]

Augustine confesses that though he was not a rich man, he has chosen the course of higher perfection and has left all to follow Christ. Yet, he makes it clear that "I have acted upon it, not by my strength but by His helping grace."[103]

Augustine's position on wealth, poverty, and the kingdom of God is consistent with that of Clement, Cyprian, and Chrysostom. However, Augustine comes out the strongest on the point that human responsibility does not achieve divine favor, and that a believer's good works, whether one sells all one has or retains one's wealth to be generous to the needy, is all due to the grace and power of God. Concerning this point, Weaver states:

> For Augustine, in contrast, the focus was not upon the individual's eternal destiny but upon the interior workings of the heart. As a result, the works of charity which merit eternal reward could never receive center stage just as the form of renunciation, whether in deed or only in intent, was only of secondary significance. These are, in fact, merely manifestations of a prior orientation of the

[100] Ibid.; *PL* 33, 687.
[101] Ibid., (Parsons, 349–50); *PL* 33, 691.
[102] Ibid., (Parsons, 344); *PL* 33, 688.
[103] Ibid., (Parsons, 352); *PL* 33, 692.

heart toward God, an orientation accomplished not by the individual but by grace.[104]

At the time that Augustine wrote this letter (414), he had been engaged in the Pelagian controversy for several years (since 411). As clarity of doctrine most often arises in the context of controversy, so it was with the way Augustine clarified the role of grace and works in light of the question of poverty and wealth.

Conclusion

Though by no means exhaustive of what the ancient Church said concerning wealth and poverty, the ideas of Clement of Alexandria, Cyprian, Chrysostom and Augustine are a representative example of some of the patristic thoughts Calvin read and integrated into his theology. Yet, none of these Fathers' opinions stand out historically as the authoritative position for the Church on poverty. Much like Calvin, these men did not sit down to write a treatise on the topic of poverty in the Christian life or the role of poverty in one's theology. The comments of the patristics on poverty are fully embedded in their preaching, letters of exhortation, and commentaries, directed at a Church who needed to hear the message of reform, always reflective of their differing situations and congregational needs. In spite of the fact that they spoke to the unique set of circumstances in their day, they do share some common perspectives on poverty that also arise in the work of John Calvin.

One of the most significant perspectives that Clement, Cyprian, Chrysostom, and Augustine share is the rejection of radical asceticism. They share the stance that one's wealth is a gift from God meant to be rightly used or bestowed upon those in need. For all these men, generosity is a mark of an obedient and repentant person. To hold on to one's resources when a person is in need, is to choose wealth over Christ, according to Augustine. Clement teaches that the Father, Son, and Holy Spirit dwell in a hidden manner within the poor, and Cyprian maintains that the only way the rich can have Christ as their partner is by sharing their abundance with the impoverished. Likewise, Chrysostom stresses that the person who withholds goods from the needy invites the harshest judgment of God upon themselves. All wealth belongs to God and what belongs to God also belongs to the poor. Therefore, to withhold one's resources from the poor is essentially robbing God.

---

[104] Weaver, "Wealth and Poverty," 380.

Another area of resemblance is the way in which these Fathers see the Christian life impacted by the conditions of wealth and poverty. They all agree that poverty or wealth, in and of itself, does not determine the quality of the Christian life for the believer. Rather, the quality of the Christian life is determined by the condition of the heart of the believer. Poverty and wealth simply provide opportunities or temptations that reveal or seek to influence a person's heart. Clement goes so far as to state that wealth in and of itself is a neutral thing. He claims that what is important to one's spiritual life is repentance and the proper condition of one's soul before God, not simply the act of divesting oneself of one's earthly things. To know God, one must be detached in one's heart from the things that he or she possesses. Cyprian stresses that this detachment from the things of this world in one's heart is of great importance because if believers are attached to their wealth, it can destroy their faith and lead them into apostasy. Furthermore he argues that the only way one is able to overcome this pitfall is by God's grace and genuine repentance. Chrysostom goes so far as to redefine the terms "poor" and "rich" in light of the condition of the soul before God: The poor person is one who has no virtue, where the rich person is one who is rich in virtue and is satisfied with what the Lord has given him or her. Chrysostom speaks of physical poverty as a way in which God purges the soul and wealth as an opportunity for the rich to be generous. He sees poverty and wealth to be masks which conceal the true spiritual identity of a person and which will be removed in death. Such masks are not to be judged in and of themselves as indications of divine favor or spiritual fitness. Likewise, Augustine stresses that wealth does not exclude a person from the kingdom of God, anymore than divesting oneself of one's goods ensure one's eternal life. He stresses that it was not the wealth of the rich man that condemned him but his lack of mercy and pride towards Lazarus. He warns that the rich must hold lightly to their riches so that they do not choose wealth over Christ and neglect to minister to those with whom Christ identifies.

The above thoughts on poverty and wealth in the thought of Clement of Alexandria, Cyprian, Chrysostom, and Augustine are significant to mention because, in one form or another, they all appear in Calvin's writings. Yet, before this study turns to examine in detail what Calvin has to say about the poverty in his theology, the following two chapters will provide further background on how the poverty was theologically interpreted in the Middle Ages and by the early reformers.

3
Poverty in the Thought of the Middle Ages

To properly evaluate Calvin's ideas on poverty, it is necessary to understand the thought patterns commonly tied to poverty throughout the Middle Ages. The history of poverty in the Middle Ages is a topic well beyond the scope of this chapter. However, some important points in this area need to be addressed as background to the Reformers' and Calvin's thoughts on this subject. This chapter shows that the cultural and religious understanding of poverty in the Middle Ages was practically and theoretically in constant flux. During this time much of the interpretation of poverty came through the lens of cultural and historical issues. As the social and economic landscape of medieval Europe changed, so did its interpretation of poverty, and as poverty's interpretation changed, so did its ethical impact on the culture at large. One of the most significant points learned in this study is that throughout the history of the Western Church the issue of poverty has been intimately related to the growth and reform of the Church.

The Words *Paupertas* and *Pauper* and Related Terms in the Early Middle Ages

Europe's Early Vocabulary of Poverty

In the literature spanning the eleventh century to the first half of the twelfth, it appears that those who are called "poor" are also rural.[1] Yet, Georges Duby argues that this reading is too simplistic. First, little evidence points to an *Unterschicht* who recognize the fact that they are an

---

[1] Murray, "Religion among the Poor," 291; Duby, "Les Pauvres," 25.

economically depressed social group.² Secondly, no matter how oppressed these people were, or how destitute their situation, the literature "never presents them as being the 'poor people.'"³ Duby explains:

> On the contrary, the words "poor" and "poverty" belong to the vocabulary of documents that describe this period's religious phenomena. It is there that one finds them in greater abundance, which concern the hermit, the pilgrim, or all movements of piety and conversion that are linked to them, and those which are based on the departure, the rupture, the eradication, and the refusal of a framed existence. It concerns all currents of popular told piety, orthodox or heretical, including the spirit of the crusade. It concerns charity and its organizations.
>
> I add that these words, when discovered in other source categories, again appear loaded with essentially religious senses. For example, in the charters of some acts of donation to Cluny emanate from so and so men called "poor." This does not concern an individual whose hierarchy of fortunes have taken a down turn. This pauper has chosen by piety to renounce his wealth. In all obviousness, in the language of those who have written documents of this time, poverty is a vocation, in all cases a notion, [and] a spiritual value.⁴

Duby observes that although most of Western Europe lived at subsistence level, by the eleventh and twelfth century the language of poverty was not applied to them, even though in reality they would indeed qualify as "poor" as we understand the term. Instead, the language of poverty was far more narrowly applied. At least in the literary heritage received from

---

² Duby, "Les Pauvres," 25.

³ Ibid.

⁴ Ibid., 26–27 (my translation). "Les mots 'pauvre' et 'pauvreté' appartiennent au contraire au vocabulaire des documents qui décrivent à cette époque des phénomènes religieux C'est là qu'on les trouve en plus grande abondance, qu'il s'agisse de l'érémitisme, du pèlerinage, ou de tous les mouvements de piété et de conversion qui leur sont liés, qui, comme eux, sont fondés sur le départ, la rupture, le déracinement, le refus d'une existence encadrée. Que'il s'agisse de tous les courants de piété dits populaires, orthodoxes ou hérétiques, y compris l'élan de croisade. Qu'il s'agisse de la charité et de son organisation.

"J'ajoute que ces mots, lorsqu'on les découvre dans d'autres catégories de sources, apparaissent encore chargés d'un sens essentiellement religieux. Par exemple, dans les chartes de Cluny, quelques actes de donation émanent de tel ou tel homme appelé "pauvre". Il ne s'agit pas d'un individu situé en bas de la hiérarchie des fortunes. Ce pauvre a choisi par piété de renoncer à ses richesses. De toute évidence, dans le langage de ceux qui ont rédigé les documents de ce temps, la pauvreté est une vocation, en tous cas une notion, une valeur spirituelles."

that time, the adjectives and nouns of poverty were reserved for those who participated in specific religious acts. In short, the concept was laden with religious connotations.

The source of this development is not difficult to identify. It was the pervasive influence of the Latin Vulgate on western thought and culture.[5] By the eleventh century, most of Europe had been Christianized, and the majority of the writings from this time were ecclesiastical. Therefore, it will be helpful to examine the language of poverty used in the Vulgate, and the way in which this vocabulary affected the West's understanding of poverty. This will partially set a cultural-linguistic context to assist in understanding of Calvin's writings.

The Vulgate's Influence on the Terms Pauper *and* Humilis

The strong religious connotations of the Latin terms *pauper* and *paupertas* have their source in the translation of the Vulgate. The large and varied Hebrew vocabulary for terms describing the social, economic, and spiritual conditions of poverty[6] became gradually narrowed by their translation into the Greek Septuagint[7] and the writings of the Greek New Testament.

---

[5] Bosl, *Armut Christi*, 16: "Durch die lateinische Vulgata, die universalste und gebräuchlichste Information des Mittelalters bis in das 13. Jahrhundert, ist der biblische Armutsbegriff im ganzen Abendland verbreitet worden." See also LeClercq, "Aux Origins," 35–42; Mollat explains that the source for this understanding of poverty is essentially Scripture. The biblical and gospel tradition acted throughout the Middle Ages "like a dormant virus," which appeared at various times only to recede again." See *Poor in the Middle Ages*, 11,

[6] LeClercq, "Aux Origins," 35–36: Summarizing LeClercq's research, there are five common terms used for poor and poverty in the Old Testament: 'ebyôn, 'ani / 'anawim, ruš, dal, and ḥasêr. 'Ebyôn designates the one who is materially poor or indigent and who lacks what it takes to have social respect. This is the group who has a preferential relationship to God and whom God defends and helps. Though this term designates an economic and/or socially oppressed group, when it is used of poverty in Israel, the stress of the context is emphasizing the spiritual sense more often than the materiel condition. Yet this word is not the most frequent word used for the poor. It appears ten times in the historical books, thirty times in the wisdom literature, and fifteen times in the Prophets. The Old Testament word that is most commonly used is 'ani, or its plural 'anawim. It means to be in a miserable condition, sorrowfully oppressed before God and man. This term appears in the Psalms alone some seventy times and forty times in the Pentateuch. Other words used to express poverty that are found less frequently are *dal*, which conveys the idea of weakness; *rus*, which means to be in need or have a lack of something; and finally *hasêr*, which expresses the idea of deficiency.

[7] Ibid., 37–38: A number of things occurred when Scripture was translated from Hebrew into the Greek Septuagint. The language of poverty acquired the dominant Hellenistic idea of gentleness and benevolence and also acquired its ennobling qualities. Also, translators did not seek a one-to-one correspondence between specific Hebrew and Greek words.

These few terms became narrowed again by the Latin Vulgate, resulting in, essentially, just two terms: *humilis* and *pauper*.⁸ Latin translators favored the term *humilis* which originally was a secondary designation for poverty. *Humilis* originally was a designation for "what belongs to the earth (*humus*)." Yet it is used in Latin translations as an attitude or disposition applied to the human spirit. With a few exceptions, the popular Greek term ταπεινός is nearly always translated into the term *humilis* in both Testaments of most Latin translations.⁹ In addition to *humilis*, there are a number of other Latin terms which translate the various biblical senses of poverty: *pauper*, referring to one who produces little; *egens* or *indigens*, one who lacks or is in need of something; *inopia/inops*, a state of barrenness or a state opposed to the abundance of resources; and *mendicus*, one having physical handicaps or infirmities that reduces him or her to begging.¹⁰ Of these terms, *pauper* occurs most frequently in both Testaments. Nearly the entire family of Greek terms for poverty are periodically translated into *pauper* and its derivatives. As with the Greek translations of the Hebrew, the Latin translators chose to translate Greek terms according to the biblical idea they expressed, rather than attempting to find word-for-word correspondences.¹¹

Jean LeClercq attributes this governing use of *pauper* and *humilis* to a number of factors, the first of which is theological. Certain texts like Matt 5:3, Luke 6:20 and Matt 11:5 "exerted decisive influence" over the success of the term *pauper* in the rest of the translation process.¹² Furthermore, the Latin Fathers consistently quote these passages using the term *pauper*, employing *egeni*, or *mendici* in only a few exceptional cases.¹³ These

---

Rather, they choose various Greek terms to summarize meanings like destitution, affliction, and humility, between which only nuances exist. There are really only three main Greek terms that are employed to translate the family of Hebrew concepts of poverty in the Septuagint; πένης, which refers to those who must work to live—used eighty times; πτωχός, which designates one who needs assistance to live often by begging—used one hundred fifty times; and finally, ταπεινός, which describes one who is weighed down by the afflictions of life—used two hundred and eighty times. LeClercq maintains that "in the use of all these words, the moral sense sweeps away the sociological signification" (38). "Dans l'utilisation de tous ces mots, le sens moral l'emporte sur la signification sociologique."

⁸ LeClercq, "Aux Origins," 38–39.
⁹ Ibid., 38.
¹⁰ Ibid.
¹¹ Ibid., 39.
¹² Ibid., 40.
¹³ Ibid., 41.

texts acted as theological anchors for the Western Church's interpretation of poverty. The second reason for the priority of *humilis* and *pauper* is practical. Jerome's Latin translation of the Psalms from the Septuagint is dominated by these terms.[14] Though Jerome had retranslated the balance of the Old Testament books from the Hebrew into the Latin, his original translation of the Psalms from the Septuagint was the text that became incorporated into the Vulgate. In Western spirituality, the Psalms have functioned as the Church's book of prayer, and consequentially, this produced effects on Western culture and language.

Pauper *and* Humilis *and the Feudal Age.*

As expressed in the Psalms, poverty is "a longing after God and his justice."[15] "The righteousness of the *pauper* [the poor] contrasts the injustice of the *viri potent* [the powerful man] and the *divites* [the rich] who dominate the unarmed and unprotected."[16] This image of the exploited poor coincided with social and ecclesiastical norms of the Middle Ages, especially during the Carolingian period. Here society was organized along a continuum of power and poverty. Social divisions were identified along the following categories: the *potentiores*, or the strongest men, the *minus potentes*, or the less strong, and finally the poorest of poor—the *pauperiores*.[17] The poorest class, the *pauperiores* is described by Mollat not as those who are indigent or without property, but as a group of persons who are vulnerable and dependent on those who are more powerful than they.[18] The widow and the orphan are obvious examples of this.[19] Mollat adds that "the only word clearly equated with the *pauper* at this time was the term humble."[20]

This understanding fit well with the Benedictine practice of poverty. The Benedictine Rule was characterized by moderation, and it became the guiding principle in early medieval monasteries. Extreme physical pov-

---

[14] Ibid., 40. Mulhern states that the vocabulary of the Psalms underlies the spiritual meaning of poverty. He argues that out of the Psalms "emerges a picture of the poor ['anawim] who are devout and fervent souls . . . who form the religious nucleus of the nation." See Mulhern, *Dedicated Poverty*, 5.

[15] Bosl, *Armut Christi*, 16 (my translation).

[16] Ibid. See also 17.

[17] Mollat, *Poor in the Middle Ages*, 33.

[18] Ibid., 33. See also Lindberg, *Beyond Charity*, 20.

[19] Bosl, *Armut Christi*, 7.

[20] Mollat, *Poor in the Middle Ages*, 33

erty was not part of Benedict's teaching. Rather, he emphasized "the self made whole in Christ."[21] Thus it has been said that St. Benedict's view of property is overshadowed by a "poverty of spirit," interpreted as a social aspect of religious poverty.[22] During the growth of the monastic movement in the ninth and tenth centuries, a large number of monks came from the knightly classes. These men left their positions of status to relinquish feudal power and become 'poor.'[23] Through the monastic movement, the Church not only evangelized Europe, but also was able to address a huge social problem of their day, namely violence.[24] When a member of a knightly family became a monk, he left behind his horses and weapons. By taking vows of poverty, monks could model peace and community, and they could protect themselves from what was seen as the chief sin of that day—the pride that comes with power.[25] Hence, the biblical notion of poverty, understood primarily as humility, when applied to the social hierarchy of the day became both a key concept in the practice of the Christian life and a force of reform within Western feudal society.

In Benedictine monasticism, poverty was defined not by one's lack of assets, but instead by one's humility of spirit. Yet Benedict was well aware that both luxury and indigence could rob a monk of his purpose and ability to grow in the knowledge of Jesus Christ. Thus, he sought to bring a balance by stressing the necessity of moderation.[26] Bede, a later Benedictine monk, once defined a wealthy individual as one who has riches and is therefore inflated, or as one who does not have wealth, yet wishes he does so that he can be exalted. Likewise, he describes a poor man as one that either has nothing and wishes for nothing, or as one that has much but conducts himself as having nothing. Bede understood that some day God will examine a person's conscience rather than one's wine cellar or coffers.[27] Lester Little says that for the Benedictines, "The test of poverty would be a state of mind and not an inventory of worldly goods. By arguing this way, Benedictines could be financially wealthy and still consider themselves as

---

[21] Mulhern, *Dedicated Poverty*, 78–79.

[22] Ibid., 79.

[23] Little, *Religious Poverty*, 197.

[24] Ibid., 198.

[25] Little, "Pride goes before Avarice," 47–46.

[26] Mulhern, *Dedicated Poverty*, 80.

[27] As cited by Little, "Pride goes before Avarice," 46. See *Lucae evangelium expositio* 4.14; *PL* 92, 515

the poor of God."[28] The result was that the Cluny and its more than 2000 daughter houses became laden with wealth, lands, and power. Eventually, the great Benedictine monasteries founded through Cluny fell into spiritual decline "because worldly splendor and poverty of spirit are uneasy partners."[29]

St. Bernard of Clairvaux (b.1090–d.1153) was a prominent impetus behind the Benedictine renewal movement referred to as the Cistercians. Bernard followed the reforms of Robert of Molesmes (b.1027–d.1110), the founder of Citeaux (1098), and became the founder and abbot of Clairvaux (1115). He established Clairvaux upon the principles of poverty, simplicity, and solitude as guided by rule of St. Benedict. The early success of the monastery can be credited to its rejection of all feudal revenues, the ownership of villas and large traces of land, and its commitment to refrain from rentals. Clairvaux's abbies and church buildings were furnished in a simple manner, and the great display of riches characteristic of Cluny were absent. Despite Bernard's reforms, by the twelfth and thirteenth centuries the Cistercians were afflicted by their wealth and large estates, just like Cluny.[30] Little comments that "Bernard's diatribes against the superfluous beauties and comforts of Cluny . . . would have been appropriate for Cistercian buildings of the late twelfth century and of the thirteenth."[31]

In spite of Bernard's administrative reforms, his understanding of poverty was still Benedictine. Little argues that the spiritual dissipation of the early Cistercian monasteries lay in the ideas held by its original leaders such as Bernard.[32] This is evident by his interpretation of spiritual poverty as it relates to charity, grace, and the involuntarily poor. Bernard believed that the kingdom of heaven belonged to those who are voluntarily poor, i.e. the "poor people of Christ," not to simply those who are poor and tend to their own affairs (i.e. the involuntarily poor). Only when poverty is voluntary can it truly be a means to perfection and hence be a means to the kingdom of God. [33] The theological ramifications of this teaching are illustrated by the following story. Bernard sent a group of monks to King

---

[28] Little, "Pride goes before Avarice," 46–47.
[29] Mulhern, *Dedicated Poverty*, 93.
[30] Ibid., 94–95.
[31] Little, *Religious Poverty*, 95. Little comments that Bernard would rhetorically use lines from Roman poetry to criticize the monks at Cluny: "Tell me, you poor men (if indeed, you are poor men), what is this gold doing in your sanctuary?" See Little, "Pride Goes before Avarice," 47.
[32] Little, *Religious Poverty*, 94.
[33] Mollat, *Poor in the Middle Ages*, 8; and Little, *Religious Poverty*, 94.

Roger of Sicily who generously gave them food, shelter, and also good land. Bernard's note of gratitude to the King said:

> These are material things, but they can be traded with, in return for heavenly things. This is the way to heaven; by such sacrifices God is won. For to these men belongs the kingdom of heaven and, in return for your material gifts, they will be able to render you everlasting life and glory.[34]

Bernard came from the knightly class, which by his day, were landed aristocracy. For him, the poor were those who had given up power and position for purposes of God's kingdom. Theirs was a poverty that required humility of spirit but was not always incompatible with the acquisition of material wealth and lands. Through these, whom Bernard called the "poor of Christ," the wealthy and powerful could vicariously participate in the kingdom of God through acts of charity which the religiously poor occasioned. Also, when thanking the Archbishop of York for the material support he provided to the Cistercians, Bernard wrote: It is one thing to fill the belly of the hungry, and another to have a zeal for poverty. The one is a service of nature the other the service of grace.[35] Bernard's words of gratitude are evidence of the critical role that voluntary poverty had in the economy of salvation and the Church. Most notably, it is Bernard's understanding of poverty that is described in sacramental language and relegates the truly hungry to an inferior level in that economy.[36]

This view of poverty had a blind side. Monasteries became trapped in the quagmire of their acquired wealth and lands. As the social landscape of the Middle Ages changed, the monasteries did not adapt.[37] They were located in rural areas far from the growing and needy urban centers. Their

---

[34] *Epistle*, 209; *PL* 182, 375, as quoted in Little, *Religious Poverty*, 94.

[35] *Epistle*, 95; *PL* 182, 228, as quoted in Little, *Religious Poverty*, 95.

[36] It is important to add a distinction here. The Cistercians did combine in their lay brotherhood the two forms of poverty: voluntary and involuntary. The lay brother led a humble life of manual labor as well as a life of simplicity, silence, and prayer. Though such a man was as poor and contemptible as a simple peasant, he nevertheless participated in a religious vocation like a monk that set his poverty apart from other peasants who were not lay brothers. See Mulhern, *Dedicated Poverty*, 104. Another important distinction concerning Bernard's understanding of poverty is that he used the term *pauperes* to refer to the involuntary poor who required material assistance as a matter of justice. Likewise he used the term *egenus* to categorize those who became needy through an accidental circumstance, like the widow or orphan. See Mollat, *Poor in the Middle Ages*, 3.

[37] Mollat reviews how the rise of the city altered the social landscape of Western Europe and contributed to the decay of monasteries and the rise of the Franciscans. Mollat, "Poverty of Francis," 27–29.

spirituality atrophied along with their social impact. Their assumption that poverty of spirit was possible even in the absence of physical poverty became morally indefensible to the larger society. In short, the biblical ethic of poverty was ready for a new interpretation. Gerhoh of Reichersberg (b. 1093–d. 1169), also Benedictine, saw the problem clearly. He argued that for the one Catholic faith there is but one rule of poverty, the Apostolic Rule which is best embodied in a return to the Benedictine Rule. He claimed that clerics possessing property were in violation of this charter and were not to be considered as *paupers Christi*; they should be sent back among the laity.[38] The reforms of Gerhoh went unheeded, and monasticism continued in its declension while new religious orders who practiced genuine poverty moved to the spiritual fore.

Paupertas, Vita Apostolica, and the New Economy

Twelfth Century Humanists and New Thoughts on Poverty

Between the eleventh and fourteenth centuries, European society underwent profound structural changes that birthed a new commercial economy, growing urban centers, and the widespread use of money. This change fostered a widespread shift in cultural and spiritual values. No longer was pride considered the worst spiritual vice. Avarice had taken its place.[39] The twelfth-century humanists re-read the Fathers, the New Testament and especially the Epistle of James. In the writings of the Fathers, they found direct instruction regarding the responsibility of the rich toward the poor. With a firm stance against the abuses of wealth, James, though rarely acknowledged in previous centuries, could no longer be overlooked.[40] The spirituality of poverty and social dimension of charity became clear, bringing a new direction to the Church's understanding of *vita apostolica* and new distinctions within the definition of *paupertas*.[41]

Gerhoh of Richersberg made the distinction between the involuntarily poor like Lazarus and the voluntarily poor like the Apostles. Others like Raoul Ardent simply referred to the involuntarily poor as *pauperes*.[42]

---

[38] The earliest work of Gerhoh of Reichersberg on this topic is the *Book Concerning the House of God* (1128–29). See Little, *Religious Poverty*, 110–11.

[39] Little, "Pride goes before Avarice," 16; See also Lindberg, *Beyond Charity*, 25.

[40] Mollat, *Poor in the Middle Ages*, 104.

[41] Mollat, "Poverty and the Service of the Poor," 53.

[42] Mollat, *Poor in the Middle Ages*, 103–4.

The canonist Huguccio, who wrote one of the greatest commentaries of the twelfth century on the *Decretum*, divided the poor into three distinct categories: First, there were those who endured their poverty for their love of God; second, there were those who gave everything up to become poor; and finally there were those who were poor but filled with "the voracity of cupidity." [43] The first two categories Huguccio called voluntary poverty, describing their situation as being spiritually beneficial. The last category he labeled involuntary poverty, and recognized that this kind of poverty "was not always productive of higher moral virtues."[44] Peter de Blois designated a man as poor if he suffered from a material need, or if his rights were violated; James de Vitry called a man poor if he had to work manually to live.[45]

Categories like these spawned further distinctions in how poverty was understood. An example of this is the language of "worthy" and "unworthy" poor. These were terms that emerged as instruments of clarification for charitable purposes. The "worthy" poor included the biblical classifications of widows, orphans, and the sick along with the "urban elite" who had fallen from their estate. The "unworthy" poor were those who were not "worthy" of charitable assistance. These folk were perceived as "vagabonds and healthy beggars." Their poverty was judged as unworthy, because they were seen as being lazy or "unwilling to work."[46] Lindberg notes that it is this later category of worthy poor to which ecclesiastical doctrine refers concerning charity and the poor.

Poverty occupied a useful place in the economy of salvation and the church. For the rich person, the poor presented an opportunity as a means of sanctification.[47] The humble state of the impoverished were a living representation of the poor and humiliated Christ.[48] Jesus' words about the difficulty of the rich entering the kingdom placed the poor in a position of favor in the divine economy. The rich were to give to the poor, and the poor were to humbly receive their gifts and pray for the souls of the rich. In this relationship the giver displayed the Christian virtue of charity,

---

[43] Tierney, *Medieval Poor Law*, 12.

[44] Ibid., 20.

[45] See Mollat, "Hospitalité et assistance," 51. This understanding of poverty has its origin in ancient Greek culture. See chapter 2 of this study.

[46] Lindberg, *Beyond Charity*, 20.

[47] Riis, "Poverty and Urban Development," 1. See also Lindberg, *Beyond Charity*, 28, 32.

[48] Lindberg, *Beyond Charity*, 28.

while the receiver displayed the virtue of humility.[49] Mollat comments: "The pauper would seem to have been created and placed in the world for the sake of the rich man's salvation."[50] The reality of the poor, charity, and practice of alms became the subject of countless writings, sermons, and letters throughout the Middle Ages. Lindberg observes that the literature never tires of the saying, "the poor carry the riches of the wealthy on their backs to heaven."[51] The only real change this teaching saw throughout the centuries was in the definition of who was considered to be rich or poor.

Poverty and the Reform Movements of the Eleventh to Thirteenth Centuries

The structural changes that swept Europe during the high to late Middle Ages not only gave rise to new thoughts on poverty, but also gave birth to new practices of poverty. The New Testament was more widely available than it was in previous centuries, and laity and clergy alike became gripped anew by the biblical ideal of apostolic poverty. Bolton comments that "in the second half of the twelfth century, considerable numbers of people appeared to behave strangely."[52]

> [They were] renouncing wealth and inheritances, living on alms or choosing to undertake manual work, starving themselves, wearing rags, going barefoot, inflicting personal suffering and generally harassing their own bodies.[53]

Ozment calls this "an ominous development in spirituality for the authority of the Church" which "rapidly produced a widespread counter-

---

[49] Tierney, *Medieval Poor Law*, 53. Lindberg calls this a "symbiotic relationship" between the rich and poor, "the social contract of the High Middle Ages" in which "the rich needed the poor to be saved and thus the poor had an obligation to remain poor." "Reformation Initiatives," 82; *Beyond Charity*, 32–33.

[50] Mollat, *Poor in the Middle Ages*, 106. See also Lindberg, *Beyond Charity*, 81–82.

[51] Lindberg, "Reformation Initiatives," 81–82; Lindberg notes that this idea may be traced back to Augustine. Augustine states, "If our possessions are to be carried away, let us transfer them to a place where we shall not lose them. The poor to whom we give alms! With regard to us what else are they but porters through whom we transfer our goods from earth to heaven? Give away your treasure. Give it to a porter. He will bear to heaven what you give him on earth." Augustine, *Sermon on the Mount*, "Sermon 60: On Almsgiving" (Kavanaugh, 268); *PL* 38, 406.

[52] Bolton, "*Paupertas Christi*," 96.

[53] Ibid.

religious culture."⁵⁴ This movement was treated with suspicion by most ecclesiastical authorities. "Those who practiced such poverty" were considered "socially dangerous."⁵⁵ These people were a direct affront to the established order of things.

In the beginning of the medieval period, the Church had faced the challenge of moderating between her duty to uphold the apostolic ideal of God's special option for the poor, while at the same time accommodating the growing power and wealth of the Church. A compromise was reached: Monks and clergy were chosen to attain this state of higher perfection by living free of material possessions, while the laity would not be held to this ethic since they would live on a lesser level of perfection.⁵⁶ But by the end of the Middle Ages, especially as the laity participated in the *vita apostolica*, they were dissatisfied with the options open to them for their spiritual lives. The reform movements of this period had "a deep appreciation for the spirituality of the laity" and helped to breakdown the idea "that religion is preformed by certain members of society."⁵⁷ The poverty ideal that gave rise to this movement culminated in essentially two groups: those whom the Church sanctioned such as the Franciscans and Dominicans, and those who organized outside of the institutional Church, commonly known as heretical groups, such as the Arnoldi, Humiliati, Waldensians, Beguine, Cathars, and others.⁵⁸ The particular contributions of these wings within this movement will be discussed below; germane for now is what they shared in common.

Little identifies a "coherent line of reform" spanning from the eleventh century Italian hermits through the early generations of the friars.⁵⁹ In the tradition of the hermitage, these movements laid heavy emphasis upon the gospels and Acts of the Apostles. They sought to translate the message

---

⁵⁴ Ozment, *Age of Reform*, 98.

⁵⁵ Bolton, "*Paupertas Christi*," 96.

⁵⁶ Hordern, "Luther's Attitude," 94.

⁵⁷ Little, "Evangelical Poverty," 16.

⁵⁸ Ozment, *Age of Reform*, 98.

⁵⁹ Little, "Evangelical Poverty," 16. Francis of Assisi and the mendicant movements of the twelfth and thirteenth century can be seen together as part of a shift in western Christendom concerning poverty that began with the eremitical movement of the eleventh century. Both movements held up the value of the impoverished itinerant preacher and sensitized the larger society to the plight of the poor. Dante was the first to link Francis to the prior eremitical movement of the eleventh century by associating his movement to that of Baldassini, a thesis which has since been demonstrated. See Bienvenu, "Préhistoire du Franciscanisme," 27–36.

of the biblical text into "codes of behavior to be literally observed."[60] The hallmark of this code was the strict observance of material poverty. Brenda Bolton presents an interesting thesis about this development. She argues that the lifestyle of "*vita apostolica* was adopted as a form of personal and social renewal and that poverty was considered to be a means towards *renovatio*."[61] She says that her second point is more difficult to demonstrate, but she asserts that it is a valid conclusion based on the evidence. Overall, says Bolton, "poverty became the distinguishing symbol of the 'new man' in the twelfth century."[62]

By her own admission, the problem Bolton faces proving her thesis is that written evidence from many of these groups is scarce. Most of the available information derives only from "contemporary observers who were openly hostile to these changes."[63] She also relies heavily upon the Fransicans who by common standards were the high point of the eleventh through thirteenth century reform movements.[64] The Franciscans saw themselves as modern day successors to the apostles by virtue of their voluntary choice of poverty and desire to live in community with one another. "To them, *paupertas* represented the hardest, most intensely personal act they could perform," Bolton argues, "poverty thus became a means whereby personal rebirth or renewal could be obtained."[65] Bolton goes one step further in her analysis of these poverty movements, asking whether those who sought this type of life and harsh treatment towards their bodies were not "visiting upon themselves a correction and deprivation which they wanted to apply to society itself," and thus participating in "a deliberate social act to recreate a new church in a new society?"[66] The proposal has merit and fits well into the overall historical and theological framework of poverty in the high to later Middle Ages. Upon closer examination of Francis and his particular application of the poverty ideal, Bolton's thesis finds the most support.

---

[60] Little, "Evangelical Poverty," 16.
[61] Bolton, "*Paupertas Christi*," 95.
[62] Ibid.
[63] Ibid., 95–96.
[64] Little, "Evangelical Poverty," 16; Ozment argues that the confirmation of the new mendicant orders of Fransicans and Dominicans were part of a move on the part of the Pope "to contain the poverty ideal and turn it into constructive use within the Church." Ozment, *Age of Reform*, 98.
[65] Bolton, "*Paupertas Christi*," 98.
[66] Ibid., 100–1.

St. Francis and the Mendicant Controversy

Though there was a great shift in the way that the West came to understand poverty in the eleventh through thirteenth centuries, no one had a greater impact on solidifying this transformation than Francis of Assisi (b.1181–d.1226). His short life—and the movement that followed him—did more to define the notion of poverty than any previous person or movement in the Western Church. The literature on Franciscan poverty and its historical evolution are far too prolific to be presented here. Yet, one should note a number of important distinctions which Francis and the mendicant movement brought to the Church's view and practice of poverty. These distinctions became a part of Calvin's cultural and theological landscape; therefore, they are important to this study.

For Francis, taking the vow of poverty was not simply a matter of the heart or of humility as it was with the Benedictines. It meant that one literally lived as a *pauper*, owning nothing and using only what is necessary for one's bare subsistence.[67] In this view, poverty was nothing short of complete physical sacrifice, described by the term *usus pauper*. It was a poverty that sought to imitate the poverty of Christ. One favorite of Francis' example of Christ's poverty was the stripping off of his garments to wash the disciples' feet. "The washing of feet is the work of Christ," and was "the sign of the true disciple" and a "sign of a true follower of the Rule."[68]

Francis' ideal was also inspired by Matt 10:8–11, where Jesus sends his disciples out to preach, commanding them to take nothing for their journey. Francis taught that poverty needs to be understood in the totality of life. He carefully outlined for his brothers what kind of garments they were to wear, and that they were to take no bags,[69] money or even a walking stick. The brothers were to work for food and lodging and were not to accept money, or even to touch it except when caring for the sick.[70] Francis

---

[67] Ozment, *Age of Reform*, 109. See also Little, "Pride goes before Avarice," 45.

[68] Lambert, *Franciscan Poverty*, 63.

[69] Lambert points out that Francis observed that the term *loculi* (or bag) is only used in the gospels in connection with Judas. Hence Francis saw the bag, or the *loculi*, as a powerful symbol of the betrayal of Christ and forbade his followers to ever carry one. To not carry a bag meant you joined the true disciples of Christ following Christ's true poverty. If you carried a bag you followed not Christ and his poverty but Judas and the wealth he sought after. Lambert, *Franciscan Poverty*, 63–64.

[70] Ozment, 99–100.

classified these rules as a "poverty of the outer things" which represent the deeper reality of his poverty.[71]

A second realm in which Francis taught the application of poverty was in the domain of human relationships. The brothers were not only exhorted to give up dependency on accumulated material goods, but they were instructed "to give up all aspirations of power and domination,"[72] thus committing themselves to never abuse or use their brothers in any fashion. Francis' teaching on the practice of poverty in human relationships became the basis for his understanding of community and brotherhood in the Christian faith. It is from this teaching that the name *minore* derived.[73]

The last area in which Francis applied the principles of poverty was his relationship to God. Francis reasoned that God as Lord and Creator possesses all things. In contrast, however, the only thing humanity possesses is sinfulness, which leaves all people as beggars before God.[74] The staggering inequality between God and humanity should eliminate all temptations of pride, jealousy and vanity. This enormous truth, humanity's spiritual destitution before God, formed the heart of Francis' perspective regarding poverty. This affected his understanding of poverty in human relationships as well as the kind of lifestyle he embraced.

Francis' practice of poverty was also related to two other distinguishing marks of his life: itinerant preaching and manual labor.[75] Following Matt 10:8–11, Francis believed that poverty was a means to ensure effective preaching. Poverty gave credibility and moral authority to both the preacher and the gospel.[76] This credo also guided Dominic and his followers, and incidentally, was also employed by Waldo and the Waldensians a generation earlier.[77] Francis made a concerted effort to go to the poor in

[71] Eßer, "Armutsauffassung," 61–65.
[72] Ibid., 66 (my translation). "Der Arme muß alles Streben nach Macht und Herrschaft aufgeben."
[73] Ibid., 67.
[74] Ibid., 68.
[75] Ozment, *Age of Reform*, 99. Francis outlines three distinguishing marks (poverty, itinerant preaching, and manual labor) for the Friars Minor in his second and definitive rule, the *Regula bullata*, composed in 1221 and approved by Pope Honorius III in 1223.
[76] Little, "Evangelical Poverty," 16.
[77] Ozment, *Age of Reform*, 99. Francis of Assisi and the mendicant movements of the twelfth and thirteenth century can be seen together as part of a shift in western Christendom concerning poverty that began with the eremitical movement of the eleventh century. The movement held up the value of the impoverished itinerant preacher and sensitized the larger society to the plight of the poor. Dante was the first to link Francis to the prior

villages and on the outskirts of urban areas, preaching the gospel as he lived and labored by their side. In a society where money ascribed worth and power to those fortunate enough to have it, and demeaned those who did not, Francis preached the poor's value as sacred images of Christ. Mollat states "this was something new: the poor and the afflicted were valued for their intrinsic human and spiritual worth and not as mere instruments for the salvation of the wealthy."[78] Therefore, as Lindberg notes, similar to the Benedictines' use of poverty to develop a moral theology in response to the power and violence of the feudal context, the Franciscans sought to integrate poverty into a moral theology that spoke to the issues involved in a developing money economy. He concludes, "The commercial revolution of 1000 to 1350 affected a theological development in the understanding of poverty and its religious significance."[79]

The consecration of manual labor by Francis and others is another twist in the reconfiguration of poverty in the eleventh through thirteenth centuries. "Monastic spirituality never regarded everyday work in the world as anything of value."[80] Though the writers of the Middle Ages did not deny the necessity of manual labor, they still saw it as demeaning and not spiritually edifying. This attitude was inherited from both the Greeks and the Romans.[81] Eusebius of Caesarea (b. 260? – d. 340?) once argued

---

eremitical movement of the eleventh century by associating his movement to that of Baldassini, a thesis which has since been demonstrated. See Bienvenu, "Préhistoire du Franciscanisme," 27–36. Little supports this thesis. He says, "There is a specific and coherent line of reform running from the Italian hermits of the eleventh century to the early generations of the Friars. Though there were many forms of spirituality there was a single program of reform" Little, "Evangelical Poverty," 16. It is also important to stress that the hermits of the eleventh century identified poverty with purity. Part of the protests against the clergy during the Gregorian reform movement was not economic in nature and only anti-clerical by accident. Rather it was the populace who insisted that the clergy forsake their wealth and "live by an ideal of poverty exemplified by the poorest of the poor." Mollat, *Poor in the Middle Ages*, 80.

[78] Mollat, *Poor in the Middle Ages*, 121.

[79] Lindberg, *Beyond Charity*, 26.

[80] McGrath, *Reformation Thought*, 223–24.

[81] Mollat states the following historical reasons for the West's traditional disdain for servile tasks: "Germanic esteem for the military life, and the Judeo-Christian predilection for the contemplative life . . ." (*Poor in the Middle Ages*, 31). The problem with this statement is that his analysis does not go back far enough. The Jews did not have a "contemplative tradition" in their history until they encountered Hellenistic culture. Rather, the source of this tradition may be attributed to assumptions about work and philosophic endeavors found in Greek philosophy and Greek aristocratic culture. As one empire conquered the next, these ideas found their way into the Roman culture influencing both Greek and Latin Fathers only to permeate all of western thought. (See also Countryman, *Rich Christian*,

that the perfect Christian life was one that was totally devoted to serving God, untainted by physical labor. Those who chose to work and live in the world became regarded as second rate Christians having forfeited a first rate calling.[82] These spiritual assumptions and values produced within medieval society a spiritual and political aristocracy, of those who worked (peasants, serfs, and servants), and those who did not (Lords and monks). This aristocracy, in turn, produced negative and dismissive attitudes towards the laborer.[83] Thus it follows why Francis instructed his followers to participate in manual labor. If *vita apostolica* meant taking on a life of no earthly importance, then according to Francis, manual labor was an essential part of this life.

Practicing this life of poverty, the Franciscan movement grew rapidly in numbers and in popularity with the people. When people saw a Franciscan teaching in their town, they were drawn to him by his affinity to the first century apostles, personally bringing the message of the gospel to them. Yet success was not always sweet. Before long the movement saw signs of struggle and internal divisions. Six months before his death, Francis composed his *Testament,* described by some as a "controversial farewell to his followers." No doubt, sensing that the movement's poverty ideal was in jeopardy, he firmly expressed the rule that the religious must deny the right to own fixed properties or hold offices invested with worldly power. In short, Francis sought to bind the movement to a strict observance of voluntary poverty.[84]

In 1228 Pope Gregory IX canonized Francis, and the order became divided between those who sought to live according to the more strict rule of the *Testament* and those who desired to live a more settled life. Pope Gregory IX was threatened by the strict rule of poverty outlined in Francis' *Testament*. Francis' views opposed the papal lifestyle of power and wealth,

---

24–25, for a description of how the Greco-Roman culture was divided between rich and poor, according to who participated in manual labor.) Furthermore, the early Church and the rabbinic tradition held a respectable attitude towards work and manual labor. Even Celsus wrote contemptuously in his polemic that Christians were uneducated "wool-workers, shoemakers and cloth makers" who wished to instruct other men. Origen, *CC* 3. 55 (Chadwick, 165). See also Hengel, *Property and Riches*, 60–73.

[82] McGrath, *Reformation Thought*, 223.

[83] Ibid. These prejudices are reflected in the development of the terms applied to the working class. Mollat discusses the synonyms for *laborator*. One was the term "*paganus* from which the term peasant is derived." This was applied to the rural pauper who was illiterate and "had not yet received the enlightenment of the Gospels." He adds, "The *illiteratus* was an uncouth rustic, hardly less stupid than his animals" (*Poor in the Middle Ages*, 31–32).

[84] Ozment, *Age of Reform*, 100.

especially with its assertions that the religious are not to own fixed properties.[85] The following year Gregory issued the bull *Quo elongati* (1229) in which he declared the *Testament* to be invalid and non-binding on Francis' followers. In it, he also asserted that Franciscans had a *usus rerum*, or a "use" of things without a real "possession" of them. Ozment writes that "under Gregory, absolute poverty became almost a legal fiction."[86] The purpose of Gregory's ruling was to confine the Franciscan order to the first rule, and also to make it clear that it is the Pope and not Francis who sets the dogma of the Church and hence the theology of movements.[87] Yet the damage had been done. The splintering of the Franciscans which had begun at Francis' death and *Testament* continued to increase until the outbreak of the *Usus Pauper* Controversy in 1279. By this time, two major factions had emerged within the movement: the Spirituals, or Fraticelli (earlier known as the Observant followers), and the Conventuals. These groups had diverse interpretations of Francis and of Lady Poverty.

Huge of Digne (d.1280) was an early Spiritual or Observant who held to the strict interpretation of Francis' Rule of poverty. He stated in his *Dispute* that when one takes the Franciscan vow of poverty, he or she is bound to the "insignia of poverty" (the "external signs of an inner quality"). Though he admitted that this "insignia of poverty" does not guarantee that one has "internal poverty. . . , yet its absence guarantees that internal poverty is absent."[88] In other words, one can be physically impoverished and not necessarily poor in spirit. Yet, one can never be poor in spirit without being physically poor. This rigorist view of the Spirituals[89] was not embraced by the order's greatest leader after Francis, Bonaventura.

---

[85] Ibid., 102.

[86] Ibid., 109.

[87] Ibid.

[88] As quoted in Burr, *Olivi and Franciscan Poverty*, 20. Burr also records a statement from Huge of Digne's writing in his *Rule Commentary* and in his work *On the Ends of Poverty*: "Where there is no adequate correlation between internal and external reality, the result is superstition or hypocrisy." Ibid.

[89] A good friend of Hughe of Digne was the first successor to Francis, the order's minister generalate, John of Parma. The whole stress of his generalate was to reform the order by stressing the Rule of poverty among his brothers without the Papal glosses that sought to lessen its rigorous nature. John failed in his mission mostly due to conflicts over his Joachimite beliefs. Upon resigning, he appointed a man who was to be a definitive leader and thinker on the question of poverty for the Franciscans, Bonaventura (b.1217– d.1274). Lambert, *Franciscan Poverty*, 103–15.

Bonaventura was a gifted thinker, leader, and administrator, which earned him the distinction of being the order's "second founder."[90] His vision was to unite the two wings of the order, though mostly at the expense of the Spirituals' ideals. He wrote the "official" biography of Francis' life and an authoritative exposition of the Rule. In both of these writings, he domesticated many of Francis' more severe statements regarding poverty while he spiritualized others.[91] He supported those who wished to substitute academic and spiritual work such as scholarship and meditation for manual labor. He did not see that upholding a life of poverty necessitated that the order remain fixed to primitive ideals of itinerant preaching that restricted the construction of buildings and meant going without food, clothing, or shelter. Bonaventura defined Franciscan poverty as something not to be measured against an "absolute standard," not even the standard of the life of Francis, but rather by "taking only those things that are necessary for the fulfillment of the role to which one is called."[92] Bonaventura could relax the Franciscan interpretation of the poverty ideal because he held to the conviction that perfection in the Christian life did not lie in poverty *per se*. In his *Apologia Pauperum*, he argues that spiritual perfection lies only in charity. Hence the "material goods of the church can be held without detriment to Christian perfection."[93] Such were the teachings of the Conventuals. Under Bonaventura, the poverty of the Franciscans "became more a spiritual ideal than a literal one, an attitude of heart

---

[90] Ozment, *Age of Reform*, 103.
[91] When Bonaventura wrote his biography of Francis, *Legenda maior* (1263), there were already two other biographies of Francis. Both were written by Francis' close friend and disciple, Thomas of Celano. The first *Vita prima* was written 1228 and the second in 1247. Celano also wrote a collection of miracle stories around 1253. Bonaventura relied heavily on Celano's work, modifying the accounts to construct his own interpretation on the significance of Francis' life and teachings. Yet, three years after his work was written, "the Paris chapter of Franciscans" not only "declared Bonaventura's biography the official life of Francis" but also "ordered" all other biographies to be "rescinded." Ozment, *Age of Reform*, 102–3.
[92] Burr, *Olivi and Franciscan Poverty*, 25.
[93] Mulhern, *Dedicated Poverty*, 124. This does not mean that Bonaventura had a disregard for poverty. He recognizes and affirms the fact that the Fathers and the New Testament hold poverty in high esteem. Bonaventure writes: "Poverty is praiseworthy; higher poverty more praiseworthy, the highest poverty—most praiseworthy, and the very highest poverty of all is that by which one holds nothing as his own either as an individual or as a member of a group." 115–16.

and mind, not an actual physical state;"[94] or, in the perspective of one Franciscan brother, this ideal was "poverty without penury."[95]

Yet Bonaventura, together with the Dominican Aquinas, came to the defense of the mendicant interpretation of poverty in the middle of the thirteenth century. William of St. Amour, head of the secular masters at the University of Paris, attempted to discredit the Franciscans' and Dominicans' practice of poverty[96] with his pamphlet *De novissimorum temporum periculis* (On the perils of the later times.)[97] William and the seculars were not against the monks practice of poverty in the cloister. Rather, they objected to the kind of mendicant poverty that was based on the providence of God with no provision for the needs of tomorrow and which depended upon begging. In short, he attacked the Franciscans' and Dominicans' way of life.[98]

In the same year (1254), a young Franciscan student, Gerard of Borgo San Donnino, published an unauthorized and heretical adaptation of the Joachimite doctrine of the ages of the world. The secular masters saw this opportunity and discredited the mendicants before the papacy.[99] At the close of his pontificate, Innocent IV withdrew the mendicants' privileges of exemptions. This brought the two great orders down to the level of the Humiliati; that is, "a co-fraternity more tolerated than approved of by

---

[94] Ozment, *Age of Reform*, 103.

[95] A. Little, *Studies*, 4.

[96] Francis and Dominic shared several things in common. They both began a life of poverty and itinerant preaching at about the same time. Both sought to emulate the apostolic life of Jesus and his disciples as part of the reform of the Church and the culture at large. Like Francis, Dominic sent his preachers off without money and instructed them to obtain their daily needs by asking others for assistance. Yet, there were some significant distinctions that set the two founders and movements apart. These pertain to the founders' view of poverty. Concerning money, Dominic saw money as something to be used where Francis saw it as something to be detested. Dominic saw nothing wrong with accepting financial support from the Bishop. He accepted only enough to cloth and feed his wandering preachers. At the end of the year any excess monies were returned. Francis would interpret such an act as not living a true life of poverty where one is fully dependent on God on a daily basis to have one's needs supplied. To accept such monies is to take oneself out of the position of a true evangelical poverty wherein faith may be fully exercised. Another great difference was that Dominic did not exclude the possibility of corporate ownership of goods. Francis did exclude this option and the Franciscans fought internally for more than a century over the interpretation of Franciscan poverty on this point. See Mulhern, *Dedicated Poverty*, 109–11.

[97] LeClercq, Vandenbroucke, and Bouyer, *Spirituality of the Middle Ages*, 337.

[98] Mulhern, *Dedicated Poverty*, 113, 122.

[99] Lambert, *Franciscan Poverty*, 107–8.

Rome."[100] Bonaventura wrote an apology on begging and poverty called *De paupertate Christi*, in which he appealed to numerous Greek and Latin Fathers. Aquinas responded to the crises by writing the treatise *Opusculum* "against those who attack the worship of God and the religious life." Yet, before Aquinas was finished, Alexander IV, Innocent's successor, restored the Mendicants' privileges and condemned William of St. Amour's actions, ordering him to leave teaching.[101] It is important to note that the treatises Bonaventura and Aquinas wrote in support of voluntary poverty stood firm in their defense until the Reformation. However, concerning this incident, Mulhern observes: "The ideal of poverty had been held in honor in the Church for almost 1300 years, but now a theology was needed to protect it."[102]

The Franciscans and Usus Pauper

Not more than five years after the death of Bonaventura, the fragile peace he had forged between the Spirituals and Conventuals vanished over a dispute concerning the order's interpretation of *usus pauper*. *Usus pauper* is a technical term that defined the obligation of Franciscans concerning their vow of poverty, namely, the restriction of their use of material things to those that can be categorized as providing or basic necessities.[103] The *Usus Pauper* Controversy[104] began between lectors in southern France. The writings of Peter Olivi (b. 1247? or 1248—d. 1298) were at the center of the dispute. Olivi argued that though a Franciscan may become a Bishop, this does not release him from the Franciscan vow of poverty, which entails an observance of *usus pauper*.[105] Olivi's definition of the state of need regarding *usus pauper* was not defined as "a state in which death is imminent unless relief comes immediately." Rather, the necessity involved in *usus pauper* was "a need manifestly existing for the present or immediate future

---

[100] Mulhern, *Dedicated Poverty*, 113.

[101] LeClercq, Vandenbroucke, and Bouyer, *Spirituality of the Middle Ages*, 337. History has judged William of St. Amour as being jealous of friars like Bonaventura and Aquinas who would take students away from the secular masters. The Friars were popular at the University of Paris and their poverty made the monks' vow of poverty look foolish. William of St. Amour's credibility was soon jeopardized when sought to label the Dominicans as the "forerunners of the Antichrist." See Mulhern, *Dedicated Poverty*, 123.

[102] Mulhern, *Dedicated Poverty*, 115.

[103] Lambert, *Franciscan Poverty*, 150. See n. 1.

[104] See Burr's book, *Olivi and Franciscan Poverty*, for a complete study on this issue.

[105] Burr, *Olivi and Franciscan Poverty*, 137.

of such a nature that one cannot remain in one's proper state without its fulfillment."[106]

The reason that Olivi held a more rigid view of voluntary poverty is that it held influence in the rest of the Christian life. Olivi saw faith and poverty as inseparable.[107] In Franciscan spirituality, humility is a key ingredient. Olivi not only saw poverty as a necessary instrument for fostering humility, but he also knew that true humility is a product of complete and absolute physical poverty and not simply about having common possessions.[108] In Olivi's reasoning a person who is void of material goods and power, and has voluntarily chosen self denial by means of a vow, has not only stripped away all grounds for pride in the present, but also for the future, since the vow kills any hope of power and wealth to come.[109] Hence, it is "only with *usus pauper* that pride may be removed and self abnegation be achieved."[110]

Poverty, for Olivi, also affects the interpretive lens one applies to Scripture, and hence one's doctrine of Christ and the Church. Poverty functions as a hermeneutical key that enables a person to read and understand Scripture and to properly understand the message of Jesus Christ revealed in the gospel. The danger of being consumed with earthly things is that they blind one to the true meaning of the wealth one has in Jesus Christ: "a spiritual wealth that is based upon the superiority of poverty over wealth." Poverty turns one's eyes from sensible things and enables one to grasp the wisdom of God that is hidden from physical eyes.[111] For Olivi, this was the reform the whole Church needed. He saw the Church as suffering from carnality stemming from an intoxication with wealth and power. He argued that luxury and heresy had the same origin, an infatuation with the things of this world. Hence, the battle for Olivi was forged on two fronts: the struggle for an evangelical poverty and the defense of doctrinal orthodoxy.[112] This meant that the man of poverty was in a perfect position to affect reform upon the Church.

From 1283 to 1285, Peter Olivi was removed from his teaching post and his writings censured. From 1285 to 1295, the order faced conflicts

---

[106] *Tractatus*, Q 9, 85 va, as quoted in Burr, *Olivi and Franciscan Poverty*, 68.
[107] Ibid., 75.
[108] Ibid., 73.
[109] Bolton, "Poverty of the Humiliati," 72.
[110] Ibid.
[111] Ibid., 76.
[112] Burr, "Poverty as a Constituent Element," 75.

over Olivi's position on *usus pauper,* but there was no attempt to censure it. Olivi never went back to teaching. The year before he died he published his *Commentary on the Apocalypse* (1297), in which he adopted much of Joachim's interpretation and periodization of history. He portrayed his time as one of transition between the period of clerics and priests, and the period of those who live in true Christian poverty. Olivi depicted St. Francis as the angel of Revelation 7:2, the apocalyptic figure who carries God's seal. Furthermore, he interpreted the struggle between the Spirituals and the Pope over poverty as the climax of the cosmic and ultimate struggle between good and evil found at the end of the age.[113] This apocalyptic interpretation of the Church was judged to be a threat. The Dominican, Thomas Aquinas lead the defense. He challenged Olivi's Joachite philosophy of history arguing that the grace of the Holy Spirit could not be received in a form more perfect than its presentation in the New Law [the New Testament] which was embodied in the papal church. Furthermore, Aquinas asserted there was no superior age of grace, save Joachim's third age, the eschatological age beyond history altogether.[114]

As a result of this conflict, Aquinas' view of poverty came to weigh heavily upon the official view adopted by the Church, and it also meant Olivi's followers were persecuted. Thomas reworked his ideas about poverty after the Paris Mendicant Controversy. In his early days, he maintained that the mendicants were following Jesus by not holding possessions in common. This teaching is noticeably absent from his later works especially in his defense against Olivi. In the *Summa,* he argues for the "fittingness of Christ's poverty and that Jesus and his disciples were fed by generous women and probably out of a common fund."[115] Thomas made some other important exegetical distinctions about poverty. Commenting on Luke 14:33, he argues that there is a difference between "renouncing all" [*renuntiare omnibus*] and "leaving all" [*relinquere omnia*]. The former is the duty of all believers, that is, to use the things of this world with an eye towards eternity; it is called "habitual poverty" or a "poverty of will." The latter describes the manner in which one can perfectly put away the temporal and focus exclusively upon the eternal. This is not only "habitual poverty" or "poverty of will," but also "actual poverty." Thomas prefers a life of both "actual" and "habitual" poverty to the practice of "habitual

---

[113] Ozment, *Age of Reform,* 112.

[114] Ibid., 112–13.

[115] Aquinas, *St* 3a, 40.3 ad 2 (Parsons/Pinheiro, 65); Mulhern, *Dedicated Poverty,* 129.

poverty" alone.[116] He detested the "cloak of the poverty of spirit for retaining riches in fact."[117] He calls those "*horribulius*" who do not view the poverty commended in Scripture as an "actual poverty" whereby one is called to renounce one's material goods, and also those who instead spiritualize the passage to mean that one has only to give them up in their heart while they may still possess them.[118]

In his later view, Thomas locates the practice of poverty within the context of the whole religious life and in relationship to the other vows and virtues. In doing this, he places charity as the end of all religious life and makes poverty superior to chastity but inferior to obedience.[119] For Thomas, poverty and spiritual perfection (charity) are not identical. Poverty can exist where spiritual perfection (charity) is missing. Hence, poverty cannot be considered an end in itself. Instead, it can only be a means to an end, that is, something that removes obstacles which hinder the exercise of virtue and one's growth towards spiritual perfection (charity).[120]

In the wake of the dispute between the Spirituals and the Conventuals and the Papacy in the opening decades of the fourteenth century, a series of papal bulls were written which effectively alienated the Spirituals from Rome and hence, the Church. In the bull *Quorundam exigit* (October 1317), Pope John XXII declared, "Poverty is great . . . but integrity is greater, and obedience is the greatest good." To the Pope, poverty involves one's response only towards worldly goods, whereas obedience to the Church involves spiritual goods—the condition of the heart and mind.[121] Three months later, he wrote the bull *Gloriosam ecclesiam* (January 1318), which accused the Spirituals of being Donatists. It charged that they confused their claim to be in a superior state of perfection with the sacramental power and authority of the Church.[122] Four years later, he wrote two more bulls, *Quia nonnunquam* and *Ad conditorem canonum*. In these, he dissolved the theological basis of the Spirituals' strict interpretation of the Franciscan Rule and vow of poverty by denying that any distinction existed between "ownership" and "use" as proposed in the bulls issued by Gregory

---

[116] Mulhern, *Dedicated Poverty*, 118–19.
[117] Ibid., 117.
[118] Ibid.
[119] Ibid., 130–31.
[120] Ibid., 128–29.
[121] Ozment, *Age of Reform*, 113.
[122] Ibid.

IX and Nicholas III a century earlier. According to John, what one ate, wore, and lived in, one also possessed and had dominion over.[123] In short, the theology of *usus pauper* was effectively declared null and void.

Pope John XXII's goal was clear. He was determined to undermine the whole teaching and way of life of St. Francis and his followers. To add insult to injury, he declared that Jesus and the Apostles possessed goods both privately and corporately in the bull *um inter nonnulles* (1323) that came the following year. Thus they did not practice an 'abject poverty' in the way taught by the Franciscans and Spirituals.[124] What began as an effort to settle an internal dispute came to discredit the whole brotherhood in the eyes of the papacy. Great dissension followed John's declarations. Conventuals found more in common with some of the Spirituals than with the Papacy. Six years later, the Pope issued *Quia vir reprobus* (1329) which condemned any form of "poor use" and asserted that spiritual perfection belongs to the realm of spiritual poverty alone and has nothing to do with the literal renunciation of property. John cited Genesis declaring that even before the fall of humanity, God gave humanity dominion over creation. Therefore, ownership of property is not a mark of sinfulness; hence, it is something no religious group need renounce.[125] Brenda Bolton writes a fitting epitaph for the demise of Franciscan poverty:

> . . . the spiritual Franciscans of the thirteenth and fourteenth centuries, with their Joachite dreams and their plans for the redemption of the whole church through the total acceptance of voluntary poverty. This vision ultimately brought discredit to this reforming group within the order, and worked fundamentally and fatally against the doctrine of the absolute poverty of Christ which had been so relevant as a force for renewal in the context of the twelfth century. The church in western society had not yet found a solution to the problem of individual rebirth and a renewal of society.[126]

Poverty and the Proliferation of Heresy

Pope John XXII may have issued the official declaration that spiritual perfection belongs to the realm of spiritual poverty alone, and that it has nothing to do with the literal renunciation of property, yet this was not

---

[123] Ibid.
[124] Ibid.
[125] Ibid., 114.
[126] Bolton, "*Paupertas Christi*," 103.

the conviction of the masses. The idealization of poverty characterized in Francis' life and teachings gripped the society at large. The poor were seen as "closer to the kingdom of God than the great and rich."[127] Large numbers of commoners and clergy alike followed the biblical ideal of apostolic poverty, which produced a "widespread counter-religious culture" that challenged the spirituality, and at times, the authority of the Church.[128] This resulted in one of the most prominent features of the high to late Middle Ages, namely, the proliferation of heretical groups.

This trend was fostered by a ruling of the Fourth Lateran Council (1215).[129] It declared that there would be no more new orders created in the Church. New orders had been the way in which the institutional Church was reformed. New orders always embodied some new interpretation and practical application of living a life of poverty for the sake of serving the Church. Throughout history, the creation of new orders was responsible for the expansion and renewal of the Church. Yet, this ruling meant that the call for reform must come from within, that is, from within the orders, the hierarchy and the ecclesial structures already in existence. To put it simply, the Council now required that new wine be placed in old wineskins. There is only one conclusion to a policy such as this: The wineskins will eventually spring leaks and finally burst. One might say that the increase in heretical groups were the leaks, and it was Luther who finally made them burst.

New orders, reform movements, and medieval heretical groups all had one thing in common: they sought change in the existing spiritual condition of the Church, and employed some practice of a life of voluntary poverty as a way to enact that change.[130] Like the others already discussed, heretical movements sprang from a "search for a fuller spiritual life."[131] From the eleventh to the fifteenth centuries, heretical groups shared many of the same perspectives as other reform groups, "namely, the desire to emulate the life and teachings of Christ and his Apostles," and more specifically, "to seek a return to the precepts of the gospel through a

---

[127] Lindberg, "There Should be no Beggars," 319.

[128] Ozment, *Age of Reform*, 98.

[129] Ibid.

[130] This is a variation on the thesis put forward by Brenda Bolton in her article "*Paupertas Christi*." She says, "*vita apostolica* was adopted as a form of personal and social renewal and that poverty was considered to be a means towards *renovatio*." Though she says this about the twelfth century Mendicants and Waldensians and hermits, I believe the statement holds true for earlier monastic and reform movements. See page 95.

[131] Leff, *Heresy in the Later Middle Ages*, 2.

life of poverty— or one of complete simplicity— and preaching."[132] Yet what is it that sets the heretical movements of the high to late Middle Ages apart from new orders and other reform movements of the Church? Ultimately, the question turns on the status of the group in the eyes of the Church. "In the Middle Ages," Gordon Leff writes:

> . . . heresy was born when heterodoxy became or was branded, dissent; and more specifically when the appeal . . . to the Bible and to the evangelical virtues of poverty and humility, became, or were treated as, a challenge to the church. It was then that protest became uppermost, conceived henceforth in directly anti-sacerdotal terms.[133]

An illustration of the above description of heresy versus heterodoxy is a comparison between Peter Waldo and Francis of Assisi.

Waldo and Francis were both laymen. Both made a decision to live as paupers with few friends and go about serving the destitute and preaching the need for penance. Both are known to have given up their goods, conferring them on the poor. Both men were from families of financial substance. Early in their ministries they consulted their respective bishops, who gave them encouragement. Yet Waldo was married and was therefore banned from preaching. When he refused to heed the authority of the Church, he and his companions were branded as heretics. Waldo decided that he was more interested in following Christ than a human authority. Francis, on the other hand, taught that the authority of the Pope and bishops was an authority delegated by Christ, and therefore true humility called one to obedience. This is where Waldo failed at an institutional level, and Francis succeeded.[134] It is this essential difference that caused

---

[132] Ibid.

[133] Ibid., 3. With the exception of the Cathars and the Free Spirit, Leff describes the development of a group's movement from dissent to that of a heretical sect. "All the main sects" he states, "began by embracing the commonly accepted tenants," and "only subsequently, in the course of growing hostility between them and the church, did they take on a more extreme, and often debased form."

[134] See Mollat, "Poverty and the Service of the Poor," 51–52; and Lambert, *Medieval Heresy*, 76. Mulhern also points out that it was not just that the Waldenses began to preach that they were persecuted by Rome and labeled heretics but that they preached against the practices of the clergy with regard to their abuse of money. Furthermore, they saw themselves as the true Church and the Roman Church as the Whore of Babylon. See Mulhern, *Dedicated Poverty*, 99–100.

the Franciscans to become an order of renewal in the church and the Waldensians to be excluded and eventually persecuted by the Church.[135]

A close examination of the proliferation of heretical groups in the Middle Ages, and how each one of them appropriated poverty into their theology and lifestyle is beyond the scope of this chapter. Yet there are some points that need to be considered as part of the medieval milieu from which Calvin emerges. Already discussed was the point that new orders, reform movements, and heretical groups practiced some form of voluntary poverty in their theology and lifestyle. Yet a tendency more characteristic of heresy than the other groups is what Gordon Leff calls "the *veneration of poverty* . . . the hallmark of most heretical movements" in the Middle Ages.[136] Poverty was not only involved in the most "universal" characteristic of "religious reform," but was the "driving force" behind nearly all heretical groups, including Wycliffe and Hus since they called the Church to divest itself of its wealth.[137] The observance of a life of poverty came to function as a moral barometer measuring the veracity of faithful discipleship and the extent to which the institutional Church had strayed from the principles of the gospel. Practicing a life of poverty ensured the moral permission to preach the gospel, and a disregard for the Church's position that restricted this privilege to the ordained.[138]

Poverty also provided heretical sects "with what may be called an historicism."[139] This outlook furnished many of these groups with a rationale for their protest against the institutional Church. Had not Christ and his disciples led lives of simplicity divested of temporal power, secular jurisdictions, material wealth, and properties? If the practices of the disciples and the early Church were normative then the endowment received by Pope Sylvester I from Constantine would have disqualified him from being a true successor of Christ. Hence, the wealth, power, and prestige of the present-day ecclesiastical hierarchy was fraudulent. "True disciples of Christ" would separate themselves from this corruption and seek to return to a way of life modeled by the apostles. This was not only the rationale of

---

[135] For more information on Waldes and the Waldensians and their view of poverty, see Little, *Religious Poverty*, 120–128; and Biller, "*Thesaurus Absconditus*," 139–60.

[136] My italics. Leff, *Heresy and the Later Middle Ages*, 9.

[137] Ibid., 8. According to Leff, the only group that this statement does not apply is the Franciscan Conventuals.

[138] Ibid., 9.

[139] Ibid.

the Waldensians, but as Leff states, "is to be found in one form or another amongst most sects."[140]

Several ramifications emerge from this perspective. First, these heretical groups, and their emphasis on poverty, among other things, "gave rise to what one may call an outlook of protest." Like the early reformers, "none of these groups thought in terms of a different Church, but rather a renewal of the present Church."[141] Second, by the thirteenth to fifteenth centuries, medieval society began to become discontented with the inability of the Church to help people with Christian practice and precept. It is estimated that by this time, upwards of thirty percent of the population of medieval Europe was pushed into vagrancy and poverty.[142] The ecclesiastical tradition, which had idealized poverty as the opportunity of the rich to gain entrance into heaven by relieving the plight of the poor, began to lose its potency as urban growth accelerated and commercial changes transpired. A growing dissatisfaction with the flagrant display of wealth within the Church, together with frustration over the limited avenues of spiritual expression for the laity, created an atmosphere of tension as the populous realized that the institutional Church could not compete with the spiritual authenticity and simplicity of life of the heretics—all of which served to undermine the moral and spiritual authority of the Roman Church.

The final point to emerge from this crisis is that poverty and the renunciation of all possessions after the example of Jesus Christ and his apostles "was physically incompatible with the continuance of the Church as a corporation."[143] As Leff notes, the "entire structure [of the Roman Church] rested upon its endowments, taxation, tithes and jurisdiction," and without these "it would have no visible identity or continuity."[144] Though a strict practice of poverty may have been implausible for the Church as an institutional structure, one cannot help but think that some simplicity would have helped to defend the integrity of the institution. In addition, the manner in which the Church dealt with the centuries-old practice of religious poverty and treated its practitioners indicates that a significant shift in the ecclesiastical posture toward reform had taken place. It would now take an Augustinian monk from Germany to begin

---

[140] Ibid. Leff makes an exception for the Cathars and the Free Spirit from this statement he makes concerning the rest of the evangelical heretical groups.
[141] Ibid., 7.
[142] Lindberg, "There Should be no Beggars," 317.
[143] Leff, *Heresy and the Later Middle Ages*, 10.
[144] Ibid.

the process of putting new wine into new wineskins. But before this study turns in that direction, the other side of the poverty question—the issue of the involuntarily poor in the high to later Middle Ages, and the culture's perception of them—needs to be examined.

The Involuntarily Poor in the High to Later Middle Ages

Poverty in the Eleventh to Thirteenth Centuries

By the eleventh century, a theology and vocabulary of poverty was well in place. The word *pauperes* was used to describe both "those who were indigent and/or needing protection; it also applied to the *paupers Christi*, those who chose destitution voluntarily for religious reasons."[145] Though specific use of the title *pauperes Christi* was largely reserved for the monks and voluntarily poor, it demonstrates how the culture respected the poor in general, as a figure of Christ, and for the theological values they portrayed.[146] The title is also indicative of another reality, namely that during the Middle Ages, the poor as a whole were primarily understood from an ecclesiological standpoint.[147] The poor fulfilled an important function. They received the alms of the rich and were required to pray for their spiritual welfare. This was the way in which the sins of the rich could be atoned.[148] Everyone knew that the poor occupied a blessed state before God, a position of favor in the divine order of things. All knew that God dwelt among the poor and promised to hear their prayers. Did not God humble God's self through the incarnation to become a fellow wayfarer and pilgrim, choosing the poor as God's own people?[149] Though this affinity with Christ in the economy of salvation gave the poor particular social significance in the Christian community, it also yielded something else, namely, a blasphemous acceptance of the state of poverty in the society[150] that not only "obscured the realities of misery," but also "perpetuated" and "maintained" them.[151]

---

[145] Mollat, *Poor in the Middle Ages*, 51.
[146] Ibid., 2.
[147] Lindberg, *Beyond Charity*, 31.
[148] Lindberg, "Reformation Initiatives," 81.
[149] Lindberg, *Beyond Charity*, 27.
[150] Hordern, "Luther's Attitude Towards Poverty," 94.
[151] Lindberg, *Beyond Charity*, 33.

There was also another twist in the theology and reality of poverty by the eleventh century. As the primary social channel for poor relief and charity, the Church had the task of receiving and dispersing alms. The *pauperes christi*, or the monks who had assumed the life of poverty by a vow, were thought to be more spiritually perfect than the laity. This included those laity who had fallen into the distresses of poverty by no choice of their own. Therefore, for a wealthy person wishing to give alms to the poor in exchange for prayers offered for his or her soul, the best recipient of those alms would be the poor who were the most virtuous or worthy. The poor who were deemed worthy were, more often than not, the clergy. This belief affected the Church's interpretation of the biblical maxims on almsgiving and charity. Church theologians and ethicists alike had already rendered numerous biblical references to the "poor," as in Luke 14:13–14, 21, to include the clergy.[152] But while the medieval society and the Church had elevated the impoverished to an honored position before God, this position had become more token than real. The alms intended for distribution among the poor fell heavily into the hands of the clergy, which meant the Church not only usurped the revenues for the poor but their spiritual role as well.[153] The result was an ever widening gap. The Church grew in wealth and was no longer effective in meeting the growing needs of the poor, especially in urban centers, and most importantly, it no longer resembled its title *pauperes christi*.

Aspects of the Church's failure were challenged by some reform movements of the high Middle Ages. Francis and others divested themselves of their goods giving them to the impoverished. As discussed previously, they preached a message of penance and called the religious to a life of strict poverty and service to the poor collecting alms only for one's immediate needs and using all other resources for the benefit of the less fortunate. Francis had indeed applied a corrective to the ecclesial improprieties of his day. Yet, by the end of the thirteenth century, even the stylized poverty of the Franciscans lost its effectiveness in achieving renewal due to its own internal battles over its definition and practice of poverty.

As the high Middle Ages waned, the numbers of impoverished swelled and attitudes changed. Lindberg states that "there was the increasing depersonalization and deprivation of the poor caused and aggravated by urban growth and the rise of the money economy. The traditional ecclesiastical

---

[152] Ibid.

[153] This is not to claim that the church never gave relief to the poor but that the lion's share of the ecclesial revenues went to support the hierarchy of the Church and not the impoverished.

idealization of poverty stemming from patristic times was unable to cope constructively with the 'commercial revolution.'"[154] In response to these changes, the vocabulary of poverty began to multiply and *pauper* took on new connotations.[155] Concerning this phenomena, Mollat writes:

> Originally a single Latin word denoted poverty throughout the West, but diversification is evident in various vernacular forms that first appeared in the thirteenth century and multiplied in the fourteenth; thus did the human mind and discourse reflect the spread and aggravation of misery and growing awareness of its effects.[156]

The linguistic changes reflected this spread of misery. "The development of a vocabulary of poverty and the poor reflects the historical development of poverty itself," Lindberg writes.[157] He summarizes the general Latin vocabulary for poverty, which is more precise in its specifications:

> For destitution . . . Latin includes the words *engens, egenus* (needy, destitute, *indigens* (in want), *inops* (helpless through poverty), *insufficiens, mendicus* (beggar), and *miser* (unfortunate and needy); for lack of food, *esuriens* (a craving hunger), *famelicus* (famished person); for lack of clothing, *nudas, pannosus* (ragged, tattered) . . . [and the] terms meaning "pitiable" or "wretched" (*miserabilis, miserabilis persona*). . . .[158]

As the vulgar languages replaced Latin, words and categories for poverty became more numerous. While this set of terms expanded, the words *pauper* and *pauvre* retained their religious significance. Yet their appearance in the diminutive forms *pauperculus* and *paupertinus* expresses the idea of condescension, which has social and theological ramifications.[159] As Mollat states, "From condescension one proceeded by degrees to distain, contempt and finally repugnance."[160]

With new words came harsher and more hostile meanings that disparaged the poor and their lot.[161] This proliferation of terms for poverty took a new turn by the thirteenth century. The "humility of the poor"

---

[154] Lindberg, "There Should be no Beggars," 319.
[155] Mollat, *Poor in the Middle Ages*, 3.
[156] Ibid., 1.
[157] Lindberg, *Beyond Charity*, 19.
[158] Ibid.
[159] Mollat, *Poor in the Middle Ages*, 3; Lindberg, *Beyond Charity*, 21.
[160] Mollat, *Poor in the Middle Ages*, 3. See also Lindberg, *Beyond Charity*, 21.
[161] Mollat, *Poor in the Middle Ages*, 4.

prized in the feudal age was not always equated with biblical virtue in the thirteenth century.[162] "The weakness of the poor was now seen as approximate to the vulgarity of the peasant, the *ignobilis* of lowly origin; the *vilis* of commonness became vileness."[163] The term *pauper* was freely interchanged with *agricola* or *laborator*, words denoting the person who lives on a subsistence level and struggles for his or her daily existence. Those clothed in "dirty, ill-smelling rags" became *abjectus* (repugnant);" and as early as the twelfth century, these people also began to be referred to as *pauperes* and were hence "distinguished from the *egeni*, the traditional biblical poor consisting of widows, orphans and pilgrims."[164] Finally, those deemed *indigentes* were judged to have some "deficiency of character."[165] Though difficult and complex to trace out, Mollat says that this process of semantic evolution continued on up to the sixteenth century and distinctly corresponds to the rise and growth of pauperism itself.[166] David Flood summarizes the situation well:

> As the Middle Ages sagged, the poor man ceased to evoke the presence of Christ as in earlier centuries. He aroused suspicion rather, and society lumped him together with the vagabond and criminal elements.[167]

By the Renaissance, Western culture had grown in its sophistication and insensitivity. The simple Latin vocabulary formerly used in a largely rural, gift-giving culture was no longer adequate for the new commercial economy, now confronted by the growing social problems which the growing urban centers engendered. The attitudes of suspicion towards the poor, sown in the thirteenth century, had come to flower in the fifteenth.

Changes in the Attitudes toward the Poor in the Later Middle Ages

By the second half of the fourteenth century, a sharp contrast between the culture's idealization of religious poverty and the squalid realities of the impoverished came into relief. In the words of Carter Lindberg, "poverty

---

[162] Ibid., 3; Lindberg, *Beyond Charity*, 21.
[163] Lindberg, *Beyond Charity*, 21.
[164] Ibid.
[165] Ibid. See also Mollat, *Poor in the Middle Ages*, 3–4, for a more detailed discussion on how the Latin vocabulary for poverty proliferated.
[166] Ibid., 2.
[167] See Flood's forward in *Poverty in the Middle Ages*, 10.

was no longer only a theological virtue; it was a major social problem."[168] This shift can be traced back to the Black Death that ravaged Europe in the mid 1300s. Some argue that the devastation wrought by the plague "substantially affected all subsequent social and economic developments."[169] Not only did a protracted agricultural crisis ensue, but also wealth became concentrated in the hands of a few who were fortunate enough to escape the pestilence.[170]

The rise of pauperism in the last three centuries of the Middle Ages presented a challenge for civil authorities. Even before the plague subsided, countries from one end of Europe to the other took measures to reduce the numbers of beggars and vagabonds. By 1350, if a vagabond was caught on an English road without a proper pass, he would be branded with a hot iron. The Parisian Parliament passed a series of laws for the control of begging and vagabonds which included penalties such as imprisonment, branding, and banishment. Many towns forbade vagrants to stay more than one night "on pain of death by hanging."[171] These laws reflect a high degree of anxiety toward the poor in the later Middle Ages. Concerning these measures, Mollat writes:

> It is but a short step from mistrust to fear, from suspicion to accusation. People were afraid not so much of the beggar's indigence as of his idleness, his rootlessness, and his anonymity. They no longer knew with whom they were dealing.[172]

This fear and anxiety occasioned the creation of new legislation. Ordinances were passed to prohibit charity and begging from anyone who was able-bodied and under the age of sixty. Wage rates were established at pre-plague levels, despite the labor shortage. At this time, the words for "poor" and "laborer" became identified with one another.[173] It is estimated from tax registers that by the fifteenth century, thirty to seventy-five percent of the urban residents owned no property.[174] This suggests that a large number of people living in and around medieval cities existed on the brink of poverty, and hard times could easily push them into destitution and beg-

---

[168] Lindberg, "Reformation Initiatives," 82.
[169] Lindberg, *Beyond Charity*, 37–38.
[170] Ibid., 38.
[171] Mollat, *Poor in the Middle Ages*, 290–91.
[172] Ibid., 251.
[173] Lindberg, *Beyond Charity*, 38–39.
[174] Lindberg, "Reformation Initiatives," 83.

ging. Lindberg uses statistics from the city of Nuremberg as one example. Around the year 1500, the city had about twenty thousand residents with about twenty thousand more in the surrounding area. Nuremberg was said to have a sound city economy, and yet its hospital claimed to feed three to five thousand people a day, and the city's poor was estimated to be around twelve to fifteen thousand.[175]

With the impoverished represented by numbers like these, it is not surprising that the theological and ethical teachings of the Church, which once held that poverty was a virtue, grew in impotence. The economic shifts and urban demographics facing the later Middle Ages fostered a significant breakdown in the poverty ideal.[176] The Church's theology of poverty had originated in a "profoundly ecclesial as well as agricultural and gift-giving society" which was now "challenged by the development of an urban society that prized wealth over poverty."[177] Lindberg notes that between the twelfth and fourteenth centuries, there was greater centralization of poor relief programs and communal laws to promote greater efficiency. However, during this time the theology or ideology of poverty was not rethought which meant that the goals of these new measures remained largely unfulfilled by the fifteenth and sixteenth century.[178] By the fifteenth century, everyone knew that the preferential means to salvation was a life of holy poverty. Yet, such a teaching begat "thousands of able-bodied beggars" which strained the resources of developing "proto-capitalist" societies seeking to consecrate work and condemn idleness.[179] The literature written near the end of the fifteenth century hurled scathing admonitions at mendicants and the like, who were "perceived to be a parasitic clergy which was avoiding ecclesial responsibility for poor relief and even worse, compounding the problem."[180] Nicholas Oresme argued "that poverty was harmful both to the state and to its subjects: to practice poverty voluntarily was to tempt Providence and violate God's laws, hence to sin."[181] In satires, Mendicants were depicted as "brokers of relics and indulgences" or as one "with his cowl pulled down over his eyes in feigned indifference

---

[175] Ibid.
[176] Lindberg, "There Should be no Beggars," 317–18.
[177] Lindberg, *Beyond Charity*, 66.
[178] Lindberg, "Through a Glass Darkly," 45.
[179] Lindberg, *Beyond Charity*, 66.
[180] Lindberg, "Reformation Initiatives," 83.
[181] Mollat, *Poor in the Middle Ages*, 254.

to the money accumulation in his purse."[182] The satirist Murner called the mendicants "tramps and hypocrites who abscond with the money of the poor."[183]

Mollat claims that all of the above attacks on religious poverty would not have undermined the institution if it were not for the arrival of something bigger, that is, the rise of humanism.[184] The last three centuries of the Middle Ages was a time of growing pessimism, party struggles, and shifts in thought. The universal values of the high Middle Ages came under attack and declined with the advent of Conciliarism and Nominalism in philosophy and theology, and Humanism in the arts and sciences.[185] One of the casualties of this intellectual shift was the sacred status of poverty. In fourteenth century Florence, many humanists chose to give their wealth to civic uses over charity to the religious and voluntary poor.[186] Though humanists looked with disdain upon the medieval practice of religious poverty, the new values bred two kinds of humanists who offered different responses towards the physically poor. First, there was the response of the cultural humanist who had a general contempt for the poor and indigent. The negative attitudes and judgments that these humanists harbored towards the voluntary poor carried over to the involuntary poor. Though contempt has followed the impoverished throughout human history, what began in the fourteenth century with the arrival of Renaissance Humanism was altogether different. The cultural humanists of the Renaissance had a thirst for the beautiful, the ornate and the pursuit of worldly pleasure. They drank deeply from the well of pagan Greek philosophy, literature, and art forms. This movement celebrated all that was glorious about humanity and culminated in the celebrated works of Michelangelo, Leonardo daVinci, Titian, and Raphael. A culture that lauds the magnificence of humanity holds contempt for that which does not conform to its ideal, and the poor did not conform to the ideal. However, among the cultural humanists of the Renaissance, contempt had joined hands with indifference.[187] The statement, "Little did it matter to us," that Jean le Bel wrote

---

[182] Ibid., 253. See also Little, "Pride Goes before Avarice," 40–44, for illustrations and art depicting the satire of the times towards money and clergy.
[183] Mollat, *Poor in the Middle Ages*, 254.
[184] Ibid., 254.
[185] Maruyama, "Simple Lifestyle," 148.
[186] Davis, "Poor Relief," 218.
[187] Mollat, *Poor in the Middle Ages*, 254.

after describing the afflictions of the involuntarily poor, demonstrates this mind set.[188] Mollat states:

> With humanism, contempt for the poor took a subtle and perfidious turn, becoming disdainful and philosophical and—height of irony—invoking the dignity of man as justification. The social failure of poverty stood at the opposite extreme from personal self-fulfillment; to those who exalted success and *fortuna* it made no sense. Eulogy of poverty gave way to praise of wealth.[189]

Poverty was not only feared and held up to contempt by the values of the Renaissance, it was now also mocked. Davis explains that "the [cultural] humanists' aesthetic commitment to classical ideals of beauty, order, and harmony made them the least able to tolerate the noise, disorder, and human ugliness on the city streets."[190] "Poverty" for these humanists, "was unworthy of man," and in the words of Agrippa d'Aubigné, "makes men look ridiculous."[191] At the hands of the intellectuals of Renaissance humanism, the breakdown of the ideal of poverty was complete. In the words of Mollat, "poverty lost its sacred status."[192]

Humanism's desacralization of the poor brought a second kind of response toward the poor's physical needs. Unlike the cultural humanists, the religious humanists were concerned for the poor and sought to meet the needs of the poor through non-traditional methods. Humanism in general bred skepticism and impatience with a merit system of salvation bound up with the performance of superstitious and mechanical good works, including those done for the poor that benefited the spiritual status of the rich.[193] Even Erasmus denounced those who superstitiously assigned a portion of their goods to the poor so that their cargo should not be lost in a shipwreck.[194] Pullman states that humanism "took the romance out of

---

[188] Ibid., 254–55.

[189] Ibid., 255.

[190] Davis, "Poor Relief," 269. Davis points out that the tastes and intellectual concerns of humanists gave them a distinctive approach to the problem of poverty. Humanists were active in community poor relief but usually promoted it for reasons other than religious, such as self-preservation. Furthermore, humanists used more secular methods than traditional almsgiving, such as taking the children of beggars and educating them with the privileged children or training them in a vocation or providing a dowry so that the cycle of poverty would be broken. See Davis' whole essay, 217–69, for more details.

[191] Mollat, *Poor in the Middle Ages*, 256.

[192] Ibid.

[193] Pullan, *Rich and Poor*, 223–24.

[194] Ibid., 224.

poverty by extolling the middle state and praising the rich man's virtue of generosity." He continues:

> ... it [humanism] was the enemy of disorder and a friend of education; it came to extol the consistent and deliberate practice of the Christian virtue of charity above all mechanical ritual.... The beggar on the streets and the chaotic distribution of alms alike offended its sense of reason and beauty."[195]

Religious humanists, both Catholic and Protestant, were at the forefront of welfare and relief reform in cities throughout Western Europe.[196] The tastes and intellectual concerns of humanism gave them a distinctive approach to the problem of poverty. There were humanists like Champier of Lyon who promoted poor relief for non-religious reasons, such as self preservation,[197] and those like Erasmus, who did so from a conviction of the message of the Evangelical gospel.[198] Regardless of the motivation, humanists employed more secular methods in poor relief than of traditional almsgiving to solve the problem of poverty. Davis cites that in Lyons, humanists would take the children of beggars to educate them with the privileged children, train young girls and boys in a vocation, or provide young women with a dowry so that the cycle of poverty could be broken.[199]

Renaissance Humanism was a significant cultural and intellectual movement which affected approaches and attitudes toward poverty in the later Middle Ages. Though there is much more that can be said about the shift in attitudes and methods of poor relief influenced by religious humanists at the close of the Middle Ages, the key for this study is to recognize that Calvin was writing at a time when poverty had lost its sacred status, and the church was grappling with the rise of pauperism. Renaissance Humanism was the intellectual milieu of the Reformation. The following chapter will examine the thought of the humanist reformers Luther, Zwingli, Melanchthon, and Bucer, and specifically, their theological understanding of poverty. It will be demonstrated that due to these individuals' revisions to the doctrine of salvation and the Church, significant changes came about in ways of viewing poverty, both physical and spiritual.

---

[195] Pullan, *Poverty and Charity*, 24.

[196] See Pullan, *Poverty and Charity*, 15, 24. See Davis's essay, "Poor Relief," 217–69; and Wandel, *Always Among Us*, 13–15. See also Steinbicker, *Poor-Relief*.

[197] Davis, "Poor Relief," 217–69.

[198] Pullan, *Rich and Poor*, 224–25; see comments on Erasmus and his *Enchiridion*.

[199] See Davis, "Poor Relief," 217–69, for more details.

Conclusion

This chapter has spanned several centuries and discussed numerous issues related to the ways in which poverty and the poor were valued in the Middle Ages. It shows that the medieval religious and cultural understanding of poverty was far from static. How spiritual poverty was understood and its relationship to the interpretation of voluntary and involuntary poverty was in constant flux. Consequently, there is no singular text, person, or group that arises out of the Middle Ages as the definitive interpretation of the biblical notion of poverty and its proper expression in the Church and Christian life. Three observations remain concerning the consistent patterns in the midst of diverse interpretations of poverty in the medieval Church. In spite of the assorted ways in which the medieval Church articulated the relationship between spiritual poverty and various forms of physical poverty, these observations become helpful to locate the study of poverty in Calvin's thought within a historical context.

The first observation pertains to how the Church sought to articulate the way in which biblical poverty, that is, the poverty of Christ and his apostles, should be manifested by the Church and lived out in the Christian life. As noted above, this quest was driven by the question of what role the physical world, or physical poverty, should play in the realization of spiritual poverty. For example, Benedictine monasticism held to a principle of moderation, while the Franciscans required that their members live in complete poverty, not even touching money unless they were dealing with the sick. Similarly, later conflicts between Pope John XXII and the Franciscans also highlight the struggle that the Church underwent in working out its biblical definition of poverty. The pope interpreted spiritual poverty in such a manner that it was not at all dependent upon the extent of one's physical poverty as the Franciscans claimed. Yet, the 'official' papal view drew another challenge. Heretical groups called upon the papacy to divest itself of all its wealth. They took the connection between physical poverty and spiritual poverty literally and with great seriousness, thus growing in numbers and credibility while undermining the moral authority of Rome.

The Western Church's struggle to define the way that spiritual poverty relates to various forms of physical poverty was a process under constant revision. It was shown that diverse interpretations of poverty and the poor were, for the most part, dependent upon the historical circumstances surrounding them. Though no one understanding of poverty comes to dominate the others during the Middle Ages, all of the interpretations presented (with the exception of some humanist views) share the motivation to meaningfully interpret the theological significance of poverty and the poor in light of Scripture and the issues of the day. This resulted in highly relative understandings of the relationship between physical poverty (voluntary or involuntary) and poverty of spirit.

The second observation concerns the way in which the Church struggled to interpret the place of poverty and the poor in the kingdom of God. The belief that the physically poor were favored by God, and that God promised to hear their prayers and vindicate injustices committed against them, were ideas that originated as expressions of the doctrine of sanctification. Yet during the Middle Ages, this belief crept its way into the heart of Christian soteriology, that is, the doctrine of justification. Thus, what began in the writings of the Patristics as an articulation of the promises of God to the poor who live the Christian life gave rise in the Middle Ages to the merit system of salvation. This point has particular significance for the next chapter. Luther and the other reformers faced the problem of how to purge Christian doctrine of its element of merit, and yet properly interpret the biblical witness of spiritual poverty and the position of the physically poor in the kingdom of God.

The final and most important observation about poverty in the Middle Ages, is its significant theological and practical role in the reform of the Church. Depending upon historical circumstances, there were those in the Church who effectively joined spiritual poverty to a life of physical poverty, voluntary or involuntary, to bring about spiritual change or renewal in the Church or in society. This can be seen in Benedict's interpretation of biblical poverty in terms of humility in order to counter the violence and abuse of power within the feudal society. This can also be seen in the reforms of Robert of Molesmes and Bernard who sought to reconfigure the Benedictine understanding of biblical poverty to include a stronger ethic of simplicity and physical moderation. Also, this is demonstrated in the way that Francis offered a fresh interpretation of biblical poverty addressing the chief sin of the new money economy, avarice. For him, biblical poverty not only meant living a life of humility, but also involved embracing true physical poverty in the manner of Christ and his disciples. All of these men, and the movements that they represent, brought reform and spiritual renewal to the Church of their day.

Conversely, when the Church resisted the call to integrate a form of physical moderation, simplicity, or poverty into its lifestyle as an expression of its spiritual poverty, or completely spiritualized its interpretation of biblical poverty, its vitality and ability to respond to needs for reform declined. This truth can be seen in the demise of the Benedictines and the Franciscans as a force of reform in the Church. It can also be recognized as a major factor in the rise of the heretical movements of the later Middle Ages. It is visible through the neglect of the physically poor as the Church grew in its wealth and power. Finally, it even manifests itself in the cynicism of the cultural humanists towards all forms of poverty, voluntary and involuntary. All of these developments were results of the Church's resistance to reform, which included its failure to appropriate a form of physical moderation and poverty to its understanding of spiritual poverty.

Seeing how the reform of the Church is connected to the biblical interpretation of poverty, it is not surprising to learn that the issue of poverty and the poor play a significant role in the Reformation itself. The following chapter will give a brief examination of the approaches of Luther and other Reformers to the issue of poverty, both voluntary and involuntary, and how they configured it in relationship to the Christian notion of poverty of spirit. This will provide the theological environment in which to assess spiritual and physical poverty in the theology of Calvin.

4

Poverty in the Thought of the Reformers

Most people do not connect poverty with the Protestant Church or with the theology of the Reformation. Yet along with the doctrine of salvation, Reformers rethought the biblical notion of poverty and the place of the poor in the Kingdom of God. There was no one standard interpretation of poverty among the Reformers. The manner in which they approached this topic largely depended upon the role that they played and the particular conflicts they encountered. Luther's ideas developed as he came to understand the way in which salvation and poverty were related. Yet in spite of their diverse interpretations, the Reformers held an important conviction in common: they all agreed that the Roman understanding of poverty desperately needed revision. This would only be achieved through a reformed understanding of the Church and the worship of God. This chapter will examine selections from the writings of Luther, Zwingli, Melanchthon, and Bucer to determine how they formulated their understandings of poverty. Before preceding with this task, it is necessary to explain some background to their views by looking at the theological implications of the virtue of poverty in the Roman Church.

The Virtue of Poverty in the Roman Church

In the previous chapter, it was shown that the notion of poverty in the Middle Ages was inextricably bound to the doctrine of salvation, and became the means of living a devout Christian life. The conviction that the poor were favored by God, and that God promised to hear their prayers and vindicate injustices committed against them were ideas that originated with the Fathers as part of the Christian life. Yet during the Middle Ages, this belief made its way into soteriology, specifically into the doctrine of justification. The consequences of this union were threefold. First, monks and those who took vows of poverty were elevated as more spiritually perfect than those who did not. This teaching divided the Church by creating two levels of spirituality. These of the higher spiritual level were guaranteed divine favor by virtue of taking vows of poverty. The lower level was occupied by everyone who did not take a vow of poverty. They were said to be distanced from God's favor. Second, involuntarily poor laity were thought to be in a blessed state.[1] This led to a cultural acceptance of poverty as well as its theological idealization. Poverty was not considered to be destructive to human life; rather, it was believed to be a virtuous state to attain. Third, the Church taught that giving alms to the poor was the most important good work that a layperson could do.[2] Yet, if the clergy were more spiritually perfect than the laity, and the impoverished were seen as being in a blessed state, then to direct charity toward either of these two groups would enable those not considered poor in either sense to participate in the poor's position of divine favor, thus earning their way to eternal life. As shown in the previous chapter, this teaching legitimized and promoted the merit system of salvation. The merit system of salvation not only depended on good works in exchange for the forgiveness of sins, but it also created what some have called the "social contract of the High Middle Ages." This describes the duty of the poor to remain poor so that the salvation of the rich could be secured.[3] In other words, in the Middle Ages, the perpetuation of poverty was thoroughly entangled with the doctrine of salvation.

Luther's Challenge to the Virtue of Poverty

An Examination of Poverty, Vows, and the Doctrine of Salvation

Given the role poverty played within medieval soteriology, it is easy to see why the association of poverty with theology was a significant concern for the reformers from the start. Luther's call for *sola fide* challenged institutional poverty at its foundation.[4] If salvation is a free gift by the grace of

---

[1] Hordern, "Luther's Attitude," 94.

[2] Ibid., 95.

[3] See Lis and Hugo, "Poverty and Capitalism," 22; as quoted in Lindberg, *Beyond Charity*, 33.

[4] Lindberg, "Through a Glass Darkly," 45. The expression *sola fide* commonly stood for the

God alone, then poverty serves no one. It does not matter if poverty is a consequence of life or if it is assumed through a vow. Either way, it possesses no special sanctity before God.[5] The rich and the poor alike stand equally before God as sinners and are both in need of God's grace. The basis of a person's relationship to God, then, shifted from one's works of charity towards the poor, to faith in God's free gift of grace through God's Son Jesus Christ. Christ's life and death on the cross became the focus of humanity's object of faith and their merit before God. The result? The giving of alms and the choice to live in poverty now had no *meritorious value* in God's economy of salvation.

Luther's assertion of *sola fide* was grounded in his declaration of *sola scriptura*. His reliance on Scripture alone as his authority in doctrinal matters displaced the authority of the Roman hierarchy and centuries of ecclesiastical tradition. By reordering the doctrine of salvation and ecclesiology, Luther produced a number of casualties to the Roman Church's system of spirituality. Among these casualties was the practice of medieval asceticism. Poverty played a significant role in medieval ascetic practices many of which involved the taking of vows. In 1521, Luther mounted an offense against the taking of vows with the writing of *De votis monasticis Martini Lutheri juicium*.[6] Besides challenging the biblical legitimacy of religious vows,[7] this treatise, in its final pages, reexamines the three vows of poverty, chastity, and obedience, and contrasts them with the virtues they ought to promote. Luther argued that if by a vow of poverty a person intends to foster spiritual poverty, then this understanding leads to one conclusion: a Christian understanding of poverty cannot see poverty as a counsel but as a precept.[8] According to Roman dogma, all believers are bound by precepts while only clergy are bound by counsels. The distinction between counsels and precepts is, in essence, a hermeneutical device

---

larger statement "justification by grace through faith alone."

[5] Lindberg, *Beyond Charity*, 165.

[6] Biot, *Rise of Protestant Monasticism*, 12.

[7] A summary of Luther's argument against vows in *De votis* is as follows: First, vows of obedience, poverty, and chastity have no scriptural support and therefore are contrary to the Word of God. Second, since vows are held to be sources of sanctification, they are contrary to justification by faith. Third, since vows are contrary to evangelical freedom of conscience, obligation to them should be abolished. Fourth, vows are contrary to God's commandments because they assume the existence of counsels that add to God's commandments. Finally, vows are contrary to reason because of their irrevocability and injurious nature to the virtues they are supposed to promote. Luther, *WA* 8, 573–669. See also Biot, *Rise of Protestant Monasticism*, 14–15.

[8] Biot, *Rise of Protestant Monasticism*, 24.

employed by the Roman Church to help interpret and apply the ethical teachings of Scripture to the Christian life. The laity were expected to follow the precepts of Christ, which, in addition to a profession of faith, prescribes a normal family life and marriage. On the other hand, clergy are held to a state of perfection and are accountable to a higher Christian ethic, that is, a life following the evangelical counsels.[9] The counsels are those principles that bind clergy by a vow to live in poverty, chastity, and obedience to the Church. On the matter of religious counsels, Luther writes, "In Holy Scripture, vows are not prescribed. The distinction between counsels and precepts is artificial; for all Christ's counsels are in effect precepts."[10] If when speaking of poverty, the religious mean spiritual poverty, then poverty cannot be interpreted as a counsel (something only the religious are to achieve); rather, poverty is a precept (something every Christian should cultivate in life). To call poverty a counsel or a virtue or something reserved only for the religious elite is, in Luther's mind, nothing short of contempt for the Lord's commandment and a failure to take seriously the promises made in baptism.[11] On the other hand, if what the religious orders intend in the language of poverty is material poverty, then the vow is made to look ridiculous.

Luther noted the fallacies and inconsistencies of the Roman approach to poverty. He observed that monasteries were brimming with possessions. Furthermore, he questioned the practice of releasing from their vows of poverty monks who were promoted to Bishop. Liberation from his vow occurred because the Church taught that the office of Bishop was in such a perfect state that a vow of poverty was no longer necessary. Biot observes:

> . . . this argument Luther could not take seriously. No, seen in its true light, the vow of poverty had to be judged as a means for avoiding having to be bothered with the misfortunate and with the "real" poor, and to divert towards one's self the aid which should have been distributed to them.[12]

---

[9] Ibid., 60. Luther's problem with this teaching was that it artificially divided the Church into two groups: the common Christians (the laity) and the elite Christians (the clergy). It also limited the spirituality of the laity.

[10] Luther, *WA* 8, 577–80; Luther is restating John Wycliffe's critique of precepts and counsels. See Chadwick, "Ascetic Ideal," 1–23.

[11] Biot, *Rise of Protestant Monasticism*, 24.

[12] Ibid.

Luther was indeed concerned about the abuse of Church offices, money, and power. Because such criticisms were popular with the masses, Luther's writings gained a large audience. Yet, the primary reason behind Luther's rejection of vows and the practice of religious poverty is far more significant.[13] George Yule explains:

> Luther's attack on medieval ascetic practices in general and on monasticism in particular was not because of asceticism as such, nor even because of the abuses that had come into monastic life, but because much of the theology that lay behind them undercut the evangelical understanding of salvation.[14]

In addition to its distortion of the doctrine of salvation, the second reason Luther attacked monasticism was his conviction that the whole of Christian spirituality should be practiced by all believers on a daily basis. This resulted in Luther's rejection of the Roman distinction between counsels and precepts which had split the clergy from the laity, leaving the Church divided. His emphasis on a life "consciously based on an evangelical understanding of the Gospel" not only released many of the clergy from a sense of guilt, but it clarified to the whole Christian community the priority of Christian discipleship.[15]

Naturally, the question arises as to why Luther was successful in reforming the Christian faith where earlier individuals like Wyclif and Hus were not. Regarding the moral decay of the Church, Luther never offered new insight. Most of his criticisms against monasticism and the wealth of the papacy had already been raised by earlier voices. Then why did Luther succeed in reform where others had failed? Luther's own analysis yields an insight:

> Doctrine and life are to be distinguished. Life is as bad among us as among the papists. Hence we do not fight and damn them because

---

[13] Biot points out that in *De votis*, Luther argues against vows primarily "because they establish a particular and superior way [to holiness or righteousness], one different from the Gospel way, which is to say different, finally, from the way of the one and only Mediator." Biot does say that Luther granted "the theoretical possibility of an authentically evangelical monastic life, with really 'free' vows—particularly as a means of education and formation of young people." "Nevertheless," Biot continues, "it remains true that in *De votis* . . . Luther's rejection of monastic life and vows rests solidly on his religious intuition. In other words, . . . it was bound up with the very essence of his conception of the major truths of religion." See Biot, *Rise of Protestant Monasticism*, 27.

[14] Yule, "Luther and the Ascetic Life," 229.

[15] Ibid., 232–33; cf. Lazareth, *Luther on the Christian Home*, 166–98. Lazareth dedicates a chapter to Luther's view of marriage and how he rejected monastic vows.

of their bad lives. Wyclif and Hus, who fought over the moral quality of life failed to understand this. I do not consider myself to be pious. But when it comes to whether one teaches correctly about the Word of God, here I take my stand and fight. That is my calling. To contest doctrine has never happened until now. Others have fought over life; but to take on doctrine—that is to grab the goose by the neck! . . . When the Word of God remains pure, even if the quality of life fails us, life is placed in a position to become what it ought to be. That is why everything hinges on the purity of the Word. I have succeeded only if I have taught correctly.[16]

Ironically, Luther succeeded in providing a Protestant understanding of poverty because the reform of the Christian life was not his focus. Rather, his focus was to correct the error into which the Church had fallen. By rectifying the doctrine of salvation and restoring the authority of the Word in the Church, Luther enabled the reform of the Christian life, the Church, and in particular, a renewed Christian understanding of poverty.

Luther's corrective of *sola scriptura* not only had consequences for vows and the practice of religious poverty, but also for his perspective on the involuntarily poor. Luther labored to reconstruct a biblical understanding of poverty, the fruits of which Calvin reaped and to which this study will now turn.

Poverty and the Poor in Luther's Writings

Poverty as Humility, the Mark of the True Christian

Luther delivered a series of lectures from 1513 to 1515 entitled *Dictata super Psalterium*, in which he referred to the poverty of the poor more than one hundred times. When Luther taught, he followed the threefold format of the medieval commentary: paraphrasing the text with interlinear glosses; noting textual observations in the margins; writing extensive remarks in the *scholia*. These forms provided Luther with ample opportunity to express his thoughts on the biblical language of poverty in the Psalms. Brummel argues that in *Dictata*, Luther rejected the socio-economic interpretation of the language of poverty.[17] Instead, Luther understood that the terms "poor" and "rich" do not designate economic or political polarities, but rather opposing spiritual goals. Those who are "poor" by the world's

---

[16] *LW* 54, 110; *WA* 1, 294–95, as quoted in Lindberg, *Beyond Charity*, 166.
[17] Brummel, "Luther on Poverty," 16. My analysis of Luther's biblical understanding of poverty relies heavily on Brummel's research because of the lack of sources on this topic in Luther studies.

standards have minds set on spiritual things and ascend to eternal realities, whereas the "rich" have carnal minds and seek only to gain more worldly possessions.[18] Hordern calls Luther's interpretation of this kind of poverty "*anawin* piety," in which the term "poor refers to a special kind of trusting disposition towards God."[19] In *Dictata*, Luther frequently equates the biblical language of the poor with "the faithful people of God . . . [or simply] true Christians." These poor or faithful ones are not those oppressed by the wealthy or powerful but are the spiritually humble and forgetful of self. Brummel calls this "the uniform argument of the *Dictata super Psalterium*."[20]

In *Dictata*, Luther spiritualizes the relationship between the poor and injustice. When the Psalms speak of those who devour people as if they were bread, Luther explained that such offenses are committed by those who attempt to exploit the faithful through wicked doctrines and hence lead them away from the true faith.[21] According to Luther, the poor man's real adversary is the heretic. Similarly, Ps 72:4 reads, "May he defend the cause of the poor of the people, give deliverance to the needy, and crush the oppressor" (*RSV*). For Luther, "the oppressors" are those who war over the hearts of the poor and seek to lure them into seeking worldly or temporal gain.[22] Luther's treatment of this passage, as well as others found in the *Dictata*, turns away from the socio-economic understanding of poverty. Furthermore, his interpretation is not allegorical. Rather, it is a construction of the symbolic meaning of the text.[23] Though Luther reads the intent of the Psalmist as referring to spiritual poverty as opposed to socio-economic poverty, he is not oblivious to the way in which one's socio-economic situation may foster spiritual poverty. A statement Luther makes in his sermon on *The Magnificat* demonstrates this point: "Humility, therefore, is nothing else than a disregarded, despised, and lowly estate, such as that of men who are poor, sick, hungry, thirsty, in prison, suffering, and dying."[24]

Luther's dialectical thinking is evident in *Dictata*. He frequently contrasts opposing ideas, such as the temporal and eternal, the present and

---

[18] Brummel, "Luther and the Biblical Language," 42.
[19] Hordern, "Luther's Attitude," 102.
[20] *WA* 3, 87, 28; *WA*, 3, 86, 13. Brummel, "Luther and the Biblical Language," 42.
[21] *WA* 3, 100, 9; Brummel, "Luther and the Biblical Language," 42.
[22] *WA* 3, 459, 27; Brummel, "Luther on Poverty," 22.
[23] Hordern, "Luther's Attitude," 102.
[24] *LW* 21, 313; *WA* 7, 560; Hordern, "Luther's Attitude," 102.

future, the manifest and hidden, the visible and invisible, the human and divine.[25] This outlook informed Luther's perception of the Psalmist's message. For centuries the Psalms had been the prayer book of the Church, the repository and heart of Christian piety and spirituality. Luther knew this. Thus, not surprisingly, he locates the language of poverty found in the Psalms in the spiritual realm, where the true Christian's life dwells. In such a dialectical interpretation, there is no regard for a poverty that is physical.

It is important to note that because the *Dictata* lectures were given before Luther nailed the *Ninety-Five Theses* to the Wittenberg Door in 1517, this work better represents Luther the Augustinian monk than Luther the Reformer. Though Luther regularly mentions monastic life in *Dictata*, to his credit, he never once draws the conclusion that the biblical language of poverty refers to making or keeping a monastic vow. Instead, he says, the spiritually poor are found throughout the whole Church.[26] When the Psalmist speaks of "a hunger that will be filled with the bread of God," Luther interprets this as meaning that the faithful will be filled by the Word of God preached and found in Scripture.[27]

Luther was frequently oppressed in his conscience by attacks he called *Anfechtungen*. He identified several sources as possible roots of the struggle: a snare set by Satan, an overwhelming sense of one's finitude, or knowledge of one's abject lostness or isolation.[28] Luther claims that the worst crisis occurs from the knowledge that a holy and majestic God confronts the human heart in all its sinfulness.[29] In the *Dictata*, Luther teaches that only true Christians are able to experience this struggle since they alone are aware of God's absolute holiness and recognize the depth of human sin.[30] Brummel concludes:

> There can be no doubt that Luther considered himself to be one of the poor subject to these *Anfechtungen*. Commenting on Psalm
>
> 34:6: "This poor man cried out," Luther wrote in the interlinear

---

[25] Brummel, "Luther on Poverty," 23.
[26] *WA* 4, 254, 18; Brummel, "Luther and the Biblical Language," 43.
[27] *WA* 4, 432, 2; Brummel, "Luther and the Biblical Language," 43.
[28] *WA* 1, 87, 14; Brummel, "Luther on Poverty," 29–30.
[29] *WA* 3, 190, 24; Brummel, "Luther and the Biblical Language," 43.
[30] *WA* 3, 87, 14; Brummel, "Luther on Poverty," 29–30.

gloss: "That is I, he who is speaking to you, have cried out in tribulation."[31]

In Luther's early writings, he symbolically interpreted the biblical language of poverty so that the text could spiritually speak to the personal and corporate life of the Church. He understood biblical poverty to be the spiritual condition of a faithful Christian, that is, the person humbled by the recognition of his or her sinful condition before a majestic and holy God. Brummel is correct in his evaluation: Luther categorically refuses to subscribe socio-economic meaning to the biblical language of poverty.[32] Yet, it is also important to note what is missing from *Dictata*. Though Luther's exposition of poverty overlooks the misery and oppression that many physically suffered, it did not idealize these conditions as did so many other writings arising out of the Middle Ages. Neither did Luther speak of human misery as being rewarded in the next life.[33] Instead, Luther's dialectic made a clear demarcation between those things concerning the spiritual realities for the redeemed in Christ, and those which belong to the experience of this world, that is, things foreign to Kingdom ideals. This dialectical teaching came to maturity in Luther's theology of the cross. Yet before this issue is discussed, an examination of Luther's stance on the problem of physical poverty is in order.

LUTHER, THE POOR, AND SOCIAL WELFARE

Brummel's research claims that Luther experienced a "hermeneutical break" with the way he understood the biblical language of poverty in the *Dictata*. This change occurred while giving his lectures on Romans which began in 1516.[34] Brummel observes that Luther's exposition of poverty in Romans assumed a greater historical-literary sense, especially beginning in chapter 12.[35] Brummel offers three reasons for this change. First, the dialectic present in the *Dictata* appears more infrequently in the lectures on Romans. Second, Luther's understanding became more aligned with the plain meaning of the text rather than its symbolical one, bringing out more of its historical sense. Third, Luther shows evidence of a growing

---

[31] *WA* 3, 185, 21; Brummel, "Luther and the Biblical Language," 43–44;

[32] Brummel, "Luther on Poverty," 15.

[33] Ibid., 50.

[34] Brummel, "Luther and the Biblical Language," 44; and "Luther on Poverty," 50–56.

[35] Brummel, "Luther and the Biblical Language," 45; and "Luther on Poverty," 55. See *WA* 56, 122, 13.

awareness of and concern for issues outside the monastery.[36] The most obvious example of this last point was Luther's posting of the *Ninety-Five Theses* one year into his Roman lectures.

Prompted by the sale of indulgences, the *Ninety-Five Theses* reflected a special concern for the welfare of the poor. The document commences with a statement about the claim that God makes upon all humanity and the radical nature of repentance. Luther addressed contradictions in the Church's system of penance, arguing that Christians need to be doing works of charity and mercy. In other words, the Church needs to concern itself with acts of compassion towards the poor.[37] Luther wrote:

> 42. Christians are to be taught that the pope does not intend that the buying of indulgences should in any way be compared with works of mercy.
>
> 43. Christians are to be taught that he who gives to the poor or lends to the needy does a better deed than he who buys indulgences.
>
> 45. Christians are to be taught that he who sees a needy man and passes him by, yet gives his money for indulgences, does not buy papal indulgences but God's wrath.[38]

Clearly, Luther argues that acts of mercy and generosity toward the poor are more fundamental to one's spirituality and ethics than the purchase of indulgences. To pass by a needy person for the sake of buying an indulgence is nothing short of damnable. Luther asserted that the sale of indulgences was a way that the Church hierarchy could raise money for the completion of St. Peter's basilica at the expense of the poor:

> 50. Christians are to be taught that if the pope knew the exactions of the indulgence preachers, he would rather that the basilica of St. Peter were burned to ashes than built up with the skin, flesh, and bones of his sheep.
>
> 51. Christians are to be taught that the pope would and should wish to give of his own money, even though he had to sell the basilica of St. Peter, to many of those from whom certain hawkers of indulgences cajole money.[39]

---

[36] Brummel, "Luther and the Biblical Language," 44–45.
[37] Hordern, "Luther's Attitude," 95.
[38] *LW* 31, 29; *WA* 1, 235.
[39] *LW* 31, 30; *WA* 1, 235.

Here, Luther was not ready to condemn the Pope for the sale of indulgences and the impact of this indiscretion on the people. Instead, he targets the hawkers and the local middlemen in his charges. By thesis 86, however, doubt regarding the Pope's judgment on the matter of indulgences creeps into Luther's remarks:

> 86. Again, why does not the pope, whose wealth is today greater that the wealth of the richest Crassus, build this one basilica of St. Peter with his own money rather than with the money of poor believers?[40]

Hostility lingers beneath Luther's words. In the words of Hordern: "Luther's indignation comes from the spectacle of a wealthy Church robbing the poor in order to build monuments of human grandeur."[41]

Several months later, Luther penned his *Explanations of the Ninety-Five Theses*. Here he further delineated his ethic of charity and poverty as well as his ideas concerning the proper approach to the construction of church buildings. He outlined three types of good works that involve money. First, he placed "giving to the poor or lending to a neighbor who is in need" as the highest good work that one can do.[42] Second, money could be given to hospitals and the building of churches only when it was clear that "there is no longer anyone in need…"; and finally, money can be given to construct public buildings.[43] Moreover, he stressed the urgency with which the Church needed to attend to the poor by discontinuing the purchase of holy vessels and decoration of the Church.[44] Luther's position follows the example of Ambrose and Paulinus, who melted down the chalices and everything of value in the churches to give the proceeds to the poor.[45]

A few years later, Luther wrote his tract on *Trade and Usury* (1524), asserting that no one should contribute more money to the institutional aspects of the Church than to the relief of poverty and suffering. Instead, the lion's share of the alms should go to the poor. He warns:

> Beware, therefore, O man! God will not ask you at your death and at the Last Day how much you have left in your will, whether

---

[40] *LW* 31, 35; *WA* 1, 237.
[41] Hordern, "Luther's Attitude," 96.
[42] *LW* 31, 199; *WA* 1, 598.
[43] Ibid.
[44] Ibid.
[45] *LW* 45, 289; *WA* 6, 46–47. See also Lindberg, "There Should be no Beggars," 329.

you have given so and so much to Churches—although I do not condemn this—but he will say to you, 'I was hungry, and you gave me no food; I was naked and you did not clothe me' (Matt. 25:42–43). Take these words to heart, dear man! The important thing is whether you have given to your neighbor and treated him well.[46]

Giving to the poor versus giving to the institutional needs of the Church was the subject of much debate between Luther and Johann Eck (b.1486–d.1543).[47] Eck contended that alms should go to the needy instead of the Church only in situations of extreme want. Otherwise such money should go to the Church, because he considered poverty to be a virtue.[48] Luther's response made Eck's position look ridiculous:

So we learn neither to help nor to give to the needy until they are perishing, starving, freezing to death, or fleeing because of poverty and debts. But this infamous gloss and supplement is confounded by a single word. "What you wish another to do to you, do so to him." No one is so foolish, however, as to be unwilling that anyone should give to him until such time as the soul is leaving the body or he has run away from his debts, and then help him when he is beyond help. But when it comes to Churches, endowments, indulgences, and other things which God has not commanded, then no one is so keen or so diligent in figuring out whether we should give to the Church before the tiles fall off the roof, the beams rot, the ceiling caves in, the letters of dispensation molder, or the indulgences rot with age; although all these things could wait more easily than people who are in need.[49]

For Luther, poverty was not a virtue to be idealized but the blasphemous result of a greedy Church. Luther's call to believers was not to sanctify poverty, but to abolish it.[50]

One of the ways Luther saw to abolish poverty was to restore the connection between worship and service to neighbor that had disintegrated during the Middle Ages. In his 1523 "Preface" to the Leisnig community welfare ordinance, Luther wrote:

---

[46] *LW* 45, 286; *WA* 6, 45. See also Hordern, "Luther's Attitude," 97.

[47] John Eck was the principal adversary of Luther who wrote a reply against *Luther's Ninety-Five Theses*, entitled *Obelisci*. Eck was behind the sale of indulgences and the lawyer for the pope and Fuggars. For more on Eck, see Nelson, *Idea of Usury*, 25.

[48] *LW* 45, 286; *WA* 6, 45. See also Hordern, "Luther's Attitude," 97.

[49] *LW* 45, 287–288; *WA* 6, 46. See also Hordern, "Luther's Attitude," 97.

[50] Hordern, "Luther's Attitude," 97.

Now there is no greater service of God [*gottis dienst*, or worship] than Christian love which helps and serves the needy, as Christ himself will judge and testify on the Last Day, Matt. 25 [31–46]. This is why the possessions of the Church were formerly called *bona ecclesiae*, that is, common property, a common chest, as it were, for all who were needy among the Christians.[51]

Christian worship, in its truest expression, always results in service to one's neighbor. Luther underscored that worship "thrusts the Christian into the world" and is characterized in "the daily life of the Christian" and by obedience to "God's commandment."[52] His treatise *The Blessed Sacrament of the Holy and True Body of Christ, and the Brotherhoods* of 1519, makes this connection in an abbreviated form. In this work, Luther attacks the medieval system of brotherhoods, wills, and the merit-piety of the mass. He stresses how "the significance or effect of [the] sacrament is fellowship of all the saints."[53] This kind of fellowship was not self-serving as the brotherhoods were, rather, it was the kind of fellowship that renders support to those in need.[54] For purposes of illustration, Luther turned to the teaching of the apostle Paul in 1 Corinthians 12 and pointed out how the whole body responds to a pain in the foot:

> So also in our natural body, as St. Paul says in 1 Corinthians 12, where he gives this sacrament a spiritual explanation, "The members have care for one another; if one member suffers, all suffer together; if anyone's foot hurts him, yes, even the little toe, the eye at once looks at it, the fingers grasp it, the face puckers, the whole body bends over to it, and all are concerned with this small member; again, once it is cared for all the other members are benefited. This comparison must be noted well if one wishes to un-

---

[51] Taken from Lindberg, *Beyond Charity*, 100; *LW* 45, 172–73; *WA* 12, 13, 26 ff.
[52] Lindberg, *Beyond Charity*, 100.
[53] *LW* 35, 50; *WA* 2, 743. Lindberg, *Beyond Charity*, 101.
[54] Brotherhoods were lay associations meant to operate for devotional and charitable reasons. However, by Luther's day, these had degenerated into "vehicles for salvation" staffed with their "own priests, altars, chapels, and festivals." Lindberg cites the example of the Brotherhood of Eleven Thousand Virgins in Cologne, which promised its participants of "6,455 masses, 3,550 entire Psalters, 200,000 Te Deums, etc." By the time of the writing of *The Blessed Sacrament of the Holy and True Body of Christ, and the Brotherhoods*, "there were twenty-one such Brotherhoods in Wittenberg." Luther criticized these as being too self centered. He argued that what was "suppose to be a special convocation of good works . . . has become a collecting of money for beer. . . . If a sow were made the patron saint of such a brotherhood she would not consent." See Lindberg, "Reformation Initiatives," 86.

derstand this sacrament, for Scripture uses it for the sake of the unlearned.⁵⁵

For Luther, reforming the sacrament would engender a reform of social ethics in general, and necessitated meeting the needs of the poor in particular. This is precisely what the Leisnig "Preface" and the treatise *The Blessed Sacrament* did; they both suggested the establishment of a common chest out of which the needs of the poor could be met.

In *The Blessed Sacrament*, Luther laments the distraction of the Church from the original focus of the "collection" the early Church took for the poor during worship:

> But in times past this sacrament was so properly used, and the people were taught to understand this fellowship so well, that they even gathered food material goods in the Church, and there—as St. Paul writes in 1 Corinthians 11—distributed among those who were in need. We have a vestige of this [practice] in the little word "collect" in the mass, which means a general collection, just as a common fund is gathered to be given to the poor. . . . This has all disappeared, and now there remain only the many masses and the many who receive this sacrament without in the least understanding or practicing what it signifies.⁵⁶

Luther found a practical solution to the problem of the neglect of the poor in the example of the early Church: Restore the "collection" during worship to be what it began as, that is, a collection for the needy, and place these funds in a common chest to minister to the poor.⁵⁷

Luther's program to reform social ethics differs significantly from both the humanists' program and that of medieval Catholicism. Like the Greeks, humanism linked social reform to education, having an optimistic

---

⁵⁵ *LW* 35:52; *WA* 2, 743–44. See also Lindberg, *Beyond Charity*, 102.

⁵⁶ *LW* 35, 57; *WA* 2, 747. See also Lindberg, *Beyond Charity*, 103.

⁵⁷ Luther's treatise *The Blessed Sacrament* contains "the first suggestion of a communal use of resources for the poor, the common chest." Lindberg, *Beyond Charity*, 101. There has been a debate over whether Luther or Karlstadt first engineered the idea of a common chest first implemented by the Wittenberg. Lindberg sorts through the facts and this debate in his article, "'There should be No Beggars Among Christians'," and effectively argues that the thoughts that underlie the Wittenberg Church order of January 1522, though they are found in Karlstadt's writings which are contemporary with the order, are actually derivative of an earlier document written by Luther sometime in late 1520 or early 1521, called *Ordnung des gemeinen Beutels*. In the *Beutelordnung* Luther gives plenty of detail on how a collection is to be taken, logistics like that the chest is to have three different keys held by the mayor, and the two stewards, and how the money is to be dispensed to the needy, etc. See Lindberg, "There should be No Beggars," 313–34.

view of the human heart and will. Education or the acquisition of knowledge could never be the key to social reform for Luther, since he could not support a view which presumed that people could make the right choices, if only they have enough knowledge. Luther held to no illusions concerning the depravity of the human heart. On the other hand, the sacramental theology of transubstantiation in the medieval Church had eroded into "an *ex opera operato* [in virtue of the action] sense of the works of charity."[58] The merit system of charity came to value the charitable acts themselves as being pleasing to God or as building up the Church instead of valuing the person in the condition of poverty. This stance changed with Luther. He saw the ethical dimension of life transformed only after right doctrine informed proper corporate worship. When right worship occurs, that is, a true celebration of the sacrament, the fellowship of the body of Christ will naturally respond in love and support to the needs it encounters—especially to those of the poor.

Poverty, Affliction, and Luther's Theology of the Cross

Brummel argues that Luther experienced a decisive shift in his interpretation of the biblical language of poverty beginning in 1519 or 1520. At this time, he categorically rejects all socio-economic connotations and instead understood the language of poverty to describe "Christians who suffer."[59] Brummel cites a series of reasons why this occurred. One is that Luther's socio-economic statements in his polemical writings were not seen as threatening to Rome. His insistence on eradicating poverty in Germany may have gained popular support among the German people but was a non-issue to the pope. Instead, the concern of Leo X was Luther's challenge to the Church's doctrine and authority.[60]

Another more significant reason was the relationship between poverty and Luther's understanding of justification by faith. Luther strongly rejected any notion that good works have a part in salvation, maintaining that this position was antithetical to justification by faith. Righteousness is alien to the believer. At justification, it comes from outside the person and

---

[58] Lindberg, *Beyond Charity*, 101.

[59] Brummel, "Luther and the Biblical Language," 47. Two significant studies that outline Luther's "theology of the cross" are McGrath, *Luther's Theology of the Cross*; and Loewenich, *Luther's Theology of the Cross*.

[60] Rome's accusation of Luther was that he "perverts the faith, seduces the simple, and relaxes the bonds of obedience, continence, and humility." Brummel, "Luther and the Biblical Language," 47–48.

is imputed to them from the righteousness of Christ. This alien righteousness is both the basis of and prior to a person's proper righteousness, which finds its expression in living a life according to the Spirit and not according to the flesh. Proper righteousness produces good works. According to Luther, "this righteousness hates the self and loves the neighbor" and does not seek the good of the self but that of the neighbor.[61]

The key term here is "neighbor." Luther began to substitute the term "neighbor" for his earlier use of the term "poor" to designate someone in need who receives the works of Christian love. More specifically, Luther used the language of "neighbor" to refer to Christ as encountered in others.[62] To love and serve our neighbor is to love and serve Christ through our relationship to others. Luther's theology of the cross brings us in direct contact with the incarnation through our neighbor. This realization had implications for Luther's language of poverty. The ethical and theological dimension now given to the term "neighbor" was removed from the connotation of "the poor"; and "the poor," exegetically understood, became "the Christian under the cross." [63]

Luther used his theology of the cross as a forceful line of defense when accused of unorthodox theology. It was also an effective tool to stand "the medieval motif of ascent on its head."[64] Luther's position was an affront to the structures of Roman ecclesiology and the dogma that supported them. Luther knew well that the cross and the doctrine of the Church were fundamentally related.[65] Luther's theology of the cross emphasized that a believer's relationship with God through Jesus Christ cannot be

---

[61] Brummel, "Luther on Poverty," 102–3. See *WA* 2, 247, 12.

[62] Hordern, "Luther's Attitude," 106.

[63] Brummel, "Luther and the Biblical Language," 48. There are five basic components to Luther's theology of the cross: First, God desires to be known by that which God has disclosed and not by that which is invisible. Second, what is known of God is veiled in revelation and may only be apprehended by faith. This revelation of God is found in God's humanity and weakness, revealed indirectly through the cross. Third, though God is revealed, God still remains hidden under the suffering of the cross. Fourth, the knowledge of God is grasped only in suffering and by the cross, not only the passion of the cross of Christ but the suffering of the Christian as well. Therefore, both the suffering of the Christian and the passion of Christ belong together. Fifth, this way of knowing God necessitates suffering for the believer and excludes all works of righteousness because God only accepts those who are meek, lowly, and despised. The content of this outline was taken from Brummel's synopsis of "the meaning of Luther's program of theology of the cross" that appears in Loewenich, *Luthers Theologia Crucis*, 12–18.

[64] Lindberg, "Through a Glass Darkly," 45.

[65] Brummel, "Luther and the Biblical Language," 51.

influenced by structures of human wealth, power, and privilege as the medieval "theology of glory" had erroneously posited.[66] The true Church is a Church that experiences the oppression of the ungodly and though small and weak, endures through suffering. The true Church resists the ungodly not by force of arms but by tearful prayers that ask God to overcome her enemies.[67] Luther describes this community of believers who depend upon God as being exclusively "hidden in the world . . . [and as those who] . . . live by the mystery of faith." It is this community that Scripture "described as poor and afflicted."[68] Luther buttressed his theology of the cross by annexing the biblical language of poverty to his concept of the suffering, humble, and despised Christian under the cross. He taught that it is through human suffering, oppression, weakness, and poverty that we grasp the knowledge and salvation of God as revealed in Jesus Christ. Brummel concludes, "The biblical language of poverty was thus emptied of socio-economic content and used in a spiritual and ecclesiastical struggle."[69]

This view is supported by Luther's interpretation of the biblical language of poverty in his most important commentary of the period between 1519 to 1525, the *Operationes in Psalmos*. In this work, Luther identifies the suffering of the cross with the biblical language of poverty and characterizes this suffering as something that occurs exclusively within the believer's soul. When he mentions the kind of distress that comes with economic poverty and bodily pain, he treats it as something passing and not as critical as the spiritual issues involved with someone's salvation or damnation. When discussing Ps 22:26, "The poor shall eat and be satisfied . . . ," Luther not only stipulates that the verse has nothing to do with physical hunger, but he also argues that it has an eternal reference. These poor are oppressed by sin, struggle under temptation, and desire grace. The promise of being filled with the Word of God applies to them. For Luther, the poor are always those who are hungry to be filled with the God's Word.[70] Even in his Christmas Eve sermon of 1521, Luther praised the poverty of the shepherds over the rich living in Bethlehem because the poor more than the rich were "able to hear the gospel" since they were "prepared by a theology of the cross."[71] It is this hearing of the gospel, this

---

[66] Hordern, "Luther's Attitude," 103.
[67] *WA* 5, 314, 4; *WA* 5, 468, 13; Brummel, "Luther and the Biblical Language," 51.
[68] *WA* 5, 305, 25; Brummel, "Luther and the Biblical Language," 52.
[69] Brummel, "Luther and the Biblical Language," 49.
[70] Brummel, "Luther on Poverty," 110–12, 114.
[71] *LW* 52, 13, 25; Lindberg, "There Should Be No Beggars," 331–32.

word of the cross, that works to crucify the old man in the poor and to change them through suffering into the people of God.[72]

Concerning "the poor" in Ps 22, Luther writes, "And 'the poor' signifies those who are afflicted, that is, those who are evangelical and faithful, who elsewhere are called 'the miserable,' elsewhere 'the humble,' elsewhere 'the meek.'"[73] He understands poverty as the determining factor in a person's relationship to God. Luther writes, "God's eyes are ever upon the afflicted and the poor. The more abject the man, the nearer and more present God is to him. But the proud he knows from afar."[74] The proud person is the ungodly person, the one who is filled with self-confidence and arrogance that comes from idle speculations about the Christian faith and results in the practice of false religion. The proud people persecute the godly ones, the ones whom Scripture calls poor, whose confidence rests faithfully in God. Luther saw the Pope as the epitome of this impiously proud man which Scripture condemned. In response to Luther the Pope declared that those who affirmed such doctrine were to be considered heretics and disobedient to the Church. In reply, Luther identified the Pope as the anti-Christ.[75]

Emptied of its socio-economic meaning, the biblical language of poverty took on a new life and became firmly embedded in Luther's theology of the cross. This theological motif became Luther's primary instrument in challenging the doctrinal abuses of the Roman Church. Yet one of the biggest tragedies of the Reformation occurred when Luther's theology of the cross was applied to a struggle outside of the confines of his program of ecclesiastical reform—the Peasants' War. The peasants were among Luther's most loyal supporters, and Luther considered them as the core of the social defense of the Reformation.[76] Not surprisingly, they requested that Luther respond to their *Twelve Articles*, a list of grievances supported by biblical texts, which the peasants had drafted against their feudal lords. Luther's response frustrated the peasants. Instead of recognizing the peasants' need for just treatment by the feudal lords, Luther argued that the Bible had nothing to do with secular life, and that the biblical language of poverty referred instead to the suffering and misery people experienced in

---

[72] *WA* 5, 249, 37; Brummel, "Luther on Poverty," 118.
[73] *WA* 5, 664, 24; Brummel, "Luther on Poverty," 119.
[74] *WA* 5, 660, 7, as quoted in Brummel, "Luther and the Biblical Language," 50–51.
[75] Brummel, "Luther on Poverty," 130–31.
[76] See Luther's letter to Melanchthon in May 26, 1521 in *LW* 48, 233; Brummel, "Luther and the Biblical Language," 52–53.

their spiritual and not physical lives. Scripture, he stated, calls believers to act as Christians and in no way sanctifies insurrection or a change in their present social status.[77] In *Admonition to Peace* (1525), Luther could only emphasize "Suffering! suffering! Cross! cross! This and nothing else is the Christian law."[78] Luther argued the same idea in a key text of his critique of the *Twelve Articles*:

> Not one of the articles teaches anything of the Gospel. Rather, everything is aimed at obtaining freedom for your person and for your property. To sum it up, everything is concerned with worldly and temporal matters. You want power and wealth so that you will not suffer injustice. The Gospel, however, does not become involved in the affairs of this world, but speaks of our life in the world in terms of suffering, injustice, the cross, patience, and contempt for this life and temporal wealth. How, then, does the Gospel agree with you?[79]

The consequences of Luther's judgments were considerable. A whole sector of German society departed from Lutheranism and engaged in a war of disastrous proportions. Some 100,000 peasants were put to death, and unknown thousands were disfigured and maimed by the feudal princes.[80] Luther's failure of the peasants had several causes. One was that he had been unable to overcome the contextualization of his own thought. Luther's sharp line of demarcation between the two kingdoms left social ethics in the hands of the princes.[81] He treated a person's placement in society within the unchangeable framework of the natural order instead of the ever-fluid framework of human history.[82] But most significantly for the peasants and this study, Luther had drained the biblical vocabulary of poverty of its socio-economic significance. By spiritualizing the biblical language of poverty as referring to Christians under the cross, he neutralized its ethical content and, as a result, had no biblical grounds with which to answer the peasants.[83] Luther could not theologically justify the aboli-

---

[77] Brummel, "Luther on Poverty," 236–240.
[78] As quoted in Maruyama, "Simple Lifestyle," 153.
[79] *LW* 46, 35–36; *WA* 18, 321. Brummel, "Luther and the Biblical Language," 54.
[80] Hordern, "Luther's Attitude," 107.
[81] Maruyama, "Simple Lifestyle," 152.
[82] Hordern, "Luther's Attitude," 107.
[83] Brummel, "Luther and the Biblical Language," 56. Lindberg states that he does not share Brummel's evaluation that Luther "spiritualized" his understanding of poverty during the critical years of the 1520's. Yet Lindberg does not offer an alternative explanation

tion of the peasants' serfdom because he did not recognize that its abolition was "an evangelical requirement."[84] Hence, his theology of the cross, an instrument designed to combat ecclesiastical battles, was unwittingly used to reinforce the injustice of the secular powers.[85]

To this day, the Peasants' War "hangs as an albatross around the neck of Lutherans."[86] Luther blamed Müntzer and Karlstadt as being responsible for "this whole great calamity."[87] Perhaps, finally realizing the plight of the peasants' situation, in 1530 Luther wrote a commentary on Psalm 82 in which another shift in his understanding and interpretation of the biblical language of poverty became apparent. Brummel cites that one of the most dramatic changes in this commentary was the near disappearance of the theology of the cross. It was as though Luther had realized that such a theological motif could not alleviate the misery of the oppressed. He also gave more attention to the socio-economic situation of the poor. Luther arranged his commentary around three tasks that every government should foster: the first task was to "protect and promote the preaching of the Gospel"; the second was to ensure the "wellbeing and protection of the poor"; and the third was to restrain the unjust use of force.[88] No laws in Germany protected the poor from being exploited, or guaranteed that they had the basics of life. Luther protested that secular governments do "not provide the poor and wretched with law and protection. In this way they are not only heedless and negligent; but they vex their subjects with force and wrong, or wink at it when others do so. And yet no one must say that this is wrong!"[89] Later in the commentary, Luther argues that, apart from the Gospel and the ministry, a realm can have nothing greater than a lord who makes the cause of the poor his own.[90]

Though Luther taught that the responsibility for changing the situation of the poor was the job of the secular government, he complained that no one paid attention to what he said when he spoke of the needy. Luther laments:

---

for the evidence Brummel presents or explain his perspective in contrast to Brummel's. See Lindberg, *Beyond Charity*, 107–8 n. 127.

[84] Scholl, "Church and the Poor," 238.
[85] Brummel, "Luther and the Biblical Language," 55.
[86] Hordern, "Luther's Attitude," 106.
[87] *LW* 13, 64; *WA* 31–1, 210. See Brummel, "Luther on Poverty," 256 n. 1.
[88] Brummel, "Luther on Poverty," 257.
[89] *LW* 13, 69; *WA* 31–1, 214. Brummel, "Luther on Poverty," 258.
[90] *LW* 13, 72; *WA* 31–1, 218. Brummel, "Luther and the Biblical Language," 58.

But how could it be worse, when neither silence nor speech helps? If we are silent, they become worse day by day; if we speak, they become still worse. Then the poor and wretched must suffer and be unsuccoured. This is all the fault of the princes and lords . . .[91]

Luther missed the critical time in history (1520–25) to influence change in the structure of German society. His commentary shows evidence of a significant shift in the way he understood the biblical language of poverty, and his interpretation of the poor regained its socio-economic connotations. He contended that only the proclamation of the Gospel had priority over service to the poor. This, he stressed, was a necessary Christian pursuit that must be attended to in both kingdoms.[92] Though Luther remained steadfast against a return to the medieval system of almsgiving, he continued to promote measures to support the poor through common funds.

Luther's influence on the Church's understanding of poverty was extensive. His corrective of *sola fide* and *sola scriptura* weakened not only the idealization of poverty but also its theological legitimization. Monasteries emptied and were turned into hospitals for the poor. Numerous clergy married in adherence to Luther's teaching on councils and precepts. He encouraged the new means of supplying the needs of those in want through the establishment of the common chest. Through his theology of the cross, Luther successfully challenged the medieval theology of glory and the doctrinal abuses of the Roman Church. He annexed the biblical language of poverty to his concept of the suffering, humble, despised Christian under the cross, the echoes of which can be heard in Calvin's writings on the Christian life and the Church. This spiritual interpretation gave Luther the credibility he needed to bring about ecclesiastical reform successfully. Though his former teaching on poverty played a disastrous role in the Peasants' War, the progress Luther made in his thought as a whole on this subject was something from which the Church reformed could never retreat. Calvin inherited many of Luther's insights on poverty. Calvin had the benefit of being a young university student in Paris in the days when Luther was writing his mature works. It is not surprising, then, to find many of these themes in Calvin's writings. However indebted Calvin may be to Luther, it will become apparent that Calvin's understanding of poverty is far more integrated and consistent than were Luther's teachings. For now, the rest of this section will address Zwingli's, Melachthon's, and Bucer's thoughts on poverty.

---

[91] *LW* 13, 61; *WA* 31–1, 207. Brummel, "Luther on Poverty," 259–60.
[92] Brummel, "Luther and the Biblical Language," 56.

Poverty and the Poor in Zwingli's Writings: The Poor as True Images of God

Like Luther, Huldrych Zwingli (b.1484–d.1531) was a first generation Reformer who also attacked the whole notion of monastic vows. In his work, *Commentary on True and False Religion* [*De vera et falsa religione commentarius*], published in 1525, Zwingli addressed this topic in a stinging and satirical style.[93] Zwingli argued that religious vows are an evasion of the divine law. He contended that the charge given in Matthew 5:3, "Blessed are the poor in spirit," is a command for the whole Church, which makes a vow superfluous. Furthermore, it is not necessary to make a vow of poverty if a person is rich, because Christ already said in Matt 19:21 to sell all one has and give to the poor. Likewise, if a person is poor, a vow of poverty is meaningless because God has already given him poverty to bear. In addition to these arguments, Zwingli had an even greater reason for rejecting the kind of voluntary poverty that is undertaken by a vow. Zwingli asks:

> Again, when the Lord has refused you riches, but given you a patient heart, so that you can endure cheerfully, and you then vow poverty, are you not more likely to ascribe your bearing a very hard situation with equanimity to your vow than to the grace of God? For if you credited all things to the grace of God, you never would make the vow, but would constantly accommodate yourself to His will.[94]

The Monastic vow of poverty avoids God's law and will because it seeks to do what is already commanded in Scripture, but does not give glory to God for the result. In the end, Zwingli rejects religious poverty because the fulfillment of a vow essentially ascribes merit to the person's vow made rather than to the power and grace of God.[95]

---

[93] Zwingli's *Commentary on True and False Religion*, is regarded as his "most mature and comprehensive work, containing a whole system of doctrine—a dogmatic and an ethics" and has been compared to Melanchthon's *Loci Communes* of 1521 and Calvin's *Institutes* of 1536. See Richards, "Introduction," in Zwingli, *Commentary*, 3–4. See also Wandel, *Always Among Us*, 59.

[94] Zwingli, "[22] Vows," *Commentary*, 264; *CR* 90, 830.

[95] See also Zwingli's "Thirtieth Article," in *Writings: Defense*, 221. In this passage Zwingli states that the vow of poverty is idolatrous because to fulfill such a vow is outside of the power to keep it. He continues, "All our good works are not good, if they are ours; but inasmuch as they are God's, they are good. How then can a person promise anything to God which is not his, unless it be given him by God?" See *ZW* 1, 331–32. Cf. Locher, *Theologie Huldrych Zwinglis*.

As a true humanist, Zwingli rejected the practice and institution of religious poverty. Nevertheless, he did not ignore the needs of the involuntary poor in Zurich. In fact, he developed an ethic based upon the doctrine of the image of God in humanity that served a dual purpose: it attacked the problem of icons and image worship while it challenged the Church to not neglect its ministry to the poor. On October 28, 1523, Zwingli preached the sermon *The Shepherd* [*Der hirt*] to the ministers who attended the Second Zurich Disputation. In this work, Zwingli contrasted the true shepherd with the false shepherd in defense of the reformed pastor against the unreformed priest.[96] In addition to the true shepherd's primary responsibility of preaching the Word, he is also obliged to care for the poor.[97] Criticizing the activities of the false shepherds of the Church, Zwingli remarks:

> If they only knew that bought—masses are a horror to God and that for the honoring of God one should clothe the living images of God—poor Christians—and not wooden and stone idols . . . that their indulgences have been nothing more than a permit for all vices, for with them they have robbed, stolen, practiced usury, fought, betrayed, indeed begun all great evils; that it is harmful for there to be so many loafers, priests, monks and nuns among the Christian people. . . . Also if they consider that other than that of the only Lord Jesus Christ, . . . no human work can be considered above another; that the highest honor to be offered the virgin Mary is not the building of high walls, the riding of the cathedral canons on beautiful horses and eating with beautiful women, but that it is to be found among all those who hope in her Son, obtaining his help, and when all that which is spent on the walls is given over to the protection of the godliness of poor daughters and women whose beauty is led into danger through poverty.[98]

In the midst of a passage which challenges people with properly judging their clerical leaders, Zwingli speaks about the clergy's moral responsibility towards the poor. He contrasts their wealthy and opulent standards of living with the proper way that the Church should administrate its resources: caring for the poor. It is important to note that the poor to which he refers are destitute Christians. Zwingli is concerned that the Church not simply

---

[96] Stephens, *Theology of Huldrych Zwingli*, 276.

[97] Wandel, *Always Among Us*, 39. Wandel also notes that when the sermon was published the following year, the border of the title page depicted Christ and his Apostles along with "detailed images of poor people."

[98] Zwingli, "The Shepherd," in *Writings: In Search*, 112–13; *CR* 90, 49–51.

promote ties between a giver and a receiver as in the medieval system of almsgiving, but should herald that through ministering to the poor, brothers and sisters in Christ may be spiritually joined.[99] He speaks of destitute Christians as "living images of God," and argues the Church should be more concerned about clothing them than their images made out of wood and stone. Wandel notes that Zwingli's criticism of ecclesial art and adornment is not only an ancient one, but this criticism was also recently voiced by Luther and the iconoclasts of Zurich.

In his *Commentary on True and False Religion*, Zwingli argues against the purchase of costly images and statues for worship, and states that such resources belong to the poor:

> But if it nowhere in the Scriptures has been commanded that statues and images if worshipped should be destroyed, love would be enough, which certainly admonishes every faithful heart to convert to the use of the needy that which is spent on the worship of images. For as soon as human reason says, "thou shalt set up this statue in honor of God or of some Saint," faith certainly contradicts declaring that all the moneys you expend for the honor of the Lord ought to be converted to the use of the poor. For when Christ in reply to the insulting words of Judas said to all the disciples [Jn.12:8], "The poor ye have with you always; but me ye have not always, and ye can do good to them," He turned aside all material service from Himself to the poor. Let us then, not weary God with any of these marks of honor which He transferred to the poor, but bestow them where He directed.[100]

Significantly, Zwingli used John 12:8 to contend that the Church needs to minister to the poor. The Roman Church had long used this text and its parallels to justify its extravagant worship, pompous ceremonies, and self-adornment. Zwingli's argument is directed against this ostentatious worship in general and the use of images in worship in particular. In his mind, a Church that spends money on images to be used in worship

---

[99] See Wandel, *Always Among Us*, 50. In his *Reply to Valentin Compar* [*Eine Antwort, Valentin Compar gegeben,*] Zwingli writes: "[The images] had to be gilded or totally of silver or of gold or clothed in gold and gemstones, all of which one should have hung on the poor. Yes, all patrons of idols will have to give account to God, that they have let his own images go hungry, freeze, etc. and have so extensively adorned their own idols" (*Always Among Us*, trans. Wandel, 63). As above, Zwingli draws attention to the poor as the true images of God whom the Church needs to clothe and adorn. Wandel interprets that Zwingli uses this metaphor to draw "attention to the divine origin of the poor and reaffirm the bond they share with all men" (64).

[100] Zwingli, "[29] Statues and Images," *Commentary*, 331; *CR* 90, 900.

is not a Church that serves the poor. Zwingli understood the medieval mindset well. Religious images were erected as material acts of service to God. People felt that they were in contact with God through images of Christ, Mary, or a particular saint. Zwingli argues that this thinking is confused. To attempt to honor God through the use of images in worship is to misunderstand the command of Christ. God had provided a way for the Church to render material service—by serving the needs of the poor. Zwingli interprets Christ's statement in John 12:8, "The poor you will always have with you," as an injunction which directs the material gifts of the Church, not toward the purchase of images, but toward fulfilling the needs of the poor.

Apart from his teaching on voluntary poverty and vows, Zwingli's theological discussion of poverty mainly appears in the context of his discourse on images in worship. Zwingli argues against the use of images in worship because they usurp the role of the poor in the worship of the Church. It is with good reason that he calls destitute Christians the living images of God. According to John 12, Christians in need are the objects whom Christ designated should receive any material honor the Church may wish to bestow upon Him. This perspective would keep the worship of God free from extravagance and provides a place of honor for the poor in the Church.

John Calvin's thoughts on John 12:8 echo those of Zwingli. Though Calvin does not emphasize the poor's relationship to images in worship as Zwingli does, it will be shown in the final chapter that Calvin does share Zwingli's interpretation of John 12:8, believing that destitute Christians should receive material service from the Church as an act of worship to give honor to Christ.[101] For now, it is important to note that Zwingli's particular theological emphasis places the needs of the poor against the extravagance spent on images as a way to challenge the understanding of worship in the Roman Church.

Poverty and the Poor in Melanchthon's *Loci Communes*

Out of all of Melanchthon's writings, his *Loci Communes* contain his clearest statement on the topic of poverty. Phillip Melanchthon (b.1497–

[101] See Willis-Watkins, "Second Commandment and Church Reform," 1–80, for Calvin's understanding and approach to the iconoclast movement. Also see Eire, *War against the Idols* and "True Piety Begets True Confession."; Payton, "Calvin and the Legitimation of Icons."

d.1560) wrote three Latin editions of his *Loci Communes*.[102] In the first edition of 1521–22,[103] he treats the topic of poverty in a brief paragraph under the heading "The Vows of Monks" and approaches it in the following manner:

> Furthermore, poverty is demanded of all Christians by divine law, and pertains not only to monks. What is meant, however, is evangelical poverty, not that vulgar mendicancy, but to have one's property in common with all, to bestow gifts, to give to all the needy, and to conduct one's business in such a way that you alleviate another's want. It is not evangelical poverty to possess nothing, but to possess in such a way that you feel that you are acting as an administrator of someone else's property, and not your own. . . . Christ desired that man to be poor in such a way that he might nevertheless give. But now *we* call "poverty" only that state when men receive from others. Do you see how far removed from the Gospel the institution of mendicancy is? For both poverty and taking care of our business are demanded not for our own sakes, but for the sake of the brethren. This is a far cry from approving mendicancy.[104]

Melanchthon redefined a biblical understanding of poverty. Evangelical poverty is different from monastic or mendicant poverty. It is a requirement for all believers and has nothing to do with selling all and going about begging. According to the Melanchthon, evangelical poverty is just another name for what is commonly understood to be Christian stewardship. Stewardship involves the idea of holding on to one's property as a person who administers it for someone else so that it can be given freely to fellow believers in need. According to Melanchthon the true definition of

---

[102] The first edition was published in 1521–22; the second was published in 1535–43; the third and final Latin edition was published from 1543 to 1560 when Melanchthon died. Melanchthon also write a German edition of his *Loci Communes* and published it in 1555. This German edition is altogether different from his 1543 last Latin edition. See Preus' translator's preface in Melanchthon, *Loci Communes 1543*, 7–8. See also chapter 3, "The Terms 'Loci Communes' and 'Loci' in Melanchthon," in Breen, *Christianity and Humanism*, 93–105, for an analysis of Melanchthon's *Loci Communes* as the first book in Protestant theology.

[103] For a brief analysis and historical background on Melanchthon's 1521 *Loci Communes*, see Reed, "Melanchthon's 1521 *Loci Communes*," 191–204; Reed describes the *Loci Communes* of 1521 as the first Protestant apology "for the Reformation at the time of its infancy, when it had not yet entered into the period of internal disputes and a new Protestant Orthodoxy," 191.

[104] Melanchthon, *Loci Communes Theologici*, 60; *CR* 21, 127.

biblical poverty, then, is the state in which the believer gives out of abundance in order to alleviate another's want, not the state of a person who receives from another.

By Melanchthon's final Latin edition of his *Loci Communes* (1543),[105] he greatly expanded his remarks on poverty. He removed the locus entitled "The Vows of Monks," and treated poverty as a separate topic under "Locus Six—The Divine Law," following his explanation of the distinction between counsels and precepts.[106] Though Melanchthon was still concerned about refuting voluntary poverty, this is not how he begins his discussion on poverty. He wrote:

> The confession of the Gospel brings many dangers to the life and fortunes of men, since zeal for the Gospel is in disrepute and unprofitable. In this common life among other common misfortunes, poverty is a very common kind of misfortune, and it often attacks the church with great harshness. Therefore it is necessary for us to have a teaching and comfort on the matter, so that we do not think that we have been forgotten by God because of our poverty. For this reason many sermons are found in the prophets and in the Gospel regarding the subject of poverty. And precepts are laid down concerning constancy, so that we do not cast off the Gospel in our weariness of being poor, and so that in our desire for wealth and power we do not allow ourselves to be drawn away into the company of evil things. Comforts are also given in which God promises that He will enrich the needy, as, for example, the statement [Matt 19:29], "He who leaves home and field will receive a hundred-fold," but He adds the words "with tribulation."[107]

Twenty-plus years passed between the time Melanchthon wrote his first edition of *Loci Communes* and his third edition, and during this time his understanding of biblical poverty had enlarged. The persecutions of the Church brought new insight to the prophetic language of poverty found in Scripture. Melanchthon's primary concern was for the spiritual health of believers. The Church's affliction was now understood as being due to its confession of faith and not because God had forsaken his people.

---

[105] For a good background and textual analysis of Melanchthon's *Loci Communes* of 1543, see Preus, translator's preface to Philip Melanchthon's *Loci Communes 1543*, 7–14.

[106] See Melanchthon, *Loci Communes 1543*, 76–79; *CR* 21, 724–28. Actually, Melanchthon began to treat poverty under its own heading in the second, 1533 edition of the *Loci Communes*. By the 1533 edition this section like many others in his Loci had expanded. Compare *CR* 21, 409–11 and 724–28.

[107] Melanchthon, *Loci Communes 1543*, 76; *CR* 21, 724.

Wishing to bring comfort to those undergoing difficulty, he quoted from Matt 19:29 to encourage the Church to resist the temptation to forsake the Gospel.

Melanchthon contrasts this understanding of poverty, that is, the believer's experience of "exercises of faith" versus the voluntary poverty of the religious:

> The statements of the Gospels are filled with these important matters. They contain salutary doctrine or teaching regarding the great exercises of faith and other virtues. They are not to be distorted toward monkish hypocrisy, toward the forsaking of our property, or toward a confusion of the social order of men. For the Gospel neither commands nor counsels that we leave our property, if it is not forcibly taken from us. It neither commands nor counsels that we put all things in common; especially since it is certain that there is distinction of ownership and property which has been established by God. Godly people should know that property rights are pleasing to God, and that this entire distinction and exchange of property is legitimate. For God wills that in these civil duties our faith be manifested and our love exercised along with other virtues.
>
> Finally, the very ridding of our selves of property brings on either begging, which in healthy and idle people is a form of robbery.... For no society can live without something of its own....[108]

Melanchthon concludes that a twisted understanding of poverty comes from an inadequate understanding of Scripture. It does not require or instruct believers to forsake their property, or to hold it in common with other people.[109] Melanchthon also asserted that selling all one has does not produce a virtuous life, but rather leads to idleness and begging. This behavior is not only destructive to a person's spirituality, but it also harms the very fabric of society. For Melanchthon, voluntary poverty is parasitic. It robs from those who have not disposed of their property. God's require-

---

[108] Ibid., 76–77; *CR* 21, 724

[109] Melanchthon seems to contradict this point in his first edition *Loci Communes Theologici* of 1521: "What is meant, however, is evangelical poverty, not that vulgar mendicancy, but to have one's property in common with all, to bestow gifts, to give to all the needy, and to conduct one's business in such a way that you alleviate another's want." See Melanchthon, *Loci Communes Theologici*, 60; *CR* 21, 127. When Melanchthon refers to having "one's property in common with all," he does not mean that there are counsels or commands that require that "we put all things in common," but that believers' understanding of Christian stewardship means that they are generous with those who are in need like one who administers the property of another.

ment for his people is not to dispose of their property and go about begging, but instead to use it to manifest Christian faith and love. In short, Melanchthon had expanded his earlier idea of "Evangelical poverty," otherwise defined as Christian stewardship.

Melanchthon outlines how a Christian is to handle both poverty and wealth correctly. God commands believers not to defraud other people or increase their wealth through sinful business practices. Most importantly, the Christian must be generous to the poor. From Prov 5:15–18, he explains what it means for Christians to manage their property in a way that shows their generosity to the needy:

> "I do not want . . . your inheritance to be squandered or your basic possessions thrown away. . . . Hold on to your principal and preserve your inheritance for the sake of your children and the public good. But help those in need out of your profits, and do so generously." . . . Exercise your faith in these activities. If you realize that these benefits and their preservation are a gift of God, then you will defraud no one. You will be generous and you may expect blessing from God. This is the true teaching of the church of Christ regarding this matter.[110]

Melanchthon argues that being generous is the way for believers to exercise their faith and lead a virtuous life. Private property is a gift from God that should not be forsaken in order to achieve some superficial form of godliness. Christians are to be wise stewards of their wealth, using its profits to increase the resources of those in need. Melanchthon continues:

> But each aspect of this matter requires great skill, great care, and virtue—to be able to bear both wealth and poverty correctly. . . . But just as it requires great skill to own property in the right way, so it requires great skill and is a mark of distinction to endure poverty in the right way. Regarding poverty, we must first recognize that it is the will of God that we be subjected to these common afflictions such as diseases, death, and need. And we must also understand that these afflictions are not signs for the godly that they have been cast off by God. They are exercises which instruct us regarding the sin on account of which our nature is subjected to death. Repentance and prayer also are exercises. Therefore you must learn that it is obedience to God, who has willed that you be exercised in this way, just as this obedience is required in a general

---

[110] Melanchthon, *Loci Communes 1543*, 77; *CR* 21, 725.

way, in keeping with the statement [1 Pet 5:6], "Humble yourselves under the mighty hand of God."[111]

Melanchthon sees that poverty and wealth bring distinct challenges to a believer's faith. Whereas wealth presents opportunities for the Church to minister to its needy, and thereby exercise faith and manifest virtue through the expression of generosity, the experiences of poverty and affliction issue another call. Melanchthon describes poverty and affliction as a type of school into which God places the godly. This school instructs believers about their sinful nature, and spiritually exercises them through adversity so that they will learn humility and obedience to God. When those within the Church experience affliction, they are not to become discouraged. Such experiences occur only by the will of God and are meant for the spiritual health of believers. This is a discipline not unlike those of prayer and repentance.

Melanchthon's view of poverty is different from that of Medieval Catholicism. For him, wealth is a gift from God requiring generosity from believers, not a vice to be shunned. Physical poverty is a problem to be solved, and a discipline endured with humility and obedience, but not a virtue. The important factor for Melanchthon is the manner in which believers respond to the material existence God has chosen for them. Both poverty and wealth provide unique opportunities for the Church to be exercised in its faith, and to express its humility and obedience to God. Though Melanchthon sees no merit in the wealthy selling away their property, he does make an important concession on this matter. He admits that there are exceptional circumstances in which believers must renounce their possessions:

> There is a two-fold desertion here, the one out of God's command in confession or vocation, as when tyrants command them either to reject the Gospel or give up their possessions; the other when a person who has been called to rule over the churches hesitates to do so because he might encounter dangers and hatred, or would rather preserve his personal property. In such cases the laudable thing is to renounce one's property. For we must give precedence to the confession of the Gospel and the calling to teach it over all human things, above our life and our fortune.[112]

---

[111] Ibid.; *CR* 21, 724–25.
[112] Ibid., 78; *CR* 21, 726.

Forsaking possessions is required by the Christian faith only when believers are confronted with a choice between the Gospel and their personal property. Melanchthon does not soften the difficulty of this situation for believers.

> There is very good reason why this concept is repeated so commonly in the Gospel. For instances often occur where confession not only compels us to give up our property, but it compels us to do the much harder thing of offending those who are very dear to us, as well as the wishes of great honorable princes and other prominent people whose judgment it is very difficult to disregard. That is, it is hard to be called the authors of discord in our country. These things cannot fail to torment our minds terribly, whenever God commands us to put the Gospel first. Our consolation must be that He has promised help and rewards.[113]

To embrace the Gospel oftentimes means that believers not only lose their personal property but also embrace the social stigma attached to their faith. In the face of such societal pressure, Melanchthon insists on the need for believers to be consistent:

> Further, there must be constancy so that in the desire to escape poverty we do not act against God. Christ is preaching this constancy when he says [Matt 5:3], "Blessed are the poor in spirit," for they are obeying God by enduring their poverty and the other difficulties which accompany poverty. For there are heavy loads which come to us when we are pressed down and despised by the powerful, when we become liable to injury and insults, and see the sufferings of our children. In the midst of these evils, to keep our constancy of mind, not to seek protection either of people or the power of evil counsels, not to be moved by our poverty to making a public tumult—in this situation, greatness of mind shines forth amid calamities. . . . Also godly men who had much property were treated the same way, such as Job, David and others. They knew that some people must be rich, and they carried out their calling; but yet they did not put their riches before their confession. Although they lost their riches, they did so willingly in obedience to God and in keeping with their calling. This obedience and likewise this constancy in confession are laudable. They are the worship of God.[114]

---

[113] Ibid.; *CR* 21, 726–27.
[114] Ibid., 77–78; *CR* 21, 726.

Remaining obedient to the Gospel is a believer's first priority. Melanchthon calls this obedience "constancy." Constancy may require a person to remain faithful under any number of persecutions, afflictions, or hardships. Melanchthon uses the language of vocation to describe constancy in a believer's life. According to him, the display of constancy is the only reason that a believer might be *called* by God to give up wealth or property. Wealth and poverty are tools for the sake of the Gospel; both are situations willed by God and meant to serve a purpose in the Kingdom. If God wills for believers to possess wealth, they are *called* to be generous with their profits. If God wills for others to suffer hardship and want, they are *called* to continue in faithfulness and obedience to God, not seeking to escape their poverty by acting in any way against God. Finally, if believers are faced with a choice between following the Gospel and losing their wealth or denying the Gospel and keeping their wealth, maintaining constancy in their obedience to Christ is a divine call that requires them to desert their worldly goods. Most importantly for Melanchthon, fulfilling one's call in his or her material existence is essential to proper worship.

According to Melanchthon, monasticism had done a great injustice to the way in which believers understand their material existence. Monasticism had issued a false call to desert private property:

> But the monks do a manifest injustice to the statement of Christ, because they hide behind their hypocrisy, as we see in Matt 19 [:29], "He who leaves his home or his father or his mother." There is a . . . kind of desertion of our worldly goods without a calling, indeed a superstitious desertion, when people imagine that taking an oath and becoming a beggar is the worship of God. Such desertion is in no way praiseworthy. Indeed, it is merely an opinion which arises out of superstition, a form of heathen godlessness, as it says [Matt 15:9; Isa 29:13], "In vain they worship Me with the commandments of men."[115]

Melanchthon believed that monasticism upheld a false call to desert private property because it maintained a false understanding of the worship of God. Taking an oath and becoming a beggar was not what Melanchthon considered to be a scriptural understanding of calling. If the veneration of poverty in monasticism is not based upon a correct reading of Scripture, then according to Melanchthon, it is based on superstition. Whatever arises out of superstition represents human opinion and godlessness and therefore cannot please God or be regarded as the proper worship of God.

---

[115] Ibid., 78; *CR* 21, 726.

Melanchthon provides a clear apology for an evangelical interpretation of poverty and wealth in his *Loci Communes*. The major difference between his comments in the first and third Latin editions of *Loci Communes* is the addition of his remarks on the poor and afflicted Church. He counsels believers to be prepared to voluntarily embrace poverty if they were confronted with a situation where choosing the gospel requires a sacrifice of wealth, honor, or property. However, for believers not facing this situation, their wealth is to be considered a gift of God and not meant to be relinquished in its entirety. God calls the rich of the Church to be generous with those in need, distributing the profits from their assets, but retaining the principal itself. Melanchthon said that it was the wealthy that exercise their faith and manifest their virtue in obedience to the Gospel.

Just as wealth is not a vice to be forsaken, poverty in Melanchthon's theology is not a virtue to be venerated. In both editions of his *Loci Communes*, Melanchthon was careful to distinguish his interpretation of poverty as evangelical and distinct from that of monasticism. The physical poverty and affliction of believers is a divine call, according to Melanchthon—a kind of school into which the godly are placed to be exercised in their obedience to the Gospel. The poverty engaged in by monasticism is a false calling based on superstition and human opinion. This kind of poverty was viewed by Melanchthon as spiritually and socially destructive, leading to idleness and begging.

Many of Melanchthon's ideas on the evangelical perspective of poverty are common to Calvin's writings: both men recognize that wealth is a gift from God meant to be shared with the poor; both encourage the poor to endure their poverty in faith and obedience; both are aware of the spiritual and social ills of mendicancy and begging; and significantly, both see the connection between the Church's treatment of the poor and right worship.[116] In addition, both men see that at times the Church will be impoverished through persecution and want and that God uses these crises to reveal to the Church its sin.[117] However, for Calvin, poverty is more integrated into his total theological thought than is Melanchthon's

---

[116] Most of what Melanchthon says about poverty in his 1543 *Loci Communes* is also found in Calvin's sermon on Deut 15:11, delivered in October of 1555. One of the subjects Calvin adds in this sermon that is missing from Melanchthon's comments on poverty is his critique of pomp and ceremony in Roman worship. However, Melanchthon treats this topic under "Locus 21—Human Ceremonies in the Church." Melanchthon also spends more time than Calvin criticizing the institution of monasticism. See chapter 9 of this study.

[117] See chapter 9 of this study for Calvin's views on the subject.

because of Calvin's attention to the role poverty plays in the revelation of Christ. This emphasis of Calvin's is not explicitly evident in Melanchthon's *Loci Communes*.

Before examining Calvin's thought on some background topics to the subject of poverty like monasticism, vows, and the right use of this world, this chapter will conclude by examining the last Reformer in this study, Martin Bucer, and his thought on poverty in his work *De Regno Christi*.

Poverty and the Poor in Bucer's *De Regno Christi*

While exiled in England, Bucer (b.1491–d.1551) wrote *De Regno Christi* (*On the Kingdom of Christ*). In October of 1550, he presented the book as a gift to young King Edward VI in response to pleas from several of his English friends to write a treatise on how the Reformation should be established in England.[118] Concerning *De Regno Christi*, Pauck writes, "It reflects his entire career insofar as in it he sets forth that doctrinal and practical understanding of the Reformation which he had achieved in connection with his work and experience."[119] Hall states that Bucer had been working out the patterns of relationship between the Church and the rest of the social order for years, but that "it was the English situation which focused them."[120] Bucer wrote *De Regno Christi* in the form of two books. Book One presents his rationale for reform based on Scripture and his understanding of how the Kingdom of Christ bears on the Church and Christian government. Book Two embodies Bucer's practical outline of his program of reform for the Church and State of England. Because *De Regno Christi* is Bucer's mature work and contains chapters on meeting the needs of the poor, it is a reasonable place to begin to explore Bucer's theological treatment of the topic of poverty in light of the Kingdom of Christ.

In Book One, the main thesis for Bucer's chapter entitled "Care for the Needy" is that caring for the poor is "proper to the kingdom of Christ" because God "forbids his people to allow anyone among them to be in

---

[118] See Pauck, "Introduction," in Bucer, "*De Regno Christi*," 157–58. Bucer's work had little influence, historically speaking, upon English poor relief. Hopf points out that most of Elizabethan poor laws were based on the preceding laws of King Henry VIII and King Edward VI. See Hopf, *Martin Bucer*, 116–17; cf. Hall, "Martin Bucer in England, " 155.

[119] See Pauck, "Introduction," in Bucer, "*De Regno Christi*," 157. Spijker writes concerning *De Regno Christi*: "It cannot be denied, however, that the deepest motives of his theology and work come to their full development here." Spijker, "Bucer's Influence on Calvin," 43.

[120] Hall, "Martin Bucer in England, " 154.

need (Deut 15:4)."[121] Bucer's style of argumentation is to cite scriptural injunctions and examples in support of his thesis, and then to exhort his readers concerning how these precepts are to be instituted by the Church and state. Bucer's chapter on helping the needy reads like a handbook, a how-to manual for the reform of poor relief in England. As a result, it does not provide much theological reflection on the role of the poor in the kingdom of God or provide theological reasons why it is important to minister to their needs in the light of the nature of God's kingdom.[122] Bucer simply asserts the scriptural charge to care for the poor and states that the Church should follow its directive.

However, Bucer does provide a few clues regarding his theological assumptions concerning the poor, but never develops them in this work. Even though he sets aside theological exposition, clarification, and reflection for the sake of ethical practicality and instruction some traces of his thought may be discerned from his remarks. He wrote:

> For when each person wishes to distribute his own alms for himself, there is violated, first of all the institution of the Holy Spirit and the legitimate communion of saints. Secondly, alms due to the least of Christ's brethren, and therefore to Christ Himself, are more often given to the unworthy than to the worthy. . . .[123]

Bucer instructed that ministry to the poor is not a task to be undertaken by private citizens, but rather by the Church.[124] Those people who disregard this fact violate what Bucer called above "the institution of the Holy Spirit and the legitimate communion of saints." He indicates that the wor-

---

[121] Bucer, "*De Regno Christi*," 256; For Latin text, see *BOL* 15b, 87. For French text, see *BOL* 15a, 87.

[122] That Bucer did not provide more theological reflection on the role of poverty and place of the poor in the Kingdom of Christ is unfortunate. At the time, he was occupied with the pressing situation of the Church of England and how to communicate a basic plan of Reform to King Edward VI. Four months after Bucer sent *De Regno Christi* to the King, he died. Three thousand people attended his funeral. Edward himself died two years later (1553); his half sister Mary ascended the English throne and acted to reverse the reform of the Church in England. In 1556, Bucer was posthumously tried and condemned as a heretic and his bones were exhumed and publicly burned in the market square at Cambridge—a testament to his reputation as a Protestant Reformer of the Church. Bucer's name was cleared of heresy charges and rehabilitated in a public ceremony in Cambridge, February 6, 1560. See Pauck, "Introduction," in Bucer, "*De Regno Christi*," 160, n. 12.

[123] Bucer, "*De Regno Christi*," 257, 258; *BOL* 15b, 89. cf. *BOL* 15a, 89.

[124] Hopf remarks that the idea that poor relief is a public affair and not one left up to the private individual is the main characteristic that binds together the poor law under Henry VII, Edward VI, and Elizabeth. Hopf, *Martin Luther*, 117.

ship and the fellowship of the Church are violated when the relief of the poor is left to the private individual. When he calls the poor "the least of Christ's brethren," stating that giving alms to the poor is like giving alms to "Christ Himself," he further underscores that ministry to the poor is essential to the proper worship of the Church. By suggesting that supplying the needs of the poor personally ministers to Christ, Bucer reveals another fact: his theological understanding of the poor is Christologically grounded. Unfortunately, Bucer does not expand or reflect upon these ideas in his treatise. He does however, leave some clues which suggest that his theological understanding of poverty and the poor is integral to his perspective regarding Christ's Kingdom and to the life and worship of the Church.

In Bucer's second book, a chapter entitled "The Sixth Law: Poor Relief" provides further evidence that ministry to the poor is integral to his view of worship and is informed by his Christology. Bucer opens his chapter saying:

> When the things long consecrated to his name and worship have been thus preserved and sanctified to Christ the Lord, as much as possible and to the degree that we trust him and love him as our Savior and the giver of all good things, and when equitable assets have been set aside and by ample patrimony constituted by the laying down of law VI for the churches of Christ in his Kingdom, Your Majesty will restore that holy provision for the poor and needy which the Holy Spirit has prescribed and commended to us. Without it there can be no true communion of saints, and your majesty will see to it that each church has its deacons in charge of providing for the poor. . . .[125]

Bucer again instructs that without restoring a ministry of the Church to the poor, "there can be no true communion of saints." As the King of England, Edward was the head of the Church, and therefore responsible for restoring what was necessary for correct worship. Monasteries had grown rich from benefices that were meant to be used in the service of the impoverished. Bucer counseled that if proper worship were to be restored, those assets consecrated to the Lord for the poor long ago needed to be reinstated. Without these resources, the deacons of the Church would not be able to conduct their ministry and, according to Bucer, such a condition would preclude a "true communion of saints." Bucer's comments concerning the ministry to the poor reflect his concern for a correct wor-

---

[125] Bucer, "*De Regno Christi*," 306–7; BOL 15,143; cf. BOL 15b, 141.

ship in the Church. Correct worship demanded that the Church minister effectively to the needs of the poor.

In another paragraph Bucer instructs:

> No Christian, even though he has fallen into poverty (and regardless of the high social standing which he once enjoyed) should be ashamed of the cross of Christ and the salutary remedy administered by the Lord through need. It is even less proper for Christians to find it distasteful to accept alleviation of their need through the ministry of his Church as from the very hand of the Lord, by whose most righteous, and to them no less salutary, judgment they have been plunged into poverty and humility of life.[126]

Bucer makes a number of significant statements which illumine his theology of poverty. He has a name for the poverty of believers: "the cross of Christ." This association suggests that believers are to not be ashamed of their situation, because their experiences of poverty and affliction are what Christ himself experienced. In other words, for Christians to be ashamed of their poverty means that they are ashamed of their Lord. They are not to refuse the assistance of the Church. Bucer indicates that the Church's giving to the poor is a way in which it extends the hand of Christ to those in need. To refuse the generosity of the Church is to refuse Christ. Finally, he states that poverty may fall upon believers as a result of God's judgment. Bucer does not explain what he means by the term "judgment." In this passage, the word "judgment" could be interpreted in its broader sense to describe the experience of poverty and humility as an expression of God's will; or it could be understood more narrowly that it is a result of their sin. Bucer leaves this point unclarified.

Though statements of theological clarification and reflection are scarce in *De Regno Christi*, it is noticeable that what Bucer does reveal about his theological understanding of poverty is similar to what one finds in the writings of Calvin. Both men insist that meeting the needs of the poor is essential to right worship and a proper expression of the kingdom of Christ, believing that when the needs of the poor are met, Christ is served.[127] Both men Christologically interpret believers' poverty and afflictions by referring to them as the cross of Christ. Both affirm that these afflictions ultimately come from the hand of God.[128] Yet the most significant correlation between Bucer's thought and that of Calvin is that

---

[126] Ibid., 313; *BOL* 15, 149; cf. *BOL* 15b, 147.

[127] See the study on Calvin's sermon on Deut 15:11 in chapter 10 of this project.

[128] See chapter 8 of this study.

Bucer discusses his program for poor relief in a book entitled *De Regno Christi* [*On the Kingdom of Christ*]. In Calvin's theology, the kingdom of Christ stands at the center of his interpretation of the meaning of poverty. Though Bucer does not provide theological reflection on the role of poverty, or on the place of the poor in the Kingdom of Christ, it is clear in *De Regno Christi* that his ethical understanding of poverty is anchored in his theological understanding of the nature of Christ's kingdom, as is his whole program of reform. It is the thesis of this project that Calvin's understanding of poverty is rooted in his interpretation of Christ's kingdom; that is, his understanding of poverty is based upon the way in which Christ's poverty and affliction demonstrate the spiritual nature of Christ's kingship and become the distinguishing mark of His kingdom. Though there is not enough information available in *De Regno Christi* to determine whether Calvin's theological understanding of poverty was influenced by Bucer, it is a significant observation that both theologians saw that Christ's kingship comes to bear upon the way that the Church responds to the poor.[129]

Conclusion

When Luther challenged the merit system of salvation with his call for *sola fide*, the medieval understanding of poverty was also called into question. By reforming the doctrine of salvation, Luther also confronted the Roman Church's institutionalizing of spirituality, which included the medieval practices of asceticism. In his treatise *De votis monasticis*, Luther attacked the Roman dogma on counsels and precepts. His argument was simple: Because vows are not prescribed in Scripture, the distinction between counsels and precepts is artificial. Luther argued that if the poverty in Roman spirituality were the poverty of spirit, then poverty could not be interpreted as a counsel but as a precept, since it is something everyone living the Christian life should possess. Yet if Roman spirituality intended a material form of poverty, then the vows of monks look foolish in the light of the monasteries' abundance of extravagant possessions. In Luther's judgment, the Roman vow of poverty was nothing more than an excuse to divert funds to themselves and away from ministering to those in genuine need.

---

[129] Calvin's relationship and admiration for Bucer is well known. The friendship between the two reformers deepened during the years 1538–41, when Calvin stayed in Strasbourg. In Spijker's article, "Bucer's Influence on Calvin," he discusses how Christ's kingship functions in Bucer's ethic articulated in *De Regno Christi* and contrasts this with Calvin's understanding of Christ's kingship in his ethics. See pages 42–44.

Luther's criticisms became a standard for the Evangelical Reformers. Zwingli, Melanchthon, and Bucer added their particular emphases to Luther's basic argument. Zwingli rejected vows of poverty because they circumvented the divine command; according to him, Matt 5:3 was a rule intended for the whole Church, not for just a few. Furthermore, fulfilling a vow of poverty credits merit to the person who made the vow, not to the power and grace of God. Melanchthon also built on Luther's approach. He rejected vows of poverty because he believed that poverty is demanded of all Christians. The true practice of biblical poverty, according to Melanchthon, does not require the poor to receive resources from others, but does require believers to give out of their abundance in order to alleviate another's want. Melanchthon described the nature of evangelical poverty in language analogous to that which teaches Christian stewardship. In his view, Christians are forbidden to relinquish private property in order to go about begging because their calling asks them to be generous with their profits. Though Bucer did not specifically address the issue of vows as did Melanchthon and Zwingli, his comments demonstrated that he ascribed to Luther's critique. In *De Regno Christi*, Bucer was not interested in writing a polemical treatise against the practices of Roman spirituality. Instead, he provided practical guidelines for the way in which the Kingdom of Christ could be practically manifest in England. Bucer instructed King Edward to restore ecclesial assets for the ministry of the poor, resources which had been seized by greedy clergy and monasteries for their own enjoyment.

Though Luther, Zwingli, Melanchthon, and Bucer agreed in their rejection of the kind of poverty assumed by a vow and embraced in monasticism, they varied in their theological interpretations of poverty and in their expressions of its implications for the Church. The writings of Luther, Zwingli, Melanchthon, and Bucer demonstrate a broad range of interpretation of poverty among the early Reformers. Their approaches to the issue of poverty differed according to their respective contexts and the roles that they played in the Protestant Reformation. These differences in their perspectives are particularly evident in the Reformers' ecclesiology.

In the years during which Luther developed his theology of the cross, he interpreted the poor as Christians under the cross. The afflictions which the poor experienced occurred not in their bodies but in their souls as a result of sin. The poor were those who hungered after God and desired to be filled with God's Word. Those who persecuted the poor were not the rich, but rather the proud who were filled with arrogance and self-confidence. For Luther, true poverty was the determining factor in one's relationship to God. He regarded the poor as being the evangelical faithful in the Church. His interpretation of poverty was an effective tool in combating the doctrinal errors of Rome; however, it brought lamentable results as Luther ignored the social and economic plight of the physically poor. Because of Luther's spiritualization of the poor, Scripture's language of poverty was neutralized and emptied of its socio-economic force. This left Luther no biblical grounds on which to defend the afflicted peasants before their German princes.

Unlike the way that Luther spiritualized the poor in his theology of the cross, Zwingli implemented his program of reform in Zurich by bringing the full socio-economic force of the biblical teaching on the poor to bear on the extravagant worship practices of the Roman Church. Zwingli used the poor in his attack on the use of icons in worship. In his perspective, God had ordained poor Christians, the true images of God, to receive any material honor the Church wished to bestow upon Christ. This focus had two benefits. It kept the worship of God free from extravagance and provided a place of honor for the poor in the Church. Images in worship, according to Zwingli, not only usurped the resources of the poor but also usurped the role that the poor played in the life of the Church.

Luther and Zwingli included theological discussions about the poor as part of their polemics. Luther's and Zwingli's approaches to dealing with the poor were as unique as their styles of ministry. Melanchthon's didactic approach to the poor reflected his career as an academician who shied away from controversy. In his *Loci Communes,* the controlling factor concerning poverty was his conviction that the first priority of the Church is to remain obedient to the Gospel. He recognized that poverty and affliction could befall the whole Church in times of persecution. God could choose to bestow poverty and afflictions on the Church to instruct believers concerning their sinfulness and to strengthen their faith. Melanchthon argued that adversity teaches the Church humility and obedience to the Gospel. These difficulties did not mean that God had forsaken the Church. Melanchthon knew that experiences of poverty and affliction could also tempt believers to forsake the Gospel. Therefore, he taught that affliction and poverty are part of what it means to follow Christ and to remain obedient to the Gospel.

Melanchthon also discussed the role of the physically poor in the life of the Church. In the poor, he argues, the rich are presented with the opportunity for exercising their faith and manifesting their virtue through generosity. The poor, on the other hand, are called to endure their experience with patience, waiting on God to fulfill their needs. The most important aspect of Melanchthon's thinking in regards to the role of poverty and wealth is not how believers respond to either of these, but their steadfast obedience to the Gospel regardless of their poverty or wealth. Remaining obedient to the Gospel, is always the first priority of the Church; a Church that upholds this priority will be patient in affliction and poverty, and generous in abundance and wealth. Likewise, a Church that is obedient to the Gospel will also relinquish its wealth and property if keeping these possessions compromises the message or the faithfulness of the Church to the Gospel.

Bucer's approach to the poor within the Church assumes a different tone than the emphases of Luther, Zwingli, and Melanchthon. Bucer did not use the poor or the biblical language of poverty to bolster a polemic as did Luther and Zwingli. Unlike Melanchthon, Bucer did not instruct his readers on the spiritual significance of poverty for the Church. Rather, Bucer's approach to the issue of poverty entails an outline of practical directives for the English Church and state to follow in serving needs of the poor. As a result, he did not concern himself with theological reflection on the spiritual significance of poverty, but instead assumed this knowledge. Nevertheless, Bucer's comments provide a window into his thought on the significance of poverty in the Church.

First, Bucer's conviction that ministering to the needs of the poor is a task to be taken on by the Church alone, and not by private individuals, comes out of an ecclesiological conviction that the poor possess a special role in the worship of the Church. Bucer calls the act of giving alms to the poor *giving alms to Christ Himself*. This association explains why Bucer is emphatic that a ministry to the poor needs to be an intentional ministry of the Church, and not left up to the whim of individuals. Ministering to Christ through the poor is an act of corporate worship. This association between Christ and the poor also explains why Bucer insists that the king should restore to the deaconate the assets confiscated by greedy monks. If giving alms to the poor is truly giving to Christ, then the poor are ordained to receive the material gifts the Church wishes to bestow upon Christ as part of its worship of God, an argument both Zwingli and Calvin articulate.

Second, Bucer called the poverty and afflictions of believers the *cross of Christ*. This analogy indicates that Bucer understands the theological significance of poverty from a Christological perspective. The poverty and afflictions of Christ are something in which believers participate. Furthermore, because this participation gives spiritual meaning to their hardships, Christians should not be ashamed of their hardships. For

Christians to be ashamed of their poverty and afflictions is to be ashamed of Christ. Furthermore, needy believers should accept the benevolence of the Church. For a believer to refuse the ministry of the Church is to refuse the ministry of Christ. Finally, Bucer discloses a Christological perspective on the issue of poverty and the poor in his treatise *De Regno Christi*. There, Bucer seeks to outline the practical directives for the way that the kingdom of Christ is to be manifest in the daily lives of the English people. Though Bucer does not theologically delineate the role of the poor in the kingdom of Christ, the fact that major sections of his work are dedicated to the relief of poverty suggest that his spiritual understanding of poverty is grounded in his Christology and in the nature of Christ's Kingdom.

Since Calvin was younger than Luther, Zwingli, Melanchthon, and Bucer, he had the benefit of being acquainted with these men through their writings, and some he knew personally or through correspondence. By the time that Calvin wrote the first edition of *Institutes* in 1536, the Reformation had been underway for nearly twenty years; Luther was writing his mature works, and Zwingli was already dead. It is not surprising, then, to find in Calvin's theology of poverty parallels to some of the views expressed by these Reformers. Though much work is yet to be done to understand the thought on poverty that Luther, Zwingli, Melanchthon, and Bucer expressed within in their writings, it can be safely concluded that all of these Reformers, including Calvin, agreed that the Roman understanding of poverty needed revision and that a proper understanding of the poor was only possible through a reformed understanding of the Church and its practice of worship.

Religious Poverty and Stewardship in the Thought of John Calvin

No discussion of Calvin's thought on poverty would be complete without some mention of his views concerning the right use of the material world. For centuries, the Church debated the relationship of possessions to the Christian life largely in terms of taking a religious vow of poverty. In the Middle Ages, this tension gave rise to a two-tiered ethical interpretation of the Christian life which distinguished between precepts and counsels. The laity were responsible to fulfill the precepts: "love thy neighbor" and the ten commandments. The clergy were expected to display a greater level of sacrifice and commitment to Christ and his church. They were responsible for fulfilling the counsels which aimed at spiritual perfection by taking vows of chastity, poverty, and obedience. The Reformation undermined this two-tiered ethic, primarily through Luther's doctrine of the priesthood of all believers. This doctrine removed any theological distinction between laity and clergy in terms of the Christian life and thus did away with all holy orders. As a result, monasteries emptied, priests married, and the Reformers had to rethink how a believer should relate to his or her material life.

This chapter will examine two topics in Calvin's thought: first, his evaluation of the institution of monasticism, and second, his theology regarding the right use of this world. Though monasticism is best known for its ascetic stance toward the material world, it will be seen that even though Calvin rejects asceticism, his main problem with the institution does not concern this. Calvin rejects monasticism primarily because it corrupts a sound ecclesiology, and more specifically, it goes against his understanding of worship. Likewise, Calvin's ecclesiology plays a fundamental role in his theology of the right use of this world, otherwise known as his theology of stewardship. Though Calvin's view of the material world is founded upon the teaching of the goodness of all God's creation, it will be shown that his understanding of stewardship is guided by his ecclesiology and theology of worship. Finally, this chapter will show that Calvin places the poor and the Church's obligation to them in the midst of his understanding of stewardship and the worship of the Church.

Calvin's Perspective on Vows

When reading Luther's writings, it is not difficult to determine his views of religious poverty. Disparaging remarks toward religious vows and the monastic life are littered throughout his works. Yet when one reads the writings of Calvin, a different picture emerges. One must search Calvin's works to find comments that address religious poverty. For example, in this passage on Christian freedom, Calvin taught:

> The third part of Christian freedom lies in this: regarding outward things that are of themselves "indifferent," we are not bound before God by any religious obligation preventing us from sometimes using them and other times not using them, indifferently. And the knowledge of this freedom is very necessary for us, for if it is lacking, our consciences will have no repose and there will be no end to superstitions. Today we seem to many to be unreasonable because we stir up discussion over the unrestricted eating of meat, use of holidays and of vestments, and such things which seem to them vain frivolities.[1]

Had this been Luther writing, this topic would surely have at least one reference to the problems that arise for Christian freedom with the practice of religious poverty. Yet Calvin is silent in this regard.[2] Even if Calvin's statement, "we are not bound before God by any religious obligation" is understood as a veiled reference to voluntary poverty, one could still say that Calvin missed a perfect opportunity to discuss this ecclesial question, choosing instead to speak in more general terms about the subject of Christian freedom. This same pattern typifies Calvin and may be observed in other passages.[3]

Calvin never wrote a treatise akin to Luther's *De votis monasticis*, and early editions of the *Institutes* failed to discuss the nature of religious life altogether. It was not until 1543, in the third Latin edition of the *Institutes*,

---

[1] *Institutes* 3.19.7 (Battles, 838–39); *OS* 4.286.12–34.

[2] This point is made by Biot, *Rise of Protestant Monasticism*, 29–30.

[3] See, for example, Calvin's comments on 1 Cor 13:3.

that Calvin wrote a significant passage on the subject of religious life by discussing the topic of vows.[4] Even so, throughout this brief passage, it is evident that Calvin's goal is not one of polemics against errant Church practices but rather one of instruction and guidance for the believer truly desiring to know God's will.

In the *Institutes*, Calvin compares a vow made to God to a promise one makes to another person.[5] He outlines three things for his readers to consider so that they may avoid error when making a vow.[6] The first is in regard "to whom the vow is made." Calvin stresses that a vow is made to God and that God hates any worship that is not first approved by the Word. When someone makes a vow that goes beyond what is found in the Word, this vow can be characterized as "self-made religion," and is thus accursed in the eyes of God.[7] Second, when Calvin states that a person must understand "who we are who make the vow," he means is that one needs to take stock of one's strength to fulfill the vow, and more importantly, one needs to consider one's calling. A vow should not hinder a person's calling and gifting, but rather should work to serve them.[8] Finally, Calvin maintains that one must consider "with what intention we make our vow." Here he offers "four ends to which our vows ought duly to be directed."[9] The first two ends refer to the past: a vow can be made either as a response in gratitude to God for God's benefits, or as an act of repentance. An example of the former would be the ancient peace offerings which pious kings of the Old Testament made when God delivered them from their enemies in battle. Calvin points out that such a vow has use today when one has been snatched from calamity. He illustrates the latter with the example of a person who is convicted of his or her gluttony and makes a vow to avoid "dainty foods." Calvin stressed that this was permissible as long as it was understood that it was optional for the person.[10] The final "two ends" to which vows ought to be directed are in regard to the future. The first situation occurs when one recognizes that the use of a particular thing is dangerous to him or her. Calvin approved of cutting off the use

---

[4] This small treatise was expanded a bit by Calvin's final 1559 Latin edition of the *Institutes* and appears in this edition at 4.13.1–21 (Battles, 1254–76); *OS* 5.238–58.

[5] Ibid., 4.13.1 (Battles, 1255); *OS* 5.238.32–33.

[6] Ibid., 4.13.2 (Battles, 1255); *OS* 5.239.16–19.

[7] Ibid., (Battles, 1255–56); *OS* 5.239.19–22.

[8] Ibid., 4.13.3 (Battles, 1256–57); *OS* 5.240.40–241.31.

[9] Ibid., 4.13.4 (Battles, 1258–59); *OS* 5.241.35–242.7.

[10] Ibid., (Battles, 1258–59); *OS* 5.241–42.

of things for a limited amount of time so that the person may regain some discipline in his or her life. The final situation in which the vow is appropriate is when a lazy or forgetful person makes a vow in order to "wake up his memory and shake off his laziness."[11]

This is the essence of Calvin's teaching on vows. What is remarkable in this passage is Calvin's systematic and biblical treatment of the topic of vows apart from the abuses of the monastic institutions. Calvin's objective thus far hardly uses the kind of polemics Luther engaged in *De votis monasticis*. Instead, Calvin is committed to right teaching concerning vows so that he may discourage any "self made religion." In the remainder of the chapter just discussed, he deals with the incongruities of monastic piety in his day, along with a number of theological problems he had with the institution itself.[12]

Calvin's Perspective on Monasticism

Calvin compares the present institution of monasticism with the character of the institution time of Augustine.[13] There are a few arguments in this later section on monasticism that are worth noting. One such argument concerns Calvin's perspective on the Roman doctrine of precepts and counsels. Like Luther, Calvin criticized the artificial division between precepts and counsels.[14] He claimed that monks "openly teach that they shoulder a greater burden than Christ laid upon his people, seeing that they promise to keep the evangelical counsels to love one's enemies, not to seek vengeance, not to swear, etc.—by which Christians are not commonly bound."[15] Calvin challenges this reasoning. "All [the ancients] declare with one voice that man must obey every little word uttered by Christ,"[16] he contends. He censured the monasticism of his day for the erroneous opinion "that a more perfect rule of life can be devised than the common one committed by God to the whole church."[17] Calvin can only

---

[11] Ibid., 4.13.5 (Battles, 1259); *OS* 5.243.5–7.

[12] Ibid., 4.13.11–21 (Battles, 1265–76); *OS* 5.248–58.

[13] Ibid., 4.13.8–10 (Battles, 1261–65); *OS* 5.244–48.

[14] See Mulhern, *Dedicated Poverty*, 137–38; and Biot, *Rise of Protestant Monasticism*, 31.

[15] *Institutes* 4.13.12 (Battles, 1266); *OS* 5.249.

[16] Ibid.; *OS* 5.249.14–16.

[17] Ibid.; *OS* 5.249.21–23. For a good discussion on Thomas Aquinas' teaching in the *Summa Theologia* on the higher state of perfection which monks have even over that of priests, see Steinmetz, "Calvin and the Monastic Ideal," 606–7.

regard "whatever is built upon such a foundation" as nothing other than "abominable."[18]

Monasticism's claim to perfection and their division between precepts and counsels were concepts which Calvin clearly opposed. Even so, he took greater issue with what he called the "double Christianity" that monasticism created by its abuse of the sacraments. Calvin asserts that its claim to perfection spawned the "sacrilegious doctrine . . . which compares the profession of monasticism to baptism, and even openly declares it a form of second baptism."[19] Calvin considers this teaching to be "blasphemous," and he condemns it for violating the Eucharist by administering it privately in their own worship services apart from the rest of the community of believers. Calvin continues:

> If this is not to break the communion of the church, what is? And to pursue the comparison which I have begun, and to finish it once for all, what resemblance in this respect do they have to the ancient monks? Even though they dwelt apart from others; they attended solemn assemblies; there they were part of the people. By erecting a private alter for themselves, what else have present day monks done but broken the bond of unity? For they have both excommunicated themselves from the whole body of the church and despised the ordinary ministry [*ordinarium contempserunt ministerium*] by which the Lord willed to preserve peace and love among his people. For every monastery existing today, I say, is a conventicle of schismatics, disturbing the order of the church and cut off from lawful society of believers.[20]

Calvin regards the separatism of the monks as a departure from the monastic practices of the ancients and theologically inexcusable. Because monasteries in Calvin's day celebrated the Eucharist apart from the rest of the body of believers, they threatened the unity of the Church and excommunicated themselves from the rest of the Christian community. In Calvin's ecclesiology, this kind of behavior was "schismatic."

Calvin's main problem with monasticism is its violation of the unity of the Church through its separatistic worship practices and its "contempt for the ordinary ministry" [*ordinarium contempserunt ministerium*] of the Church. The bonds of unity in the Church which monasticism had broken

---

[18] *Institutes* 4.13.12 (Battles, 1266); *OS* 5.23–24.
[19] Ibid., 4.13.14 (Battles, 1268). See also Tamburello who discusses this point in *Union with Christ*, 95.
[20] *Institutes* 4.13.14 (Battles, 1268–69); *OS* 5.251.34–252.9.

were clear enough, but what does Calvin mean by the term "ordinary ministry"? Calvin uses the term "*ordinaria Sacramenta*" when speaking of the sacraments in 4.14.20 of the *Institutes*. He uses the phrase to distinguish the Lord's Supper and baptism as the two "ordinary sacraments," different from that of the laying on of hands when initiating ministers into their offices.[21] Calvin also uses the term "ordinary" in his comments on Mary's anointing of Jesus in John 12:7. Calvin calls the Church's ministry to the poor the "ordinary service" [*ordinarium cultum*] of the Church.[22] Whether Calvin's statement refers to the way monasticism fractured the Church by establishing a separate altar or to its neglect of the poor, he believes the institution of monasticism has a blasphemous ecclesiology.

Though Calvin praises the ecclesiology of ancient monasticism and its connectedness to the worship of the larger Church, he still expresses a number of reservations about the institution's manner of life as a whole. In speaking of "the ancient form [of monasticism] that Augustine commends," Calvin remarks:

> It was a beautiful thing to forsake all their possessions and be without earthly care. But God prefers devoted care in ruling a household, where the devoted householder, clear and free of all greed, ambition, and other lusts of the flesh, keeps before him the purpose of serving God in a definite calling.[23]

Calvin admired the life of voluntary poverty the monks of old practiced, calling it a "beautiful thing." Yet he believed that such a lifestyle falls short of the divine will for human beings. These men would have done better if they "ruled a household" in a godly manner while they sought to fulfill their divine calling.

Calvin's other difficulty with ancient monasticism pertains to its escapism. Calvin writes:

> It is a beautiful thing to philosophize in retirement, far from intercourse with men. But it is not the part of Christian meekness, as if in hatred of the human race, to flee into the desert and the wilderness and at the same time to forsake those duties which the Lord has especially commanded. Though we grant there was noth-

---

[21] Ibid., 4.14.20 (Battles, 1296); *OS* 5.278.19.

[22] *Commentary on John* 12:7 (Pringle, 13); *CO* 47, 279. See chapter 10 for a more detailed examination of Mary's anointing of Jesus.

[23] *Institutes* 4.13.16 (Battles, 1271); *OS* 5.253.28–32.

ing else evil in that profession, it was surely no slight evil that it brought a useless and dangerous example into the church.[24]

Again, Calvin has nothing against the solitary exercise of philosophical thinking. There is nothing inherently wrong in such acts. Yet he argues, to practice this as a lifestyle not only fails to model the Christian virtue of meekness but also is negligent to fulfill the tasks God commands for one to engage in the world. The result is a "dangerous example" for the Church at large concerning the nature of the Christian life.

This "dangerous example" of forsaking all possessions in order to contemplate the higher things away from the human community climaxed in the medieval ascetic tradition. Calvin rejects both the practices and theological basis of asceticism. Jean-Daniel Benoît offers this definition of asceticism:

> In general, asceticism is conceived of as a way of attaining a mystical union, or an ecstasy; it implies denial of the world, mortification designed to subdue the flesh, fasts, watches, states of slavery voluntarily imposed on the body, and subjection of our most natural tendencies.[25]

Asceticism aims to separate a person from the material or external world so that he or she may obtain "a kind of inner withdrawal, a wonderful contemplation of God and a union with him."[26] This exercise in the mortification of the flesh and its desires was thought to be meritorious before God and was believed to contribute to one's salvation. Calvin rejects asceticism not only because of the merit system of salvation it embraces and fosters but also because this spiritual path is largely inaccessible to the ordinary believer hence further dividing the Church.[27] Thus apart from the reading of Scripture and prayer, Calvin does not emphasize the outward exercises of mortification. He states that most of these practices were "lesser helps" in the Christian life.[28] He explains: "Throughout its course, the life of the godly ought to be tempered with frugality and sobriety, so that it bears

---

[24] *Institutes* 4.13.16 (Battles, 1271); *OS* 5.253.33–254.2.

[25] Benoît, *Calvin Directeur*, 75.

[26] Ibid., 175–76.

[27] Ibid.

[28] Calvin writes: "Indeed, fasting is not otherwise useful than when it is joined as a lesser help to these [i.e. acts of repentance, true humility and the fear of God]." See *Institutes* 4.12.19 (Battles, 1245); *OS* 5.228.15–19. See also Benoît, *Calvin Directeur*, 180

some resemblance to a fast."[29] Calvin believes that the material world is a good gift that God gives to his people.[30] However, this gift needs to be used with moderation, resisting both extremes of asceticism and excess,[31] knowing that one must use it as a steward in light of one's calling.[32]

Calvin reserves his strongest language for his attack on the spiritual life and moral failures of monks. In reference to 2 Cor 10:12, Calvin notes the particular spiritual snares of the order. He refers to monks as "unlearned asses" who are full of pride and vanity because "they measure themselves by themselves." He recognizes that the ascetic lifestyle tends to promote pride and self-righteousness rather than a humble poverty of spirit. Calvin quips, "It is not to be wondered, if the man that has but one eye is a king among the blind."[33] Though he despises their vanity and self-importance, he has a particular contempt for their vow of celibacy. In his comments, Calvin holds nothing back:

> But what use would it be to explain in detail what a great discrepancy there is in their morals? This is clear: that no order of men is more polluted by all sorts of foul vices; nowhere do factions, hatreds, party zeal, and intrigue burn more fiercely. Indeed, in a few monasteries men live chastely, if one must call it chastity where lust is suppressed to the point of not being openly infamous. Yet you will scarcely find one in ten which is not a brothel rather than a sanctuary of chastity. But what sort of frugality is there in their diet? They are fattened just like pigs in a sty.[34]

By Calvin's estimation, a monk's vow of chastity gives rise to all sorts of depravity within the monastery. He is against this vow of chastity primarily because it was assumed by those to whom God had not given the power of restraint.[35] Calvin suggests that this special gift should instead be used by whomever to whom it has been truly granted. Yet "if at any time they feel themselves troubled by their flesh, . . . let them not despise the remedy

---

[29] *Institutes* 4.12.18 (Battles, 1244); *OS* 5.255.30–33.

[30] Ibid., 3.10.2 (Battles, 720); *OS* 4.178.11–14.

[31] Ibid., 3.10.5 (Battles, 723); *OS* 4.180.6–9.

[32] Ibid., 3.10.6 (Battles, 724; *OS* 4.180.36–38.

[33] *Commentary on 2 Corinthians* 10:12 (Pringle, 333); *CO* 50, 120. See also Tamburello's discussion of this text in *Union with Christ*, 95.

[34] *Institutes* 4.13.15 (Battles, 1269–70); *OS* 5.252.23–31.

[35] Ibid., 4.13.18 (Battles, 1273); *OS* 5.256.10–12.

which is offered them. For those who are denied the power of continence are called to marriage by God's clear word."[36]

In spite of Calvin's reproach for the institution of monasticism, he is honest in his assessment that his charge above concerning the despicable moral conditions of monasteries did not apply unilaterally to all monks. He concedes that the institution could hold a vestige of what the order was like in antiquity cultivating a few "good ones in their flock."[37] Yet the problem was that "these few lie hidden, scattered in that huge multitude of evil and depraved men. And they are not only despised but also wantonly molested, and even at times cruelly treated by others."[38] Calvin uses the language of his own ecclesiology to describe the righteous few within monasticism. Oddly, it is a description similar to the one he gives of the persecuted French Evangelical Church. In the *Institutes*' "Prefatory Address to King Francis I," Calvin offers his plea:

> For ungodly men have so far prevailed that Christ's truth, even if it is not driven away scattered and destroyed, still lies hidden, buried and inglorious. The poor little church [*pauperculus*] has either been wasted with cruel slaughter or banished to exile, or so overwhelmed by threats and fears that it dare not even open its mouth.[39]

The conceptual parallels are as follows. The monks who are among the "good ones in the flock" are described as "few" in number, and are portrayed as a politically weak spiritual minority group. In his "Prefatory Address," Calvin uses a form of the diminutive *pauperculus* to suggest the wretched and pitifully feeble state of the French evangelicals.[40] Like the monks, this "poor little church" is weak in numbers as well as in political strength. The result was that these righteous monks "lie hidden" just as

---

[36] *Institutes* 4.13.17 (Battles, 1272); *OS* 5.254.25–29. Biot argues that Calvin is primarily against the vow of chastity because "one cannot know with certainty whether the gift of continence is permanent." Biot goes on to give the following quote from Calvin's French 1541 edition of the *Institutes* but neglects to give it a footnote and thus offer any more specific information as to where in the work it may be found. Biot quotes Calvin; "We are uncertain of God's will for the future. Let us use the gift for the space of time it is lent us; yet let us commend ourselves to God, and be ready to follow wherever he calls." From this quote Biot concludes that Calvin rejects vows, "that of chastity in particular" because they "bear upon an uncertain future 'which is never in the hands of men, but ever in the hands of God.'" See *Rise of Protestant Monasticism*, 42.

[37] *Institutes* 4.13.15 (Battles, 1270); *OS* 5.253.11–15.

[38] Ibid.; *OS* 5.253.15–19.

[39] Ibid., "Prefatory Address to King Francis I" (Battles, 11); *OS* 3.11.9–13.

[40] ". . . paupercula vero Ecclesia aut crudelibus caedibus. . . ." *OS* 3.10–11.

the truth of Christ to which the French evangelical Church adheres "still lies hidden." "Depraved men" have persecuted these monks in a manner similar to the oppression of the "poor little church" by "ungodly men." The afflictions born by both groups are also similar. Calvin sketches how these monks have been "despised," "wantonly molested," and "cruelly treated." Likewise, the "poor little church" has been "wasted with cruel slaughter or banished to exile, or so overwhelmed by threats and fears that it dare not even open its mouth." Though more attention will be given to the "Preface" of the *Institutes* concerning the "poor little church" in chapter 9, for now one should take note that the persecution of French evangelicals and these monks is for the same reason—for the sake of righteousness.

There is one final point worth mentioning here. When Calvin speaks of this righteous monastic minority, he commends these men for imitating the monastic practices of the ancients.[41] Earlier in the passage, Calvin summarizes the character of ancient monasticism from the "eyewitness" reports of Gregory of Nazianzus, Basil, Chrysostom, and especially Augustine.[42] He recounts their austere and disciplined lifestyle in which they shared their goods in common, and he praises their distribution of any surplus to the needy. He especially stressed their "diligent piety" and "brotherly love" whereby those who were strong worked to uphold the weak because "no one is urged to hard things which he cannot bear."[43] He explains that monasticism in its ancient form did not inspire a "double Christianity" in its theology of a second baptism or in segregated worship.[44] Calvin emphasized that "Augustine is sketching for us a holy and lawful monasticism, which would dispense with all ridged requirement of those things left free to us by the Lord's Word."[45] For Calvin, this was not simply a life in retreat from the world to contemplate the things of God. These ancient monastics engaged the world by service to the poor and were more integrated with the Church in their worship and ministry. Even though he pays such respect to the ancient form of monasticism, in the final estimation, Calvin regards a faithful life engaged with the world as esteemed over any expressed monastic ideal.

Calvin is equitable in his assessment of monasticism. He recognized that it was Scripture that gave the monasticism of antiquity its authority

---

[41] *Institutes* 4.13.15 (Battles, 1270); *OS* 5.253.13–14.
[42] Ibid., 4.13.8–10 (Battles, 1261–65); *OS* 5.244.22–248.15.
[43] Ibid., 4.13.9 (Battles, 1264); *OS* 5. 245.33–36; 247.12–15.
[44] Ibid., 4.13.14 (Battles, 1268–69); *OS* 5.251.15–17.
[45] Ibid., 4.13.10 (Battles 1264); *OS* 5.247.29–32.

as a viable pattern of Christian spirituality. He recognized that it was the ancient devotion to Scripture that fostered a monasticism that worshiped with the church and served the poor. Any guide other than the Word of God results in "self-made religion," an alternative Calvin despised but readily saw in the ecclesiology and spirituality of the monks of his day.

Calvin's Perspective on the Right Use of This World

Calvin's Rejection of Asceticism

Along with his rejection of religious poverty, Calvin sought to construct a theology balancing the Christian's relationship to this world with believers' freedom in Christ. Calvin's theology of "a right use" does not disparage creation, while it is also responsive to the demands of the gospel. In his 1539 edition of the *Institutes*, Calvin writes a brief but highly influential section on the "Life of the Christian Man." Due to the popularity of Calvin's perspective on the Christian life, this section of the *Institutes* was published and circulated independently from the rest of the work as early as 1550.[46] In the final chapter of this short discourse, Calvin expressed his views on "How We Must Use the Present Life and Its Helps." Here he sketches his understanding of a Christian's proper relationship to the material world. Calvin warned, "this topic is a slippery one and slopes on both sides into error."[47] The errors of strictness and laxity, severe depravation, or unbridled excess in regards to the use of things are the two dangerous slopes of which he warns. Calvin offers a guiding principle concerning the use of the material world: "Let this be our principle: that the use of God's gifts is not wrongly directed when it is referred to that end to which the Author himself created and destined them for us, since he created them for our good, not for our ruin."[48] This means that God created food not only to provide for people's necessities "but also for delight and good cheer."[49] Just as God endowed all of nature with beauty apart from necessity, even clothing may serve a function beyond that of basic need and convey comeliness and decency.[50] Calvin declares:

---

[46] See Calvin, *Golden Booklet*, 9.
[47] *Institutes* 3.10.1 (Battles, 720); *OS* 4.177.22–24.
[48] Ibid., 3.10.2 (Battles, 720); *OS* 4.178.11–14.
[49] Ibid.; *OS* 4.178.16–17.
[50] Ibid., 3.10.2 (Battles, 720–21); *OS* 4.178.17–18.

Away, then, with that inhuman philosophy which, while conceding only a necessary use of creatures, not only malignantly deprives us of the lawful fruit of God's benefices but cannot be practiced unless it robs a man of all his senses and degrades him to a block.[51]

Calvin's reference to "creatures" in the above text pertains to all things animate and inanimate that God created. Clearly, Calvin did not support the ascetic lifestyle propagated by "inhuman philosophy." Asceticism demeans the individual and denies one of the divinely sanctioned experience of creation through one's bodily senses. Thus, it forbids believers to use what God created for their benefit and must be rejected. Ultimately, Calvin discarded asceticism because it violates the freedom that believers have in Christ. Though Calvin grants that he admires the original vision of asceticism, that is, the commitment to use only those things necessary for life, he asserts that the severe restrictions of the ascetic lifestyle bind the consciences of individuals beyond that which the Word of God instructs, a practice Calvin will not tolerate.[52]

In Calvin's theology, binding the conscience of a believer ultimately becomes a serious hindrance to one's faith. As seen above, Calvin clearly stated that "regarding outward things that are of themselves 'indifferent,' we are not bound before God by any religious obligation preventing us from sometimes using them and other times not using them . . . ."[53] In his discussion vows, Calvin argues that when a person makes the kind of vow that binds the conscience beyond that which the Word approves, it is "self-made religion."[54] When people construct worship practices and requirements apart from what God commands, this is always detestable to God and destructive to one's faith and the Church.

Calvin's Teaching on Moderation and Simplicity

The other error that Calvin cannot bear is the wanton intemperance and unbridled excess to which human nature is inclined. People succumb to this trap under the "pretext of freedom" when they do not recognize guid-

---

[51] Ibid., 3.10.3 (Battles, 721); *OS* 4.178.35–39.

[52] Calvin writes: "This one plan occurred to them: they allowed man to use physical goods in so far as necessity required. A godly counsel indeed, but they were far too severe. For they would fetter consciences more tightly than does the Word of the Lord—a very dangerous thing." Ibid., 3.10.1 (Battles, 720); *OS* 4.177.28–32.

[53] Ibid., 3.19.7 (Battles, 838); *OS* 4.286.27–29.

[54] Ibid., 4.13.2 (Battles, 1255); *OS* 5.239.21.

ing principles in their lives and justify that all things are permitted.[55] Calvin corrects this mistaken interpretation by qualifying that though all things may be created for one's benefit, they are also created that one might "recognize the Author and give thanks for his kindness."[56] Thus Calvin asks, "Where is your thanksgiving if you gorge yourself with banqueting or wine that you either become stupid or are rendered useless for the duties of piety of your calling?"[57] Excess consumption not only impairs one's ability to be grateful to the Giver of the gifts of creation, but it also prevents one from fulfilling one's divine calling. Furthermore, such excessive indulgence "infects the mind with its impurity," so that the individual "cannot discern anything that is right and honorable."[58]

Calvin establishes four rules to help the individual correct this problem. The first rule relates to the perspective believers need to have towards the material things that they use in their lives. Calvin's guideline is simple: "Those who use this world should be affected as if they did not use it."[59] This principle not only eliminates excessiveness in food, drink, clothing and buildings, but it also abolishes pride, arrogance, over fastidiousness and the kind of ambition, "care and inclination that either diverts or hinders you from thought of the heavenly life," encouraging that which cultivates the soul.[60] Calvin's second rule focuses on the attitude one should have towards his or her economic circumstances. Calvin instructs that one "should know how to bear poverty peaceably and patiently, as well as to bear abundance moderately."[61] This principle guards the poor from "immoderate desire" and teaches them to advance in "the Lord's school" while demonstrating to everyone their integrity and commitment to their discipleship in Christ.[62] On the other hand, Calvin observes that those who bore poverty with impatience, and were not content with little, also abused the use of things when they prospered. Calvin writes:

> This is my point: he who is ashamed of mean clothing will boast of costly clothing; he who, not content with a slender meal, is troubled by the desire for a more elegant one, will also intem-

---

[55] Ibid., 3.10.3 (Battles, 721); *OS* 4.179.2.
[56] Ibid.; *OS* 4.179.4–5.
[57] Ibid.; *OS* 4.179.5–7.
[58] Ibid., (Battles, 722); *OS* 4.179.7–10.
[59] Ibid., 3.10.4 (Battles, 722); *OS* 4.179.25–26.
[60] Ibid.; *OS* 4.179.33–35.
[61] Ibid.; *OS* 4.179.28–30.
[62] Ibid., 3.10.5 (Battles, 723); *OS* 4.180.8–9.

perately abuse those elegances if they fall to his lot. He who will bear reluctantly, and with a troubled mind, his deprivation and humble condition if he be advanced to honors will by no means abstain from arrogance. To this end, then, let all those for whom the pursuit of piety is not a pretense strive to learn, by the apostle's example, how to abound and to suffer want [Phil 4:12].[63]

Calvin desires to hold a number of things in tension. He acknowledges that in regards to "external matters," the believer was not subject to "fixed formulas" that curb the freedom a person has in Jesus Christ. Yet he sees the nature of this freedom as "indulging oneself as little as possible"; as maintaining an "unflagging effort of mind to insist upon cutting off all show of superfluous wealth"; and as diligently guarding "against turning helps into hindrances."[64] For Calvin, to rightly use of this world is to live such that one's material life does not hinder one's spiritual life or calling, but rather serves God in every way. For Calvin, the Christian life is not lived in voluntary poverty or self-indulgence. Rather, the right use of this world, according to Calvin, is marked by moderation and simplicity. These are what preserve the believer from facing the temptations that arise from intemperance and the binding of the conscience.

Calvin suggests a third rule which is based upon the precepts of love. "It decrees that all those things were given to us by the kindness of God, and so destined for our benefit, that they are, as it were, entrusted to us, and we must one day render an account of them."[65] A strong motivation for living a life of moderation is, for Calvin, the knowledge that he is a mere steward of the earthly things in his possession. This means that these are gifts from God to be used as property entrusted to him for a brief period of time. Then, after his death, he will be called before God to give an account of his choices. This God who hates "excess, pride, ostentation, and vanity" and "greatly commended abstinence, sobriety, frugality, and moderation."[66] Thus Calvin's advice is simple: "we must so arrange it that this saying may continually resound in our ears: Render account of your stewardship [Luke 16:2]."[67]

Calvin's teaching on the right use of this world does not end with his rejection of the ascetic lifestyle or with his instruction on stewardship.

---

[63] Ibid.; *OS* 4.180.14–21.
[64] Ibid., 3.10.4 (Battles, 722–23); *OS* 4.179.40–180. 5.
[65] Ibid., 3.10.5 (Battles, 723); *OS* 4.180.24–26.
[66] Ibid.; *OS* 4.180.31–35.
[67] Ibid.; *OS* 4.180.27–28.

Calvin also gives his readers a positive ethic. He explains that these material gifts were given to be used for the greater kingdom. In other words, a life of moderation and simplicity is lived for a greater purpose. A believer is to use his or her material resources properly so that the work of God may be advanced.

Calvin's Teaching on Stewardship and Worship

Calvin's fourth rule builds on this reality. It pertains to how the believer is to use the material gifts God has given in order to serve God and do his work:

> But Scripture, to lead us by the hand to this, warns that whatever benefits we obtain from the Lord have been entrusted to us on this condition: that they be applied to the common good of the church. And therefore the lawful use of all benefits consists in a liberal and kindly sharing of them with others. No surer rule and no more valid exhortation to keep it could be devised than when we are taught that all the gifts we possess have been bestowed by God and entrusted to us on condition that they be distributed for our neighbors' benefit [cf. I Peter 4: 10].[68]

Calvin saw that the material goods God entrusted to believers were actually God's way of blessing the Church through its individual members. These gifts are divinely bestowed on believers for the good of the Church. The right use of this world in Calvin's theology is never about a personalistic ethic. Rather, according to him, things in this world only find their value in their advancement of the kingdom by ministering to the corporate body of Christ. He instructs that a person's material resources may be distributed for the benefit of his or her neighbors. Calvin acknowledges that this practice is contrary to nature. People naturally desire to fill their own needs and look after their own goods. Following Paul, Calvin stipulates that the only possible way to achieve such selflessness is if "you renounce yourself, and give yourself wholly to others."[69] Thus, Calvin reasons, "right stewardship is that which is tested by the rule of love."[70] This means that the Christian should not only look after another's benefit

---

[68] Ibid., 3.7.5 (Battles, 695); *OS* 4.155.27–36.
[69] Ibid.; *OS* 4.155.17–19.
[70] Ibid.; *OS* 4.156.8–9.

with an eye to one's own advantage "but shall subordinate the latter to the former."[71]

Calvin's position on stewardship is directly connected to his biblical teaching on alms. He argues that in the Old Testament, people were commanded to bring the first fruits of their labors and consecrate them to the Lord. This consecration sanctified the harvest and enabled the people to enjoy the benefits of their labor. Yet since one cannot add anything to God by such an offering or acts of generosity, Calvin taught "as the prophet says, practice it towards the saints on the earth [Ps 16:2–3]."[72] Thus the way in which a believer exercises this aspect of the law in the present age is by giving alms to the needy.[73]

The subject of alms in the context of a believer's stewardship of his or her resources introduces another avenue of Calvin research. The body of historical and theological material in this area is important to the study of Calvin and poverty because it demonstrates the manner in which Calvin's ideas on stewardship as an act of worship and ethical responsibility were embraced by the Genevan Church and community. Yet this scholarship is far too vast to be discussed in detail here. What can be said is that the Genevan Church effectively ministered to those in need during Calvin's tenure. Robert Kingdon notes that Geneva underwent radical reforms in which the laity were granted real power and were doing the ministry to the needy.[74] In the mid-sixteenth century, Geneva experienced a constant flow of French refugees who fled the religious persecution in France. Fred Graham estimates that the city may have swelled to twice its size all within the original city walls.[75] He indicates that the majority of these people were not nobility but rather those in the artisan and the lower classes who often came with their families. These people had to be housed, fed, and—for those who stayed—provided with jobs.

---

[71] Ibid.; *OS* 4.156.9–11.

[72] Ibid., (Battles, 696); *OS* 4.156.22–23.

[73] Ibid.; *OS* 4.156.23–25.

[74] Kingdon, "Social Welfare," 68–69.

[75] Geneva's population was estimated to be about 10,300 around 1542 and thought to have swelled to around 20,000 by 1559, which was a peak year for refugees. See Graham, *Constructive Revolutionary*, 105–6. However Kingdon writes, "Many of the refugees to Geneva were relatively well-to-do. Some of them were wealthier than most Genevans. But there were bound to be some who needed assistance, men who had been unable to bring with them their tools of their trade, families that had lost a bread-winner through accident or disease." See Kingdon, "Calvinism and Social Welfare," 86.

The Diaconate of the Genevan Church responded to these needs as part of the mandate of the church written by Calvin in the *Ecclesiastical Ordinances*.[76] Calvin distinguished between two kinds of deacons, the *procureurs* (those who collect alms for the poor) and the *hospitallier* (those who distribute the alms).[77] For Calvin, the diaconate was an office of the Church dedicated solely to meeting the needs of the poor. Jeannine Olson's work on the *Bourse française*, or "French Fund," describes how this common purse was an essential element in the successful ministry of the diaconate's task to meet the ever demanding needs of French refugees.[78] Out of the Fund, deacons paid wet nurses to nurse babies whose mothers had died in childbirth, provided foster homes for orphans, gave clothing and bedding to needy travelers, and cared for the sick. They supplied dowries for poor young women, tools for artisans to start businesses, and even books for cash-strapped pastors back in France.[79] The success of this early form of social welfare system shows the extent to which Calvin's teachings were applied in the ministry of the Genevan Church.[80] Chapter 10 will detail in greater depth Calvin's understanding of the role of the poor in the worship of the Church. Calvin's theology on the right use of this world was not just lofty rhetoric for sermons and books. This thought directly influenced the Church's ministry to the poor in Geneva who had found their way to the gates of this remarkable city.

---

[76] See Calvin, "Draft Ecclesiastical Ordinances," in *Calvin: Theological Treatises*, 58–72; CO 10a, 15–30. There are a number of studies that illuminate Calvin's theology and teaching on deacons. First among them is the work of McKee, *John Calvin on the Diaconate*. For other studies on the diaconate at the Geneva Church see Graham, *Constructive Revolutionary*, esp. chapter 6; Olson, "Calvin and the Diaconate," 242–47; Kingdon, "Calvin's Ideas, 119–38, and Kingdon, "Deacons of the Reformed Church," 255–64.

[77] Calvin, "Draft Ecclesiastical Ordinances," *Calvin: Theological Treatises*, 58–71; CO 10a, 15, 23–25. See also Kingdon, "Social Welfare ," 60.

[78] See Olson, *Calvin and Social Welfare*; or a good summary of her work and findings can be found in Kingdon, "Calvinism and Social Welfare," 86ff.

[79] Kingdon, "Social Welfare ," 58.

[80] Kingdon shows that there was some development in the area of social welfare in Geneva before Calvin arrived. However, no one disputes the advances that were made by the Genevan Church in the diaconate under Calvin's tenure in Geneva. See Kingdon, "Was the Protestant Reformation a Revolution?," 213. See the following for background on the social welfare system in Geneva: Wallace, *Calvin, Geneva and the Reformation*; Innes, *Social Concern*; Kingdon, "Calvinism and Social Welfare" ; and "Social Welfare in Calvin's Geneva "; and "Was the Protestant Reformation a Revolution?"; Scholl, "Church and the Poor"; Alves, "Christian Social Organism"; Lang, "City of God"; Olsen, "Reformation and Revolution," *Calvin and Social Welfare*, and "The Bourse Française."

Conclusion

For Calvin, the worship and ministry of the Church is about expressing its oneness or unity in Christ. This is the main reason why Calvin rejects the institution of monasticism and grants measured support for the way the monks of antiquity practiced their faith. He argues that the monks of his day broke the communion of the Church embodied in the sacraments by setting up their own altars and teaching a second baptism. Among the ancients, this was not the case. They worshiped together with the larger Church and tended to the needs of the poor. In Calvin's day, however, any vestiges of the righteous practices of ancient monasticism were gone. The ascetic practices of these monks produced attitudes of self-righteousness rather than spiritual poverty and service towards the needy. Even though the institution may have had a few godly members, its separatism, pride, and disregard for the poor convinced Calvin that the monasticism of his day was guilty of bringing a schism to the body of Christ and thereby also disturbing its order by introducing a "double Christianity."

Calvin recognizes that depending on believers' use of this world, their spiritual life and the unity of the Church can either be assisted or impeded. Calvin rejects asceticism not only because creation is a good gift which believers ought to use in gratitude but because he is unwilling to bind people's consciences with a vow of poverty and thereby go beyond the requirements of the Word. Calvin recognizes a true danger to both the Christian life and the Church when one goes beyond the Word: this danger is in creating a "self-made religion." Instead, Calvin embraces moderation and simplicity. Moderation protects the believer against "wanton intemperance" which impairs one's ability to give thanks to God or to fulfill one's calling. Yet most importantly for the Church, Calvin teaches moderation and simplicity in life so that those in whom God bestows material blessings may more easily renounce themselves and generously take up serving the needs of others. It was shown that this understanding of stewardship is rooted in Calvin's ecclesiology. Thus it is not surprising to discover that Calvin's theology of the right use of this world is a result of his theology of worship and thus directed the ministry of the Genevan Church. Alms gathered as part of the Church's worship—a response in gratitude to God for his good gifts—met the needs of the poor. Through the ministry of a lay diaconate and the generous gifts of the people of Geneva to the *Bourse française*, the hungry were fed, orphans were placed in families, refugees were housed, and the sick were cared for. History indeed bears witness to the effects of Calvin's pastoral leadership and teachings on the social ministry of Geneva, as well as on the power of the gospel to reform the Church.

Part II

Spiritual and Physical Poverty in Calvin's Theology

6

Introduction to Part II

Distinctions in Calvin's Thought on Poverty

CALVIN'S Christology directs his understanding of poverty in the broader contours of his exegesis and theological thought. For Calvin, what is revealed in Christ must be made manifest in Christian life, the Church, and one's social ethics. The fact that Calvin's thought on poverty touches all these doctrines should not be surprising. In the Middle Ages, the Church's view of poverty and the poor affected all these areas. Being a French Catholic, Calvin was immersed in these ideas and their connections. Like Luther, he was aware of the role poverty played in the merit system of salvation and how it influenced the praxis of the Church. Knowing the theological value and power contained in the biblical language of poverty, he did not hesitate to rework classic biblical texts as well as more obscure ones to bring forward new theological interpretations on the topic.

When Calvin uses poverty language in his writings, often his physical and spiritual usages intersect. When Calvin speaks of poverty, he often does so with the understanding of the way a believer's physical needs affects his or her spiritual needs and vice versa. When Calvin refers to physical poverty in a socioeconomic sense, he may indeed be doing more than addressing his social ethics. He may, in fact, be speaking of his ecclesiology, Christology, soteriology, or even his doctrine of the Christian life. Though Calvin's thought moves freely between describing the physical reality of poverty and our spiritual condition before God, there is one thing that needs to be stressed about Calvin's method: Calvin uses a whole range of terms for poverty at his disposal in order to communicate humanity's desperate situation before God.

Two sources influenced Calvin's understanding of poverty. The first was the historical and socioeconomic reality of poverty in medieval western society. The sixteenth century into which Calvin was born was well equipped with a colorful and nuanced vocabulary of poverty. As chapter 3 discusses, this was a direct result of the growth of pauperism in the West during the later Middle Ages, which fostered an unfavorable shift in people's attitudes towards the poor.[1] The rising problem of pauperism was a difficulty universally recognized in Calvin's day. With the spread of pauperism came the growth of the Latin vocabulary of poverty. Calvin does not hesitate to employ this plethora of late medieval Latin terms at his disposal. Calvin's other formative source is his Christology. Calvin uses his Christology as a theological hermeneutic both in his reading and exegesis of Scripture and in his evaluation of the Church of his day. The poor and afflicted Christ, better known as the theology of the cross, is fundamental to understanding his thoughts on the spiritual and physical dimensions of poverty and how these two intersect. Though Calvin uses the common Latin vocabulary applied to the poor of his day, his theological uses and significations of these terms are determined by his Christology and the nature of the gospel and its message.[2]

Distinctions in Calvin's Vocabulary of Poverty

Calvin's Vocabulary of Physical Destitution and Need

The reason for discussing the scope of Calvin's vocabulary of poverty is that it illustrates just how nuanced Calvin's thought was on poverty. Calvin's vocabulary of poverty can be divided into three categories. The first and most central category contains those words which refer to those who are left destitute or describes those left with great physical needs and little means to satisfy them. Calvin's favorite terms in this category are *pauper* (poor, not wealthy, meager, of small means, scanty), *inopia* (want, lack, scarcity, need), *egestas* (penury, necessity, want, meanness), *indigens* (in want of, needing, poor), and to a lesser extent *penuria* (want, need, scarcity, destitution), *mendicus* (beggarly, needy, in want, indigent), *orbitas* (destitution, bereavement, childlessness, widowhood, orphanhood), *orbus* (deprived, bereft, destitute, devoid), *spoliatus* (despoiled, stripped, impov-

---

[1] Mollat, *Poor in the Middle Ages*, 3.

[2] Cocks neglects to take account of Calvin's theological context. When she examines what she calls Calvin's "economic model" of images, which includes metaphors of poverty, she does not recognize how Calvin's Christology governs the way he uses poverty language. See Cocks, "Metaphors and Models," 248–54; esp. 248 and 254.

erished, bare), *necessitas* (necessity, need, want, distress) and the figurative sense of *angustia* (scarcity, want, poverty, distress).

Outside of these terms, Calvin's vocabulary of destitution becomes more specific. He uses the following terms to describe the manner in which one is physically destitute: If one is lacking health or some physical ability, Calvin uses the terms *tabidus* (wasting away, melting, decaying), *imbecillus* (weak, feeble, helpless, perishable), and *infirmitas* (want of strength, weakness, feebleness). If he wishes to communicate an appalling sight or a lack in someone's appearance, he uses *deformis* (ugly, misshapen, hideous, loathsome, unsightly), and *pravitas* (crookedness, distortion, deformity) which he may often employ to denote the perverse nature of someone's character. The words Calvin uses to denote someone's destitution regarding food and water are *famelicus* (famished, starved, hungry), *ieiunus* (fasting, abstinent, hungry, meager), the verb *esurio* (to hunger, to desire to eat, to suffer hunger, to be hungry), and *sitiens* (thirsty, dry, parched). On occasion, Calvin will use *ieiunus* in its figurative sense to describe someone who is powerless, insignificant, low, and contemptible. When a person is destitute in regards to clothing, Calvin almost always applies the terms *nudus* (naked, bare, stripped, uncovered, exposed), and sometimes uses the terms *spoliatus* (despoiled, stripped, impoverished, bare) or *exuo* (to draw out, take off, pull off, in regards to clothing or possessions it means to unclothe, strip, despoil, deprive). *Nudus* may also carry the sense of someone who is without property, in need, destitute, deprived, or defenseless. At times, when Calvin speaks of a title being "stripped" from someone, he will use the term *inanus* (empty, void, stripped). *Inanus* may carry the figurative connotation of being empty, useless, worthless, and vain.

Calvin's Vocabulary of Social and Experiential Destitution

The second group of Latin terms denoting poverty in Calvin's writing are those words which describe the social and experiential destitution of the poor. These terms are *ignobilis* (unknown, obscure, undistinguished), *plebeius* (vulgar, common, mean, low), *infimus* or *infumus* (one of the lowest in condition or rank, last, at the bottom, meanest, basest, most humble) or its verb form *infimo* (to make low, to lower). There is also *orbus* (deprived, bereft, destitute, devoid), *despectus* (contemptible, scorned, looked down upon), *despicatus* (in contempt, despised), *spretus* (disdain, scorn, contempt), *afflictus* [or *adflictus*] (cast down, miserable, unfortunate, wretched, distressed, ruined, dejected, discouraged, troubled, base, vile, low), *aerumnosus* (full of trouble, miserable, wretched, distressed), or the words *afflicto* [or *adflicto*] (to break into pieces, destroy, shatter, damage, injure), *reiectaneus* (to be rejected, repudiated, spurned), *desperatus* (given up, despaired of, irremediable, desperate), and *perditus* (lost, hopeless desperate, ruined), a term often applied to one's spiritual or moral character, thus describing one who is morally lost, corrupt, sinful, or incorrigible. A few terms that Calvin regularly uses for their figurative meanings to quantify the social and experiential destitution of the poor include *deiectus* (thrown down, low, sunken, depressed), which can denote one who is cast down, dejected, dispirited; the term *demissus* (lowered, sunken, low-lying, drooping, falling, hanging down low), which can be used figuratively to mean downcast, dejected, dispirited, humble, low, unassuming and modest; the term *abiectus* (low, crouching), which can figuratively describe one who is low, common, without elevation, of low rank or condition; the term *tenuis* (draw out, meager, slim, thin, slender), which may be used figuratively for one who is lessened, diminished, reduced, weakened, enfeebled, and degraded. The verb *exinanito* (to empty, to make empty, to desolate), in its figurative sense may be applied to the act of being exhausted, consumed, weakened or made powerless, and *orbo* (deprive, strip, spoil, rob, make destitute). Finally, Calvin uses the term *humilis* (low, lowly, small, slight) in its figurative sense to describe one who is reduced, weakened, degraded, insignificant, enfeebled, or made abject or base. He also regularly uses the term *humilis* to describe the person who possesses the correct spiritual posture, disposition, or attitude towards God and humanity.

Calvin's Vocabulary of Derision and Offensiveness

A third category of terms that Calvin often uses along with his vocabulary of poverty contains words of derision used by those not poor to describe the poor offensively. These adjectives belong to a group of terms that have a wider application than those strictly applied to the impoverished. These terms, then, may be used in contexts unrelated to poverty. Yet Calvin frequently employs these words of derision alongside words of physical and social destitution to convey the dismal and offensive reality of poverty. When Calvin uses these adjectives in contexts relating to poverty, they signal a derogatory attitude or value judgment against the poor. In short, they are used to convey a strong sense of rejection and disgust toward the poor's social worthlessness. Some of Calvin's favorite terms in this category are *contemptus* (despised, despicable, vile, abject, contemptible), *miserabilis* (pitiable, miserable, deplorable, lamentable, wretched), *misellus* (poor, wretched, unfortunate), *probrosus* (shameful, ignominious, infamous), *de-*

spectus (scorned, despised), *dedecorus* (dishonoring, disgraceful), *detestabilis* (exerable, abominable, detestable), *foedus* (foul, filth, loathsome, repulsive, ugly), *probrosus* (shameful, disgraceful), *dispudet* or *dispuere* (it shames, is shameful), *ludibrium* (mockery, derision, wantonness), *horrendus* (dreadful, terrible, fearful, horrible, awful), *horribilis* (terrible, fearful, dreadful, horrible, astonishing), *vilis* (vile, worthless, cheap, base, mean, of small value), *aerumnosus* (full of trouble, miserable, wretched, distressed), and sometimes *vitiosus* (full of faults, faulty, defective, invalid), and the term *tenuis* in its figurative sense (to make small, lessen, diminish, reduce, or degrade). Though several of the above adjectives appear in noun and verb forms in Calvin's writings, two nouns in particular stand out as frequently appearing in texts in which Calvin uses the language of poverty: *scandelum* (scandal, offense, stumbling block, shocking, repulsive) and *offendiculum* (offense, stumbling block, repulsive).

Calvin's Vocabulary of Wealth, Power and Success

Another class of words should be mentioned that often appear in the same context as Calvin's comments on poverty and the poor. When Calvin comments on power, wealth, and success, these terms serve as a point of contrast for his discussion of the theological meaning and significance of poverty. From the perspective of his vocabulary of poverty, these terms can be described as a collection of antonyms: *dives* (rich, wealthy, opulent), *ops* (means, property, substance, wealth, riches, treasure, resources, might, power), *opulentus* (rich, wealthy, opulent, prosperous), *praedives* (very rich, affluent), *copiosus* (abundant, well supplied, rich, plentiful, abounding), *splendidus* (bright, shining, glittering, brilliant, magnificent, impressive), *pompa* (solemn procession, parade, display, ostentation, array), *magnificus* (magnificent, great, elevated, noble, distinguished, eminent, splendid, rich, costly, sumptuous), *maiestas* (greatness, grandeur, dignity, majesty, elevation), *dignitas* (worth, merit, value, authority, honor, distinction, reputation, greatness), *gloriosus* (full of glory, glorious, famous, renowned), *decorus* (becoming, fitting, beautiful, fine, handsome), *formosus* (finely formed, beautiful, handsome), and *potens* (able, mighty, strong, powerful, potent, influential). All these words communicate the sumptuousness, beauty, splendor, and glory of wealth. In addition to these words, there are a number of terms that denote a certain air or attitude of the rich. The most common adjective Calvin uses to denote the prideful disposition of the wealthy is *superbus* (haughty, proud, vain, arrogant, domineering), its noun form *superbia* (pride, arrogance, haughtiness, loftiness), or its verb form *superbio* (to be proud, to be haughty, to plume oneself). Another favorite noun Calvin uses to denote the attitude of pride is *fastus* (disdain, haughtiness, arrogance, pride). At times, Calvin also employs the adjectives *iactans* (boastful, vainglorious), or *iactito* (to make a show of or display), and *arrogans* (assuming, arrogant, haughty), as well as the adverb *elate* (lofty, proud) and the verb *effero* (to bring forth, to carry out, take out) to carry the figurative meaning to raise, elevate, exalt, laud, praise, extol, puff up, or inflate.[3]

Calvin's Latin vocabulary of poverty and wealth is extensive to say the least. It not only shows how considerable the terminology for the poor became in the sixteenth century, but also indicates Calvin's command of the language and the nuance in his thought. Even good English translations of Calvin's Latin writings cannot always clarify the nuanced vocabulary he used.

---

[3] This list of terms was compiled from reading across Calvin's corpus of writings.

7

Poverty and Calvin's Christology

CALVIN'S Christology lays the foundation for his thought on poverty. Christ is his interpretive key. His birth, life, and death function as a theological hermeneutic which guides Calvin's exegesis of Scripture, especially on the topic of poverty. This does not mean that Calvin neglects the immediate contexts of the biblical texts he studies. Instead, Calvin approaches Scripture with respect for the historical situation as well as with an eye to how it illumines the course of salvation history as it culminates in Christ.[1] This chapter will examine a number of Calvin's writings in order to demonstrate the central and defining role that poverty plays in Calvin's understanding of Christ. It will show that Calvin interprets Christ's physical poverty at times as a simplicity or moderation of life, and at other times, as suffering and affliction. Whether Calvin understands Christ's poverty as simplicity or suffering, it becomes a prevalent framework in his theology. For Calvin, Christ's poverty reveals the divine nature of his kingship, and specifically defines the spiritual character of his kingdom. In other words, it will be shown that in Calvin's theology, Christ's poverty is an essential component of who Christ revealed himself to be.

In this vein, Calvin relied primarily on texts from the Gospel narratives with a few exceptions in Isaiah and 2 Corinthians. Aside from a few scattered comments, the majority of Calvin's discussion of Christ's poverty falls into three categories according to the progression of his life: his birth and incarnation; his triumphal entry into Jerusalem; and, finally, the prophecies, events, and reflections surrounding Christ's death on the

---

[1] Puckett's study substantiates Battle's suggestion that Calvin attempted to find a middle way between the historical exegetical method's of his Jewish contemporaries and the Christian exegesis that read the New Testament into the Old Testament that neglected the natural sense of the text. See Puckett, *John Calvin's Exegesis*.

cross. This progression of events will be examined in the following study, beginning with a discussion of poverty and the birth of Christ.

Poverty and the Advent and Incarnation of Jesus Christ

Calvin's teachings on Christ's poverty occur throughout his comments on the birth narratives. Yet he discusses this topic only where certain textual observations warrant its mention. In these passages, Calvin neither dismisses Christ's poverty as a secondary issue nor elevates it above other essential elements in the text. Instead, Calvin skillfully works this aspect of the evangelists' message into the larger fabric of his interpretation, carefully using it to illuminate the coherence and genius of the Gospel.

Included in his numerous comments surrounding the two genealogies of Jesus, Calvin makes a point that is particularly relevant to this study. It concerns the fundamental reason why the Evangelists saw a need to set Jesus within a genealogy. Given the social location of Mary and Joseph, Calvin writes:

> One matter, however, might appear incredible, that this very poor and despised couple belonged to the posterity of David, and to that royal seed, from which the redeemer was to spring...[T]he genealogy traced by Matthew and Luke... was the design of both Evangelists to remove the stumbling-block arising from the fact, that both Joseph and Mary were unknown, and contemptible, and poor, and gave not the slightest indication of royalty.[2]

Calvin recognizes that the genealogy plays a crucial role. Matthew and Luke wanted to prove to their readers that Jesus descended from the royal blood line of David despite the peasant status of Mary and Joseph. Yet Mary and Joseph "were unknown, and despised and poor." In fact, "Mary and Joseph were in such deep poverty [*inopiam*]" that they did not "have it in their power to offer a lamb" for the redemption of their first born but brought two young pigeons instead.[3] Calvin realized that Mary and Joseph's poverty could present a stumbling block to some people's faith. People in the first century as well as in the sixteenth were well aware that royalty were born of rulers, having kings and queens as parents. Calvin

---

[2] *Commentary on Matthew* 1:1 (Pringle, 82–83); *CO* 45, 55. All the English translations of Calvin's Commentaries used in this study are from the 22 volume set of *Calvin's Commentaries*. In some cases I have made minor modifications to the English from the Latin for the sake of clarity.

[3] *Commentary on Luke* 2:24 (Pringle, 141); *CO* 45, 88.

maintains that the Evangelists used the genealogy to overcome this apparent discrepancy for the reader.

Christ's poverty as a stumbling block is a theme in Calvin's exegesis of the birth narratives. Calvin's comments on the shepherds' encounter with the Christ Child demonstrate this point:

> This was a revolting sight, and was sufficient of itself to produce an aversion to Christ. For what could be more improbable than to believe that He was the King of the whole people, who was deemed unworthy to be ranked with the lowest of the multitude? or to expect the restoration of the kingdom and salvation from Him, whose poverty and want were such, that He was pushed into a stable? Yet, Luke writes, that none of these things prevented the shepherds from admiring and praising God. The glory of God was so fully before their eyes, and reverence for his Word was deeply impressed upon their minds, that the elevation of their faith easily rose above all that appeared inglorious and despicable in Christ. [4]

Every circumstance surrounding Jesus' birth went against what common sense would suggest. The lack of beauty in the scene should have turned the shepherds away.[5] For kings were to be born in palaces and placed on clean linen beds, receiving the finest care available. Yet, here was the "King of the whole people, who was deemed unworthy to be ranked with the lowest of the multitude . . . [and] whose poverty and want were such, that he was pushed into a stable." Calvin marvels that the shepherds' faith was not shaken by "all that appeared inglorious and despicable in Christ." The poverty of Christ was not a stumbling block for the faith of the shepherds. According to Calvin, their faith rose above these obstacles because they were able to perceive the fullness of God's glory out of their reverence for the Word. Here is a theme that will be repeated throughout Calvin's exegesis. On passages that refer to the poverty of Christ, Calvin will occasionally emphasize this important point: Faith is the key element which keeps a person from being turned away from Christ who appears to us in a lowly estate.

Calvin offers a reason why the shepherds responded in faith as they did. He explains, "though God had, at His command, many honorable and distinguished witnesses, he passed by them, and chose shepherds, per-

---

[4] Ibid., 2:16 (Pringle, 123); *CO* 45, 78–79.

[5] In Calvin's *Sermon on Luke* 2:1–4, he writes: "For our Lord Jesus Christ is here in a manger and He is, as it were, rejected by the world. He is in extreme poverty without any honor, without any reputation, as it were subject to servitude." See *Deity of Christ*, 37; *CO* 46, 957.

sons of humble rank, and of no account among men."[6] In other words, it was the humility of the shepherds, the fact that they were men "of no account," that enabled them not to be revolted by the sight of a pauper king lying in a manger. Calvin draws the following conclusion: "If then we desire to come to Christ, let us not be ashamed to follow those whom the Lord has taken from among the dung of cattle to be our instructors, in order to cast down the pride of the world."[7] The shepherds teach Calvin that Christ's kingship is not recognizable amidst his impoverished state except by the humble of heart.

If the shepherds modeled a humility of faith, then the Magi modeled the conviction of faith. Calvin was equally impressed that these men were not ashamed to offer their royal gifts to a child found in such lowly circumstances. Their conviction that this was indeed the King of Israel led them to worship Christ in spite of the fact that this child did not possess the external display of royalty:

> So scandalous a sight might naturally have created an additional prejudice; for Christ was so far from having aught of royalty surrounding Him, that He was in a meaner and more despised condition than any peasant child. But they are convinced that He is divinely appointed to be a King. This thought alone, deeply rooted in their minds, procures their reverence. They contemplate in the purpose of God his exalted rank, which is still concealed from outward view. Holding it for certain, that He will one day be different from what He now appears, they are not at all ashamed to render to Him the honors of royalty.[8]

Because the Magi were convinced that the Christ Child was the divinely appointed king, the sight of his unbecoming condition was no obstacle to their worship. They did not hesitate to "render to Him the honors of royalty" in spite of the fact that his royalty was concealed under the conditions of poverty. The Magi's faith had the conviction of things not seen. For Calvin, the poverty of Christ's birth brought out two essential elements concerning the nature of faith: First, faith's humility, or its ability not to be offended at Christ's destitution; and second, faith's conviction of

---

[6] *Commentary on Luke* 2:8 (Pringle, 113); *CO* 45, 73. See also *Sermon on Luke* 2:1–4; *CO* 46, 958.

[7] *Commentary on Luke* 2:8 (Pringle, 114); *CO* 45, 73. See also *Sermon on Luke* 2:1–4; *CO* 46, 959.

[8] *Commentary on Matthew* 2:11 (Pringle, 137); *CO* 45, 88.

things not seen, namely, the conviction that the Christ Child is the King of Israel in spite of his despised condition.

In every scriptural passage that Calvin discusses regarding Christ's poverty, he does so from a particular *theological* vantage point. This vantage point is Calvin's conviction that Christ's poverty *reveals* the nature of his kingship:

> This is a very remarkable narrative. God brought the Magi from Chaldea, to come to the land of Judea, for the purpose of adoring Christ, in the stable where He lay, amidst the tokens, not of honor, but of contempt. It was a truly wonderful purpose of God, that He determined his Son should enter into the world attended by obscurity and humility, and yet bestowed upon Him illustrious ornaments, both of commendation and of other outward signs, that our faith might be supplied with everything necessary to prove His Divine Majesty.
>
> A beautiful instance of real harmony, amidst apparent contradiction, is here exhibited. A star from heaven announces that He is king, to whom a manger, intended for cattle serves for a throne, because He is refused admittance among the lowest of the people. His majesty shines in the East, while in Judea it is so far from being acknowledged, that it is visited by many marks of dishonor. Why is this? The heavenly Father chose to appoint the star and the Maji as our guides, to lead directly to His Son: while He stripped him of all earthly splendor, for the purpose of informing us that His kingdom is spiritual.[9]

Calvin writes as if he finds the irony of Christ's birth amusing: "A star from heaven announces that He is king," while this king rested on a throne "intended for cattle." This king's "majesty shines in the East," while Judea has refused him "admittance among the lowest of people." Calvin is finally able to make sense of this paradox. It provides the reader with a fundamental *theological* insight that defines the character and significance of poverty for his Christology and the rest of his thought: God permitted the Son to be "stripped . . . of all earthly splendor," so that the world would know the true nature of his kingdom, or as Calvin concluded, that "His kingdom is spiritual." In other words, the poverty of Christ was an *elected* aspect of Christ's incarnation meant to serve a specific divine purpose. Christ's impoverishment was providentially engineered into the circumstances of his birth in order to reveal something special about the character

[9] Ibid., 2:1 (Pringle, 128); *CO* 45, 81.

of the kingdom as well as the King, namely, that he is not an earthly king, and that the kingdom he rules is not an earthly realm. For Calvin, Christ's kingship and kingdom are *spiritual*.

Christ's birth into poverty specifically demonstrates this point.[10] Speaking of the "illustrious ornaments" given to Christ by the Magi, Calvin reminds his readers that these should only be seen as "outward signs . . . necessary to prove his Divine Majesty" which function as to embolden our faith. They do not conflict with the fact that Christ's material poverty points directly to the spiritual reality of his kingship and kingdom. This is important for Calvin's Christology because he believes that Christ's ignominious birth can only serve to illumine the kind of king that Christ is and what kind of kingdom he rules. Christ is a king who was not only "emptied" of the splendor of heaven but also of the splendor of earth so that he could fill humankind with his spiritual riches. Calvin discusses this connection between the purpose of the incarnation and the physical poverty of Christ's birth in his comments on Luke 2:7:

> We see here . . . the great poverty of Joseph . . . [and] we see, at the same time, what sort of beginning the life of the Son of God had, and in what cradle He was placed. Such was His condition at his birth, because He had taken upon him our flesh for this purpose, that He might "empty Himself" on our account. When He was pushed into a stable, and was placed in a manger, and a lodging refused Him among men, it was that heaven might be open to us, not as a temporary lodging, but as our eternal country and inheritance, and that angels might receive us into their abode.[11]

The impoverished circumstances surrounding Christ's birth manifests the spiritual purpose of his incarnation. The circumstances surrounding Christ's entrance into this world reflect the work of the atonement. The reason for Christ's poverty and rejection was "that He might 'empty himself' on our account" so "that heaven might be open to us."[12] Christ's pov-

---

[10] The point that Calvin regarded the kingly office of Christ as being spiritual in nature is not a new observation. See Stroup, "Relevance of the Munus Triplex," 24; Wallace, *Calvin's Doctrine*, 8; and Peterson, *Calvin's Doctrine*, 32. What is unique about the above discussion is that Calvin regarded the poverty of Christ as evidence that His kingship was of a spiritual, not a physical or earthly nature.

[11] *Commentary on Luke* 2:7 (Pringle, 112); *CO* 45, 72–73.

[12] In the following passage (Ibid., 2:8 [Pringle, 113]; *CO* 45, 73), Calvin maintains that this "emptying of Himself" does not assert that "any part of Christ's glory should be taken away by it," but rather that "it should lie in concealment for a time." The topic of Christ's emptying will be taken up in more detail at the end of this chapter.

erty, then, stands as tangible proof that he is God's gift for our salvation. His poverty *is* physical evidence for the redemptive nature of his life, a reminder of the sacrifice God made to reclaim humanity.

Also in his remarks on Luke's narrative, Calvin discusses the nature of the Gospel using language which is similar to the way in which he describes the nature of Christ's incarnation. He writes, "the Gospel is mean according to the flesh," in order "'that our faith should stand' in the power of the Spirit, not in the 'lofty words of human wisdom,' or in any other worldly splendor."[13] The parallels that he uncovers by comparing the nature of the Gospel and the birth of Christ are remarkable. Calvin said that the Gospel comes to us in a manner similar to Christ's coming— humble and stripped of all worldly splendor. This lack of glory is meant to inform our faith regarding the nature and power of God's Spirit. Calvin draws on this point in his commentary on Luke 2:12. In this passage, he makes a direct comparison between "the mean and despicable condition of Christ" and the Word of the Gospel embodied in the signs of the sacraments:[14]

> The angel anticipates the scandal which might naturally hinder the faith of the shepherds; for what a mockery is it, that He, whom God has sent to be King, and the only Savior, is seen lying in a manger! That the vile and abject condition in which Christ was might not deter the shepherds from believing in Christ, the angel tells them beforehand what they would see. This method of proceeding, which might appear, to the view of men, absurd almost ridiculous, the Lord pursues toward us every day. Sending down to us from heaven the word of the Gospel, he enjoins us to embrace Christ crucified, and holds out to us signs in earthly and fading elements, which raise us to the glory of a blessed immortality. Having promised to us spiritual righteousness, He places before our eyes a little water: by a small portion of bread and wine, He seals the eternal life of the soul. But if the stable gave no offense whatever to the shepherds, so as to prevent them from going to Christ to obtain salvation, or from yielding to His authority, while He was yet a child; no sign, however contemptible in itself, ought

[13] Ibid.
[14] Peter Auksi remarks that Calvin repeatedly notes how Scripture lacks the brilliance, eloquence, and polish of unrefined literature. Calvin sees Scripture as humble, lowly, simple, and unrefined. Auksi's thesis is that Calvin's aesthetic of simplicity stems from his view of Scripture. Auksi is correct in his analysis of how Calvin understands the simple nature of Scripture and that Calvin's aesthetic is congruent with his view of Scripture. What Auksi fails to recognize is the way Calvin's Christology participates in his aesthetic of simplicity and how the Word of God written and the Word of God incarnate are aesthetically parallel in their lowly, humble, unrefined, simple estate. See Auksi, *Christian Plain Style*, 216–28.

to hide His glory from our view, or prevent us from offering to Him lowly adoration, now that He has ascended to heaven, and sits at the right hand of the Father.[15]

The sacraments, for Calvin, also reflect the nature of the incarnation. They appear "mean" to us. The simple signs of water, bread, and wine employ the same aesthetic quality as Christ and the Gospel do to communicate God's Word to us. Their lack of splendor and beauty ought not to keep us from "offering to Him lowly adoration." Calvin regards these elements as signs of God's "promised . . . spiritual righteousness." Just as the spiritual nature of Christ's kingship is made known by his lowliness, so the mean and simple elements of the sacraments reveal the spiritual nature of God's promise and the believer's faith. As the humble faith of the shepherds took no offense at the commonness and poverty of the Christ Child, so the Church should not take offense at the "fading elements which raise us to the glory of a blessed immortality."[16] Calvin's interpretation of the simple nature of the sacramental signs clearly has its roots in his Christology, specifically in ability of the poverty of Christ's incarnation and atonement to reveal the spiritual nature of his kingship.

That which Calvin observes as embedded in the historical detail of Christ's birth narratives and expressed in the nature of the Gospel, both in word and in sacrament, he explicitly states of the incarnation in his exposition of 2 Cor 8:9–10. The following passage comes as an explanation and a rationale for believers to be generous to those in need. He engages a discussion of the nature of Christ's incarnation, poverty, and divine kingship:

> "Though He was rich," says he, "He resigned the possession of all-blessings, that He might enrich us by His poverty." . . . Christ was rich, because He was God, under whose power and authority all things are; and farther, even in our human nature, which He put on, as the Apostle bears witness, (Heb. 1:2; 2:8), He was the heir of all things, inasmuch as He was placed by His Father over all things, inasmuch as He was placed by His Father over all creatures, and all things were placed under His feet. He nevertheless became poor, because He refrained from possession, and thus He gave up His right for a time. We see what destitution and penury as to all things awaited Him immediately in His coming from His mother's womb. We hear what He says Himself, (Luke 9:58): 'The foxes have holes, and the birds of the air have nests: the Son of Man does

---

[15] *Commentary on Luke* 2:12 (Pringle, 117–18); *CO* 45, 75–76.
[16] Ibid., (Pringle, 118); *CO* 45, 75–76.

not have a place to lay His head.' Hence He has consecrated poverty in His own person, that believers may no longer regard His poverty with horror. By His poverty He has enriched us all for this purpose, that we may not feel it hard to take from our abundance what we may lay out upon our brethren.[17]

Calvin offers some critical reflection on the theological significance of Christ's poverty. He interprets Paul's remarks about Christ's riches as pertaining to Christ's divine kingship. Calvin writes, "Christ was rich, because He was God." He possessed all "power and authority" and "was placed by His Father over all things." Calvin also acknowledges the paradox: "He nevertheless became poor." Christ's poverty was evident from the day that he entered the world and throughout his whole life. Unlike the animals of the fields and birds of the air, the Son of Man did not have "a foot of earth on which He could lay His head."[18] Calvin sees that the paradox of Christ's divine kingship and his extreme poverty had a purpose. He states that Christ's intent was to consecrate poverty "in His own person" so that people would not "regard it with horror."[19]

The key word in Calvin's statement is *consecro* or "consecrate."[20] *Consecro* means to provide something with honor or sacred status because it has been offered or dedicated to God.[21] Calvin recognized that something unique had happened that brought significance to poverty and elevated the status of the poor in Christ. Though he does not elaborate on this point, he indicates to the reader that because of Christ, poverty and the poor now possess a sacred status in the divine economy. God

---

[17] *Commentary on 2 Corinthians* 8:9 (Pringle, 290–91); *CO* 50, 98–99. An outstanding study has been conducted on the various views of the Fathers on 2 Cor 8:9 by LeClerq, "Les Controverses," 45–56.

[18] *Commentary on Matthew* 8:20 (Pringle, 388); *CO* 45, 241. It is interesting to note that Calvin's comments on Matt 8:20 and Luke 9:58 do not elaborate on the poverty of Christ even though the text provided a perfect verse for him to do so, i.e. "the Son of Man has nowhere to lay His head." Instead Calvin sticks to the context of the verse in his explanations and notes only that this refers to the conditions in which Jesus lived and essentially that those who follow him as disciple should be prepared to expect this sort of life. What can be learned from this passage is that Calvin does not over-extend his understanding of poverty and its relationship to Christology. If anything, Calvin lets several opportunities like this go by where he could have elaborated on the theological significance of Christ's poverty.

[19] *Commentary on 2 Corinthians* 8:9 (Pringle, 291); *CO* 50, 98–99.

[20] Ibid.; *CO* 50, 99. The sentence reads: "Ergo paupertatem in se ipso *consecravit*, ne ipsam amplius horreant fideles sua paupertate: nos ideo omnes ditavit, ne durum sit nobis detrahere ex nostra abundantia quod in fratres erogemus." Emphasis mine.

[21] Lewis, *Latin Dictionary*, 426.

bestows honor upon the poor, removing the contempt from their poverty because it is the way that God has elected for Christ to be born into this world. The idea that Christ consecrated poverty in his own person, and thereby has changed the status of poverty from a thing of horror to a sign of honor, can be traced throughout Calvin's theology. This motif becomes especially noteworthy in his doctrine of the Christian life and the Church. Nevertheless, Calvin lifts up poverty and the poor as having great value because they mirror God's own physical self-expression in the incarnation of Christ.

Calvin's exegesis of the birth narratives stresses the way that the divine nature of Christ's kingship and the spiritual nature of his kingdom are revealed in the poverty of Christ. Christ's poverty *is* the visible sign in the divine revelation of Christ's royal position as King, and thus the identifying mark of his kingdom. The proof of this reality for Calvin rests in Christ's lack of splendor and beauty. Calvin grants that Christ's poverty is a stumbling block for those who merely look upon his physical appearance. It is only by the humility of faith, such as that which the shepherds demonstrate, that a person will overcome the obstacle of Christ's physical poverty. Instead, the person of faith will see the poverty of Christ as a tangible symbol of the gift of our salvation, that is, the physical evidence for the redeeming work of Christ.

The Poverty of Christ and his Triumphal Entry: A Revelation of his Kingship

In his commentaries, Calvin makes specific references to Christ's poverty when he encounters texts that address Christ's kingship. The pericope of the triumphal entry is one of those texts. Two passages in Calvin's commentaries focus on Christ's triumphal entry.[22] The first one is found in his analysis of Matt 21:1–9, and the second is located in Zech 9:9. Calvin's remarks on these two texts overlap; Calvin wrote his *Harmony of Matthew, Mark and Luke* prior to his production of the *Commentaries on the Twelve Minor Prophets*. Also, the writer of the Gospel of Matthew cites Zech 9:9 to inform the reader of the prophetic nature of Jesus' actions.[23] This means

---

[22] A third passage on the triumphal entry of Christ is found in John 12:14–15 (Pringle, 21–23); *CO* 47, 284–85. Though Calvin refers to this passage in his *Commentary on John*, he does not specifically mention the poverty of Christ as he does in his *Harmony of Matthew, Mark, and Luke*.

[23] Calvin's *Harmony of the Gospels* originated out of lectures he delivered from 1553 to 1555 and published in 1555. Calvin's *Commentary on the Twelve Minor Prophets* was published four years later in 1559, though it is not certain when Calvin delivered these lectures.

that Calvin had to study Zech 9:9 in order to comment on Matt 21:1–9. Even though Calvin wrote his comments on Matt 21:1–9 prior to those on Zech 9:9, this study will begin with an examination of Calvin's comments on Zech 9:9 as a context for his interpretations on Matt 21:1–9. This is because, in Calvin's mind, the Matthew text could not be understood apart from the prophecy of Zechariah.

The Poverty of Christ as Evidence for his Kingship

According to Calvin, the prophecy of Zech 9:9 revealed "the manner in which the Church was to be restored."[24] A king would arise from the family of David to "order all things to their original state."[25] This promise was especially important to the faithful of Zechariah's day, who suffered much grief over the depressing situation of the Jews. Zechariah exhorts his people to persevere in faith by encouraging them to "rejoice greatly, and shout without interruption."[26] Their King would not come to his own people in the manner of earthly kings who ruled according to their own pleasure or for their own benefit.[27] Rather, this King was to provide for the wellbeing of the Church; and his kingdom would benefit the whole people in common.[28]

Calvin sees that the poverty of Christ is central to what Zechariah says regarding the nature of Christ's kingship. He observes that this relationship extends to the very manner in which this king presents his royalty

---

See Parker, *Calvin's New Testament Commentaries*, 28; and *Calvin's Old Testament Commentaries*, 29.

[24] The following is my English translation of Calvin's Latin translation of Zech 9:9 (*CO* 44, 269) from which Calvin drew his comments:

Rejoice greatly, O daughter of Zion!   *Exulta valde filia Sion,*
Shout aloud, O daughter of Jerusalem!   *Iubila filia Ierusalem:*
Behold, your king comes to you;   *Ecce, rex tuus veniet tibi,*
He is just and preserved,   *iustus et servatus ipse (vel, idem),*
poor, and riding upon an ass,   *pauper, et equitans super asinum,*
upon a colt the foal of an ass.   *et super pullum filium asinarum.*

[25] *Commentary on Zechariah* 9:9 (my translation); *CO* 44, 269.

[26] Ibid., (my translation); *CO* 44, 271. "laetari valde, et usque ad iubilum."

[27] Ibid., (my translation). See text below.

[28] Ibid.: "Quum autem Deus consuluerit totis ecclesiae saluti, dum statuit mittere Messiam, atque hoc se facturum pollicitus est, hinc potuit populus colligere solidam fiduciam Non est igitur haec particula levis momenti, ubi propheta docet regum hunc venturum Sioni et Ierosolymae: quasi diceret, regem hunc non venturu m sua causa, sicuti terreni principes dominanter vel pro sua libidine, vel pro suis commodis: sed hoc regnum toti populo commune fore admonet: quia scilicet secum trahet beatum statum."

to his people. Calvin regards the following lines of the biblical text "and riding upon an ass, upon a colt the foal of an ass" as a way of embellishing the concept of the king's poverty. He concludes that Zechariah's intention for including this clause was specifically "to explain the Hebrew word *oni* [poor]" in the text. This phrase reveals that the king will not have a "magnificent and splendid appearance like earthly princes, but would appear in a sordid or at least an ordinary condition so as not to differ from the humblest and the lowest of the people."[29] Calvin continues:

> . . . this king would be poor; for He would ride on an ass, and would not appear in great eminence, nor be distinguished for arms, or for riches or for splendor, or for number of soldiers, or for royal trappings which dazzle the eyes of the vulgar. . . .[30]

This display of humility has a specific purpose. Calvin regards the king's simple and unassuming appearance as an incentive for "the faithful to raise up their eyes to heaven, in order to come to the true knowledge of Christ's kingdom, and to feel assured that righteousness and salvation are to be expected from Him." Therefore, the poverty of the king is meant to move the believer past various physical realities toward spiritual ones. Only when a person raises his or her eyes to heaven can a true knowledge of Christ's kingship be gained and with this the conviction that Christ's righteousness and salvation are yet to come. Such confidence is possible "because He will be accompanied with nothing that may strike men with fear, but will serve as an humble and obscure individual."[31]

Calvin perceives that the poverty and humility of Christ's kingship are important because they are necessary to remove the obstacle of fear. If a king appears ordinary and without riches and splendor, the common person will not be fearful of him and can receive the righteousness and salvation that he brings. The poverty of Christ not only strips away the reluctance and fear of the common person but also serves to emphasize that the character of Christ's kingdom is not bound up with what is "temporal or what passes away" in the manner of the kingdoms of this world. Instead, the nature of Christ's kingship and kingdom is one that offers a salvation and righteousness that "is to be perpetual."[32]

---

[29] *Commentary on Zechariah* 9:9 (Pringle, 255); *CO* 44, 272.
[30] Ibid., (Pringle, 256).
[31] Ibid.
[32] Ibid.

Calvin delves further into Zechariah's phrase "and riding upon an ass, upon a colt, the foal of an ass." He identifies two levels on which the prophet's words can be understood: a metaphorical or figurative level, and a historical level. He insists that both are fulfilled by Jesus Christ and neither interpretation conflicts with the other. Calvin explains:

> Now we, who are fully persuaded and firmly maintain that the Christ promised has appeared and performed His work, do see that it has not been said without reason that He would come poor and riding on an ass. It was indeed designed that there should be a visible symbol of this very thing; for He mounted an ass while ascending into Jerusalem a short time before his death. It is indeed true that the Prophet's words are metaphorical: when he says, A king shall come, riding on an ass, the words are figurative; for the Prophet means, that Christ would be as it were an obscure person, who would not make an appearance above that of the common people. That this is the real meaning is no doubt true. But yet there is no reason why Christ should not afford an example of this in mounting an ass.... We now then understand how well do these things agree, that the Prophet speaks metaphorically of the contemptible appearance of Christ; and yet that the visible symbol is so suitable that the most ignorant must acknowledge that no other Christ but he who has already appeared is to be expected.[33]

Calvin understands that the prophecy of Zechariah did not need an actual or literal fulfillment for the prophet's words to come to pass. The mere fact that Christ came as an "obscure person" who did not "make an appearance above that of the common people" was enough to testify to the truthfulness of the prophecy. Yet what Calvin argues here is that Jesus' actions in the triumphal entry were unique. According to Calvin, though it was not necessary for the fulfillment of the prophecy, Christ elected to make his actions specifically conform to the words of the prophet so that there would be no mistake about his identity. In a word, it was life imitating prophecy. In Calvin's mind, Jesus' mounting of the ass serves to unveil that which could have remained hidden or difficult to grasp because of Christ's obscurity and poverty. Calvin said that the poverty of Christ displayed in riding the ass was a "visible symbol" confirming the words of Zechariah, showing that he was indeed the King of Israel.

In his discussion of Zech 9:9, it is evident that Calvin sees the condition of poverty as a key fulfillment of the prophecy concerning the character of the Messiah's kingship and kingdom. The poverty of this Son of

[33] Ibid., (Pringle, 256–57); *CO* 44, 272–73.

David stands as a sign that the kingdom rules is very different from all earthly realms. his poverty invites the common person to banish the fear that a vassal would have towards an earthly king. Calvin recognizes that the Messiah's poverty spoken of in Zechariah was clearly manifested when Christ mounted an ass just a short time before his death. He calls Christ's act a "visible symbol" for good reason. By coming as a "poor" and "obscure person" it communicates that Christ's kingdom does not function according to the rules of this world.

Calvin sees God's subversion of human social stratification and the symbols of power and glory as evidence that God's kingdom is not of this world. What Calvin does not articulate strongly enough is that Christ's poverty challenges the social powers that are in this world. Like all of the other Magisterial Reformers, Calvin was willing to challenge the hierarchy of the Roman Catholic Church, but he never challenged the authority of kings or civil magistrates in the same way. They were revered as divinely appointed servants, and Christ's kingdom was never to supplant human government or the prevailing social system. For Calvin, Christ's poverty points beyond the physical hierarchy of his day and sets the believer's hope not on what is seen, but on that which is spiritual and unseen.

The Poverty of Christ and the Nature of his Kingdom

Exegeting Matt 21:1–9, Calvin posits why Christ requested that his disciples bring him an ass. It was not because he was exhausted from a journey. Christ asked for an ass to demonstrate the nature of his kingdom. Though Christ sought to demonstrate this with his baptism, Calvin sees that it was at this occasion in particular that Christ fully revealed his calling. Christ resisted the title of "King" throughout his ministry, yet on this day in the final week of his life, he openly declared himself to be king. Calvin muses whether Christ chose this time to profess his kingship because he was "not far from the end of His course" and therefore "intended to commence His reign openly on earth." Finally, Calvin suggests that Christ's request for his disciples to bring him an ass "would have been a ridiculous display, if it had not been in accordance with the prediction of Zechariah."[34] With this prediction in mind, Calvin describes the absurd nature of the triumphal entry:

> In order to lay claim to the honors of royalty, He enters Jerusalem, "riding on an ass." A magnificent display of splendor! more especially when "the ass" was borrowed from some person, and when

[34] *Commentary on Matthew* 21:1 (Pringle, 447); *CO* 45, 572.

the want of a saddle and of accouterments compelled the disciples to "throw their garments on it," which was a mark of mean and disgraceful poverty. He is attended, I admit, by a large retinue; but of what sort of people? Of those who had hastily assembled from the neighboring villages. Sounds of loud and joyful welcome are heard; but from whom? From the very poorest, and from those who belong to the despised multitude.[35]

Everything about this situation seems preposterous to Calvin. Christ "lays claim" to his rightful "honors of royalty" in a way by which no earthly king would be taken seriously, especially in the sixteenth century. The regal appearance of rulers in the Middle Ages was taken with utmost seriousness. Calvin exclaims, "A magnificent display, truly! more especially when 'the ass' was borrowed. . . ." Christ was so impoverished that the disciples had to throw their coats on the beast because he did not possess the necessary accouterments. In Calvin's mind, this is a scene that should astonish any person from any time in history. Here was a king actively bearing the "mark of mean and disgraceful poverty."[36] As if this were not base enough, Calvin marvels that Christ went yet another step lower. His large retinue was attended not by dignitaries of state or the bastions of power but by peasants who had been "hastily assembled from the neighboring villages," people who were "the very poorest, and from . . . the despised multitude."

Calvin calls the scene in verse eight "a ludicrous exhibition" where "an uproar of obscure persons, by cutting down trees, and laying down their garments, bestowed on Christ the empty title of King."[37] He refers to Christ's title of King as "empty" because commoners are not the kind of people who crown kings, let alone confirm one as a rightful sovereign. Kings were to be born of royal families and crowned by dignitaries or those in power. Yet Calvin recognizes that Christ looked upon these commoners as fit heralds of his kingdom.[38]

[35] Ibid., (Pringle, 448).
[36] "turpis ac pudendae inopiae signum est." Ibid., (Pringle, 447); *CO* 45, 572. Calvin makes a similar comment in Matt 21:5. He refers to the fact that Christ rode on an "ass or the foal of an ass" was another mark or indication of poverty. He supports this conclusion by stating that this was "the manner of riding which belongs to the common people" and that it "is contrasted with [the manner of riding which belongs to] royal splendor." See *Commentary on Matthew* 21:5 (Pringle, 450); *CO* 45, 572. Calvin makes similar observations in his lecture notes on Zech 9:9, see above.
[37] Ibid., 21:8 (Pringle, 451); *CO* 45, 574.
[38] Ibid. Calvin makes the application here that "even in the present day, . . . He commissions from the heavenly throne obscure men, by whom His majesty is celebrated in a despicable manner."

Calvin insists that "it was altogether necessary for Him to take this method" to proclaim his kingship. As his lecture notes on Zech 9:9 indicate, the display of poverty in Christ's triumphal entry was proof positive that his kingdom did "not consist of the fading riches of this world."[39] Yet he acknowledges that the wicked would not find this method to be acceptable even though this was testified by God's prophet. Calvin takes this opportunity to exhort his readers:

> Therefore, in order that the contemptibleness of Christ may not hinder us from perceiving in this exhibition His spiritual kingdom, let us keep before our eyes the heavenly prediction, by which God conferred more honor on His Son under the deformed aspect of a beggar, than if He had been decorated with all the dazzling ornaments of kings.[40]

In this text, Calvin underscores the importance of seeing Christ's poverty as a fulfillment of prophecy. Christ's poverty, or "contemptibleness," is really an "exhibition of His spiritual kingdom." Stated another way, Christ's poverty acts as a mark or a sign[41] that his kingdom is spiritual. But this understanding may only be achieved by one's keeping "the heavenly prediction" always before him or her. This is how Calvin speaks about faith. If believers keep the words of the prophet before their eyes, they will never need the dazzling ornaments of kings to recognize Christ's kingship. Calvin made a similar point in a more abbreviated manner in his notes on a parallel passage from the Gospel of John. He states:

> When he describes Christ as "riding on an ass," the meaning is, that His kingdom will have nothing in common with the pomp, splendor, wealth, and power of the world; and it was proper that this should be made known by an outward manifestation, that all might be fully assured that it is spiritual.[42]

Again according to Calvin, Christ's ministry embraced poverty so that his kingdom would be visibly distinguished from the kingdoms of this world. By "riding on an ass," Christ provides tangible evidence for Calvin that

---

[39] Ibid., 21:1 (Pringle, 447); *CO* 45, 572.

[40] Ibid. "Ergo ne impediat contemptibilis Christi habitus, quominus in hoc spectaculo cernamus spirituale eius regnum, nobis ante oculos versetur oraculum coeleste, quo Deus filium suum sub illa deformitate mendici magis ornaverat quam si cunctis regum insignibus fulgeret."

[41] "inopiae signum est." See ibid., 21:1 (Pringle, 448); *CO* 45, 572.

[42] *Commentary on John* 12:15 (Pringle, 23); *CO* 47, 285.

his kingship and kingdom are spiritual. This challenges the believer to not seek the "pomp, splendor, wealth, and power of the world." The spiritual nature of the kingdom of Christ sets itself over and against these worldly ideals. This is a recurring theme in Calvin's writings, especially in his ecclesiology, and will receive more attention in chapter 10 of this study.

Calvin realizes that the poverty Christ displayed could interfere with people's ability to grasp the spiritual nature of the kingdom. Considering the ridiculous manner in which Christ proclaimed his kingship, Calvin believes that Matthew feels the same awkward tension that he does:

> Perceiving that it was hardly possible that men, who are too much devoted to wealth and pomp, should derive any advantage from this narrative, when viewed according to the feeling of the flesh, he leads them away from the simple contemplation of the fact to the consideration of the prophecy.[43]

How one approaches the text makes all the difference concerning whether a person will receive its message. Calvin sees that Zechariah's prophecy had the power to overcome the materialism which afflicted people's hearts. The Renaissance culture of the sixteenth century highly valued the classical forms of beauty and splendor. In the triumphal entry, Calvin sees Matthew gently directing his audience "away from the simple contemplation of the fact of Christ's poverty to the consideration of the prophecy," that is, the prophecy of Zech 9:9. The Zechariah text removes the tension believers may sense regarding Christ's poverty so that they may recognize his divine kingship.

Calvin's findings warrant several conclusions. Calvin's analysis of the Gospel accounts reflects the fact that by the sixteenth century, the idealism of poverty had fallen into disrepute. From the manner in which Calvin highlights the irony of the socioeconomic and cultural aspects of Christ's triumphal entry, it is safe to say that there was nothing in this event that should draw the sixteenth-century person to give allegiance to such a king. In fact, Calvin appears to be highly sensitive to Christ's flagrant display of poverty riding into Jerusalem as her king. He argues convincingly that Matthew intentionally placed the comment concerning Christ's fulfillment of the Prophet's words where he did because it was just as true in his day as it was in Calvin's: "people are devoted to wealth and pomp" and therefore will not understand the intent of the text. Calvin uses dramatic phrases like "ludicrous exhibition," "ridiculous display," "the deformed aspect of a beggar," and "disgraceful poverty" to describe Christ's triumphal

---

[43] *Commentary on Matthew* 21:1 (Pringle, 448); CO 45, 572.

entry as the King. With expressions such as these, Calvin plays on the humanist disdain for poverty and the poor as well as the growing middle class urbanites' contempt for the indigent. Calvin knowingly uses the material values of his readers, confirming their prejudices with his colorful use of language, and then strategically placing Christ in the midst of them. This challenged his reader to evaluate their culture and understand how God's values reorder it. Yet Calvin's manner of exegesis and method of communicating his results have an even more significant motivation behind it.

The main reason that Calvin believes Christ chose to proclaim his kingship in the midst of an obvious display of his poverty was so that "all might be fully assured that it is spiritual."[44] His appeal to Zech 9:9 establishes that the display of poverty in Christ's triumphal entry was a "visible symbol" for Christ's kingship.[45] According to Calvin, Matt 21:1–9 clearly shows that this "visible symbol" which Christ displayed in his poverty points to the spiritual essence of his kingship and kingdom. The fact that Christ's rule is spiritual in nature means that it is fundamentally different from what one sees in the kingdoms of this world. The lack of physical splendor in Christ's procession to Jerusalem confirms that his kingdom cannot consist in the fading riches of this world, but rather must lie in a completely different sphere. Calvin said that Christ is the kind of king that the wicked and those devoted to riches, pomp, and display will despise and find deformed. Likewise, he is the kind of king that the needy multitudes will joyfully embrace. This leads one to understand that poverty is not only an intentional aspect of Calvin's Christology but also that it is something embedded within the larger structure of his theology.

A final point arising out of the previous discussion deserves comment. If the physical poverty of Christ is indeed a "visible symbol" of Christ's spiritual reign, then Christ's poverty is revelatory of who he is. In other words, Christ's poverty is an instrument or vehicle of revelation, something like a window through which humanity might look to see something of the configuration of Christ's divine nature and the spiritual character of his kingdom. Calvin develops this point in his reflection on Christ's suffering and death, something which this chapter will now address. The passion and death of Jesus Christ on the cross is the pivotal event for all of Calvin's theology. The following section will demonstrate not only the degree to which Christ's kingship was impoverished in regards to the things of this world but also how the revelation of the spiritual

---

[44] *Commentary on John* 12:15 (Pringle, 23); *CO* 47, 285.
[45] *Commentary on Zechariah* 9:9 (Pringle, 256); *CO* 44, 272–73.

nature of Christ's kingdom is accomplished by his extreme poverty and abasement in Calvin's understanding.

The Poverty of Christ and Affliction of the Cross

The Cross and the Vocabulary of Poverty

When Calvin discusses the details of Christ's passion and crucifixion, the Latin term *pauper* and its derivatives conspicuously disappear from virtually all of his writing. It is as if this term is too mild to communicate the extent of the abasement that Christ suffered. This change does not mean that Calvin does not recognize the poverty of Christ in these passages. The language and vocabulary of poverty had grown extensively by Calvin's day, especially in its specificity. Calvin uses many of these words when he comments on Christ's final hours. Furthermore, there is a marked difference between Calvin's perception of what happens to Christ in the crucifixion, and how he describes other events in Christ's life.

In Calvin's analysis of the nature of Christ's birth, incarnation, and triumphal entry, two themes predominate: Christ's kingship and his appearance as an ordinary person. The term *pauper* and its related forms may fit the picture of a king who is born of peasant parents and lives simply and obscurely like a common man. But when Calvin studies the texts concerning Christ's passion and crucifixion, he is aware that Jesus' life has moved beyond the general experience of a *pauper* or that of an *obscurus hominis*. On the cross, Christ's impoverishment extended to every level that a human being can experience, and Calvin's vocabulary reflects this change. With this extreme impoverishment experienced by Christ come new elements in Calvin's theological understanding of poverty.

This section will consider two distinct areas in Scripture that have specific relevance for Calvin's understanding of poverty and of the abasement of Christ. The first area is the accounts of Christ's crucifixion in the gospels; the second is the prophecy concerning Christ's abasement in the Suffering Servant passages of Isaiah. The following segment will review these passages and explore Calvin's reflection on the gospel accounts of Christ's crucifixion.

The Abasement of the Cross

Calvin uses Christ's passion as a special opportunity to discuss the spiritual nature of his kingdom and to clarify that it may only be seen and understood by those who have faith. One of the first gospel passages which he interprets as emphasizing this theme is Luke 23:11.[46] This verse is placed in the context of Christ's appearance before Herod and his court. Calvin chose to describe Christ as one "who had at that time nothing but what was contemptible in His appearance."[47] In other words, Jesus was poor. He did not exhibit the "luxury . . . royal dignity and wealth" that characterized Herod and his retinue. Calvin notes that this is the reason why Herod "despised" him:[48]

> Luke relates not only that Christ was despised by Herod, but also by the whole of his retinue; and this is intended to inform us, that the honor which is due to God is seldom rendered to Him in courts of kings. For almost all courtiers, being addicted to pompous display, have their senses preoccupied by so great vanity, that with closed eyes, they carelessly despise, or pass by the spiritual favors of God.[49]

Herod and his court demonstrate the perception of spiritual things by those who value wealth and are "addicted to pompous display." Calvin remarks that these people had preoccupied senses which prevented them from recognizing "the spiritual favors of God." The poverty of Christ did not elicit faith from Herod, but rather derision and mocking. He who values "his luxuries and royal dignity and wealth" is blinded to spiritual realities. To men such as these, Calvin concludes, the poverty of Christ and the understated nature of his kingship look ridiculous.

This passage introduces a core theme for Calvin: those who have faith are not addicted to pompous display and wealth and are the same people who can recognize God's grace. On the other hand, those who are caught up in luxuries and ostentation are those who not only lack faith but also are unable to see the grace of God before them. Pompous people are blinded to God's spiritual nature because the physical presentation of God's grace to us in the gospel comes to us as simple, and even in some sense impoverished. Therefore, those who are arrogant despise the gospel for its simplicity, just like Herod's court despised Jesus for his lack of splendor.

Referring to the passage in which Christ's garments were stripped from him, Calvin explains why Christ's impoverishment and abasement

---

[46] "And Herod, with his soldiers treated Him with contempt and mocked Him; then, arraying Him in gorgeous apparel, he sent Him back to Pilate" (*RSV*).
[47] *Commentary on Luke* 23:11 (Pringle, 279); *CO* 45, 753.
[48] Ibid.
[49] Ibid.

are essential to his very identity and mission. Though he notes that "nothing happened to Christ in this respect but what was done to all who were condemned to die . . . ,"[50] Calvin sees in the Evangelists' renderings more than a simple expression of the facts:

> For the Evangelists exhibit to us the Son of God stripped of His garments, in order to inform us, that by this nakedness we have obtained those riches which make us honorable in the presences of God. God determined that his own Son should be stripped of His raiment, that we, clothed with His righteousness and with abundance of all good things, may appear with boldness in the company of angels, whereas formerly our loathsome and disgraceful aspect, in tattered garments, kept us back from approaching to heaven.[51]

The event of the Son of God being stripped of his clothes is more than just an unfortunate historical circumstance for Calvin. It is an image of the atonement. The fact that he was "stripped of His garments" serves to illustrate that Christ's righteousness was imputed to believers because "our loathsome and disgraceful aspect, in tattered garments, kept us back from approaching to heaven." He purposely uses the language of poverty for two reasons: to portray our own spiritual poverty, that is, our inward destitution, and to show the riches Christ relinquished and the want he assumed for our sake. Thus, the "visible symbol" of Christ's poverty has far-reaching consequences for Calvin's theology. To the person of faith, Christ's stripping stands as material evidence that Christ's righteousness and spiritual riches are imputed to the believer.

In his discussion of Matt 27, Calvin introduces John's recognition that these events unfolded in accordance with the words of David in Ps 22:18. He examines the words, "they part my garments among them, and cast the lot upon my vesture," and contends that "what David complained of, as having been done to himself metaphorically and figuratively, was literally, as the common phrase is in reality, exhibited in Christ." Calvin argues that David spoke metaphorically about his property. By the term "garments," David meant "his wealth and honors." By saying that they

---

[50] *Commentary on Matthew* 27:35 (Pringle, 298); *CO* 45, 766.
[51] Ibid. See also *Commentary on John* 19:23 (Pringle, 298); *CO* 47, 416: "Let us also learn that Christ was stripped of His garments [*nudatum fuisse Christum suis vestibus*], that He might clothe us with righteousness; that His naked body [*Nudum eius corpus*] was exposed to the insults of men, that we may appear in glory before the judgment-seat of God."

were "divided," Calvin maintains that the cruelty of David's enemies was "represented even more strikingly by the metaphor":[52]

> Now as he [David] was a shadow and an image of Christ, he predicted, by the spirit of prophecy, what Christ was to suffer. In His person, therefore, this is worthy of observation, that the soldiers plundered His raiment, because in this pillage we discern the signs and marks by which He was formerly pointed out. It serves also to remove the scandal with which the sense of the flesh might otherwise have regarded His nakedness, since He suffered nothing which the Holy Spirit does not declare to belong truly and properly to the person of the Redeemer.[53]

Though David's prophecy was written from a metaphorical standpoint about his personal affliction, Calvin recognizes that its literal fulfillment was in Christ's suffering. The correspondence of David's prophecy with the plunder of Christ's raiment serves an important theological purpose. It is a 'sign and mark' which demonstrates that Christ is indeed the Redeemer. The prophecy "serves . . . to remove the scandal" of His nakedness by disclosing the true identity of Christ. Calvin sensed the importance of this evidence. The faithful require a witness confirming Christ's identity so that their faith would not be deterred by His physical appearance. In Calvin's thinking, the significance of poverty as the distinguishing mark of Christ's kingship and kingdom is the fact that it reveals Christ as "the person of the Redeemer."

The events in Christ's humiliation—being mocked by Herod and his court and being stripped of his garments—are indeed significant in Calvin's mind. Yet the greatest shame Christ suffered was that he was portrayed as a criminal in his death. As Calvin notes, it was one thing to be crucified and quite another "to be crucified as if He had been the basest of men."[54] Not only was Christ's life exchanged for the life of a convicted murderer,[55] but he was also crucified between two criminals.

---

[52] *Commentary on Matthew* 27:35 (Pringle, 299); *CO* 45, 766.

[53] Ibid.

[54] Ibid., 27:18 (Pringle, 282); *CO* 45, 766.

[55] Calvin writes concerning the exchange between Jesus and Barabas in his *Commentary on Matthew* 27:15 (Pringle, 282); *CO* 45, 755: "God had appointed Him to be a sacrifice . . . to atone for the sins of the world, He permitted Him to be placed even below a robber and murderer. That the Son of God was reduced so low none can properly remember without deepest horror, and displeasure with themselves, and detestation of their own crimes. But hence also rises no ordinary ground of confidence; for Christ was sunk into the depths of ignominy, that He might obtain for us, by His humiliation, an ascent to the heavenly glory:

It was the finishing stroke of the lowest disgrace when Christ was executed between two robbers; for they assigned Him the most prominent place, as if He had been the prince of robbers. If He had been crucified apart from the other malefactors, there might have appeared to be a distinction between His case and theirs; but now He is not only confounded with them, but raised aloft, as if He had been by far the most detestable of all. . . . [F]or the prophet expressly says concerning Christ, that He will deliver His people, not by pomp and splendor, but because He will endure the punishment due to their sins. In order that He might free us from condemnation, this kind of expiation was necessary, that He might place Himself in our room.[56]

Christ's crucifixion between the two robbers identifies him as "the prince of robbers." Calvin regards the fact that Christ died in this manner to be the "finishing stroke of the lowest disgrace."[57] Yet Calvin sees that Christ's complete humiliation, his placement between two criminals, serves an important theological purpose. It graphically portrays the substitutionary aspect of Christ's atoning work. It stands as a visual reminder that it was for *their* sake Christ experienced this abasement. It was an impoverishment "due to *their* sins" because Christ "placed Himself in *our* room."[58] Such is the unexpected pattern of a king who miraculously delivers his people "not by pomp and splendor" but by a shameful death.

The substitutionary aspect of the atonement displayed in the events of Christ's crucifixion also has another function:

> The supreme and sole Judge of the world is placed at the bar of an earthly judge, is condemned to crucifixion as a malefactor, and, what is more, is placed between two robbers, as if He had been the prince of the robbers. A spectacle so revolting might, at first sight, greatly disturb the senses of men, were it not met by this argument, that the punishment which had been due us was laid

---

He was reckoned worse than a robber, that He might admit us to the society of angels of God."

[56] Ibid., 27:38 (Pringle, 302); *CO* 45, 768.

[57] Calvin makes reference to this point in his *Commentary on Isaiah* 53:12. Concerning the phrase "And was ranked with the transgressors. . . " he writes, "But the Prophet spoke in general terms, in order to show that Christ did not die an ordinary death. For the purpose of disgracing Him more, those two robbers were added; that Christ, as the most wicked of all of them might be placed in the midst of them." *Commentary on Isaiah* 53:12 (Pringle, 130); *CO* 37, 266.

[58] Emphasis mine. *Commentary on Matthew* 27:38 (Pringle, 302); *CO* 45, 768.

on Christ, so that, our guilt having now been removed, we do not hesitate to come into the presence of the Heavenly Judge.[59]

The offensive element of the cross is such that Calvin recognizes that it is great enough to prevent a sinner from embracing Christ. What transforms this picture of the "Judge of this world," condemned as a criminal and displayed as the "prince of the robbers" is that in that moment Christ was our substitute: "The punishment which had been due *us* was laid on Christ."[60] This truth rescues Calvin's faith in Christ. If it were not for this point, the death of Jesus Christ would be nothing but a massive scandal.

Calvin's description of the outrageous nature of Christ's humiliation continues in his discussion of the taunting crowd. Concerning the jeer in Matt 27:42, "If He is the King of Israel, let Him now come down from the cross, and we shall believe Him," Calvin writes:

> For they ought not to embrace as King any one who did not answer to the description given by the prophets. But Isaiah (52:14; 53:2) and Zechariah (8:7) expressly represent Christ as devoid of comeliness, afflicted, condemned, and accursed, half dead, poor, and despised before He ascends the royal throne. It is therefore foolish for the Jews to desire one of an opposite character, whom they may acknowledge as King; for by so doing, they declare that they have no good-will to the King that the Lord has promised to give. But let us on the contrary, that our faith may firmly rely on Christ, seek a foundation in his cross; for in no other way could He be acknowledged to be the lawful King of Israel than by fulfilling what belonged to the redeemed. . . . For the Jews, in consequence of having imagined to themselves a king who had been suggested to them by their own senses, rejected Christ crucified, because they reckoned it absurd to believe in Him; while we regard it as the best and highest reason for believing, that He voluntarily subjected Himself on our account to the ignominy of the cross.[61]

---

[59] Ibid., 27:24 (Pringle, 288); *CO* 45, 759.

[60] Emphasis mine. Ibid., 27:24 (Pringle, 288); *CO* 45, 759.

[61] *Commentary on Matthew* 27:42 (Pringle, 305–6); *CO* 45, 770–71. See also ibid., 16:20 (Pringle, 299–300); *CO* 45, 479: The Jewish leaders were not the only ones who expected the Messiah to appear in the splendor of earthly kings. Calvin writes: "And first of all, it was necessary to inform them that Christ must commence His reign, not with gaudy display not with magnificence of riches, not with the loud applause of the world, but with an ignominious death. But nothing was harder than to rise superior to such an offense; . . . for they imagined that He would procure for them earthly happiness. So far were they from having ever adverted to the ignominy of the cross, that they considered it to be utterly unsuitable that He should be placed in any circumstances from which He did not receive

The scandalous nature of Christ's cross is fundamental to the essence of Christ's kingship. Calvin demonstrates that the only way for Christ to truly be the King of Israel was fulfill the prophecies of the Redeemer. This is not an arbitrary point. The prophets predicted that the king would be "devoid of comeliness, afflicted, condemned, and accursed, half dead, poor, and despised *before* He ascends the royal throne."[62] The prophets saw that it was Christ's role as Redeemer—the affliction he endured on the cross for our account—that gave him legal claim to the throne of Israel. Yet ironically, this is what caused the Jews to reject him as King. The Jews desired a type of king "who had been suggested to them by their own senses" instead of someone who fit the unbecoming description of the prophets. According to the senses, Christ had no majesty, power, wealth, or pomp. He had none of the splendor and power of an earthly king. In short, the Jews rejected Christ as king because they wished to see with their eyes and not by faith. They thought it was absurd to believe in a king who was crucified.

While the scandal of Christ's abasement drove the Jews to reject Christ as their king, it gave Calvin and his readers "the best and highest reason for believing" in Christ's kingship. According to Calvin, this disgraceful impoverishment marks Christ as the Redeemer-King.[63] For Christ "voluntarily subjected Himself on *our* account to the ignominy of the cross."[64] Concerning this point, John Frederick Jansen writes:

> In any discussion of the reign of Christ, it is well to begin with Calvin's most recurrent theme, the regal conquest of Christ over the devil, death and sin. . . . The Cross is not only a sacrifice for sin. It is a royal victory. . . . While later Calvinism has tended to formulate the atonement primarily in sacrificial and penal terms, Calvin himself never separated it from the kingly office.[65]

---

honor." Even though Peter's confession stated that Christ was the promised king, Peter and the others could not conceive of a king undergoing the humiliation and suffering of which Christ spoke. Calvin recognizes that the disciples were caught in the same confusion as the Jews over the significance of what it meant for Jesus to be the Christ.

[62] Emphasis mine. Ibid., 27:42 (Pringle, 288); *CO* 45, 770.

[63] See Jansen, *Calvin's Doctrine*, 89. Stroup argues that Christ redefines the kingly office as it was known by Israel: "He [Jesus Christ] is not only one of Israel's anointed kings: He is the one who reigns until the end 'when He delivers the kingdom to God the Father after destroying every rule and every authority and power (1 Cor. 15:24).'" Stroup, "Relevance of the *Munus Triplex*," 29.

[64] Emphasis mine. *Commentary on Matthew* 27:42 (Pringle, 306); *CO* 45, 771.

[65] Jansen, *Calvin's Doctrine*, 88, 89.

Jansen correctly observed that Calvin does not separate the cross from his kingly office. Yet Jansen fails to explain the reasons for this shift, except to say that "since the cross effects the work of redemption, it must necessarily be a kingly work as well as a priestly work."[66] We may, however wish to add a point of insight from the present study that may enhance Jansen's reasoning. Calvin does not separate the cross and Christ's work of atonement from his kingly office because together Christ's poverty and his afflictions are the "visible symbol" of his kingship. Calvin sees that Christ's poverty and afflictions mark his kingship as divine, while at the same time they reveal him to be the Redeemer. This means that Christ's kingship, and by necessity his divinity, is most fully disclosed on the cross.

Calvin marvels that the true nature of Christ's kingship was revealed to the most unlikely man in the gospels. This was one of the two criminals between whom Christ was crucified. Calvin declares: "I know not that, since the creation of the world, there ever was a more remarkable and striking example of faith":[67]

> A robber, who not only had not been educated in the school of Christ, but, by giving himself up to execrable murders, as endeavored to extinguish all sense of what was right, suddenly rises higher than all the apostles and the other disciples whom the Lord Himself had taken so much pains to instruct; and not only so, but he adores Christ as a King while on the gallows, celebrates His kingdom in the midst of shocking and worse than revolting abasement, and declares Him, when dying, to be the Author of life.[68]

Calvin stands amazed at the incongruity of the situation. The greatest insight into Christ's true identity comes at the most unexpected time, in the midst of his utter abasement on the cross. The greatest profession of faith in Christ as "King" and "Author of life" comes from a most unlikely source, a convicted criminal. Calvin writes concerning this individual, "With a mangled body, and bleeding to death, he is looking for the last stroke of the executioner, and yet he relies on the grace of Christ alone."[69]

---

[66] Ibid., 89.

[67] *Commentary on Luke* 23:42 (Pringle, 311); *CO* 45, 774.

[68] Ibid. Jansen mentions this text in his section on "Christ our King," however he does not examine Calvin's understanding of how Christ's abasement as king is revelatory for the spiritual nature of His kingship. See Jansen, *Calvin's Doctrine*, 85–88.

[69] *Commentary on Luke* 23:42 (Pringle, 312); *CO* 45, 774. "Lacero corpore iam exsanguis extremam manum carnificum expectat, et tamen in sola Christi gratia acquiescit."

He wonders, "For what marks or ornaments of royalty did he see in Christ, so as to raise his mind to His kingdom?"[70] Calvin responds:

> And certainly, this was, as it were, from the depth of hell to rise above the heavens. To the flesh it must have appeared to be fabulous and absurd, to ascribe to one who was rejected and condemned, (whom the world could not endure), an earthly kingdom more exalted than all the empires of the world. Hence we infer how acute must have been the eyes of his mind, by which he beheld life in death, exaltation in ruin, glory in shame, victory in destruction, a kingdom in bondage.[71]

Calvin notes that the robber saw no "marks or ornaments of royalty" in Christ. He did not look on Christ with the eyes of the flesh. Instead, the robber looked on Christ with the eyes of faith. This is the only possible way for such a person to proclaim Christ as "the Author of life" in the midst of such horror. Only by faith can one behold life in the face of death, exaltation in the midst of ruin, glory in shame, victory in destruction, and a kingdom in bondage. Calvin reminds us that this criminal's insight places him in a special relationship to the rest of the Church:

> ... that if any man disdain to abide by the footsteps of the robber, and to follow in his path, he deserves everlasting destruction, because by wicked pride he shuts against himself the gate of heaven. ... If each of us shall truly seriously examine the subject, we shall find abundant reason to be ashamed of the prodigious mass of our crimes, so that we shall not be offended at having for our guide and leader a hopeless man, who obtained salvation by free grace.[72]

For Calvin, the story of the thief on the cross is scandalous because he obtained salvation "by free grace." This is the reason that Calvin declares

---

[70] Ibid. Stroup states that one of the most interesting conversations going on today between Reformed theologians and theologians from oppressed communities and from the third world is over diverse understandings of Christ's prophetic office. However, Stroup maintains that though the Reformed Church has much to learn from liberation theology about the nature of Jesus' prophetic office, "liberation theology can learn something from the Reformed claim that Jesus' prophetic office must not be separated from his equally important roles as priest and king." See Stroup, "Relevance of the *Munus Triplex*," 30. However, this author believes that it may be Christ's kingly office that has the most to say about how spirituality and the nature of poverty and affliction relate in the person of Christ.

[71] *Commentary on Luke* 23:42 (Pringle, 311); *CO* 45, 774. The last sentence reads: "Hinc colligimus quam perspicaces ei fuerint mentis oculi, quibus vitam in morte, celsitudinem in ruina, gloriam in probro, victoriam in exitio, regnum in servitute intuitus est."

[72] *Commentary on Luke* 23:43 (Pringle, 312–13); *CO* 45, 776.

this "hopeless man" to be the Church's "guide and leader." For an onlooker not to recognize him as such is a serious offense deserving everlasting destruction. What makes this man special in the eyes of Calvin? The thief perceived that the one hanging on the cross next to him was not a loathsome criminal, or even an earthly king who had lost his realm. Rather, this man looked upon Christ and his suffering with faith, perceiving Christ as the king of Israel because he was the Redeemer from sin. Calvin affirms that this man's "assurance of pardon" came because as Jesus died he beheld Christ as "a sacrifice of sweet savor, efficacious for expiating the sins of the world."[73]

According to Calvin, this is the example for the believer to follow. This criminal understood that Christ's kingship was divine and that his kingdom was spiritual. He understood that his suffering on the cross was an act of his redemption, an act that manifested his kingship. Unlike Herod and the other thief who mocked the Lord, this man saw the utter humiliation of Christ as a mark of his kingship. The Jewish leaders had stumbled over the offense of Jesus' death but as Calvin notes, this hopeless sinner saw the scandal of Christ's crucifixion as the way in which the kingdom would be brought forth. This thief saw what the prophets had foretold, that the suffering of Christ was something that identifies him as the Redeemer. Thus, Calvin commends this criminal: "From this teacher, therefore, whom the Lord has appointed over us to humble the pride of the flesh, . . . for the more eagerly any man follows him, so much the more nearly will he approach to Christ."[74] In this criminal, according to Calvin, God provided a human witness to Christ's spiritual kingship and redemption of the sins of the world at a time when few others were found.[75]

---

[73] Ibid., 23:42 (Pringle, 312); *CO* 45, 774–75.

[74] Ibid.; *CO* 45, 775.

[75] Commenting on the final verses of Matt 27, Calvin speaks of some of the other witnesses to Christ's spiritual kingship and glory in the midst of his abasement. Calvin relates: "Although in the death of Christ the weakness of the flesh concealed for a short time the glory of the Godhead, and though the Son of God Himself was disfigured by shame and contempt, and, as Paul says, was emptied, yet the heavenly Father did not cease to distinguish Him by some marks, and during His lowest humiliation prepared some indications of His future glory, in order to fortify the minds of the godly against the offense of the cross. Thus the majesty of Christ was attested by the obscuration of the sun, by the earthquake, by the splitting of the rocks, and the rending of the veil, as if heaven and earth were rendering the homage which they owed to their Creator." Ibid., 27:45 (Pringle, 316); *CO* 45, 777–78. Also, Calvin interprets that the eclipse, the earthquake and the rending of the veil were more than just coincidence. It was "as if heaven and earth were rendering the homage which they owed to their Creator." He calls these events "marks" or "indications of His majesty," because of the shame, contempt and humiliation in the death of Christ. Just

Thus far the reader has seen that Calvin understands Christ's physical poverty to be a "visible symbol" of his spiritual kingship. Christ's poverty acts as an instrument of revelation, a physical sign that reveals to the believer something regarding the nature of Christ's dominion. Calvin's exegesis of Christ's passion narratives does much to disclose this reality. His conclusion regarding the narratives essentially is that Christ's poverty in his suffering and death identify him as the Redeemer from sin. This means that for the person of faith, Christ's physical poverty is visible evidence that his righteousness and spiritual riches have been imputed to the believer. It means that Christ has placed himself in our room, has taken on our spiritual destitution, and has substituted himself as the sacrifice for our sin. Yet Calvin maintains that this truth is not apparent to everyone. Just as Christ's impoverishment has the power to make him known as the King and Redeemer, it also has the power to conceal this knowledge. Calvin teaches that only those with faith are able to recognize the grace and knowledge of God because they are not distracted by the wealth and luxury and do not despise the simple and impoverished Christ.

The Poverty of Isaiah's Suffering Servant

In the closing pages of his commentary on Isa 52, Calvin defines what the prophet means when "he calls Christ 'His Servant.'"[76] The designation, "His Servant," Calvin writes, needs to be understood "as holding the office to which the Father has appointed Him," meaning that he will be "a leader of the people and restorer of all things" and that he will be exalted for it.[77] Calvin explains that "Christ ought not to be regarded as a private individual" but as one "we ought to understand as belonging also to us."[78] In his analysis of chapter 53, he provides a framework by which the exegesis of Isa 53 and its theology of the "Servant" will be interpreted.

---

as God uses the word of the prophets to help remove the scandal of Christ's poverty and abasement, Calvin believes that God also sent these "marks" to help remove the offense of the cross and testify to Christ's glory and majesty. See Calvin's remarks in on Matt 27:35 (Pringle, 299); *CO* 45, 766; and on Matt 21:1 (Pringle, 447–48); *CO* 45, 572.

[76] *Commentary on Isaiah* 52:13 (Pringle, 106–7); *CO* 37, 252. Calvin's comments on Isaiah 53 are extensive. Therefore this section will review only a selection of those that are judged to have particular relevance to the issue of Christ's poverty. Due to the way in which the author of Isaiah writes, some of Calvin's remarks are repetitive in ideas and language. Therefore the texts selected for this section are not exhaustive of what pertains to Christ's abasement (and thus poverty) in Isaiah but are representative of it.

[77] Ibid., (Pringle, 107).

[78] Ibid.

He shows that the restoration can be accomplished only through a Servant who experiences great suffering. Concerning the phrase, "As many as were astonished by him," Calvin states:

> . . . the exalted state of Christ was not visible at first sight, and on this pretense it might be rejected. On this account, he [Isaiah] informs them that Christ must first be rejected and humbled, and anticipates that doubt which might have arisen from His debased and deformed condition.[79]

Calvin sees the dilemma which Christ's visible appearance presents for those who saw him as the prophet Isaiah described. Christ's glory and exalted state were not evident given "His debased and deformed condition."[80] The Prophet wisely anticipates the doubt that arises concerning a Messiah who is rejected, humbled, and abased. He explains the nature of this humiliation. The phrase, "So marred by men," Calvin writes, describes how "Christ was disfigured among men," that is, "that His form was defaced by the perverse judgment of men."[81] He asserts that this "perverse judgment" which Christ bore was directly related to the nature of the incarnation:

> He came into the world so as to be despised everywhere; His glory effaced under the humble form of the flesh. For though a majesty worthy of "the only begotten Son of God" shone forth in Him, yet the greater part of humanity did not see it, but on the contrary, they despised that deep abasement which was the veil or covering of His glory.[82]

---

[79] Ibid. Calvin employs a vocabulary used of the poor and disenfranchised: The words *abicio, humilis, abiectus,* and *deformis* all describe, in particular, in what way Christ was abased or impoverished.

[80] Ibid.

[81] *Commentary on Isaiah* 52:14 (Pringle, 107); CO 37, 252. Calvin makes this point in contrast to how other interpreters have understood it. According to Calvin, these others read the Hebrew *mem* to be a particle denoting comparison, making the phrase read that Christ's appearance was marred "beyond" that of other men. Instead, Calvin reads the particle according to its "simple" meaning thus translating the text to read "so marred 'by' men."

[82] Ibid. The Calvin Translation Society translation reads: "He came into the world so as to be everywhere despised; His glory lay hid under the humble form of the flesh. . . ." The term behind the words "lay hide" is *deleo* which means "to erase, efface, obliterate, blot out, abolish, annul, extinguish, and put an end to." Though the translation of the word as "laid hid" is accurate in regards to Calvin's explanation of how the two natures relate in his Christology and fits well with the imagery of the "veil" or "covering" mentioned in the following phrase, Calvin chooses to use a stronger Latin term. This author has chosen to

In his sufferings, Christ certainly did not look like the Messiah or resemble a king of Israel. He came to his people only to be despised and rejected by them, his humble flesh disguised his majesty and glory. Drawing on the imagery of Heb 10:20, Calvin refers to all that belonged to his flesh as a veil. Inasmuch as poverty and suffering belonged to Christ's flesh, these also contributed to the veil which hid his true nature. According to Calvin, this fleshly veil did not diminish or remove Christ's glory from him; it merely concealed it so that it was not visible to the human eye. The result was that "many were astonished at Him."[83]

Calvin equates the astonishment with Christ's appearance in Isaiah's prophecy with the historical response of the Jews. He describes Christ as one who "lived among men without any outward show."[84] He often juxtaposes the idea of "outward show" or "pomp" against aspects of Christ's poverty and simplicity. In this case, he writes that the Jews were particularly astonished because they "did not think that the Redeemer would come in that condition or attire." In other words, they were astonished that he came in lowliness without all of the customary trappings of royalty.[85] In his remarks on Isa 42:2, Calvin specifically states that the reason pomp and great display are missing from Christ's kingship is so that people would not form earthly conceptions of his identity and mission.[86] In Isa 53:2, Calvin elaborates this point while explaining how Christ's flesh can both reveal and conceal a knowledge of God. Regarding the passage, "Yet He shall grow up before Him as a twig," he writes:

---

translate *deleo* as "efface," meaning that the substance of Christ's glory is still there but it was unrecognizable or effaced in the way it was presented under His flesh. This is meant to be more in keeping with Calvin's conviction that Christ's glory (and thus His divine nature) was not extinguished by the incarnation, as well as keeping the force of his vocabulary. See *Commentary on Philippians* 2:7–11 (Pringle, 56–63); *CO* 52, 26–30.

[83] *Commentary on Isaiah* 52:14 (Pringle, 107); *CO* 37, 243.

[84] Ibid., (Pringle, 108); *CO* 37, 252.

[85] Ibid.

[86] Calvin writes "He [Isaiah] demonstrates what the nature of Christ's coming will be; certainly, without pomp [*sina pompa*], such as commonly attends earthly kings, at whose arrival there are uttered various noises and loud cries, as if heaven and earth were about to be mixed. But Isaiah says, that Christ will come without any noise or cry; and that not only for the sake of applauding His modesty, but, first that we may not form any earthly conception of Him; secondly, that having known His kindness by which He draws us to Him, we may cheerfully hasten to meet Him; and, lastly that our faith may not languish, though He be contemptible and humiliated [*quamvis contemptibilis sit eius humilitas*]." See *Commentary on Isaiah* 42:2 (Pringle, 287); *CO* 37, 60.

> This verse refers to what was formerly said, that Christ will at first have no splendor or outward show among men; but that before God He will nevertheless be highly exalted, and will be held in estimation. Hence we see that we must not judge the glory of Christ from a human perspective, but must discern by faith what is taught us concerning Him by the Holy Scriptures; and therefore the phrase "before Him," is here contrasted with human senses, which cannot comprehend that great lofty greatness.[87]

Christ's flesh will conceal his divine glory if we approach him according to "human senses" and judge him "from a human perspective." According to Calvin, the poverty of Christ is only revelatory for those who have faith. If we approach the poverty of Christ in the way that Scripture commends, we will comprehend such a knowledge of Christ's glory and exaltation as the witness of this earthly life affords. To all others, Christ's poverty conceals his identity and glory. Those who do not come to Christ with the eyes of faith only see a suffering and impoverished man. Therefore, the humble form of Christ's flesh, or "the veil" that covered his glory while he was on earth, has both a revealing and concealing function. The prevailing effect depends on the perspective of the individual person who considers Christ.

Calvin repeatedly marvels that Christ's abasement is a paradox both concealing and revealing a knowledge of Christ. The fact that Christ's manifestation was "astonishing" to the Jews was not only because he lacked the outward show or splendor of a king but also because Christ suffered and was abased. "When He came to be crucified, their [the Jews'] horror was greatly increased."[88] Calvin recognizes that Christ's abasement was a necessary element in his glorification. In fact, concerning the phrase "For he poured out His soul to death," Calvin concludes that "Christ's emptying was the beginning of this supreme dominion"[89] because it was the "victory which He obtained for us, . . . the fruit of His death."[90] Calvin continues:

> Therefore, He shows that this was done in order that He might take our sins upon Him; and His object is, that whenever the death of Christ shall be mentioned, we may at the same time remember the atonement made for us. And this fruit swallows up all

---

[87] Ibid., 53:2 (Pringle, 113); *CO* 37, 256.

[88] Ibid., 52:14 (Pringle, 108); *CO* 37, 252.

[89] Ibid., 53:12 (Pringle, 130); *CO* 37, 266. "Postea addit exinanitionem Christi fuisse huius summi imperii principium."

[90] Ibid.; *CO* 37, 267.

the shame of the death of Christ, that His majesty and glory may be more clearly seen than if we only beheld Him sitting in heaven; for we have in Him a striking and memorable proof of the love of God, when He is so insulted, degraded, and afflicted with the utmost disgrace, in order that we, on whom had been pronounced a sentence of everlasting destruction, may enjoy along with Him immortal glory.[91]

What ultimately enables the person of faith to perceive Christ's royal glory and majesty in the midst of his afflictions is an understanding of the atonement. Calvin's remark is stunning: All the shame and disgrace displayed in the death of Christ communicates more about the majesty and glory of God than what a person would learn if one "beheld Him sitting in heaven." Could Calvin mean that Christ's heavenly glory conceals a knowledge that may only be revealed in his crucified flesh? Could God's splendorous glory actually hide from our minds God's true nature? Calvin would answer that such knowledge is hidden because of our fallen condition. The Word of God incarnate is an accommodation to our spiritually impoverished state. Thus, seeing Christ spiritually with the eyes of faith in the midst of his affliction enables us to better perceive who Christ is than if we physically saw him on his heavenly throne. This would mean that if the poverty of Christ is perceived from the standpoint of the atonement, and his abasement is understood as being experienced for our sake, then the offensiveness of the cross disappears, and knowledge of Christ's glory and majesty replaces it.

To summarize, so far it has been established that Christ's flesh and his abasement veiled his divine glory. Calvin interprets this veil of the flesh and its role in the crucifixion as the reason for the Jews' disbelief. They viewed Christ from the standpoint of the human senses, not with eyes of faith. They had expected their Messiah to be a king adorned with outward splendor. Yet Christ came as a suffering servant, as one who would accomplish the work of atonement through great shame and disgrace. Calvin maintains that if a person views Christ from a divine perspective, not only will the astonishment and offensiveness of the cross disappear, but this person will also perceive the glory of Christ through the veil of his flesh.

There is a deeper significance to Calvin's comments on the affliction and disgrace Christ experienced in the atonement. By using the figure of "the veil," Calvin communicates something about the mystery of the

---

[91] Ibid., (Pringle, 130–31).

incarnation.[92] The veil is Calvin's way of describing Christ's humanity in relationship to his divinity.[93] More specifically, the veil is the humbled form of Christ's flesh, the poverty and afflictions that he bore in his body. The image of a veil conveys the idea that Christ's humbled and afflicted humanity conceals his heavenly majesty while not rendering it inoperative.[94] While the veil of Christ's flesh hides his glory, it still has the ability to reveal to certain people a knowledge of Christ's divinity. Its revelatory effect becomes apparent when the veil of Christ's humbled flesh falls most heavily which occurs in the event of Christ's work of atonement on the cross. It is precisely there that the veil of Christ's humanity simultaneously reveals and conceals his divinity. For the person of faith, Christ's sacrifice is the ultimate window into the nature of Christ's kingship, and ultimately, also into the character of his divinity. Yet when an unbeliever approaches the event with the eyes of the flesh, Christ's impoverished humanity becomes an impenetrable veil that completely obscures his divinity. Christ's poverty was indeed an attribute of the veil that never subtracted from his divinity or glory[95] but only served to disguise his glory for the purposes of redemption.

[92] See *Institutes* 2.12.2 (Battles, 476); *OS* 3, 438–39; and *Commentary on Philippians* 2:7 (Pringle, 57); *CO* 52, 26–27.

[93] See Willis, *Calvin's Catholic Christology*, 8–25, 61–100; for a detailed explanation of how Calvin construed Christ's humanity and divinity as well as the theological and historical implications of his position. See also Bromiley, "Reformers and the Humanity of Christ," 79–104; for a brief comparative perspective on how Calvin and other Reformers treat the humanity of Christ in particular.

[94] See *Commentary on Philippians* 2:7 (Pringle, 57); *CO* 52, 26: According to Calvin, Christ's abasement did not "empty" Christ of His divinity or of His glory but only "concealed" it under the weakness of His flesh. The "form" of the servant that Christ assumed could not have been exchanged with His previous "form" of the majesty of God. Instead, the "form" of the servant was joined to the Second Person of the Trinity and acted as a covering, as something placed over Christ's glory to conceal it from the "view of men." Therefore, this concealing of Christ's glory and divine nature did not in any way lessen it but rather only hid it for a time from human eyes. Willis writes of Calvin's understanding of Christ's "*kenosis*" in his comments on Phil 2:7: "This full humanity was enabled by the Eternal Son's emptying Himself in the sense of freely concealing Himself and withholding the exercise of His powers through the flesh to which He was fully joined. The '*kenosis*' was the concealment, not the abdication, of the Eternal Son's divine majesty. Calvin says that when Paul uses the term '*kenosis*' (*exinanitio*), he means Christ was brought to nothing (*in nihilum redigi*)." See Willis, *Calvin's Catholic Christology*, 80.

[95] He supports this in his *Institutes,* where he makes a remark about how the two natures of Christ were influenced by Christ's suffering: "Surely, when the Lord of glory was is said to be crucified, Paul does not mean that He suffered anything in His divinity, but he says this because the same Christ, who was cast down and despised, and suffered in the flesh,

Because Christ's humiliation and impoverishment is so central to Calvin's Christology, it is not surprising to see its theological implications extend beyond its revelatory and concealing functions described earlier. The significance of Christ's humiliation, in Calvin's theology, extends beyond the important point that this was the way in which Christ accomplished the work of redemption. It extends even beyond the person of Christ himself. Calvin writes of the phrase "he hath no form or comeliness," that it

> ... must be understood to relate not merely to the person of Christ, who was despised by the world, and was at length condemned to a disgraceful death; *but to His entire kingdom*, which in the eyes of men had no beauty, no comeliness, no magnificence, which, in short, had nothing that could direct or captivate the eyes of men to it by its outward appearance.[96]

For Calvin, Christ's poverty and afflictions expand the reaches of "His entire kingdom." This interpretation is a direct result of his understanding of the term "Servant." For Christ is not to be regarded as a "private individual" and if his office is one by which his Father has appointed him to be "the restorer of all things," then "whatever He affirms concerning Himself we ought to understand as belonging also to us."[97] Since the faithful are members of his kingdom, it makes complete sense for Calvin to extend the character of Christ's incarnation and kingship to his kingdom and those he rules. However, Calvin issues a warning to his audience. Just as one is not to judge "the glory of Christ by human views," in the same way, one is not to judge his kingdom "by human conceptions."[98]

This notion that Christ's poverty is also a mark of his kingdom is an idea that may be traced throughout Calvin's theology, and is particularly evident in his doctrine of the Christian life and the Church. Calvin always regards the believer as one who is "in Christ," that is, a member of Christ joined to his body, the Church.[99] This union of believers in Christ means that they participate in Christ's sufferings as well as in his glory. Though

---

was God and Lord of glory" (*Institutes*, 4.17.30 [Battles, 1402]; *OS* 5, 389). See also Niesel, *Theology of Calvin*, 115–18, for a concise explanation of the 'unity but not fusion of the two natures in Christ' in Calvin's Christology. For more on the topic of how Christ's divine nature was affected by Christ's suffering and abasement see Minnema, "Calvin's Interpretation of Human Suffering," 146–53.

[96] Emphasis mine. *Commentary on Isaiah* 53:2 (Pringle, 114); *CO* 37, 256.
[97] Ibid., 52:13 (Pringle, 107); *CO* 37, 252.
[98] Ibid., 53:2 (Pringle, 113); *CO* 37, 256.
[99] See Kennedy, *Union with Christ*.

the following chapter will examine how Calvin's Christological understanding of poverty and affliction affects his doctrine of the Christian life, let it suffice for the present to say that Calvin's exegesis of Isaiah 52 and 53 recognizes that the poverty and abasement of Christ leave a mark on the nature of his kingdom as a whole.

Conclusion

From cradle to crucifixion, Calvin believes Christ's poverty is evidence for his kingship and is the distinguishing mark of his kingdom. In Calvin's estimation, Christ's poverty and despised condition demonstrate that his kingship is not like that of earthly kings. It is not consumed with magnificent displays. It is not dependent upon political power or military force. The poverty of Christ was an elected aspect of his incarnation meant to serve a specific purpose, which was to reveal that Christ's kingship is divine and that the kingdom he rules is spiritual in nature.

Calvin's exegesis demonstrates this thesis in five ways. The first concerns Calvin's recognition that because of Christ, something unique happened to the status of the poor and afflicted, and also to the perception of poverty. Calvin claims that Jesus consecrated poverty in his own person. In other words, because God elected for Christ to be incarnate, not only into human flesh but into impoverished and afflicted human flesh, the poor are now endowed with a sacred status in the divine economy. God chooses to bestow honor on the poor, removing their contempt since theirs is the very way that God chose for Christ to come into the world. In short, God bestows a sacred status on poverty and the poor because it is the poverty and afflictions of God's Son that revealed his kingship to be divine and his kingdom as spiritual.

The second point concerns Calvin's observation that Christ's poverty is tangible proof of the gift of our salvation, physical evidence of his redeeming work, and an indication of the sacrifice God made to reclaim humanity. Christ emptied himself of the splendor of heaven and earth so that he could fill us with his spiritual riches. The poverty of Christ's abasement and Calvin's understanding of the atonement go hand in hand. The stripping of Christ's garments serves to illustrate that his righteousness was imputed to the believer. Christ's physical poverty displays our spiritual poverty. It testifies to the riches Christ relinquished and the destitution he assumed on our behalf. Nearly every time that Calvin mentions the humiliation and disgrace Christ suffered in his crucifixion, he reminds his readers that it was for *our* sake Christ experienced this abasement; it was an impoverishment due to *our* sins. According to the prophets, Christ's poverty and afflictions serve as a sign that Christ is king of Israel because he is their Redeemer. His suffering gave him legal right to claim the throne of Israel. The poverty and humiliation of Christ are not only what distinguishes Christ's rule, but they also serve to mark him as "the person of the Redeemer."

Third, Calvin recognizes that the scandal of Christ's poverty can be a stumbling block for faith. Every detail concerning Christ's birth, life, and death was unexpected. Kings should be born in palaces, not in stables. They should ride on horses, not on borrowed asses. Most importantly, kings are not crucified. Calvin observes that the scandal of this abasement produces two kinds of responses from people: some are offended by Christ's destitution, and some are not. Calvin instructs that if we approach Christ's poverty from the standpoint of the humility of Christian faith, as directed by Scripture, we will comprehend a knowledge of Christ's glory and exaltation. When we approach Christ in faith, the atonement dissolves the offensiveness of Christ's sufferings to reveal his glory through his work as the Redeemer. Yet this was not the case with the Jews. Calvin points out that they desired a king such their own fleshly wisdom would have suggested rather than of the prophets' descriptions. They rejected Christ because he had none of the splendor and power of an earthly king. Because they approached Christ according to human senses, and judged him from a human perspective, the poverty of Christ to them had a concealing effect on the nature of his divine kingship. The result was that the Jews found it impossible to believe in a king who was crucified.

Fourth, the afflictions of Christ communicate something about the mystery of the incarnation. Calvin uses the metaphor of the veil to refer to the form of Christ's humbled flesh, which acted to conceal his glory and divinity to the human eye. He maintains that while this veil covered Christ's glory, it did not render it inoperative. Instead, it acted as a vehicle of revelation through which the viewer might look to see something of the configuration of Christ's divinity. It clarified how Christ's humanity participates in the accomplishment of God's plan of salvation, that is, how Christ's humanity functions in the work of redemption. For Calvin, Christ's condition of poverty, although distinguished from his divine essence, can never be separated from the person and work of the One Mediator.

Fifth, Calvin perceives that the poverty of Christ has an important effect outside of Christology. The poverty of Christ has significant implications not only for Calvin's understanding of the incarnation and the atonement, but also for Christ's entire kingdom. What was manifested in the character of Christ's incarnation and work of redemption is now extended over those whom he rules. Calvin recognizes that Christ's poverty leaves its mark on the nature of the Christian life, as it does on the Church. The following chapters will examine these connections and propose that Calvin's Christological convictions underlie his understanding of spiritual and physical poverty in the Christian life and the Church.

8

Poverty in Calvin's Doctrine of the Christian Life

CALVIN believed that Christ's poverty marks Him as the Redeemer-King and Deliverer from sin who demonstrates His reign with an ignominious death. The cross reveals that Christ's poverty and affliction not only reveal the divine nature of Christ's kingship but also the spiritual nature of His kingdom. Jansen explains:

> Certainly the cross is a sacrifice, but it is more. We may add that its character as a royal conquest over sin has important implications for Christian life, for it points us beyond unresolved tension and dialectical conflict towards a positive and victorious life. . . .We are not only forgiven; we are to share in the conquest of sin.[1]

Christ's "royal conquest over sin" has important implications for the Christian life. The focus of this chapter is Calvin's understanding of the role of spiritual and physical poverty in the Christian life in the light of Christ's "royal conquest over sin" as the Redeemer-King. When Calvin discusses the cross and the Christian life, the language of poverty and affliction is often close at hand. In fact, Calvin's doctrine of the Christian life is most noticeably influenced by Christ's poverty and affliction in his exhortation for the believer to bear the cross. To bear the cross, according to Calvin, is to imitate Christ. This chapter will show that cross-bearing, in Calvin's thought, is a theological category that allows poverty and affliction to benefit a believer's spirituality. Calvin believed Christ's poverty and suffering represented by His cross bearing assumes a sacramental dimension when it is applied to the Christian life. This means that the experi-

---

[1] Jansen, *Calvin's Doctrine*, 90.

ence of poverty in the Christian life has potential as a vehicle of divine grace and blessing for the believer. Calvin holds that hardships in this life present opportunities for believers to gain knowledge of God's glory. This idea is alluded to in Calvin's comments examined in chapter 7. In his *Commentary on 2 Corinthians* 8:9, Calvin teaches the following about Christ's poverty:

> The foxes have holes, and the birds of the air have nests: the Son of Man does not have a place to lay His head. Hence He has consecrated poverty in His own person [*Ergo paupertatem in se ipso consecravit*], that believers may no longer regard His poverty with horror.[2]

This chapter will examine what it means that Christ "has consecrated poverty in His own person" for Calvin's doctrine of the Christian life. It will demonstrate that the experience of poverty and affliction occupies a significant place in Calvin's understanding of the Christian life because of the way it relates to humility and the law and fosters the conditions necessary for growth in faith.

One of the best texts on the role of poverty in the Christian life is found in Calvin's exegesis of the beatitude found in Matt 5:3 and Luke 6:20. Considering the lack of passages that directly address the issue of the role of poverty in the Christian life, that is, how physical poverty and poverty of spirit are related in light of cross-bearing, this text is crucial for grasping Calvin's understanding of the matter.

The Relationship Between Physical and Spiritual Poverty: Matthew 5:3/Luke 6:20

In Matt 5:3, Jesus states, "Blessed are the poor in spirit, for theirs is the kingdom of heaven."[3] Its parallel, Luke 6:20, states, "And he [Jesus] lifted up his eyes on his disciples, and said: 'Blessed are you poor, for yours is the kingdom of God.'"[4] Throughout the history of the Church, these two verses have been recognized as significant texts that speak to the role of poverty in the Christian life. Historically speaking, these texts were used to support the poverty ideal of the Middle Ages. In particular, they were used for the veneration of the involuntarily poor and inspired the practice of voluntary poverty. They are, therefore, important texts in determining

---

[2] *Commentary on 2 Corinthians* 8:9 (Pringle, 291); *CO* 50, 98–99.
[3] Matt 5:3 (*RSV*).
[4] Luke 6:20 (*RSV*).

the direction of Calvin's theology concerning the place of poverty in the Christian life.

Calvin approaches Matt 5:3/Luke 6:20 with the classic discipline of his commentary style. After reviewing some of the historical detail of the text, he delineates the "object" of Christ's address in this Beatitude. He draws attention to the fact that among the general public as well as among the philosophers, there existed a common belief about the nature of happiness. This belief claimed "that the happy man is he who is free from annoyance, attains all he wishes, and leads a joyful and easy life." Christ's address sought to correct this illusion. He said that people who are truly happy do not always "lead an easy and prosperous life." Instead, Christ desired for His disciples to learn to bear the cross. This is a significant insight. For if the disciples were to assume that the life of blessedness is something contrary to suffering, then they would bypass the way of the cross. However, if the disciples would place "their happiness beyond this world, and above the affections of the flesh," then they would have happiness "in the very midst of [their] miseries."[5]

Calvin's discussion of the nature of true happiness, and what it means to be a disciple, in addition to the necessity of bearing the cross sets the context for his exposition of the phrase "Blessed are the poor."[6] He opens this discussion with several observations, some of which concern textual differences between Matt 5:3 and Luke 6:20. First, Calvin notices that the Lukan text is "simple" in that "the poverty of many is accursed and unhappy." Therefore, he contends that Matthew expresses Christ's intention "more clearly." Calvin makes a distinction: "Many are pressed down by distresses, and yet continue to swell inwardly with pride and cruelty." Stated another way, many can be caught in the clutches of poverty and yet are not subdued and humbled by their woes. This contrast brings Calvin to conclude that Matthew has a fuller understanding of Christ's meaning. Christ pronounces a blessing upon those who "submit themselves wholly to God and with inward humility to commend themselves to him for protection."[7]

---

[5] *Commentary on Matthew* 5:2 (Pringle, 260); *CO* 45, 161.

[6] Calvin's Latin translation of Matt 5:3 from the Greek reads: "Beati pauperes spiritu: quoniam illorum est regnum coelorum" (*CO* 45, 159). [Blessed are the poor in spirit, for theirs is the kingdom of heaven.] Calvin's Latin translation of Luke 6:20 reads: "Beati pauperes: quia vestrum est regnum Dei" (*CO* 45, 160). [Blessed are the poor, for yours is the kingdom of God.]

[7] *Commentary on Matthew* 5:3 (Pringle, 260); *CO* 45, 161.

Next, Calvin responds to the interpretations of "others" who "explain poor in spirit to be those who claim nothing for themselves, and are even so completely emptied of the confidence in the flesh, that they acknowledge their poverty." Such a reading of the text not only is incomplete but also spiritualizes the intensity of the adjective "poor." Furthermore, it also does not take seriously the affects of adversity upon the human spirit. Calvin does not succumb to this temptation. He does not interpret the term "poor" in a strictly spiritual sense as Matthew's version can be construed, and he does not spiritualize the meaning of Luke's version, which lacks the qualifier "in spirit." Instead, Calvin chooses an alternative route. He argues that the words of Luke and Matthew "must have the same meaning." He retains the existential force of the word "poor" in Luke's text, asserting that there can be no doubt that poor describes "those who are pressed and afflicted by adversity." The only reason why Matthew adds the qualifier "in spirit," he states, is to clarify that Christ's blessedness is restricted "only to those who under the discipline of the cross, have learned to be humble."[8]

Calvin's interpretation that both evangelists see Christ as addressing the physically poor with this utterance is noteworthy. Calvin's acknowledgment that physical poverty has the potential to generate beneficial spiritual consequences is also significant. He dispels any ambiguity concerning this idea in his exegesis of the following phrase: "For theirs is the kingdom of heaven." Christ does not tell those undergoing hardship that they should be "harden[ed] . . . by unfeeling obstinacy" as the Stoics teach.[9] He does not require the afflicted to find any resources within themselves to face their trials. Christ's method is different. He holds out the "hope of eternal life" that "animates them to patience . . . [so] that in this way they will pass into the heavenly Kingdom of God."[10] In conclusion, Calvin adds:

> It deserves our attention, that only he who is reduced to nothing in himself, and relies on the mercy of God, is poor in spirit, for they who are broken by despair murmur against God, and this proves them to be of a proud and haughty spirit.[11]

---

[8] Ibid., 5:3 (Pringle, 261); *CO* 45, 161–62.

[9] Greek Stoicism taught that suffering is inconsistent with the principle of human perfection. Instead, human perfection lies in a rational state that was unaffected or indifferent to suffering. Calvin rejects this position. See Minnema, "Calvin's Interpretation," 156; see also Kraye, "Moral Philosophy," 364–70.

[10] *Commentary on Matthew* 5:3 (Pringle, 261); *CO* 45, 162.

[11] Ibid.

Poverty in Calvin's Doctrine of the Christian Life   193

This statement cannot be interpreted apart from what Calvin has already said about the meaning of the words "poor in spirit." He does not revert to spiritualizing the text just after making a concerted effort to avoid this error. Instead, he guards against the opposite danger—to maintain that the mere fact that one is poor and crushed by circumstances entitles him or her to receive the blessings of the Kingdom of Heaven. Nothing could be further from Calvin's reading of the text. The kingdom belongs to those who are poor in spirit. It belongs to those who have been "broken by [the] despair" of their poverty and hopeless circumstances *and* to those who also "rest upon the loving kindness of God."[12]

André Biéler reflects on Calvin's analysis of poverty in Christ's Sermon on the Mount: "he [Calvin] teaches us that destitution and poverty can be received in faith as a grace."[13] Does this mean that Calvin believes that the experience of poverty and affliction have a sacramental dimension for the believer? On this question it is important to remember Calvin's theology of the sacraments. He teaches that the elements themselves *do not* contain the grace of God within them. Bread, wine, and water are all common elements. Only through the promise and power of the Holy Spirit can these simple elements offer to us the grace of God. Thus, the bread and wine of the Lord's Supper and the waters of baptism have sacramental value only because they are instruments through which the Spirit of God has chosen for the administration of God's grace.[14] When Biéler states that "poverty can be received in faith as a grace,"[15] he does not mean that Calvin believes that poverty in and of itself is good or intrinsically contains God's grace. Instead, he claims that in Calvin's thought, poverty and affliction strip away all human securities and false assurances, drawing a person to rest upon divine promises alone,[16] thereby allowing the Holy Spirit to work in their lives.

Calvin's comments on the parallel texts of Matt 5:3 and Luke 6:20 are unusual passages in Calvin's writings in which he links physical and spiritual poverty together with the notion of bearing the cross. His exegetical integrity handling these texts is impressive. Unlike Augustine and Luther, Calvin does not dismiss the physical component of poverty by spiritual-

---

[12] See also Calvin's *Sermon on Matthew* 5:1–4 and *Luke* 6:20–21, especially *CO* 46, 773–74.

[13] My translation. Biéler, *Pensée Économique*, 311. "il nous apprend que le dénuement et la pauvreté peuvent être reçus dans la foi comme une grâce."

[14] See Calvin's *Commentary on Matthew* 4:4 (Pringle, 215); *CO* 45, 132.

[15] Biéler, *Pensée Économique*, 311.

[16] Ibid.

izing the term "poor."[17] He recognizes how physical hardship and affliction can influence the Christian life bringing a person to depend upon the mercy of God seen at the cross. Furthermore, what Calvin does not say here is almost as important as what he does say. He does not discuss whether this text supports the practice of voluntary or religious poverty. It is as though the centuries of religious poverty and the use of Matt 5:3 to legitimize its practice never entered his mind, and if it did, it is as though these arguments were not worth refuting.[18] Instead, Calvin chooses to refute the "empty arguments of the Stoics" and, most importantly for his readers, decides to focus his efforts on explaining what he believes the Evangelists say about being poor in spirit.

The Imitation of Christ: Self-Denial and Bearing the Cross

In Calvin's theology, the consequence of Christ's poverty and suffering reach far beyond Christ's earthly ministry. Calvin understood that the Christian's experience of sanctification is patterned after Christ's life of

---

[17] It is interesting to note that Calvin's exegetical approach to this text is quite different from that of his favorite theologian, Augustine. In Augustine's *Commentary on the Lord's Sermon on the Mount*, he understands Christ's words "Blessed are the poor," in Matt 5:3 and Luke 6:20 to mean "Blessed are the poor in spirit." Nowhere in his comments does he refer to the relationship between physical poverty and suffering and poverty of spirit. Instead he spiritualizes the verse and limits 'poor' to mean humble and God-fearing, the opposite of arrogant and proud. See Augustine, "Commentary on the Lord's Sermon on the Mount" (21–22), "Sermon 53: On the Beatitudes" (211–12), and "Sermon 11: On the Beatitudes" (358–59) in *Commentary on the Lord's Sermon on the Mount*. Likewise, Calvin's approach to this text differs from Luther. Like Augustine, Luther maintains the distinction between the earthly realm and the spiritual realm in this matter. Luther understands Christ's blessing upon the poor to mean those who are spiritually poor and not those who are spiritually and physically poor. Commenting on Matt 5:3, Luther writes: "So be poor or rich physically and externally, as it is granted to you—God does not ask about this—and know that before God, in his heart, everyone must be spiritually poor." See *LW* 21, 13; *WA* 32, 307.

[18] One comment Calvin makes on verse 2 indicates how far the sixteenth century values had traveled from the original poverty ideal: "We know that not only the great body of people, but even the learned themselves, hold this error, that he is the happy man who is free from annoyance, attains all his wishes, and leads a joyful and easy life" (*Commentary on Matthew* 5:2 [Pringle, 259]; *CO* 45, 161). Materialism has been a problem for the Church throughout its history. Yet with the growth of urban centers and the rise of the new money economy in the twelfth century, the danger of avarice reasserted itself. This may be why Calvin does not spend time on voluntary poverty. The issue his readers face is not a defection into a monastery, but being seduced by the culture's materialism to believe that true happiness lies in the acquisition of things and an easy life.

poverty. Christ's life is a guide for how the Christian life is to be lived.[19] Only within the context of Christ's poverty and suffering are the hardships experienced by believers given meaning. Calvin uses two categories to frame his understanding of the Christian life, namely, the notions of self-denial and bearing the cross. Calvin entitled book 3 chapter 7 of the *Institutes*, "The Sum of the Christian Life: The Denial of Self."[20] The subsequent chapter is entitled "Bearing the Cross, A Part of Self-Denial."[21] Given the order in which these passages occur, Calvin appears to consider self-denial as fundamental to his doctrine of the Christian life. Bearing the cross defines what it means to deny self. Because of the centrality of these ideas in Calvin's thinking, it is essential to identify first, what Calvin meant by these terms, and second, how poverty and suffering relate to them.

Calvin's analysis of Peter's confession in Matt 16:24 provides direction for the Christian's cross-bearing and self-denial.[22] Calvin wrote that Christ presents Himself "as an example of self-denial and patience."[23] It was necessary for Christ to undergo what Peter thought to be inappropriate treatment of the Messiah in order to invite the rest of His followers to imitate Him.[24] Calvin writes:

> The words must be explained in this manner: If any man would be my disciple, let him follow me by denying himself and taking up his cross, or, let him conform himself to my example. The meaning is that none can be reckoned to be the disciples of Christ unless they are true imitators of Him, and are willing to pursue the same course. He lays down a brief rule for our imitation, in order to make us acquainted with the chief points in which He wishes us to resemble Him. It consists of two parts, self-denial and a voluntary bearing of the cross.[25]

To imitate Christ, or be conformed to His example, means two things for Calvin: self-denial and voluntarily bearing the cross. Both of these acts are essential to discipleship. Though they are both found in the example and

---

[19] See *Institutes* 3.6.3 (Battles, 686); *OS* 4, 148; and *Commentary on Philippians* 2:9 (Pringle, 58–59); *CO* 52, 27.

[20] *Institutes* 3.7.1 (Battles, 689); *OS* 4, 151.

[21] Ibid., 3.8.1 (Battles, 702); *OS* 4, 161.

[22] Matt 16:24 reads: "Jesus told His disciples, 'If any man would come after me, let him deny himself and take up his cross and follow me'" (*RSV*).

[23] *Commentary on Matthew* 16:24 (Pringle, 303); *CO* 45, 481.

[24] Ibid.

[25] Ibid.

person of Christ, self-denial and bearing the cross have different emphases for the Christian life.

Calvin underscores the distinctions between self-denial and bearing the cross in his comments on Phil 3:10.[26] He maintains that when a believer becomes a partaker of Christ's benefits, he or she must "acknowledge that a condition is presented to him—that his whole life be conformed to his death."[27] Calvin continues:

> There is, however, a twofold participation and fellowship in the death of Christ. The one is inward—what the Scripture terms the "mortification of the flesh," or the "crucifixion of the old man," of which Paul treats in the sixth chapter of Romans; the other is outward—what is termed the "mortification of the outward man." It is the endurance of the cross, of which he treats in the eighth chapter of the same Epistle, and here also, if I do not mistake.[28]

Calvin understands two kinds of mortification. The first, or "inward . . . mortification of the flesh," is used in Rom 6 and refers to a person's old sin nature that must be crucified with Christ.[29] This mortification targets the inner life of the believer in his or her sinful desires and passions. The kind of mortification that may only be achieved through the power of the Holy

---

[26] *CO* 52, 24; Phil 4:10 reads ". . . that I may know Him and the power of his resurrection, and may share his sufferings, becoming like him in his death . . ." (Pringle, 93); *CO* 52, 24.

[27] *Commentary on Philippians* 3:10 (Pringle, 99); *CO* 52, 50.

[28] Ibid.

[29] See *Commentary on Romans* 6:7 for a summary of this point (Pringle, 226); *CO* 49, 108. *Institutes* 2.16.7 of the *Institutes*, Calvin explains that the "mortification of our flesh" is when Christ's "death mortifies our earthly members so that they may no longer perform their functions; and it kills the old man in us that he may not flourish and bear fruit" ([Battles, 512]; *OS 3*, 491–92). In his comments on John 3:6, Calvin gives a more detailed description of what he means when he refers to the term "flesh": "By the 'flesh [*caro*],' therefore, in this place means not only the body [*non corpus*], but also the soul [*animam*], and consequently every part of it. . . . But if flesh [*caro*] is contrasted with the Spirit,' as a corrupt thing is contrasted with what is uncorrupted, a crooked thing with what is straight, a polluted thing with what is holy, a contaminated thing with what is pure, we may readily conclude that the whole nature of man is condemned [*damnari*] by a single word" ([Pringle, 112]; *CO* 47, 56). Calvin's comments throughout Romans 6 focus on the question of the old sin nature in humanity known as the "flesh." Concerning Paul's phrase in verse 6 "that our old man is crucified with Him," he states "what he [Paul] means is that the whole nature which we bring from the womb, and which is so incapable of the kingdom of God, that it must die so far as we are renewed to real life." Calvin continues: " 'The body of sin,' which he afterwards mentions, does not mean flesh and bones, but the corrupted mass; for man, left to his own nature, is a mass made up of sin" ([Pringle, 224]; *CO* 49, 107–8).

Spirit[30] involves a daily struggle of following Christ, otherwise known as the process of sanctification. This kind of inner mortification of the flesh is equal to what Calvin calls self-denial.[31] The language of self-denial stresses the positive aspects of what a person's life will look like if his or her "old man" is truly crucified with Christ and if, inwardly speaking, the flesh is really mortified.

The second kind of mortification, "mortification of the outward man," is often called the "endurance of the cross." Calvin understands the endurance of the cross to involve the suffering of external afflictions, persecutions, or hardships that may come to a believer as he or she follows and becomes conformed to Christ.[32] These afflictions have a special role in the Christian life. For now it is important to note that Calvin finds a connection between the endurance of the cross and the mortification of the outward man. For the moment, the topic of cross-bearing will be left aside in order to discuss Calvin's understanding of self-denial.

Self-Denial

In his reflections on Matt 16:24, Calvin describes what it means to deny one's self:

> This self denial is very extensive, and implies that we ought to give up our natural inclinations, and part with all the affections of the flesh, and thus give our consent to be reduced to nothing, provided that God lives and reigns in us.[33]

When Calvin says that "self denial is *very extensive*," he means that the concept is both fundamental to the Christian life and encompassing of the kind of relationship a believer is called to have towards God and neighbor.[34] Believers can only relate to God properly if they are willing to for-

---

[30] Calvin writes: "For how much we may be harassed by the sting of sin, it cannot yet overcome us, for we are enabled to conquer it by the Spirit of God . . . " (*Commentary on Romans* 6:14 [Pringle, 224]; *CO* 49, 113).

[31] See Wallace, *Calvin's Doctrine*, 52–53; Minnema, "Calvin's Interpretation," 154–55; and Leith, *John Calvin's Doctrine*, 76.

[32] Wallace states, "Self-denial is the inward or direct aspect of this twofold conformity and participation, bearing one's cross is the outward or indirect aspect." See *Calvin's Doctrine*, 52. Also in Calvin's *Commentary on Romans* 8:28–30. He links the ideas of election, bearing the cross, and affliction in the believer's life (Pringle, 314–20); *CO* 49, 158–59).

[33] *Commentary on Matthew* 16:24 (Pringle, 303–4); *CO* 45, 481.

[34] Emphasis mine. See *Institutes* 3.7.4 (Battles, 693); *OS* 4, 154. "Now in these words we perceive that denial of self has regard partly to men, partly, and chiefly, to God."

sake the values and affections of the flesh. Dedication to God is the basis of this teaching. If something is considered sacred, it cannot be used profanely without doing harm to oneself or to one's relationship to God.[35] For Calvin, self-denial is an attitude of the heart and an affection of the soul. Self-denial is an ever-present understanding that one belongs to his or her God, not to oneself. It is demonstrated in the daily choices believers make informed by knowledge of what God wants them to do and say. If men and women of faith cannot follow this leading, they are living according to their own "carnal sense" and not according to God's Spirit and cannot be said to be following Christ.[36]

In Luke 14:33, Christ warns His disciples about counting the cost. Calvin considered the meaning of this verse with regard to self-denial.[37] He recognized that the verse speaks to renouncing everything in order to follow Christ:

> It would be absurd to insist on a literal interpretation of the phrase, as if no man were a disciple of Christ, till he threw into the sea all that he possessed, divorced his wife, and bade farewell to his children. Such idle dreams led people to adopt a monastic life, as if those who intend to come to Christ must leave off humanity. Yet no man truly forsakes all that he possesses till he is prepared at every instant to leave all, gives himself free and unconstrained to the Lord, and rising above every hindrance, pursues his calling. Thus, the true self-denial which the Lord demands from His followers does not consist so much in outward conduct as in the affections; so that every one must employ the time which is passing over him without allowing the objects which he directs by his hand to hold a place in his heart.[38]

According to Calvin, true self-denial pertains to an individual's affections and not to his or her material wealth. When Christ said, "Whoever of you

---

[35] Calvin describes this in a memorable way in the *Institutes*: "If we are not our own but the Lord's, it is clear what error we must flee, and to where we must direct all the acts of our life. We are not our own: let not our reason nor our will, therefore sway our plans and deeds. We are not our own: in so far as we can, let us therefore forget our selves and all that is ours. Conversely, we are God's: let us therefore live for Him and die for Him. We are God's: let His wisdom and will rule all our actions. We are God's: let all the parts of our life accordingly strive toward Him as our only lawful goal." (*Institutes* 3.7.1 [Battles, 690]; *OS* 4, 151).

[36] *Institutes* 3.7.1 (Battles, 690); *OS* 4, 151.

[37] Luke 14:33; "So therefore, whoever of you does not renounce all that he has cannot be my disciple" (*RSV*).

[38] *Commentary on Luke* 14:33 (Pringle, 475); *CO* 45, 296.

does not renounce all that he has cannot be my disciple," Calvin contends that He refers to a believer forsaking the affections and desires for things, not the physical possessions themselves. He argues that if Christ's words were meant to be taken literally, they would lead believers to behave foolishly as like many of the monks: divorcing wives, abandoning children, and divesting themselves of every possession. Instead, true self-denial takes hold of a believer's values and desires. Only then do the objects in his hand not hold a place in his heart; only then is there no need to dispose of one's earthly goods.

There is a logical connection between Calvin's description of self-denial and the mortification of the flesh to which Calvin refers in Phil 3:9. If self-denial is practiced, then "mortification of the flesh" will follow in a believer's life. Self-denial is the attitude; "mortification of the flesh" is the outcome. The former pertains to imitating Christ's life, and the latter pertains to participation in Christ's death. Both are concerned with the inward life of the believer. Both affect a believer's response to his or her external world.[39]

Bearing the Cross

The second part to the imitation of Christ is "taking up the cross." Calvin discusses this concept in his comments on Matt 16:24:

> He lays down this injunction, because, though there are miseries common to all which the life of men is indiscriminately subjected, yet as God trains His people in a peculiar manner, in order that they may be conformed to the image of His Son, we need not wonder that this rule is strictly addressed to them. It may be added that though God lays the burden of the cross on both good and bad men, unless they willingly bend their shoulders to it, they are not said to bear the cross; for a wild and refractory horse cannot be said to admit his rider, even though he carries him. The patience of the saints, therefore, consists in willingly bearing the cross which has been laid on them.[40]

Calvin describes the relationship between "the cross," "ubiquitous miseries," and situations to which people are "indiscriminately subjected." Yet he qualifies this relationship concerning the Christian. Suffering and

---

[39] See Wallace, *Calvin's Doctrine*, 51–67, for a more extensive essay on Calvin's understanding of self-denial in the Christian life. See also Leith, *John Calvin's Doctrine*, 74–82.

[40] *Commentary on Matthew* 16:24 (Pringle, 304); *CO* 45, 481–82; and see also *Commentary on 2 Corinthians* 1:5 (Pringle, 112); *CO* 50, 11.

hardships are experienced by the godly and the ungodly alike. In Calvin's reasoning, though suffering is "the burden of the cross" which God lays upon all people, only the believer can be said to carry this cross willingly. He restricts true cross-bearing to believers because only they will become "conformed to the image of the Son" through their suffering. Believers must endure their suffering with patience. Unbelievers, however, cannot be said to "bear the cross" even though God has laid upon them the "burden of the cross." Calvin uses the illustration of a wild horse. He may be saddled in order to be ridden, though he may not "admit his rider even though he carries him."[41] So it is with unbelievers. They may have the cross laid upon them, but like a wild horse, they seek to throw it off rather than be trained by it.

These ideas also appear in Calvin's analysis of Matt 10:38. He shows that the willingness of some to bear the cross and "endure many afflictions" is directly related to becoming considered a disciple of Christ.[42] As with his interpretation of Matt 16:24, he contends that unbelievers, just like unbelievers, are "firmly bound to their cross, and cannot with their most violent struggles shake it off."[43] To unbelievers, "the cross is accursed." They have no hope, and "a mournful end awaits them."[44] The difference between believers and unbelievers according to Calvin is that the former have this consolation: "In bearing the cross we are companions of Christ—which will speedily have the effect of allaying all its bitterness."[45] Calvin instructs:

> Let us therefore learn to connect these things, that believers must bear the cross in order to follow their Master; that is, in order to conform to His example, and to abide by His footsteps like faithful companions.[46]

The burden of the cross is not optional for anyone. Poverty, suffering, and hardships happen to everyone. Yet believers have a special advantage over unbelievers. Believers can understand the larger significance of their miseries. Theodore Minnema writes:

---

[41] See also Wallace, *Calvin's Doctrine*, 73.

[42] *Commentary on Matthew* 10:38 (Pringle, 472); *CO* 45, 294. Wallace writes, "To be one of the elect of God means to be appointed to slaughter." See *Calvin's Doctrine*, 68–69; and Leith, *John Calvin's Doctrine*, 74–82.

[43] *Commentary on Matthew* 10:38 (Pringle, 472); *CO* 45, 294.

[44] Ibid.

[45] Ibid.

[46] Ibid.

The suffering of the believer is always in Christ. Only in that relation and on its basis can the believer's suffering be faced and interpreted.... The pattern of suffering in the life of Christ issues in His death on the cross. The cross is a summation of the pattern of suffering in Christ. To this pattern of suffering the Christian must conform his life. Living in Christ means bearing the cross.[47]

Just as Christ's suffering was never meant to be an end in itself, so it is with the trials of believers. They take comfort in knowing that because of the adversity that Christ experienced, their afflictions are able "to make them conform to His example, and to abide by His footsteps like faithful companions." Furthermore, they have the benefit of knowing that they partake in Christ's own sufferings. Wallace explains:

> In the process of being conformed to Christ by bearing their cross, the faithful are thereby brought into a special relation to Christ and His death. Calvin can speak in such a way of this communion with Christ and His death which is given through the Cross as to imply that the suffering of the Cross for the Christian has the value of a sacrament.[48]

Wallace does not say that believers' poverty, suffering, and afflictions *are* sacraments in the same way that baptism and the Lord's Supper are sacraments. Rather he says that the suffering of believers provides them with a kind of special communion with Christ and His afflictions, and therefore has "the *value* of a sacrament."[49] In other words, Calvin maintains that poverty and afflictions are means which God uses to conform the believer to Christ. They are vehicles chosen by God to impart divine grace and provide the fellow sufferer with a communion with Christ.

The communion that a believer shares with Christ by virtue bearing the cross, in Calvin's thought, comes as the result of being a disciple. This association is discussed in Calvin's discussion of the scribe who asked Jesus if he could follow him in Matt 8:19–20.[50] Calvin remarks that because this

---

[47] Minnema, "Calvin's Interpretation," 154.

[48] Wallace, *Calvin's Doctrine*, 70. See also Graham, *Constructive Revolutionary*, 67. Graham says, "It would not be too strong to say that for Calvin both wealth and poverty were sacramental—that is, they were channels of grace from God, and means of evidencing faith on the part of man."

[49] Emphasis mine. Wallace, *Calvin's Doctrine*, 70.

[50] Matt 8:19; "And a scribe came up and said to Him, 'Teacher, I will follow you wherever you go.' And Jesus said to him, 'Foxes have holes, and birds of the air have nests; but the Son of man has nowhere to lay His head'" (*RSV*).

man was a scribe, he was "accustomed to a quiet and easy life, had enjoyed honor and was ill-fitted to endure reproaches, poverty, persecutions, and the cross."[51] Calvin considers this man's hesitation to follow Christ:

> . . . the disciples of Christ must walk among thorns, and march to the cross amidst uninterrupted afflictions. The more eager he is, the less he is prepared. He seems as if he wished to fight in the shade and at ease, neither annoyed by sweat nor dust, and beyond the reach of the weapons of war. There is no reason to wonder that Christ rejects such persons: for, as they rush on without consideration, they are distressed by the first uneasiness of any kind that occurs, lose courage at the first attack, give way, and basely desert their post.[52]

Calvin uses an illustration from war to show how a person accustomed to luxuries and ease may respond when confronted with the hardships of discipleship. Those who wish to be disciples of Christ can expect to "walk among thorns, and march to the cross amidst uninterrupted afflictions." Because communion with Christ results in freedom to suffer with Christ, this assumes that the believer will experience Christ's cross. It is not the kind of life for the one who is unprepared. As with an army, a person who is not fit for the rigors of battle will not persevere. Calvin implies that when an army enlists a man who is not prepared for combat, it faces the possibility that he may desert his post and become a liability for the rest of the troops. This illustration explains Calvin's concept of discipleship well. He admonishes his readers:

> Let us therefore look upon ourselves as warned, in his person, not to boast lightly and at ease, that we will be disciples of Christ, while we are taking no thought of the cross, or of afflictions; but on the contrary, to consider early on what sort of condition awaits us. The first lesson which He gives us on entering His school is to deny ourselves, and take up His cross.[53]

Calvin enjoins his audience to take stock and consider whether they can commit to a cross. Following Christ costs something. It is an illusion to think that one can follow Christ and yet remain free from afflictions. A disciple can expect to experience "reproaches, poverty, persecutions,"—in

---

[51] *Commentary on Matthew* 8:19 (Pringle, 388); *CO* 45, 241.
[52] Ibid.; *CO* 45, 241. See also *Institutes*, 3.8.1 (Battles, 702); *OS* 5, 133.
[53] *Commentary on Matthew* 8:19 (Pringle, 388); *CO* 45, 241.

short, all manner of hardship that Christ experienced as He lived His life in the shadow of the cross.[54] Wilhelm Niesel writes:

> ... we cannot escape this destiny. God wills thus to test His own so that they become conformed to the image of His Son. ... By sending us misfortune and sorrow God breaks our resistance to His will and trains us to obedience. The cross of circumstance which He lays upon us promotes our self-renunciation and brings us to cast ourselves wholly upon Christ.[55]

If, by bearing the cross, the believer engages in imitating Christ while persevering under affliction, then bearing the cross becomes for Calvin a theological pattern revealing that suffering can positively influence a believer's spirituality. Through such hardships, God imparts his grace, enabling the believer to experience communion with Christ.

The remainder of this chapter will show how Calvin equates physical poverty with the endurance of the cross. This will demonstrate that Calvin perceives a believer's poverty and afflictions to be related to Christ's suffering on the cross so that these distresses might become an opportunity for a believer to draw closer to Christ and foster piety.

Physical Poverty and Bearing the Cross

The Reason for Poverty and Afflictions

Calvin is unequivocal when it comes to naming a reason for poverty and affliction: the "prime reason for bearing the cross" is to reflect the judgments of the divine will.[56] "The conclusion will always be: the Lord so willed, therefore let us follow His will."[57] Calvin says that adversity comes from God alone, and that through affliction, a believer sees how God is testing him or her.

> Whether poverty or exile, or prison, or insult, or disease, or bereavement, or anything like them torture us, we must think that none of these things happens except by the will and providence of God, that He does nothing except with a well-ordered justice.[58]

---

[54] Ibid.
[55] Niesel, *Theology of Calvin*, 145.
[56] *Institutes* 3.8.10–11 (Battles, 711); *OS* 4, 168–69.
[57] Ibid., 3.8.10 (Battles, 711); *OS* 4, 169.
[58] Ibid., 3.8.11 (Battles, 711); *OS* 4, 170. In his *Commentary on Romans* 8:28 Calvin writes: "Paul, however, no doubt made here this express declaration—that ... the afflic-

Calvin reasons that if poverty, exile, prison, insult, disease, or bereavement comes from the hand of God, it must be for the believer's good. Furthermore, if this is so, believers can yet take comfort knowing that "in the very act of afflicting us with the cross He is providing for our salvation."[59]

This conclusion is especially true regarding the believer's persecution for the sake of his or her faith in Christ. Calvin believes "that not only they who labor for the defense of the gospel but they who in any way maintain the cause of righteousness suffer persecution for righteousness."[60] These people will be offensive to the world and hated. They will risk losing their lives, fortunes, or honor for the sake of doing what is right. Calvin encourages such people:

> Let us not grieve or be troubled in thus far devoting our efforts to God, or count ourselves miserable in those matters in which He has with His own lips declared us blessed. Even poverty, if it be judged in itself, is misery; likewise exile, contempt, prison, disgrace; finally death itself is the ultimate of all calamities. But when the favor of God breathes upon us, every one of these things turns into happiness for us.[61]

Calvin believes that Christians should embrace a unique attitude toward affliction. Yet he does not deny the pain or difficulty of these situations.[62] As he states: "If there were no harshness in poverty, no torment in diseases, no sting in disgrace, no dread in death—what fortitude or moderation would there be in bearing them with indifference?"[63] Calvin teaches believers to view their sufferings from a divine viewpoint. In the midst of suffering the disgrace of others, believers are assured that their righteous deeds bring pleasure to God. In the same way, they can gain comfort knowing that the Lord is glorified, and God's favor rests upon them when they endure hardship for the sake of righteousness. Calvin asks:

---

tions, which conform us to Christ, have been appointed; and he did this for the purpose of connecting, as by a kind of necessary chain, our salvation with the bearing of the cross" ([Pringle, 316]; *CO* 49, 159).

[59] *Institutes* 3.8.11 (Pringle, 711); *OS* 4, 170. See also *Sermon on Luke* 2:1–4; *CO* 46, 968.

[60] *Institutes* 3.8.7 (Battles, 707); *OS* 4, 166.

[61] Ibid.

[62] See ibid., 3.8.8 (Battles, 708); *OS* 4, 167.

[63] The whole phrase in Latin reads: "Si nulla esset in egestate asperitas, nullus in morbis cruciatus, nulla in ignominia punctio, nullus in morte horror: cuius foret vel fortitudinis vel moderationis, ea susque deque habere?" (Ibid.).

What then? If, being innocent and of good conscience, we are stripped of our possessions by the wickedness of impious folk, we are indeed reduced to poverty among men. But in God's presence in heaven our true riches are thus increased.[64]

The comfort a believer receives is not the hope that these evils will cease. Instead, his comfort comes from knowledge of God's favor. Stated another way, God's favor does not change the fact that in *reality* the believer may continue to suffer, any more than Christ's knowledge of His Father's favor towards His obedience mitigated the suffering of the cross. Calvin likens the suffering of believers to scattered seeds. Unless a seed that is sown falls into the ground and dies, the fruit can never be harvested.[65] Therefore, even though believers may be "reduced to poverty among men," their "true riches are thus increased" or "sown" in heaven.

The Result of Poverty and Afflictions: 2 Corinthians 12:10

POVERTY AND AFFLICTION AND A KNOWLEDGE OF GOD'S GLORY

If the reasons for bearing the cross belong to the judgments of the divine will, then the result of bearing the cross is to reveal the glory of God. Calvin makes this argument in his comments on 2 Corinthians 12:10. The verse occurs in a passage in which Paul discusses the sufficiency of grace to overcome the thorn in his flesh. Calvin's remarks open with a discussion of the relationship between physical poverty and its ability to reveal the glory of God.[66] He notes Paul's varied use of the term "weakness" [*infirmitatis*]. Paul had previously used this term to refer to "the punctures that he experienced in the flesh," but now Calvin argues that Paul uses the term

---

[64] Ibid., 3.8.7 (Battles, 707); *OS* 4, 166.

[65] In his *Commentary on John* 12:24, Calvin states: "for not only do we think that we perish in death, but our life also is a sort of continual death. We shall therefore be undone, unless we are supported by that consolation which Paul holds out: if our outward man decays, the inward man is renewed from day to day. When therefore, the godly are distressed by various afflictions, when they are pressed hard by the difficulties of their situation, when they suffer hunger, or nakedness, or disease, when they are assailed by reproaches, when it appears as if they would every hour be almost overwhelmed by death, let them unceasingly consider that this is a sowing which, in due time, will yield fruit" ([Pringle, 28];*CO* 47, 288).

[66] Calvin's Latin text of 2 Cor 12:10 reads: "Therefore I take pleasure in infirmities, in insults, in necessities, in persecutions, in distresses for Christ's sake: for when I am weak, then I am strong" ([Pringle, 372]; *CO* 50, 138). [Quamobrem placeo mihi in infirmitatibus, in contumeliis, in necessitatibus, in persequutionibus, in anxietatibus pro Christo. Quum enim infirmus sum, tunc robustus sum.]

infirmitatis "to denote those external qualities, which deliver contempt in the sight of the world." He concludes that the word *infirmitatis* is used by the apostle as "a general term, and that under it is comprehended the feebleness of our nature as well as all tokens of abasement."[67] Concerning Paul's outward abasement, he states:

> Now the point in question was Paul's outward abasement. He proceeded farther, for the purpose of showing, that the Lord humbled him in every way, that, in his defects, the glory of God might shine forth the more resplendently, which is in a manner, concealed and buried when a man is in an elevated position. He now again returns to speak of His excellences, which, at the same time, made him despicable in public view, instead of procuring for him esteem and commendation.[68]

Calvin argues that God's glory was revealed to those around Paul through Paul's "outward abasement."[69] It was the kind of glory that otherwise lies hidden to a person who occupies an "elevated position." He believes that without Paul's suffering, God's glory could not have been seen by those around him in the same manner.

It should be noted that here Calvin uses the imagery of burial or concealment. Calvin says that the glory of God lies dormant in the believer, somewhat like a seed buried in the ground. When the storms of adversity come, the glory of God bursts from its place of concealment into the believer's life, much like a plant that emerges from the dry ground after being watered. This imagery is patterned after Christ's death, burial, and resurrection. He argues that God's glory in Christ could never be made manifest to the extent that it was revealed in His resurrection if Christ had not descended from His heavenly glory, taken on human flesh, suffered, and died.[70] As exemplified by Christ, the glory of resurrection *always* follows the death and the apparent defeat of God's children, both in physical and spiritual senses. Calvin suggests that when Paul was not experiencing hardship, poverty, or persecution, God's glory was present in him but was buried or concealed. In this state, God's glory could not be made known to others. Just as with Christ's death and resurrection, God revealed his glory in the midst of Paul's utter humiliation and weakness in a way that would have remained hidden if Paul stayed in his elevated position. Calvin iden-

---

[67] *Commentary on 2 Corinthians* 12:10 (Pringle, 379); *CO* 50, 142.
[68] Ibid., (Pringle, 379–80).
[69] Ibid., (Pringle, 379).
[70] *Commentary on Philippians* 2:7 (Pringle, 56–58); *CO* 52, 26.

tifies the resulting divine glory from poverty and suffering as the ultimate reason why the Lord wills the impoverishments of God's children.

This point is significant for Calvin. Suffering, persecutions, humiliation, and poverty are not meant simply to conform a believer to the life and death of Christ through to the cross. Being conformed to Christ through suffering serves a much greater purpose in the divine plan. Affliction and poverty open opportunities for God's glory to be revealed to the world in ways that could not occur if hardships were absent from a believer's life. In effect, they are a kind of revelatory vehicle showing who God is. Thus, suffering and poverty serve the kingdom by revealing a particular knowledge of God—a knowledge of God's glory that is concealed when suffering and poverty are absent. This reality also means that suffering, poverty, and affliction may be a vehicle of the knowledge of God's glory *only* if the person undergoing hardship is a believer. Though Calvin would say that the suffering of an unbeliever under the burden of the cross is according to the will of God, this person's suffering is not the kind of experience that reveals a knowledge of God's glory. That revelation only is effective for the believer who *willingly* bears the burden of the cross as a disciple of Christ.

In Calvin's thought, there is a correlation between one's perception of Christ's poverty and afflictions and how one perceives one's own afflictions. To the unbeliever, Christ's humbled flesh is offensive. It veils his true identity and the glory of His divine nature. Just as the lowliness of Christ blinds the unbeliever to his true nature, by the same principle the unbeliever cannot grasp the greater purpose in his or her own afflictions. Conversely, to the believer, Christ's humbled flesh reveals who Christ truly is. It is a visible symbol that identifies Him as the Redeemer from sin. Christ's poverty demonstrates that His kingship is not of this world and that His kingdom is a spiritual one; similarly, the poverty and suffering of believers reveal the glory of God and their true identity with Christ. The afflictions of believers enable the treasure of God's glory, deposited within them, to shine forth. Calvin says that believers must not throw off the bridle and bit of hardship, as unbelievers may, but instead they are to be trained by it. This way, God's glory may be made manifest in the lives of the faithful.

Calvin's insight is not without precedent to the Reformation. His understanding of poverty and suffering in the Christian life is rooted in Luther's theology of the cross. In the Heidelberg Disputation of 1518, Luther declared:

19: The man who looks upon the invisible things of God as they are perceived in created things does not deserve to be called a theologian.

20: The man who perceives the visible backside of God [*posteriora Dei*] as seen in suffering and the cross does, however, deserve to be called a theologian."[71]

What Luther asserted in the above theses was a distinction between a theology of glory versus a theology of the cross. A theology of glory seeks to discern a knowledge of God through a form of speculative theology. This theology believes that reason is able to "see through" what is visible to the eye, that is, what is visible in created things[72] in order to discern the invisible nature of the divine. For Luther, such wisdom is nothing but folly. It only results in "dissolving the power of the cross in a sea of abstract universals."[73] Luther argues instead that a true knowledge of God is revealed in the very place where human wisdom would never think to seek it, namely, in the weakness, suffering, and shame of the cross. It is here, in the cross, where a knowledge of God's glory lies concealed, hidden from the eyes of flesh, only to be discerned with the eyes of faith. Furthermore, Luther argued that this knowledge of God is grasped only in the suffering of the Christian. Thus, for Luther, the passion of Christ and the suffering of the believer belong together.[74]

Calvin stands convinced of Luther's theological insights. According to Calvin, the unbeliever's blindness to this reality is rooted in his or her lack of faith. When one has faith in Christ, Christ becomes the reference point for the interpretation of all of life. Hence, the cross stands for the be-

---

[71] This translation is McGrath's with one exception. In thesis 20, I have translated "posteriora Dei" as "backside of God" where McGrath renders it "rear parts of God." Alister E. McGrath, *Luther's Theology*, 149; WA 1.354.17–21.

[72] Though there is some dispute among Luther scholars as to what Luther meant by "visible created things" or literally "those things that have been made [*ea, quae facta sut*]." Some argue that this statement refers to looking for a knowledge of God in creation that would be gained by analogy. Another interpretation of Luther's meaning would be that "the knowledge a theologian of glory arrives at can be understood as both divine perfections and therefore also goals for human 'works.'" See Forde, *On Being a Theologian*, 72, n.3. In thesis 21 Luther provides the categories of a "theology of glory" and a "theology of the cross": He writes, "The theologian of glory says bad is good and good is bad. The theologian of the cross calls them by their proper name." see "The Heidelberg Disputation," in *Luther*, 291–92.

[73] Forde, *On Being a Theologian*, 73.

[74] Brummel, "Luther and the Biblical Language," 48; and Loewenich, *Luthers Theologia Crucis*, 12–18.

liever as a testimony that poverty, suffering, and affliction are never wasted in God's economy. Like the cross, they are redemptive and will result in God's glory.

POVERTY AND AFFLICTION AND A KNOWLEDGE OF SELF

Poverty and affliction not only provide an opportunity for knowledge of God's glory to be revealed but also serve to reveal a knowledge of self. Regarding Paul's conclusion in 2 Cor 12:10, "for when I am weak, then I am strong," Calvin writes:

> Should any one object, that Paul speaks here, not of a failure of strength, but of poverty, and other afflictions, I answer, that all these things are means for making our own feebleness clear to us; for if God had not exercised Paul with such trials, he would never have perceived his weaknesses so clearly. Hence, he has in view not merely poverty, and hardships of every kind, but also those effects that arise from them, as for example, an awareness of our own feebleness, self-distrust and humility.[75]

Calvin realizes that Paul addresses more than just the nature of poverty and hardships in and of themselves. He identifies their "effects" as bringing about "an awareness in our own feebleness, self-distrust and humility." Poverty makes "our own feebleness clear to us." The feebleness that is shown to us is not a physical feebleness. Rather, our physical poverty and affliction reveal another form of weakness—our spiritual feebleness.

The above truth brings full circle this discussion of Calvin's understanding of poverty in the Christian life. Just as poverty and hardships reveal a kind of knowledge of God's glory, at the same time they reveal a knowledge of self, that is, a knowledge of one's weaknesses that should foster humility.[76] Calvin incorporates this topic in his analysis of Luke 14:28, and what it means to count the cost of following Christ. Here, he further clarifies how bearing the cross reveals a knowledge of self:

> This doctrine reproves the rashness of those who foolishly proceed beyond their capacity, or flatter themselves without thinking of bearing the cross. Yet, we must take care lest this meditation, to which Christ exhorts us, should fill us with alarm or retard our progress. Many persons, not having from the outset laid their account with suffering, relax their zeal through cowardice: for they

---

[75] *Commentary on 2 Corinthians* 12:10 (Pringle, 380); *CO* 50, 142.
[76] See *Institutes* 2.7.6–8 (Battles, 354–57); *OS* 3, 332–34.

cannot endure to be Christians on any other conditions than that of being exempted from the cross. . . . But there is no good reason for being discouraged *by a knowledge of our poverty*, for the Lord grants to us seasonable aid. I readily acknowledge that, if we calculate the expense, we are all destitute of power to lay a single stone, or to wield a sword against the enemy. . . . The design of Christ, therefore, is to warn His followers to bear the cross, that they may prepare themselves with courage.[77]

Calvin says that suffering and afflictions reveal a knowledge of a person's "poverty." In other words, physical poverty has the power to reveal a poverty of spirit. Poverty of spirit is a person's spiritual inability "to wield a sword against the enemy." It is a person's inability to change one's spiritual bankruptcy. Suffering reveals a knowledge of self that manifests a person's spiritual destitution and emptiness before God. Calvin states above that this knowledge should not discourage the believer or "retard our progress," rather, it should drive the Christian to depend upon the "seasonable aid" that the Lord grants. Though Calvin does not specifically identify that seasonable aid in this text, in other writings he indicates that it is the grace of God that comes to a person through faith in the gospel of Jesus Christ by the power of the Spirit.[78] To use Wallace's expression, this is where the experience of poverty and affliction in a believer's life has the "value of a sacrament."[79] Part of what it means to be conformed to Christ is to have a knowledge of our own spiritual poverty. In Calvin's thought, only when we grasp the depths of our spiritual poverty will we be driven to Christ to receive the seasonable aid of His grace—a grace that reveals a knowledge of God's divine glory and brings us into communion with Him. In Calvin's theology, a believer's physical poverty and affliction can act as an instrument of revelation, disclosing one's spiritual poverty, that is our inner need for the grace of Jesus Christ.[80]

---

[77] Emphasis mine. *Commentary on Luke* 14:28 (Pringle, 474–75); *CO* 45, 296.

[78] For a clear statement what Calvin means by "seasonable aid" see *Commentary on John* 6:29, 7:37 (Pringle, 244–45, 306–7); *CO* 47, 180, 141.

[79] Wallace, *Calvin's Doctrine*, 70.

[80] The centrality of this idea in Calvin's theology is underscored by the fact that Calvin writes about this in the opening paragraph of the *Institutes*. See *Institutes* 1.1.1 (Battles 36–37); *OS* 3, 31–32; Calvin says: "Indeed our very poverty better discloses the infinitude of benefits reposing in God. The miserable ruin, into which the rebellion of the first man prostrated us, especially compels us to look upward. Thus not only will we, in fasting and hungering, seek thence what we lack; but, in being aroused by fear, we shall learn humility. For, as a veritable world of miseries is to be found in mankind, and we are thereby despoiled of divine raiment, or shameful nakedness exposes a teeming horde of infamies.

The Nature of Poverty and Afflictions: Lazarus and the Rich Man

The discussion above pertains to the role of hardships in the Christian life and how they function theologically in Calvin's thought. Calvin also addresses the nature of poverty and suffering in his exegesis of Christ's parable of "Lazarus and the Rich Man."[81] Calvin begins with a full description of the diverse conditions in which both men lived. He observes the rich man, that he was "clothed in purple and fine linen, and enjoying splendor and luxury every day." According to Calvin, this "denotes a life spent amidst delicacies, and superfluity, and pomp."[82] Calvin qualifies that God does not condemn elegant furnishings, fine clothing, or the work expended to make such items. Yet the problem as he sees it is that "seldom . . . such things are kept in moderation."[83] Though this kind of indulgence is not pleasing to God, Calvin sees that this rich man is guilty of a much greater sin: "The chief accusation brought against this man is his cruelty toward suffering Lazarus, poor and full of sores, [left] to lie out of doors at his gate."[84] Calvin cannot ignore the contrast:

Each of us must, then, be so stung by the consciousness of his own unhappiness as to attain at least some knowledge of God. Thus, from the feeling of our own ignorance, vanity, poverty, infirmity, and what is more—depravity and corruption, we recognize that the true light of wisdom, sound virtue, full abundance of every good, and purity of righteousness rest in the Lord alone. To this extent we are prompted by our own ills to contemplate the good things of God; and we cannot seriously aspire to Him before we begin to become displeased with ourselves . . . . Accordingly, the knowledge of ourselves not only arouses us to seek God, but also, as it were, leads us by the hand to find Him."

[81] Calvin prefaces his comments on the text with some remarks about Christ's intention for telling the story. He states: "He [Christ] points out what condition awaits those who neglect the care of the poor, and indulge in all manner of gluttony; who give themselves up to drunkenness and other pleasures, and allow their neighbors to pine with hunger; nay who cruelly kill with famine those whom they ought to have relieved, when the means of doing so were in their power. Some look upon it as a simple parable; but as the name Lazarus occurs in it, I rather consider it to be the narrative of an actual fact. But that is little consequence, provided that the reader comprehends the doctrine which it contains" *(Commentary on Luke* 16:19 (Pringle, 184); *CO* 45, 407).

[82] Ibid.; *CO* 45, 407–08.

[83] Ibid., (Pringle, 184–85); *CO* 45, 408. Calvin writes: "He who has a liking for fine dress will constantly increase his luxury by fresh additions; and it is scarcely possible that he who indulges in sumptuous and well garnished tables shall avoid falling into intemperance."

[84] Ibid. Bucer also stresses that the rich man was not reproached for his wealth but because of his unwillingness to help the needy. See Backus, "Church, Communion and Community," 69.

> The rich man, devoted to the pleasures of the table and to display, swallowed up, like an insatiable gulf, his enormous wealth, but remained unmoved by the poverty and distresses of Lazarus, and knowingly and willingly suffered him to waste away with hunger, cold, and the offensive smell of his sores.[85]

Calvin is outraged. Not only did the rich man remain "unmoved by the poverty and distresses of Lazarus," allowing him to waste away at his doorstep, but he also refused to learn piety from the dogs. Calvin is indignant about the rich man's indifference:

> There can be no doubt that those dogs were guided by the secret purposes of God, to condemn that man by their example. Christ certainly produces them here as witnesses to convict him of unfeeling and detestable cruelty. What could be more monstrous than to see the dogs taking charge of a man, to whom his neighbor is paying no attention? And what is more, to see the very crumbs of bread refused to a man perishing of hunger, while the dogs are giving him the service of their tongues for the purpose of healing his sores? When strangers, or even brute animals supply our place, by performing an office which rather should have been discharged by ourselves, let us conclude that they are many witnesses and judges appointed by God, to make our criminality more manifest.[86]

Calvin was incensed at the injustice this rich man committed against Lazarus. He was appalled at his blatant neglect and insensitivity. This man had no compassion towards Lazarus, whose condition was so shocking that he accepted the ministry of the dogs' tongues!

Lazarus' death provided Calvin with an important theological point. He used it to argue that this story proves that a person whose life is full of poverty, pain, and distress is not to be regarded as "accursed by God."[87] In other words, what appears to the eye can be deceiving:

> In him the grace of God was so entirely hidden, and pressed down by the deformity and shame of the cross, that to the eye of the flesh nothing presented itself except the curse; and yet we see that in a body which was loathsome and full of rottenness there was lodged a precious soul, which is carried by angels to a blessed life. It was no loss to him that he was forsaken, despised, and destitute of

---

[85] *Commentary on Luke* 16:19 (Pringle, 185); *CO* 45, 408.
[86] *Commentary on Luke* 16:21 (Pringle, 185); *CO* 45, 408.
[87] Ibid., (Pringle, 186).

every human comfort, when heavenly spirits deem him worthy to accompany him on his removal from the prison of the flesh.[88]

Calvin discovers a significant insight about the nature of poverty and suffering. That is, a person who is impoverished will appear "loathsome and full of rottenness." The last thing we will be able to identify in such a person is the grace of God because the nature of suffering and poverty is to conceal or hide God's grace. Calvin calls this the "deformity and shame of the cross."

Calvin speaks of the phrase the "deformity and shame of the cross" in order to describe how cross-bearing veils the grace of God in the Christian life. Just as the grace of God in Christ was obscured by Christ's shocking and revolting abasement on the cross, so it was with the suffering of Lazarus. Yet this similarity twists some of Calvin's comments examined above. Reflecting on 2 Cor 12:10, Calvin states that God's purpose in Paul's hardships was that "the glory of God might shine forth more resplendently," a glory which is "concealed and buried when a person is in an elevated position."[89] The question arises, how can Calvin claim that God's glory is revealed in suffering and poverty, when at the same time he says that it acts to conceal God's grace? Do physical afflictions have a revealing effect or a concealing effect? Does poverty reveal the glory of God? Or does it merely resemble the deformity and shame of the cross?

Calvin's interpretations of Luke 16:22 and 2 Cor 12:10 do not conflict with one another, but rather reveal Calvin's grasp of the paradox at work in a believer's suffering. Part of the solution lies in the phrase, "to the eye of the flesh nothing presented itself except the curse."[90] When Calvin says "the eye of the flesh," he refers to the perception of poverty and suffering apart from faith, that is, from the perspective of the world. When suffering is viewed apart from faith, it has a concealing effect over the grace of God. Grace lies hidden, buried, and pressed down under a body that is "loathsome and rotten." If a person sees Lazarus from God's perspective—with the eyes of faith—he or she will see beyond his appearances to behold "a precious soul." So then, whether a situation is viewed with the eye of the flesh or the eye of faith determines the outcome of what is revealed and what remains concealed.[91]

[88] *Commentary on Luke* 16:22 (Pringle, 186); *CO* 45, 408–9.
[89] *Commentary on 2 Corinthians* 12:10 (Pringle, 379); *CO* 50, 142.
[90] *Commentary on Luke* 16:22 (Pringle, 186); *CO* 45, 408–9.
[91] This is also true in Paul's situation in 2 Cor 12:10. Faith plays a major role in how God's glory "might shine through more resplendently" in Paul's life. The only way Paul's

In Calvin's mind these are the two ways in which the glory and grace of God can be concealed with regard to hardship. One of these occurs when a person is in an "elevated position" and does not experience poverty and suffering. The other takes place if a person's poverty is not viewed with the eyes of faith but rather with the eyes of "flesh." In either case, an aspect of God's glory and grace lies hidden in a way that would otherwise be manifest if poverty and suffering were both present and viewed with the eyes of faith. This same principle was at work in the poverty and affliction of Christ's life and death. As in the crucifixion of Christ, the offensiveness of Lazarus' affliction acted like a veil, concealing the grace of God that rested upon him. Christ's affliction hid His glory as the king of Israel to those who did not look upon Him in faith. Yet to the thief on the cross, the spiritual nature of His kingship and the reality of God's grace and glory were apparent because of his willingness to look upon Christ in faith. Just as believers need to consider the poverty and affliction of Christ from a divine perspective, they also must judge the suffering of others in the same manner. When a person appears "loathsome and full of rottenness," a believer needs to remember that God sees "a precious soul" within.

Cross bearing and the Rich Young Ruler

THE LAW, THE CROSS, AND THE MORTIFICATION OF THE FLESH

Calvin recognized the significant role that Matt 19:21 played in supporting the practice of religious poverty as a means for achieving spiritual perfection.[92] He is well aware that the seeds of this erroneous understanding were sown in the writings of the Fathers.[93] In the *Institutes*, Calvin rebuts this argument by targeting those who "boast that they are made perfect by forsaking all their possessions."[94]

Calvin's critique focuses on the young rich man's rejoinder to Christ that he has kept all of the commandments. Calvin observes that the young

---

outward abasement can humble him is if he faces it in faith. Calvin describes faith as that which "brings nothing to God, but on the contrary places man before God as empty and poor that he may be filled with his grace" (*Commentary on John* 6:29 [Pringle, 245]; *CO* 47, 141). This is what Paul's sufferings did for him. His "defects" were used by God to "humble him," or reveal his emptiness, so that the glory of God might be displayed in him. *Commentary on 2 Corinthians* 12:10 [Pringle, 379]; *CO* 50, 142.

[92] *Institutes* 4.13.13 (Battles, 1267); *OS* 5, 249.
[93] Ibid., (Battles, 1268); *OS* 5, 251.
[94] Ibid., (Battles, 1267); *OS* 5, 249.

man asked specifically what he could do to enter into eternal life.[95] "Because the question was concerned with works," Calvin said, Christ "refers him to the law."[96] He laments that "this passage was erroneously interpreted by some of the ancients, whom the Papists have followed, as if Christ taught that, by keeping the law, we may merit eternal life."[97] In his commentary, Calvin spends considerable effort arguing that eternal life is not merited by works and that the righteousness of the law was meant to show that it is impossible for any person to attain its standard.[98] In pride and vain confidence, the young man asserted that he had kept all the precepts of the law.[99] Calvin's evaluation of this man states the truth of the matter:

> . . . for if he had not flattered himself through hypocrisy, it was an excellent advice to him to learn humility, to contemplate his spots and blemishes in the mirror of the law. But intoxicated with foolish confidence, he fearlessly boasts that he has discharged his duty properly from his childhood.[100]

Breaching the subject of the law did not cause to dawn on this young man "how little he had advanced toward . . . righteousness."[101] Calvin notes that "Christ employed other words for detecting the hidden disease of avarice."[102] Calvin sees that the young man lacked "one thing" in the keeping of the law:[103]

[95] Ibid.; *OS* 5, 250; and *Commentary on Matthew* 19:16 (Pringle, 393); *CO* 45, 537.

[96] *Institutes* 4.13.13 (Battles, 1267); *OS* 5, 250; see also *Commentary on Matthew* 19:17 (Pringle, 394); *CO* 45, 537–38.

[97] *Commentary on Matthew* 19:17 (Pringle, 394); *CO* 45, 538.

[98] Ibid., (Pringle, 394–95).

[99] *Institutes* 4.13.13 (Battles, 1267); *OS* 5, 250.

[100] *Commentary on Matthew* 19:20 (Pringle, 396); *CO* 45, 539.

[101] *Institutes* 4.13.13; *OS* 5, 250. Calvin states in his *Commentary on Matthew* 19:20, "For if he had known himself thoroughly, as soon as he heard the mention of the law, he would have acknowledged that he was liable to the judgment of God; but now, when the bare words of the law do not sufficiently convince him of his guilt, the inward meaning is expressed by other words" (Pringle, 397); *CO* 45, 539. Calvin argues that though the young man knew the law and what was required of him, he missed what the purpose of the law was for, namely to reveal his sinfulness and poverty before God. Thus the young man did not possess what Calvin would call "knowledge of self" which comes through and understanding of the law. Calvin recognizes that Christ perceives this problem in the young man and thus uses another means to reveal his sin, which had masqueraded behind the law as righteousness.

[102] *Commentary on Matthew* 19:20 (Pringle, 396); *CO* 45, 539.

[103] *Commentary on Mark* 10: 21 (Pringle, 397); *CO* 45, 539. The Calvin Translation Society has this section properly marked as Mark:10:21. However, *Calvini Opera* 45, 539,

> For though the law nowhere obliges us to "sell all," yet as it represses all sinful desires, and teaches us to bear the cross, as it bids us be prepared for hunger and poverty, the young man is very far from keeping it fully, so long as he is attached to his riches, and burns with covetousness. And He says that one thing is wanting, because He does not need to preach to him about fornication and murder, but to point out a particular disease, as if He were laying his finger on the sore.[104]

Calvin sees the connection between the law and the cross. The purpose of the law for a Christian is to teach us to bear the cross. Though this man thinks he is in good standing with the law, Calvin perceives that his is sorely lacking in his ability to bear the cross of poverty because of his affection for his wealth.

In Calvin's theology, the law's "third use" is when the law is used in the Christian life to guide and instruct the believer in all righteousness.[105] This instruction is to teach believers to "bear the cross" so that they can "be prepared for hunger and poverty."[106] Calvin's third use of the law corresponds to the outward dimension of what Calvin calls "twofold participation and fellowship in the death of Christ," otherwise known as the "mortification of the outward man" discussed above.[107] Both the law and the cross teach believers to anticipate external afflictions and persecutions—this is why they need to "be prepared for hunger and poverty."[108]

Calvin recognizes that the young man missed this lesson because his wealth had impaired his ability to keep the law fully. If the young man had learned how to bear the cross and had been prepared by the law to face hunger and poverty, Calvin predicts that "he would not have gone away in sorrow upon hearing this word. For the man who loves God with all his heart not only counts as refuse whatever opposes love of him, but flees

---

designates these comments as belonging to Matt 19:20.

[104] *Commentary on Mark* 10:21 (Pringle, 397); *CO* 45, 539.

[105] *Institutes* 2.7.12 (Battles, 360); *OS* 3, 337; Calvin's description of the third use of the law: "Here is the best instrument for them to learn more thoroughly each day the nature of the Lord's will to which they aspire, and to confirm them in the understanding of it."

[106] *Commentary on Mark* 10:21; (Pringle, 397); *CO* 45, 539.

[107] See remarks above on Calvin's *Commentary on Philippians* 3:10 (Pringle, 99); *CO* 52, 50.

[108] *Commentary on Mark* 10:21 (Pringle, 397); *CO* 45, 539.

it like the plague."[109] Thus Christ lays "His finger on the sore" and delves into this "secret wound."[110]

Mark's gospel provides Calvin with another important observation.[111] With its explicit reference to the cross, Calvin recognizes that Christ's call for the young man to "follow me" contains a requirement for "the mortification of the flesh."[112] Calvin refers to this as the "inward" dimension of how a believer participates and has fellowship in the death of Christ.[113] With "the ease, and leisure, and conveniences of home" the rich young ruler "had never experienced in the smallest degree what it was to crucify the old man, and to subdue the desires of the flesh."[114] This young man not only lacked the signs of outward mortification which the law was designed to advance in its students, but he also lacked any kind of inward mortification, which is required of those who would truly follow Christ and thus willingly bear the cross. The inward mortification aims at crucifying the sinful desires and passions which the law reveals. Furthermore, Calvin sees that the "order which Christ gave to 'sell all that he had' was not an addition to the law, but the scrutiny of a concealed vice."[115] The young man should have confronted his affection for his wealth as a hindrance to his faithfulness to God. Since the man did not recognize his sin in "the mirror of the law," Christ sought to expose his "hidden disease of avarice"[116] by challenging him to sell all of his possessions and give to the poor. Biéler

---

[109] *Institutes* 4.13.13 (Battles, 1268); *OS* 5, 250–51.

[110] *Commentary on Mark* 10: 21 (Pringle, 297); *CO* 45, 539; See also *Institutes* 4.13.13 (Battles, 1267); *OS* 5, 250.

[111] Calvin also makes another observation from Mark's text. He notices that Christ urged the young man not only to "sell all" he had, but also to "give to the poor." Calvin cites the example of "Crates, a Theban," who believed he could not be saved unless he threw all his wealth into the sea. Calvin claims that Crates would have been better off if he had distributed his wealth to the needy instead of following through with such a rash display. He argues: "Certainly, as charity is the bond of perfection, he who deprives others, along with himself, of the use of money, deserves no praise; and therefore Christ applauds not simply the selling, but liberality in assisting the poor" (*Commentary on Mark* 10:21 (Pringle, 397–98); *CO* 45, 540). The issue of the Church's responsibility for the poor and the biblical imperatives for the believer to giving to the poor will be examined in closer detail in the final chapter. For now it is important to recognize that Calvin sees Christ's injunction to the young man to sell all he has and give to the poor as equally important for his spiritual health and need to fulfill the law.

[112] *Commentary on Mark* 10:21 (Pringle, 398); *CO* 45, 540.

[113] *Commentary on Philippians* 3:10 (Pringle, 99); *CO* 52, 50.

[114] *Commentary on Mark* 10:21 (Pringle, 398); *CO* 45, 540.

[115] *Commentary on Matthew* 19:22 (Pringle, 400); *CO* 45, 541.

[116] *Commentary on Matthew* 19:20 (Pringle, 396); *CO* 45, 539.

states: "Calvin suitably noticed that the former [the rich young ruler] was not condemned by Jesus because of a moral sin, but because his faith did not penetrate into his material and social life to transform it"; thus it "appears . . . as a deceiving faith." [117]

The young ruler's despondency as he left demonstrates "how widely distant the young man was from that perfection to which Christ had called him."[118] Calvin poses an important question in this encounter for the believer to ponder:

> . . . for how is it that he withdraws from the school of Christ, but because he finds it uneasy to be stripped of his riches? But if we are not prepared to endure poverty, it is manifest that covetousness reigns in us.[119]

Calvin recognizes that a believer must be "prepared to endure poverty." He recommends that in order for believers to "persevere in the school of Christ, we must renounce the flesh."[120] Calvin uses the story of the rich young ruler to warn believers that "unless the sweetness of the grace of Christ renders all the allurements of the flesh distasteful to us, the same thing will happen to us."[121] To use the strong language of Philippians 3:8, unless our earthly riches are as worthless as dung to us, we will walk away from Christ just as this young man did.

Parallels between Physical Poverty and the Law

In Calvin's theology, marked parallels are evident between the function of the law on the one hand, and the greater purpose of suffering, poverty, and afflictions on the other. These connections are not conclusions which Calvin himself draws. They are observed correlations which arise out of Calvin's comments that are too striking to ignore. These findings suggest that there is a relationship between the way that Calvin understands

---

[117] My translation. Biéler, *Pensée Économique*, 346–47. "Calvin fait remarquer que celui-ci n'a pas été condamné par Jésus à cause d'un péché moral, mais parce que sa foi, ne pénétrant pas dans sa vie matérielle et social pour la transformer, apparaissait, de ce fait, comme une foi mensongère." Biéler goes on to concede that external charity is not always a guarantee of authentic charity, it is nevertheless true that authentic love is expressed by material acts. For the Christian, love is never only spiritual. See 347.

[118] *Commentary on Matthew* 19:22 (Pringle, 399); *CO* 45, 541.

[119] *Commentary on Matthew* 19:22 (Pringle, 399); *CO* 45, 541.

[120] Ibid., (Pringle, 400).

[121] Ibid.

the law and his perception of the effects of poverty or afflictions on the Christian life.

The first correlation pertains to the manner in which the law and poverty manifest a knowledge of self.[122] The first use of the law, according to Calvin, reveals that everyone stands empty and spiritually naked before God.[123] This is a similar result which hardship achieves. Calvin maintains that poverty and affliction "are means for making our own feebleness clear to us."[124] Furthermore, a knowledge of self, which both the law and suffering supply, has the same effect. They both are meant to humble the proud heart. Calvin states, "The law was given for the purpose of abasing proud hearts which swelled with vain confidence."[125] A similar idea is found in Calvin's writings on suffering and poverty. In his comments on 2 Cor 12, Calvin explains that "he [Paul] has in view not merely poverty, and hardships of every kind, but also those effects that arise from them, as for example, an awareness of our own feebleness, self distrust and humility."[126] Just as the law strikes our conscience and presents our weaknesses before us, like a mirror, in a similar manner poverty and afflictions have a way of striking our flesh and revealing our utter dependency and weakness. Thus poverty and afflictions have a type of "first use" in that they compel people "to know and confess his [their] own feebleness and impurity."[127] Both have a chastening effect upon a person.[128] They both have the ability to create a teachable heart because they have the ability to humble and thereby bring a person to a true knowledge of one's self by revealing their neediness.

This ability of both the law and poverty to bring about a knowledge of self leads to a second correlation between these two concepts in Calvin's thought. Because both the law and poverty are able to create a humble heart, or a poverty of spirit, they both have the ability to prepare a person

---

[122] Compare *Commentary on Isaiah* 61:1 (Pringle, 305); *CO* 37, 372; and *Institutes* 2.7.6–8 (Battles, 354–57); *OS* 3, 332–34; with *Commentary on 2 Corinthians* 12:10 (Pringle, 379–80); *CO* 50, 142.

[123] See *Institutes* 2.7.8 (Battles, 357); *OS* 3, 334.

[124] *Commentary on 2 Corinthians* 12:10 (Pringle, 380); *CO* 50, 142.

[125] *Commentary on Isaiah* 61:1 (Pringle, 305); *CO* 37, 372.

[126] *Commentary on 2 Corinthians* 12:10 (Pringle, 380); *CO* 50, 142.

[127] Quote taken from Calvin's definition of the first use of the law in *Institutes* 2.7.6 (Battles, 354); *OS* 3, 332. Compare with *Commentary on 2 Corinthians* 12:10 (Pringle, 380); *CO* 50, 142.

[128] See *Institutes* 2.7.8 (Battles, 357); *OS* 3, 334; and *Commentary on Luke* 14:28 (Pringle, 474–74); *CO* 45, 296.

for the grace found in Christ. The punitive function of the law is for a reason—to drive the individual to Christ where they may find comfort, forgiveness, and grace.[129] Calvin specifically says in his comments on Luke 14:28 that "there is no good reason for being discouraged by a knowledge of our poverty, for the Lord grants to us seasonable aid."[130] What Calvin means by "seasonable aid" is the grace of God that comes through faith in Jesus Christ in the power of the Spirit.[131] However, this leads to yet a third correlation in Calvin's thought: The universal character of both the law and poverty. Calvin teaches in the *Institutes* that the punitive function of the law is laid upon unbeliever and believer alike.[132] It acts to judge all men before a holy God and reveal, as said above, a knowledge of one's destitution before God. Yet this knowledge will only have an affect upon the believer, not the unbeliever, by leading the believer to receive the grace of Christ. In a similar way, poverty and affliction are laid upon all people.[133] Calvin writes, "God lays the burden of the cross on both good and bad men, unless they willingly bend their shoulders to it, they are not said to bear the cross." [134] Though the cross of suffering and afflictions is universally applied to all humanity, like the law, only the Christian may benefit from the experience because only the Christian may be spiritually trained by it.

The fourth correlation is the ability of poverty and the law to reveal a knowledge of God. This comparison has both a similarity as well as a distinction in Calvin's thought. Where the law reveals a knowledge of God's righteousness, and thereby warning, informing, and convicting us, the knowledge of God revealed in our hardships is different. According to Calvin's exegesis of 2 Cor 12:10, the Lord humbled Paul through his abasement because "in his defects, the glory of God might shine forth the more resplendently, which is in a manner, concealed and buried when a man is in an elevated position."[135] Though there is a difference in the content of the knowledge of God revealed by the law and hardships, it is striking that in both cases believers are to be trained by it. Both the law

---

[129] See *Institutes* 2.7.9 (Battles, 357); *OS* 3, 335.
[130] *Commentary on Luke* 14:28 (Pringle, 474); *CO* 45, 296.
[131] See *Commentary on John* 7:37; 6:29 (Pringle, 306–7); *CO* 47, 180; 141.
[132] See *Institutes* 2.7.8 (Battles, 356); *OS* 3, 334.
[133] *Commentary on Matthew* 16:24 (Pringle, 304); *CO* 45, 481–82; and see also *Commentary on 2 Corinthians* 1:5 (Pringle, 112); *CO* 50, 11.
[134] *Commentary on Matthew* 16:24 (Pringle, 304); *CO* 45, 481–82.
[135] *Commentary on 2 Corinthians* 12:10 (Pringle, 379); *CO* 50, 142.

and the experience of bearing the cross through poverty and afflictions reveal a knowledge of God that is otherwise not evident.[136] This means that poverty and affliction can be said to have a form of "third use" similar to what Calvin called the third use of the Law. Though poverty itself is unable to reveal the will of God, when joined to a knowledge of Christ's cross it provides the perfect school in which faith may grow. Calvin's third use of the law must also be joined to the cross. Without the cross, the law drives a person to despair not unlike suffering apart from the cross.[137] Both the law and poverty have the ability to conform one to God's will if joined with God's grace in Christ.

The number and pattern of these correlations suggest that there is an even deeper connection between the way in which the law and poverty function in Calvin's understanding of the Christian life. The law, afflictions, and poverty do indeed share a common root. In Calvin's exegesis of the Rich Young Ruler he discusses the relationship between the law and the selling of this man's possessions. He states that "we are no where commanded in the law to sell all."[138] However, he continues, "the law . . . teaches us to bear the cross, as it bids us to be prepared for hunger and poverty."[139] Calvin not only links the instruction of the law to what it means to bear the cross, but also he clarifies *how* the law teaches cross-bearing—that is it "bids us to be prepared for hunger and poverty." In addition, he states that the law teaches the discipline of bearing the cross, since bearing the cross is how the believer is called to imitate Christ. This raises the question: If the law instructs a believer in what it means to bear the cross, and bearing the cross is our imitation of Christ, then what is Christ's relationship to the law? Calvin's exegesis of Rom 10:4 explains:

> . . . because the law had been given for this end, to lead us as by the hand to another righteousness: that is, whatever the law teaches, whatever it commands, whatever it promises, always has a reference to Christ as its main object; and hence all its parts ought to be applied to Him. But this cannot be done, except being stripped of all righteousness, and confounded with the knowledge of our sin, we seek gratuitous righteousness from Him alone. . . . We have

---

[136] Compare on the Knowledge of God embodied in Scripture in the *Institutes* 1.6.1 (Battles, 69–71); *OS* 3, 60–61, with Calvin's *Commentary on 2 Corinthians* 12:10 (Pringle, 339); *CO* 50, 142, on suffering and poverty.

[137] Compare concepts in *Institutes* 2.7.8 (Battles, 356–57); *OS* 3, 337 on the law with Calvin's *Commentary on Matthew* 10:38 (Pringle, 474); *CO* 45, 294.

[138] *Commentary on Matthew* 19:20 (Pringle, 396); *CO* 45, 539.

[139] *Commentary on Mark* 10:21 (Pringle, 397); *CO* 45, 539.

here a remarkable passage, which proves that the law in all its parts had a reference to Christ; and thus no one can rightly understand it, who does not continually level at this mark.[140]

Calvin emphasizes Christ as the primary focus of the law. Every aspect of the law's instruction, commands, and promises must be applied first to Christ.[141] Because in all its parts the law has reference to Christ, the multiple parallels between the function of the law and believers' sufferings with Christ in the Christian life should be not surprising. They demonstrate that Calvin's Christology is the root of his understanding of the influential role of poverty and the law in the Christian life. More specifically, this foundation grows out of Calvin's theology of the cross. The cross is the deeper connection between the law and the experience of poverty and suffering in the Christian life. Christ's own utter impoverishment and suffering intersect with the law at the cross. While Christ's life satisfied the requirements of the law, his death fulfilled our judgment under the law. As a result, the believer looks to the law to be instructed in what it means to bear the cross and thus become conformed to Christ.

Conclusion

The utter poverty of Christ's cross leaves its unmistakable mark upon the character of the Christian life. According to Calvin, Christ's cross has consequences beyond the work of justification. It also applies to the work of sanctification. He teaches that the poverty and suffering of Christ present a pattern for how the Christian life is to be lived—a pattern that is summed up in the phrase bearing the cross. Calvin defines this cross as the external afflictions and hardships of life. Bearing the cross is his theological term for a believer's response to such hardships. In this view, one's response to affliction reflects one's spiritual maturity. Calvin suggests that Christ's poverty and suffering, embodied in the figure of cross bearing, has sacramental value in its application to the Christian life. He teaches that the experience of bearing the cross can become a vehicle of divine grace and blessing; his writings demonstrate this idea in several ways.

First, poverty and afflictions occasion the experience of divine grace because cross-bearing leads to a knowledge of self. Hardships strip away self-confidence and false security, fostering self-doubt and a sense of vul-

---

[140] *Commentary on Romans* 10:4 (Pringle, 384–85); *CO* 49, 196.

[141] See Hesselink, "Christ, the Law, and the Christian," 186–87. Hesselink clearly articulates the relationship between the Law and Christ in Calvin's theology and the significance of this for his thought and ethics.

nerability. Most importantly, they reveal humanity's spiritual poverty and the inability for people to change. This truth should engender a sense of humility that allows the Holy Spirit to work in the human heart. Grasping the depth of one's spiritual poverty should drive the believer to depend upon the mercy of God, that which is revealed in the cross of Christ guides him or her to receive the seasonable aid of God's grace. This grace brings to a believer a knowledge of God's divine glory and draws one into communion with God. When this union occurs, the poverty and afflictions in a believer's life have the effect of a sacrament.

Second, Calvin teaches that poverty and affliction can reveal divine grace because they present opportunities for a revelation of the knowledge of God's glory. For Calvin, this is the prime reason for bearing the cross. He maintains that although God's glory is present in believers' prosperity, it remains hidden if the believer stays in a lofty position. Yet just as a knowledge of Christ's glory could not be revealed without His utter abasement, so it is with the Christian life. Hardships in the lives of believers serve the kingdom by declaring a knowledge of God's glory. Poverty and afflictions, then, are an instrument of God's kingdom, demonstrating God's glory and sufficiency if the person under trial willingly bears the burden of the cross in obedience to Christ's example.

One reason remains as to why the experience of bearing the cross, that is, persevering in poverty and affliction, can serve as a vehicle of divine grace and blessing. This relates to the Christological connection between the law and the experience of poverty and affliction in the Christian life implicit in Calvin's thought. Calvin teaches that the law is a guide for the Christian life. The law incites the believer to bear the cross so that he or she may be equipped to face afflictions. This means there is a congruency in Calvin's thought in the way the law and hardships function in the Christian life. Both reveal a knowledge of self that compels a person to confess his or her own impotence and spiritual helplessness. In addition, both reveal a knowledge of God when they have Christ as their reference point. When the law is seen through the eyes of faith, in light of the grace found in Christ, it has the ability to reveal a knowledge of God that enables the believer to be conformed to the will of God. Poverty and afflictions function similarly. When they are experienced in light of the gospel of Christ's cross, impoverishments are meant to conform the believer to Christ. Thus, the cross of Christ brings spiritual value to believers' hardships. When believers bear the cross of their afflictions in faith, their suffering showcases a knowledge of God's glory and becomes an instrument of divine grace and blessing.

9
Poverty and Affliction in Calvin's Ecclesiology

IN the mind of Calvin, a relationship exists between the poverty and afflictions experienced by Christ and the poverty and afflictions of the Church. Chapter 7 demonstrated that Calvin regards the poverty of Christ to be a mark that His kingship is divine and that His kingdom is not of this world but is instead spiritual in nature. The thesis of this chapter is that this idea manifests itself in Calvin's ecclesiology. Calvin maintains that the Church is the expression of the kingdom of God on earth. His position suggests that poverty and afflictions are a defining aspect of his ecclesiology, similar to his Christology. Calvin interprets the experience of poverty and affliction in the Church as which reveals spiritual truth, or that which is of God: they reveal the judgment of God; they awaken the Church to its sin; they act to renew and purify its spiritual life. Suffering enables the Church to testify to the power of God while conforming believers to Christ and thus marks the Church as the true Church of God. Following the pattern Christ established in the affliction of His flesh, sufferings are part of the Church's divinely ordained purpose while it remains in this world. They disclose that the Church is established not according to the things of this world, but rather in what is divine, that which is spiritual and invisible.

This idea that the Church as the physical expression of the kingdom of God on earth, marked by trials and weaknesses in a manner similar to Christ's ministry was marked by poverty and afflictions, has two distinct expressions in Calvin's thought. The first concerns Calvin's understanding of the Church's *experience* of poverty and afflictions and the spiritual reasons for it. This is the focus of the present chapter. The second addresses the manner in which Calvin's understanding of poverty and the kingdom of Christ critiques the luxuries, ceremonies, and wealth in the Roman Church and how it prescribes proper worship and spiritual ministry. This will be the topic of the next chapter. The current chapter will begin its analysis by discussing the reason why the Church is poor and suffers affliction. Two sources in Calvin's writings deal extensively with this subject. One is in his commentaries and the other in his 1550 treatise *De Scandalis* [*Concerning Scandals*].[1] The following section will first examine what Calvin says about the suffering state of the Church in a number of passages from his *Commentaries*. Later, it will show how Calvin applies this knowledge in his 1550 treatise *Concerning Scandals*, which was written to the French Evangelicals undergoing persecution for their faith.

The thesis that the kingdom of God on earth is marked by poverty and affliction, not splendor and glory, is an essential component of Calvin's ecclesiology. This chapter will demonstrate this thesis in several ways. It will show that the affliction of the Church reveals the judgments of God. It acts to awaken the people of God to sin, and upon repentance, brings renewal to their spiritual life. Thus affliction results in the purification of the Church, which in turn causes the Church to testify to God's power, thus marking herself as the true Church of God. This chapter demonstrates that Calvin's understanding of a poor and suffering Church was no small part of his ecclesiology. He uses his Christology, informed by a theology of the cross, to interpret the struggles of the Church, and concludes that they are normative and necessary. In short, it will be shown that he believes that suffering, poverty, and affliction to be at the heart of the Church's divinely ordained purpose in this world. Finally, this chapter examines Calvin's understanding of the nature of the Church. He finds poverty and affliction to be a primary expression of the true nature of the Church.

Though this chapter focuses on the theology of Calvin regarding the suffering Church, it is important to keep in mind the context of his writings. Refugees were pouring into Geneva by the thousands, fleeing the bloody persecution by Henry II.[2] Calvin knows the how dangerous it was to be a Protestant Huguenot in France. Though Calvin made no refer-

---

[1] Calvin was well aware of the persecutions and struggles of the French Evangelicals and wanted to write a tract to bring encouragement and direction to their faith. He understood the stumbling blocks to their faith and their need to receive some guidance. In a letter he wrote to Farel in September of 1546, Calvin states that he began to write *Concerning Scandal* [*De Scandalis*]. However, in another letter to Farel dated October 2, 1546, Calvin indicates that he has laid the treatise aside to write his *Commentary on Galatians*. In a letter to Farel of August 19, 1550, he states that the treatise will soon be completed. Barth and Scheuner, Introductory note, xi; *CO* 2, 159.

[2] Henry II, Son of Francis I, was crowned king of France in 1547 and died in 1559.

ence to current events in these passages, the reader should remember that Calvin and his audience are not in a comfortable setting. The Reformed Church in Geneva was a church full of refugees fleeing the fires of persecution in France who had abandoned their homes and possessions for the sake of the gospel. And those who were native to Geneva had to cope with a city burgeoning with a flood of immigrants. Though records are sketchy, it has been estimated that Geneva's population of about 10,000 may have as much as doubled and had to be accommodated within the city walls.[3] Knowing Calvin's historical context, his teaching about the poverty and suffering of the Church becomes all the more significant. What will unfold in this study is that which informed Calvin and his parishioners regarding how to interpret their losses and suffering.

The Role of Poverty, Persecution, and the Affliction of the Church

The Reasons for the Afflictions of the Church

THEY REVEAL THE JUDGMENTS OF GOD: PSALM 9:9

Calvin notes that the context of Psalm 9[4] is David's recounting of God's former victories over his enemies and his appeal for God's further protection, given the escalating dangers around him.[5] He sees David as being especially acquainted with poverty, misery, and affliction and therefore familiar with the spiritual difficulties that accompany this condition. Calvin

---

[3] Scholars agree that in 1536, Geneva's population was about 10,300. Graham estimates that if each refugee arrived with one dependent, the population of Geneva is around 20,000 by 1559. Records show that between 1542 and 1560 some 4,776 workers legally entered Geneva and most of these had wives and children. By 1559 two new churches even had to opened because of the rise in population. See Graham, *Constructive Revolutionary*, 105–6.

[4] Calvin's comments on Ps 9:9 appears in *CO* 31, 100, as Ps 9:10. The difference in the numbering of the verses begins in Psalm 9:6, where Calvin writes "Varie exponitur septimus versus." [The seventh verse is explained in different ways] So Calvin's comments on Ps 9:9 are actually found in *CO* 31, 100–101 under Ps 9:10. Calvin's translation of Ps 9:9 into Latin reads: "Et erit Iehova munimentum pauperi, protectio opportunis temporibus in tribulatione." [Jehovah will be a refuge for the poor, and a timely protection in tribulation.] My translation. Calvin wrote his *Commentary on Psalms* from about 1553 to 1557. See Parker, *Calvin's Old Testament Commentaries*, 29. From before 1549 through 1560, Calvin regularly preached on the Psalms for afternoon sermons. See Parker, *Calvin's Preaching*, 150–52.

[5] *Commentary on Psalms* 9:1 (Pringle, 110); *CO* 31, 95–96.

reflects on this text and considers why the Church suffers affliction and why God appears to delay in providing divine assistance:

> He [David] offers a remedy for the temptation which harshly casts down the weak, when they see themselves, and those who are like them abandoned to the will of the ungodly, while God keeps silence. He admonishes us that God delays his aid and to outward appearances he forsakes his faithful ones, in order at length to help them at a more convenient time, according to the greatness of their necessity and affliction. From this it follows that he by no means ceases from the exercise of his office, although he suffer the good and the innocent to be reduced to extreme poverty, and although he exercise them with weeping and lamentations; for by doing this he lights up a lamp to enable them to see his judgments the more clearly.[6]

Calvin observes that David is an example of a person who is faithful to God and yet experiences affliction and persecution. Though by all outward appearances, it may seem that God has forsaken the faithful to the whims of the ungodly, as Calvin argues, God delays his aid for a reason. God's intent is so "he [might] light up a lamp to enable them to see his judgments the more clearly."[7] Calvin saw that poverty and persecution can bring insight to a person to understand God's ways.

As Calvin saw it, this realization was encouraging to Calvin. If poverty and affliction enable a believer to perceive the judgments of God more clearly, then this knowledge should influence a believer's attitude toward his or her circumstances. In his comments on Ps 9:9, Calvin elaborates on this idea. He states that "the greatest blessing which we can receive" from God is the "experience of his fatherly favor." This means that believers are not to "feel so uneasy at being accounted poor and miserable before the world."[8] Calvin suggests that without affliction, God's "protection" and "fatherly favor" are not experienced in the same way that they are when be-

---

[6] *Commentary on Psalms* 9:9 (Pringle, 118–19); *CO* 31, 100.

[7] Ibid., (Pringle, 119); *CO* 31, 100.

[8] In his *Commentary on Psalms* 9:9, Calvin writes: "Accordingly, he [David] expressly declares, that he [God] interposes his timely protection in the afflictions of his people [*ipsa afflictione*]. From this we are taught the duty of giving his providence time to make itself manifest in the time of need. If the protection by the power of God and the experience of his fatherly favor is the greatest blessing which we can receive, let us not feel so uneasy at being accounted poor and miserable before the world [*coram mundo pauperes et miseros*], but let this consolatory consideration remedy our grief, that God is not far from us, having been summoned to aid our afflictions [*aerumnae*]." See Pringle, 119; *CO* 31, 100–1.

lievers are "accounted poor and miserable before the world."[9] This perspective calls believers to forbearance of their suffering. He instructs believers to give God's "providence time to make itself manifest."[10] Concerning verse 10, Calvin explains:

> . . . that when the Lord delivers the righteous, the fruit which results from it is that they themselves, and all the rest of the righteous acquire increasing confidence in his grace; for unless we are fully persuaded that God exercises a care about men and human affairs, we must necessarily be troubled with constant anxiety. But as most men shut their eyes that they may not see the judgments of God, David restricts this advantage to the faithful alone, and certainly where there is no godliness, there is no sense of the works of God. It is also to be observed, that he attributes to the faithful the knowledge of God, because from this religion proceeds, whereas it is extinguished through the ignorance and stupidity of men.[11]

Calvin maintains that doctrine of God's providence, namely, the conviction that "God exercises a care about men and human affairs," is a source of comfort for believers. God delivers the righteous and provides them with an "increasing confidence in his grace." Calvin views this is as an advantage that the ungodly do not have. Godly forbearance of affliction brings about a knowledge of God from which religion proceeds. Calvin's interpretation of the parable of the fig tree in Matt 24:32 continues to enlarge his insight into God's providence, especially regarding the afflictions of the Church.[12]

They Foster Its Spiritual Life: Matthew 24:32

According to Calvin, the afflictions of the Church not only reveal the judgments of God but also foster spiritual growth and maturity in the Church. Concerning the parable of the fig tree in Matt 24:32, Calvin maintains that believers will undergo great tribulation and persecution before Christ returns to gather his Church.[13] He rejects the view that the parable merely teaches that "the state of confusion" of the persecution of the Church "will be an evident sign that the coming of Christ is near" as

---

[9] *Commentary on Psalms* 9:9 (Pringle, 119); *CO* 31,100–1.
[10] Ibid.
[11] *Commentary on Psalms* 9:10 (Pringle, 119–20); *CO* 31, 101.
[12] Matt 24:32: "From the fig tree learn its lesson: as soon as its branch becomes tender and puts forth its leaves, you know that summer is near"(*RSV*).
[13] *Commentary on Matthew* 24:29–31 (Pringle, 150–51); *CO* 45, 666–68.

it is when "the summer is at hand when the trees begin to grow green."[14] Instead, he argues that the parable teaches how persecution and affliction affect the Church. Christ likens the afflictions of the Church to the seasons of a fig tree. The tree in winter appears to be full of strength and toughness, whereas in spring the tree becomes weak and feeble as the tree softens and its bark splits to allow the growth of new twigs. Calvin contends that this softening is not a sign of the tree's decline, but rather an indication of its life. So it is with the Church. Afflictions soften the external appearance of the Church "according to the perception of the flesh." Yet this does not mean that the Church has lost its vitality. Instead, just the opposite is true. As a tree in the spring diffuses its sap throughout the whole tree and collects its strength "to break forth to renovate what was dead," so it is with the suffering Church. Through persecution and affliction, the Lord seeks to restore the people of God and renovate what was dead.[15] Calvin clarifies:

> The general instruction conveyed is, that the weak and frail condition of the Church ought not to lead us to conclude that it is dying, but rather to expect the immortal glory for which the Lord prepares his people by the cross and by afflictions; for what Paul maintains in reference to each of the members must be fulfilled in the whole body, that if the outward man is decayed, the inward man is renewed day by day. (2 Cor 4:16)[16]

The frail and afflicted Church is not a Church that is dying, but is a Church prepared by the cross to receive the Lord's immortal glory. Calvin handles the effect of tribulations on the Church and the role of affliction in the Christian life in a similar fashion. The cross represents the conforming of believers and the Church as a whole to the image of Christ. Thus, affliction prepares the Church for its future and immortal glory by renewing its inward life, though the outward appearance appears to decay.

Calvin draws upon the language and categories of 2 Cor 4:16 to define this idea of "the weak and frail condition of the Church" which prepares the Church for its destiny of immortal glory. This text also clarifies his use of the phrase "the corruption of the outward man" cited above. He admits that the term "outward man" had been ignorantly confused with the term "old man" spoken of in Romans 6.[17] Calvin understands the

---

[14] *Commentary on Matthew* 24:32 (Pringle, 150); *CO* 45, 670.
[15] Ibid.
[16] Ibid., (Pringle, 150–51), *CO* 45, 670.
[17] *Commentary on 2 Corinthians* 4:16 (Pringle, 211); *CO* 50, 58.

term "outward man" as referring to "everything that relates to this present life":[18] to a person's health, wealth, honors, friendships, and any other earthly resources. Thus, the corruption of the outward man, to which Paul refers in this passage, does not entail a corruption of a person's spiritual life by sin. The outward man is corrupted by the loss of outward and physical blessings.[19] When Calvin says that "the Lord draws from the corruption of the outward man, the perfect restoration of his people," he means that it is through *physical* and *outward* afflictions and impoverishment of the Church, God restores the Church's *inward* and *spiritual* health. This idea is made explicit in Calvin's comments on verse 17:

> He had said that the decay of the outward man ought to give us no grief, inasmuch as the renovation of the inward man springs out of it. As, however the decay is visible, and the renovation is invisible, Paul, with the view of shaking us off from a carnal attachment to the present life, draws a comparison between present miseries and future happiness.[20]

Calvin's definition of the inward man encompasses all that has to do with an individual's or the Church's spiritual life and fitness. Physical decay (or affliction) is visible for all to see, whereas the renovation of the inward man is invisible. He argues that the rehabilitation of the inward man proceeds out of the "decay of the outward man."[21] Regarding the Church, it may be said that when her outward form is afflicted and persecuted, though it may appear to the eye of the flesh to be in decay, it is in reality being renovated by the work and judgment of God.

The above texts gave Calvin two reasons why the Church suffers in this age. First, the affliction of the Church reveals the judgments of God to the faithful, and second, it also works to renew the inward man or spiritual life of the Church. These points are fundamental to understanding Calvin's perspective on the following text, Ps 25:13, which enhances another aspect of this reasoning. It provides a third answer to the question,

---

[18] Ibid.

[19] Ibid. Calvin goes on to say, "For in the reprobate, too, the outward man decays, but without anything to compensate for it." Calvin maintains that for the unbeliever, suffering and affliction do not hold the same benefit as they do for the believer. A similar contrast is found in Calvin's comments on Ps 9:10, where he argues that in affliction, a knowledge of God's judgments are not revealed to the unbeliever, but to the faithful alone ([Pringle, 120]; *CO* 31, 101).

[20] *Commentary on 2 Corinthians* 4:17 (Pringle, 212); *CO* 50, 58.

[21] Ibid.

why does God withdraw divine blessings from the Church and permit it to fall into poverty and affliction?

They Awaken the People of God: Psalm 25:13

According to Calvin, Ps 25:13[22] teaches that believers are not only spiritually blessed by God but are also blessed "as to their condition in the present life," or in regards to their physical life.[23] This observation must not be misunderstood. He is aware that the *experience* of many believers is not that of physical blessing, but rather of afflictions, sickness, and poverty. He grants "that God does not always deal with them [believers] according to their desires, and that the blessings for which they would wish do not always flow in a certain and uniform manner."[24] This apparent incongruity requires an explanation:

> But we must know, that as often as God withdraws his blessing from his own people, it is for the purpose of awakening them to how far removed they still are from that perfect fear of God. . . . It is indeed true, that all our miseries proceed from this one source—that by our sins we prevent the divine blessing from flowing down in a uniform course upon us. . . .[25]

Calvin acknowledges that there are times when "God withdraws his blessing from his own people." This divine action is not without a purpose. Blessings are withdrawn so that God's people will spiritually awaken and understand "how far removed they still are from that perfect fear of God."[26] Affliction and poverty, then, alert the Church of its spiritual needs. In a word, suffering reveals knowledge of self. It informs the corporate self-consciousness of the Church as to how far the people of God have wandered away from the purposes of the Lord. Calvin also finds another reason why the Church suffers affliction, stating that because of "our sins we prevent the divine blessing from flowing down in a uniform course upon us."[27] According to Calvin, sin in the Church is the main reason for her affliction. In this text, Calvin does not defend this statement or explain

---

[22] Calvin translates Ps 25:13: "Anima eius in bono morabitur, et semen eius haereditate possidebit terram" (*Commentary on Psalms* 25:13 [Pringle, 426]; *CO* 31, 257). [His soul shall dwell in good, and his seed shall inherit the earth.]

[23] *Commentary on Psalms* 25:13 (Pringle, 428); *CO* 31, 258.

[24] Ibid.

[25] Ibid., (Pringle, 428–29).

[26] Ibid., (Pringle, 428).

[27] Ibid., (Pringle, 429).

it further. He only suggests that God's hand of blessing is withdrawn when the Church no longer reflects Christ's kingdom on earth because of her sinfulness.

In spite of the fact that God may withdraw his blessings, Calvin encourages his readers to understand that God does not abandon the Church in its time of need. Calvin assures:

> And yet, in so far as it is expedient for them, they now enjoy the blessings of God, so that in comparison of worldly men, and the despisers of God, they are truly happy and blessed, because even in their greatest poverty, they never lose the assurance that God is present with them; and being sustained by this consolation, they enjoy peace of mind. . . . and yet, amidst such a state of confusion, his grace never ceases to shine forth, so that the condition of the godly is always better than that of others: for although they are not satiated with good things, yet they are continually made to experience a sense of the fatherly favor of God.[28]

Calvin is careful to make an important distinction. Even though divine blessings may be removed from God's people, God had not abandoned them. Even though God's children may experience hardship and poverty, they shall always have access to a comfort and happiness not available to unbelievers. This is the reassurance coming from knowledge of the reality that God is present with them in their time of struggle. It is a grace that "never ceases to shine forth." It penetrates the darkest shroud of affliction to surround believers with "a sense of the fatherly favor of God."

The poverty and affliction of the Church are not only brought on by the sins of the Church and, subsequently, the removal of God's hand of blessing, but also these trials are used by God to awaken the Church to its sinful condition. The following section introduces two additional texts, Isa 29:19–20 and Zeph 3:12–13, which further support the teaching that God uses affliction and poverty to awaken the Church to its sinfulness. It will be shown that God awakens the Church from spiritual slumber for a specific reason: so that God might use the experience of suffering to purify and correct the Church.

THEY PURIFY AND CORRECT THE CHURCH: ISAIAH 29:17–20 AND ZEPHANIAH 3:12–13

The discourse of Isaiah 29 is a prophecy against the city of Jerusalem. Calvin observes that the Jews possessed a foolish confidence in the temple

---

[28] Ibid., (Pringle, 428–29).

and the altar of God as being their strongest defense against their enemies.[29] Isaiah challenged their wickedness, hypocrisy, and superstition in life and worship,[30] and threatened the city with the judgment of God.[31] Calvin recognizes that the judgment of God falls upon the Church because of its wickedness and pride. These indulgent people in the ranks are spiritually asleep and approach the worship of God with "profound indifference." Consequently, they will experience divine judgment through "the powerful hand of God." [32] Calvin recognizes that this analysis is not true of all persons in the Church. Yet, in order that the godly will not lose hope, the prophet shifts his tone in verse 17 from an outlook of judgment to one of grace. Calvin summarizes: "That the godly may not be discouraged, he passes from threats to proclaim grace, and declares that when they shall have given evidence of the obedience of their faith, by enduring for a little the cross laid upon them, a sudden renewal is at hand to fill them with joy."[33]

Calvin's allusion to the cross is significant. It shows that he interprets the afflictions of the Church from a Christological perspective. Though the trials of the Church are brought on by the sins of her people, still God's judgment falls upon the godly and the ungodly alike. Yet the difference between the hardships of the godly and those of the ungodly is not in what is experienced but in how the experience is understood. Calvin describes the afflictions of the godly as a cross that is laid upon them for a little while. For God to afflict the righteous along with the unrighteous in the Church is not unfair of him. For the righteous, it is a path to sudden renewal and joy. It is an experience that can only strengthen the faith of the godly. For the righteous, the cross can never be separated from resurrection. For the unrighteous, however, the cross is God's way of dealing with their pride and profound indifference to spiritual things. It is a divine punishment meant to break the calloused heart. Yet, through all these difficulties, Calvin clings to the promise of God not to forsake the Church in its afflictions:

---

[29] *Commentary on Isaiah* 29:1 (Pringle, 309–10); *CO* 36, 485.

[30] *Commentary on Isaiah* 29:13 (Pringle, 323–25); *CO* 36, 493–94.

[31] Ibid., (Pringle, 326–30); *CO* 36, 495–96.

[32] Calvin writes: "The Lord now declares that he will make those wicked men to know who they are; as if he had said, 'You are now asleep in your pride, but I shall speedily awake you.' Men indulge themselves, till they feel the powerful hand of God; and therefore God will overtake such profound indifference." *Commentary on Isaiah* 29:17 (Pringle, 330); *CO* 36, 497.

[33] Ibid., (Pringle, 331); *CO* 36, 498.

He promises that the Church of God, as we have said, shall still be preserved amidst those calamities. Though the world be shaken by innumerable tempests, and tossed up and down, and though heaven and earth shall mingle, yet the Lord will preserve the multitude of the godly, and will raise up his Church, as it were, out of the midst of death.[34]

In such an embattled Church, Calvin sees the image of the crucified and resurrected Christ. Just as God raised the crucified Son of God, so God "will raise up his Church, as it were, out of the midst of death."[35]

God has a purpose in permitting the affliction and persecution of the Church to continue to the point that it has seemingly died. If the affliction of the Church is a result of divine judgment upon the sinfulness of the people of God, then the affliction itself is an agent of the purification of the Church. Calvin understands that God uses this method in a way that is unexpected,[36] allowing the Church to reach a point at which "it will appear to have altogether perished."[37] The Church is nearly obliterated in the crucible of affliction to remove the dross and to purify its members. Furthermore, it is only after the Church is purified that the renewal and blessing of God can return to the corporate Church. Calvin finds that the greatest blessing which affliction brings to the Church is that it "prepares us for receiving the grace of God."[38] This is a believer's true source of joy and gladness. When believers are "cast down," they are placed in a position to experience the grace of God when "he may afterwards raise us up."[39]

---

[34] *Commentary on Isaiah* 29:18 (Pringle, 331–32); *CO* 36, 498.

[35] Ibid., (Pringle, 332).

[36] Calvin writes: "He therefore means that the Church must first be chastised and purified, and that not in a common and ordinary way, but in a way so unusual that it will appear to have altogether perished. He therefore says, "in that day," that is after having punished the wicked and purified his Church, not only will he enrich the earth with an abundance of fruits, but by renewing the face of it." Ibid.

[37] Ibid.

[38] Calvin writes: "As if he said, 'Though they are now distressed, yet I will give them occasion of gladness, so that they shall again be filled with joy.' He speaks of the 'humble;' and hence it ought to be observed that our afflictions prepare us for receiving the grace of God; for the Lord casts us down and afflicts us that he may afterwards raise us up. Thus, when the Lord corrects his people, we ought not to lose heart, but should recall to remembrance those statements, that we may always hope for better things, and may believe that, after such calamities and distresses, he will at length bring joy to his Church." *Commentary on Isaiah* 29:19 (Pringle, 333); *CO* 36, 499.

[39] Ibid.

Thus, Calvin believes that the Church undergoes hardship to be made pure of sin so that its members can receive the grace of God.

The reasons Calvin gives for the affliction of the Church require believers to embrace a particular outlook on their hardships. The people of God need to see their struggles as a way in which the Lord brings them correction and fosters humility. However, Calvin recognizes that this is not always the outcome of the suffering of the Church:

> ... the grace of illumination does not belong indiscriminately to all; for, although all have been chastened together, yet not all have had their hearts subdued by affliction, so as truly to become "poor in spirit," or "meek."[40]

Calvin does not perceive a contrast between how those inside and outside of the Church respond to affliction. The "all" in the above text refers to all in the visible Church. His point is that God's "grace of illumination" through affliction belongs only to those who are part of the true Church, that is, those who "have had their hearts subdued by affliction" and have genuinely become poor of spirit.[41]

Calvin's use of the phrase "grace of illumination" refers to the kind of knowledge of God and self that suffering reveals. This knowledge comes from Scripture and results in meekness or poverty of spirit. Thus not everyone who undergoes affliction in the visible Church will emerge with the same results. Only a portion will be subdued by the affliction to become sensible to their own poverty of spirit, thus receiving God's grace of illumination. The mixed results show that only a portion may be considered to be the true Church.[42] Furthermore, it is those who are poor in spirit that God will honor when the Church is restored. Calvin writes:

> ... the restoration of the Church consists in this, that the Lord raises up those who are cast down, and has compassion on the poor. But that purification of the Church, of which we have already spoken, is first necessary; for so long as the Lord does not

---

[40] Ibid.

[41] Ibid.

[42] This idea that though "all" in the Church are chastised, not "all" in the Church are humbled by affliction also appears in Calvin's comments in his commentary on Zeph 3:12; Calvin states: "Let us further know, that men do not profit under God's scourges, except they wholly deny themselves and forget their own power, which they falsely imagine, and recline on him alone. But the Prophet speaks of the elect alone; for we see that many are severely afflicted, and are not softened, nor do they put off their former insolent spirit." Those who are "soften" by the experience of affliction are those who are truly elect in the visible Church ([Pringle, 295–96]; *CO* 44, 67).

execute his judgment against the wicked, and the bad are mixed with the good, so as even to hold the highest place in the Church, everything is soiled and corrupted, God is not worshipped or feared, and even godliness is trampled under feet. When therefore the ungodly are removed or subdued, the Church is restored to its splendor, and the godly, freed from misery and calamities, leap for joy.[43]

The "poor" to whom Calvin refers are those who are poor in spirit as well as those who have suffered in having the material blessing of God removed from either their corporate body or their personal life. These are the ones who "are cast down" and whom "the Lord raises up" in order to restore the Church. The affliction of the Church is necessary to subdue or remove the ungodly. In other words, the judgment of God upon the Church purges the Church of the wicked and corrupt, those who neither worship nor fear God. According to Calvin, these are the members who have invited the judgment of God upon the whole Church. Yet it is only through such hardships and through the removal of the ungodly that the true joy and splendor of the Church might be restored.

Calvin pursues this subject from another perspective in his exegesis of Zeph 3:12–13. Zephaniah was the last of the minor prophets to prophesy before the Babylonian exile. In this passage, Zephaniah lays aside his message of repentance and judgment to exhort the faithful remnant of Israel to be patient as God uses affliction to purify the nation. In verse 12, Calvin observes that God offers a promise to the faithful in the midst of their suffering.[44] He contends that the afflictions of Israel during the Babylonian exile were necessary for God to "provide for the safety of his Church." God's purpose was "to gather for himself a pure and holy Church."[45] Yet because of the moral and spiritual depths to which the people had sunk, it was necessary for God to cut off the majority of them. Calvin explains this divine action in more detail:

---

[43] *Commentary on Isaiah* 29:20 (Pringle, 333–34); *CO* 36, 499.
[44] Calvin's translation of Zeph 3:12 reads: "Et residuum faciam in medio tui populum afflictum et pauperem; et sperabunt in nomine Iehovae" (*Commentary on Zephaniah* 3:12 [Pringle, 293]; *CO* 44, 65). [I will also leave in the midst of you an afflicted and poor people, and they shall trust in the name of the Lord.]
[45] Calvin writes: "Here the Prophet pursues the same subject—that God would provide for the safety of his Church by cutting off the majority of the people, and by reserving a few; for his purpose was to gather for himself a pure and holy Church, as the city had previously been full of uncleanness." *Commentary on Zephaniah* 3:12 (Pringle, 293–94); *CO* 44, 66.

> Zephaniah takes it for granted that pride could not be torn away from their hearts, except they were wholly cast down, and thus made contrite. He then teaches us that as long as they remained whole, they were ever proud, and that hence it was necessary to apply a violent remedy, that they might learn meekness and humility; which he intimates when he says, "that the remnant of the people would be humble and afflicted for if they had become willingly teachable, there would have been no need of so severe a correction. In short, though the faithful lament that God should thus almost annihilate his Church, yet in order that they might not murmur, he shows that this was a necessary remedy. How so? because they would have always conducted themselves arrogantly against God, had they not been afflicted. It was therefore needful for them to be in a manner broken, because they could not be bent. "I will," he says, "make the remnant an afflicted and a poor people."[46]

In Zephaniah's day, the prideful and wicked state of Israel was far from possessing the ability or desire to learn meekness apart from a traumatic experience.[47] This hubris can only be corrected by one thing—by the near annihilation of the Church. Calvin understands this as necessary since "as long as they remained whole, they were ever proud." Thus God applied a violent remedy. Because they could not be bent, God fractured his people to break them of their pride. God re-formed the Church out of the remnant that was left, that is, out of a troubled and poor people. Calvin's teaching on the remnant said that through affliction, God acts to make the visible Church correspond to the invisible and true Church of God.

Toward the end of his exegesis, Calvin focuses on two Hebrew terms Zephaniah uses to speak of those who survived this purifying experience. He observes: "The word, *oni* means humble; but as he adds the word *dal*, or poor, he no doubt shows that the Jews could not be corrected without being stripped of all the materials of their glorying."[48] Thus Calvin recognizes that the Jewish remnant was both poor in spirit [*oni*] and physically poor [*dal*]. He also acknowledged that their humility came at a high price. This result could not be achieved without stripping away all of their earthly possessions. Thus, it may be said that their prideful spirit plunged them deeply into physical poverty, and their physical poverty, in turn,

---

[46] Ibid., (Pringle, 294).

[47] The Church for Calvin includes both Old Testament Israel as well as the New Testament body of believers, which includes Jews and Gentiles. Hence Calvin speaks routinely of the Church in his exegesis of the Old Testament.

[48] Ibid., (Pringle, 294).

awakened them to humility or poverty of spirit. Calvin closes his remarks on this tragic necessity with a summary and an exhortation:

> This verse contains a most useful instruction: for first we are taught that the Church is subdued by the cross, that she may know her pride, which is so innate and so fixed in the hearts of men, that it cannot be removed, except the Lord so to speak roots it out by force. There is then no wonder that the faithful are humbled so much by the Lord, and that the lot of the Church is so contemptible; for if they had more vigor, they would soon, as is often the case, break out into an insolent spirit. So that the Lord may keep his elect under restraint, he subdues and tames them by poverty. In short he exercises them under the cross. This is one thing. We must also notice that later clause, when he says, "They shall trust in the Lord," that is, those who have been reduced to poverty and want. Hence we see for what purpose God deprives us of all earthly trust, and takes away from us every ground of glorying; it is that we may rely only on his favor.[49]

Calvin's comments imply that affliction is necessary to restrain evil in the Church, the sort of evil that manifests itself in pride and rebellion against God. This is the kind of evil that will eventually corrupt the entire Church. Therefore, God reduces the Church to poverty, or "exercises them under the cross," so that the faithful will remain humble and rely on God's favor alone. Here Calvin also seems to suggest that the experience of poverty and affliction is the mark of the true Church. The Church which is "exercised under the cross" is the Church in which the elect are disciplined and subdued to trust in nothing but God's favor. Calvin also implies the opposite, namely, that the Church which is not reduced to the poverty and trials of the cross is a Church that may be in grave spiritual danger, in which "everything is soiled and corrupted."[50]

Calvin's interpretation on Isa 29:19–20 and Zeph 11:12 show that his Christology, expressed through his understanding of the cross, is fundamental to his understanding of the weakness and suffering of the Church. The cross represents God's judgment upon sin. The Church experiences affliction and poverty because the ungodly must be purged from the congregation. The cross sets the pattern for the suffering of the righteous. Just as Christ learned obedience through suffering and poverty, so the elect need to be subdued in order to learn sole dependence upon God. The cross

---

[49] Ibid., (Pringle, 295); *CO* 44, 66–67.
[50] *Commentary on Isaiah* 29:20 (Pringle, 333); *CO* 36, 499.

also represents death and resurrection. When the experience of the cross is laid upon the Church, Calvin acknowledges that sometimes God permits it to be nearly annihilated, such that to all appearances it is dead. Yet this death experience is an occasion for God to raise up a remnant and reform the Church, causing the visible Church to more closely resemble the true Church of God.

The following passage presents yet another reason why the Church suffers affliction. Calvin reads on Isa 40:29–30 as showing that the affliction and poverty of the Church occur ultimately to reveal and magnify the power of God in the lives of the elect.

They Magnify the Power of God: Isaiah 40:29–30

Calvin's exposition of Isa 40:29–30 discusses the nature of God's power and grace to the elect when the Church undergoes affliction and poverty. He observes that the prophet Isaiah chides the Jews for not "having profited more by the doctrine of the law." Calvin adds that the Lord inflicted judgment upon them so that by this reproof, God could prepare them to receive his comfort.[51] Isaiah's prediction that the Jews were about to experience a terrible judgment brought the prophet's attention to the plight of the godly. The weakness and destitution of Israel at the time of the exile opened an opportunity for God's grace and power to be revealed and magnified in the elect.[52] Because the remnant receives this assistance, they may conclude that they enjoy divine favor, and thus will not doubt their salvation. Calvin applies this scenario to his own day:

> It was indeed to the people who were held captive in Babylon that the prophet looked; but we ought also to apply this doctrine to ourselves, that whenever our strength shall fail, and we shall be almost laid low, we may call to remembrance that the Lord stretches out his hand "to the faint," who are overwhelmed by the complete lack of aid. But first, we must feel our faintness and poverty, that the saying of Paul, "The power of God is made perfect in our weakness," we cannot receive seasonable assistance from God.[53]

---

[51] Calvin writes: "for they could not receive it while their minds were occupied with wicked and foolish thoughts. It was therefore necessary first to remove obstructions, and to open up the way for comfort." *Commentary on Isaiah* 40:27 (Pringle, 236); *CO* 37, 27.

[52] Calvin writes: "Because the Jews were at that time weakened and destitute of all strength, he shows that on this account it belongs to God to give assistance to those who were thus debilitated. He therefore magnifies the power of God on this ground, that they may conclude and believe that they ought not to doubt of their salvation so long as they enjoy his favor." *Commentary on Isaiah* 40:29 (Pringle, 237); *CO* 37, 28.

[53] Ibid.

The reason why the Church undergoes affliction and poverty is that "the power of God is made perfect in our weakness." It is only when every last avenue of earthly assistance is closed that it can become fully evident that it is God who sustains and protects his people. Calvin sees this teaching to be as important for his day as it was for those who went through the destruction of Jerusalem and were marched in chains to Babylon.[54]

In verse 30, Calvin shifts his attention to the contrast the prophet makes between the strength of the strongest man and the strength which the Lord provides.[55] He observes that the strength which the Lord provides the elect is not the kind of strength that "easily fails," but rather is a strength that is "invincible."[56] Calvin recognizes that all human ability and strength comes from God. This kind of strength is generally called "human" because, as Calvin notes, "men claim as their own what God has bestowed generally on all."[57] This strength is a result of God's kindness to all nature. Nevertheless this strength is to be distinguished from the special dispensation of grace which God provides to the elect:

> And thus by men's strength he means that which is generally possessed by mankind, and by "God's assistance," he means that by which he peculiarly assists us after our strength has failed; for the Prophet speaks of the grace of God which is commonly called supernatural, and says that it is perpetual, while men can have nothing in themselves but what is fading and transitory; that by this mark [*nota*] he may distinguish between the Church of God and the rest of the world, and between spiritual grace and earthly prosperity.[58]

---

[54] Calvin states in his comments on verse 31: "The Jews who were oppressed by that cruel captivity, had great need of this doctrine; but for us also, during this wretchedly ruinous condition of the Church, it is exceedingly needful." *Commentary on Isaiah* 40:31 (Pringle, 239); *CO* 37, 30.

[55] Isaiah 40:30 reads: "Even the youths shall faint and be weary, and the young men shall fall exhausted" (*RSV*).

[56] Calvin writes: "By this comparison the prophet illustrates more powerfully what he had formerly said, that the strength which God imparts to his elect is invincible and unwearied; for men's strength easily fails, but God's strength never fails." *Commentary on Isaiah* 40:30 (Pringle, 237); *CO* 37, 28–29.

[57] Calvin writes: "It is indeed certain that all the vigor which naturally dwells in us proceeds from God; but since men claim as their own what God has bestowed generally on all, the Prophet thus distinguishes between strength of men which appears to be born with them, and that strength by which God peculiarly supports his elect; for God's kindness, which is diffused throughout all nature is not sufficiently perceived." Ibid., (Pringle, 237–38).

[58] Ibid., (Pringle, 238).

Two observations are readily found in this excerpt. First, Calvin calls the strength God provides the elect in their affliction and poverty the "grace of God." It is a spiritual and a supernatural strength that comes only after one's personal strength has failed. This text confirms what Biéler says regarding Calvin's understanding of the poverty Christ commended in the Sermon on the Mount: Calvin "teaches us that destitution and poverty can be received in faith as a grace."[59] Calvin's comments on Isa 40:30 support the idea that the experience of poverty can have a sacramental dimension for the believer. Wallace explains:

> Calvin can speak in such a way of this communion with Christ and His death which is given through the Cross as to imply that the suffering of the Cross for the Christian has the value of a sacrament. . . . The sufferings of the Church under the Cross have so close a relation to the death of Christ, and to His suffering, that in partaking of these sufferings both the Church and the individual within the Church may be said "to hold fellowship with the sufferings of Christ."[60]

Poverty and suffering are able to strip away false assurances and human securities, thereby drawing people (or the Church) to depend upon divine strength and promises alone and to allow the Holy Spirit to work in their lives.

Secondly, Calvin affirms that this strength may only be recognized by the fact that "it is perpetual" when all else is "fading and transitory." Most significantly, Calvin calls this strength a *nota*, or a "mark" by which one "may distinguish between the Church of God and the rest of the world, and between spiritual grace and earthly prosperity."[61] Calvin's use of language is noteworthy here. By using the term *nota*, Calvin signals to the reader that he speaks about what marks or distinguishes the Church as *true*. He contends that the Church is recognized (or marked) as being of God by the fact that it is perpetual and not transitory. Divine grace sustains the perpetual nature of the Church of God. This mark of the true Church, or the fact that the Church is perpetually sustained by God's grace, is particularly recognizable in settings in which the Church is impoverished or undergoing hardship. Calvin gives two reasons for this conclusion: First, everything else that *appears* to sustain the Church is in fact

---

[59] My translation. Biéler, *Pensée Économique*, 311. "il nous apprend que le dénuement et la pauvreté peuvent être reçus dans la foi comme une grâce."

[60] See Wallace, *Calvin's Doctrine*, 70. See also Biéler, *Pensée Économique*, 311.

[61] *Commentary on Isaiah* 40:30 (Pringle, 238); *CO* 37, 28–29.

transitory is stripped away. Second, the nature of Christ's kingdom, of which the Church is the earthly expression, is marked by poverty and affliction. Therefore, one way that a person recognizes this poor and afflicted remnant as the true Church of God indeed is its perseverance when there is no earthly reason for its continuation. In Calvin's mind, the poverty and afflictions of the Church essentially mark the Church of God as *true*. It is only through the experience of suffering that God's grace may be identified and thus *reveal* the Church as truly belonging to God. When the Church bears the *mark of the kingdom and its king* in its steadfastness through poverty and affliction, this is when the grace of God—that is, what is *spiritual* and *invisible*—can be revealed to human eyes. Thus, trials provide the necessary conditions under which God's grace marks the Church as true through its perpetuity.[62]

The implications of this observation for Calvin's ecclesiology are far from trivial. For Calvin, the marks of the church are the way in which the true church, which is a spiritual body, is made known. By these marks, the invisible "face of the church comes forth and becomes visible to our eyes."[63] In the *Institutes*, Calvin identifies only two marks of the Church, namely "the pure preaching of God's Word and the lawful administration of the sacraments."[64] Calvin's interpretation of Isaiah 40 does not mean that he has a third mark of the Church in his theology.[65] However, call-

---

[62] Calvin is prudent about the way he uses the language of *nota* or "marks" of the Church. In his "Prefatory Letter to King Francis," Calvin writes: "Rather, it [the Church] has quite another mark [*nota*]: namely, the pure preaching of God's Word and the lawful administration of the sacraments" (Calvin, *Institutes*, "Prefatory Address to King Francis" [Battles, 24–25]; OS 3, 24, 2–6). In 4.1.10 of the *Institutes*, when Calvin calls the preaching of the Word and the observance of the sacraments "distinguishing marks of the Church," the Latin term behind the English word "marks" is *symbola* (see *Institutes* 4.1.10 [Battles, 1024]; OS 5,14). At the beginning of paragraph eight, Calvin uses the phrase "Dominus certis notis et quasi symbolis nobis designavit," meaning "the Lord by certain marks and tokens has pointed out to us" how the Church becomes visible (see *Institutes* 4.1.8 [Battles, 1022]; OS 5, 12, 28–29). It is evident that Calvin uses the Latin terms *nota* and *symbola* as synonyms. The definition of the term *nota* is similar to the definition for *symbola* (which is a transliteration of the Greek term συμβολον.) The definition of *symbola* is "a sign or a mark, token, or symbol by which one gives another to understand a thing." *Nota* is defined as a "a sign, a mark or a token" or "a distinguishing mark or feature." See Lewis, *Latin Dictionary*, 1217, 1829.

[63] *Institutes* 4.1.8–9 (Battles, 1023); OS 5, 13:21–27

[64] *Institutes*, "Prefatory Address to King Francis" (Battles, 24–25); OS 3, 24:6

[65] Milner notes that Calvin adds two more marks to his well know marks of correct preaching and hearing of the Word and correct administration of the sacraments in his *Commentary on Acts* 2:42 (Pringle, 126); CO 48, 57–58. These two additional marks "whereby the true Church might be judged," are "fellowship and prayer." Milner goes on to argue that

ing the grace received by the Church a "mark" should signify the central role that faithfulness in suffering has in Calvin's ecclesiology. The issue of Calvin's marks of the Church is beyond the limits of this chapter and will be addressed in more detail at a later point.[66] For now, it is important to note that the poverty and affliction of the Church play an essential role in marking or authenticating the Church as true. Thus, it may be concluded that the perpetuity of the Church under the conditions of poverty and affliction witnesses to those in and out of the Church that the true Church is sustained by the power and grace of God alone.

The Purpose of the Church's Persecution: An Examination of "The Poor State of the Church" in De Scandalis

Background and Definition of Scandals

Evidence of a poor and afflicted Church was all around Calvin. Geneva was flooded year after year with refugees who fled the religious persecutions in France. The flock that Calvin shepherded in Geneva was primarily composed of these poor and displaced refugees. A significant part of his French correspondence was directed toward those who suffered hardship and persecution for their faith.[67] Through letters, Calvin encouraged numerous

---

such remarks "do not throw into question the clear and fixed position taken up by Calvin in the *Institutes*, but they do suggest that he is more concerned with the marks as realities than as abstract criteria" Milner, *Calvin's Doctrine*, 100. This author agrees with Milner on this point. The fact that, in this text, Calvin calls the divine grace that becomes evident in the Church during times of poverty and affliction, a mark of the Church, does not challenge the theological place of the two marks of the Church given in the *Institutes*. However, it shows that Calvin is concerned with being true to the biblical text and to the historical reality in which the Church exists.

[66] A sizable amount of literature in Calvin studies and Reformation research, more than can be reviewed here, concerns this question of what are the marks of the Church and how many there are. Kingdon points out that together with the Augsburg Confession of 1530, and the majority of Lutherans, Calvin (in every edition of his *Institutes*), and Bullinger, stressed two marks of the Church–right preaching and administration of the sacraments; where Bucer, in his work *Scripta duo adversaria D. Bartholomaei Latomi*, published in 1544, added a third–discipline. Later, Peter Martyr Vermigli, John Knox, Pierre Viret and Beza argue for three marks of the Church, though not consistently. Maruyama maintains that Calvin and Bullinger stressed two marks because they saw that discipline comes out of a correct preaching of the Word and administration of the sacraments. Furthermore, there were apologetic reasons. Keeping the marks of the Church to two marks distinguished the position of the Reformers from that of the Annabaptists who included discipline. See Kingdon, "Peter Martyr Vermigli," 199–214; See also Maruyama, *Ecclesiology of Beza*, 24; Milner, *Calvin's Doctrine*, 175.

[67] See Benoit, *Calvin in His Letters*, 49–62.

believers in prison, some of whom were eventually burned at the stake.[68] So when he speaks of the poor and afflicted Church, it must be remembered that he speaks as a French exile ministering to those who left everything to come to Geneva. Calvin was conversant with those Evangelicals "dispersed over Europe, outnumbered, and under constant persecution."[69] This is the general setting for Calvin's treatise *De Scandalis*.[70]

In the treatise itself, Calvin relates the specific reason why he wrote *De Scandalis*: The Gospel was under attack, and the Evangelical Church was caught in the crossfire. The assault came from two sources. One was the "humanist circles who disdained the gospel and believed they were

---

[68] Wallace records a moving letter to Calvin from five of his students of Lyons who had been captured in 1552 by the Henry II army. Calvin was in correspondence with them to encourage them in their faith. After languishing in jail for a year these young men were burned at the stake. See Wallace, *Calvin, Geneva*, 216–18. See also Hughes, *Register*, 191–92.

[69] See Heller, *Conquest of Poverty*, 121; and Oberman, "Pursuit of Happiness," 282. Ganoczy, *Calvin Théologien*, 184ff.

[70] Only a few studies take a serious look at Calvin's treatise *De Scandalis*. Oliver Millet's study examines the treatise for how Calvin translated and adapted his Latin version to the general French reading public. He is more interested in Calvin's literary and rhetorical style than in penetrating the theological issues at hand in the treatise. See Millet, *Calvin*, 787–808. Wulfert de Greef's book, *The Writings of John Calvin*, also provides some brief comments on the treatise that are helpful for understanding its historical background. Another source is the introductory note by Barth and Scheuner, originally published in *Opera Selecta*, v. II, edited by Barth and Niesel, 159, found in Fraser's English translation of Calvin's *Concerning Scandals*, xi. Barth and Scheuner write that due to reports from those who fled to Geneva from France, Calvin "felt constrained to write a tract" about the stumbling blocks the French had to endure for their faith. Calvin wrote Farel in September of 1546 saying that he had begun the book (*CO* 12, 380 n. 826) and by October 2 he wrote Farel again to say that he had laid it aside to work on his *Commentary on Galatians* (*CO* 12, 390 n. 832). Calvin did not resume and complete his work on the treatise until the summer of 1550. See letter to Farel dated August 19, 1550, *CO* 12, 623 n. 1398, in which Calvin explains that the treatise is to be finished in a short time. One fact that may be of importance in Calvin's initial undertaking of this treatise is that he received a letter from François Balduinus (who later came to Geneva and became Calvin's secretary for a time), who wrote from Paris in December of 1545. He urged Calvin to write to the French Churches to console those who are enduring the scandal of being dashed to pieces by their enemies (see *CO* 12, 230 n. 738). The year before Calvin began the treatise, in the vicinity of Rouen (1545), and under King Francis I, Calvin was shocked by the news that a terrible bloodbath of persecution broke out against the Waldenses in which several thousand people were slaughtered. In 1547, Henry II succeeded Francis I. By 1548, he began to persecute the Protestants Christians with greater intensity than what Francis had done. See de Greef, *Writings*, 66. It is hard to say what exactly motivated Calvin to write *De Scandalis*. Yet it is clear that the Evangelical Church in France was experiencing an especially difficult time at the end of the 1540s.

really not learned if they did not mock God."[71] The other was the Roman Catholic circles who wished to harm the cause of the Reformation.[72] Calvin intended *De Scandalis* to fortify the true believers to enable them to endure suffering and to respond to the various arguments brought against the gospel.[73]

Calvin's treatise centers around this question: "how can it be that the teaching of the gospel, which is the one and only way to salvation, [be] constantly bound up with many scandals?" Calvin defines "scandals" as "obstacles of all kinds, whether they divert us from the right direction, or keep us back by being in the way or provide the means for making us fall."[74] He explains that it is the nature of Christ and the gospel, to "remove all obstacles and open up an easy entrance into the kingdom of God for us."[75] Yet he concedes that scandals do arise when people encounter Christ, not because Christ "provides any occasion for stumbling," but because of the "perversity of men."[76] To those who wish to have a gospel and a Christ without scandal, Calvin replies:

> Do they want Christ free from every scandal? Let them invent a new Christ for themselves! For he can be no other Son of God than

---

[71] de Greef, *Writings*, 142.

[72] Ibid. Persecutions in France had been mounting the year before Calvin wrote *De Scandalis*. In April of 1545 Parliament received letters asking that it enforce the edicts against heresy. By May 1545 some Calvinists desecrated some 65 images in the cemetery of St. Maur. They also attacked an image of the Virgin Mary used in processions. This resulted in mass arrests and imprisonments in 1546 (Heller, *Conquest of Poverty*, 22); In December of 1545, François Bauduin wrote Calvin from Paris, urging him to comfort the Evangelicals in France and strengthen them against scandal: "Consolar quoque omnes ecclesias, ne percellantur adversorium improbitate, aut illis scandalis frangantur. Tu es unus inter primos quem Dominos excitat suo classico: in te omnis domus inclinata recumbit" (*CO* 12, 230); Heller, 129–30; See Heller for further background on the emergence and consolidation of Protestantism in France during the years of 1545–1546. Heller, *Conquest of Poverty*, 17–22.

[73] de Greef, *Writings*, 142.

[74] *De Scandalis* (Fraser, 8); *OS* 2, 166.

[75] Ibid., (Fraser, 8–9); *OS* 2, 166. In 1543, Melanchthon published his third and last Latin edition of his *Loci Communes*. In Locus 23 he addresses the topic of "offense" or the Greek word *skandalon*. This demonstrates that Calvin's undertaking of such a treatise on the subject of "scandals" was a common *topus* of the day. Melanchthon defines "scandal" in the following manner: "A thing is called a scandal or a scandalous example when a person becomes worse, or because he is confirmed in his error, or because he imitates a bad example, or because he develops even greater feelings of hatred against the gospel." See Melanchthon, *Loci Communes*, 236; *CR* 21, 1029.

[76] *De Scandalis* (Fraser, 9); *OS* 2, 166.

the one made known in the Scriptures. Or let them at least change men's natures and make the whole world different![77]

Calvin argues that the name of Christ will be bound up with scandals until the end of time, not because this stems from the nature of Christ, but because of the sinfulness of humanity.

This study will analyze a small portion of Calvin's treatise on "scandals." It will probe only the passages in which Calvin speaks about scandal in conjunction with the poverty of the Church. He addresses this subject under what he calls the first class of scandals, those that arise from the nature of the gospel itself.[78]

Persecution and the Ordained Purpose of the Church

Calvin is fully aware that when unconfessed sin encounters the gospel in a believer's life, scandals arise. At the heart of the matter, he sees that Christians succumb to scandals in times of persecution because of their reluctance to follow Christ to the cross and deny their fleshly desires.[79] Calvin exclaims:

> Oh! if we were to grasp the meaning of "Blessed are those who are persecuted for righteousness sake" (Matt 5:10), how easy it would be for us to surmount not merely this particular stumbling block but whatever the world and the flesh inflict upon us! To you persecution is so grievous that you are retreating from Christ. Why? You have no idea how valuable Christ is. Concern for this present life is dragging you away from him, doubtless because you have no taste for the life to come. Avarice is burning you up, doubtless because you do not yet grasp what true riches are. You are intoxicated with ambition because clearly, you have not yet learned to glory in the Lord. Gluttony, sexual lust, displays, or other empty delights lure you because you are still ignorant of that sweetness which the prophet declares is "laid up for them that fear" God (Ps 31:20). Finally, it is not surprising that few Christians are in fact to be found, seeing that there are few who have come to realize that

---

[77] *De Scandalis* (Fraser, 10); *OS* 2, 166.
[78] Calvin delineates three kinds of scandals: The first class of scandals is described as "intrinsic" and arises because these seem to "spring from the gospel itself." The second class of scandals "follow the appearance of the gospel on the scene." These scandals entail things that conflict with the gospel from disturbances to doctrinal errors and impiety. The third class of scandals are called "extrinsic" because they "flow from unrelated sources" outside of the gospel. These scandals involve the slander of Roman Catholics as well as the contention over methods of reform by Protestants. *De Scandalis* (Fraser, 12–14); *OS* 2, 168–70.
[79] Ibid., (Fraser, 26–28); *OS* 2, 177–79.

> Christ is so precious that they regard everything else as so much filth.[80]

It should be remembered that Calvin speaks such words not to a Church which is comfortable and at peace but to a persecuted Church! Calvin is not sympathetic toward those who experience difficulty reconciling their suffering with their faith in Jesus Christ. He holds nothing back from exhorting these believers concerning the heart of the problem. His intention is to use this rebuke to prepare his readers for what he is about to teach them concerning the nature of the afflicted Church.

Calvin claims that the "Church Universal contains in itself far greater grounds for offense" than "the private afflictions of the individual."[81] He introduces the topic of the offensiveness of the Church to bring believers' private afflictions into perspective with the nature and history of the Church. He offers two reasons for the Church's loathsome appearance: First, "it never shines with that splendor, which would enable the minds of men to recognize the kingdom of God," and second, "if ever it succeeds in rising to some modest position, soon afterwards it is either crushed by the violence of tyrants or collapses of its own accord. . . ."[82] Calvin explains that the kingdom of God is different from the kingdoms of this earth. The kingdom of God cannot be recognized in the same way that earthly realms are known. It not only lacks the visible splendor of earthly realms but also is constantly being crushed by violence or hardship. Calvin affords that "true religion [has always been treated] . . . with contempt and abuse" by prideful men such as Cicero who "scoff at the law of God."[83]

The persecuted state of the Church should not be a reason to shrink back "from making a genuine profession of the gospel."[84] People who are concerned with the fact that "we are few in number and also have very little authority–indeed no power" are people who value the wrong things.[85] Calvin continues:

> And certainly, as things are today, there is no need to be surprised if such a deformed state of the Church is frightening them away, but the brilliance that shines in its opponents is blinding their eyes. In truth, the only people who stumble on this stone and the

---

[80] Ibid., (Fraser, 28); *OS* 2, 178–79.

[81] Ibid.; *OS* 2, 179.

[82] Ibid.

[83] Ibid.

[84] Ibid., (Fraser, 29).

[85] Ibid., (Fraser, 28–29); *OS* 2, 179.

only people kept back by this stumbling block are those who do not discern the spiritual kingdom of Christ. For those who allow neither the stable in which Christ was born nor the cross on which He hung to prevent them from giving honor to the king Himself, will not in the least despise the poor condition of His Church [*illi humilem Ecclesiae euis fortunam minime despicient*].[86]

Believers who are driven away from Christ over the "deformed state of the Church" stumble at this point because they fail to recognize an essential reality: the kingdom of Christ is a *spiritual* kingdom, and therefore is marked by physical poverty and affliction. Some are blinded to this truth because they listen to the opponents of the true Church who value splendor and all that shines. Yet from "the stable in which Christ was born ... [to] the cross on which He hung," Christ's earthly life was devoid of splendor because the nature of his kingship was not after the manner of earthly kings. The splendor and wealth of earthly kings symbolizes their earthly power and authority. Christ's poverty, on the other hand, reveals His utter rejection of earthly power and authority, marking His kingship as being spiritual and not of this world.[87] Calvin concludes, therefore, that those who do not take offense at the detestable nature of the stable or the cross "will not in the least despise the poor condition of his Church."

Calvin's Christology clearly directs his ecclesiology. The way Calvin alternates between his observations regarding the poor and afflicted Reformed Church and its parallels in Christ's birth and death shows that his ecclesiology is theologically formed and controlled by his Christology. For Calvin, the Church must always be judged by the two great Christological events, the incarnation and the cross. If the Church does not bear the mark of the poverty Christ demonstrated in His birth, or mirror the afflictions of Christ in His death, the Church should be considered suspect. Thus Calvin describes the kind of Church these people, who wish to divorce the church from scandal, seek: a Church that is "well favored in every way, flourishing with wealth and influence, enjoying unbroken peace . . . ." Yet of such a Church he asks, "will it not have the appearance of an earthly power?" His question goes to the heart of the issue. Calvin ob-

---

[86] Ibid., (Fraser, 29); *OS* 2, 179.
[87] See *Commentary on Zechariah* 9:9 (Pringle, 256); *CO* 44, 272–73: Calvin writes about Christ's kingship; "that he would come poor and riding on an ass. It was indeed designed that there should be a visible symbol of this very thing." And again he states: "that the visible symbol is so suitable that the most ignorant must acknowledge that no other Christ but he who has already appeared is to be expected." See chapter 7 pages 163–64 of this study.

serves: "Accordingly, the spiritual kingdom of Christ will have to be sought elsewhere; and furthermore, the Church will be cut off from its head." Again, Calvin said that the Church is not to be modeled after an earthly power. To pursue power, influence, and wealth is to sever the Church from her Lord.[88] Instead, the Church must witness to a spiritual power, that is, to the power and grace of God through people's lives.[89] Calvin attests to the authenticity of the Church that suffers:

> However, let us remember that the outward aspect of the Church is so contemptible that its beauty may shine within; that it is so tossed about on earth that it may have a permanent dwelling-place in heaven; that it lies so wounded and broken in the eyes of the world that it may stand, vigorous and whole, in the presence of God and his angels; that it is so wretched in the flesh that its happiness may nevertheless be restored for it in the spirit. In the same way, when Christ lay despised in a stable, multitudes of angels were singing his excellences; the star in the heavens was giving proof of his glory; and the Maji from a far off land realized his significance. . . . when the sun failed, it was proclaiming him—hanging on the cross—King of the world; and the open tombs were acknowledging him Lord of death and life. Now, if we see Christ in his own body tormented by the insults of the wicked in their arrogance, crushed by cruel tyranny, exposed to derisive behavior, violently dragged this way and that, do not let us be frightened by any of those things, as if they were unusual. *On the contrary, let us be convinced that the Church has been ordained for this purpose, that as long as it is a sojourner in the world it is to wage war under the perpetual cross.*[90]

For Calvin, the theology of the cross defines the beauty of the true Church. Only when the Church is conformed to the image of Christ, whether at His cradle or in His cross, does the Church shine with splendor in God's presence. Just as with Christ, the physical countenance of the Church can be deceiving. God's standard of beauty is always at odds with the aesthetic values of this world. What appears contemptible to the eye of the flesh is

---

[88] See *Institutes*, "Prefatory Address to King Francis" (Battles, 24–27); *OS* 3, 23–26.

[89] See *Commentary on Isaiah* 40:29 (Pringle, 237); *CO* 37, 28. This text stresses that as long as the Church appears like an earthly power, which enjoys wealth and influence, "the mark" of God's grace and power is obscured. It is only when "men have nothing in themselves," and "after our strength has failed" that God's grace is revealed, enabling one to "distinguish between the Church of God and the rest of the world, and between spiritual grace and earthly prosperity."

[90] Emphasis mine. *De Scandalis* (Fraser, 29–30); *OS* 2, 180.

really beautiful in his eyes. What seems to be wounded and broken is vigorous and whole. If Christ's sufferings hail Him as the promised King and Messiah, as the Lord of heaven and earth, then why should the Church, the expression of God's kingdom on earth, expect to be exempt from this pattern? Therefore, the poverty and affliction of the Church, like that of Christ, mark the Church as the true Church of God. As with Christ, the suffering of the Church enables the Church to testify to a power and grace that is godly and spiritual in nature and not of this world and thereby to shine within.

Calvin draws another important conclusion in this text. He says, "let us be convinced that the Church has been *ordained for this purpose*, that as long as it is a sojourner in the world it is to wage war *under the perpetual cross*."[91] What exactly does Calvin mean by this? What is the "perpetual cross"? Perhaps Calvin elucidates his meaning in a passage from the *Institutes* on the Christian life:

> It is the Heavenly Father's will thus to exercise them so as to put his own children to a definite test. Beginning with Christ, his firstborn, he follows this plan with all his children. For even though that Son was beloved above the rest, and in him the Father's mind was well pleased, yet we see that far from being treated indulgently or softly, to speak the truth, while he dwelt on earth he was not only tried by a *perpetual cross* but his whole life was nothing but a *perpetual cross*. The apostle notes the reason: that it behooved him to learn obedience through what he suffered.[92]

Calvin's phrase "perpetual cross" refers to the suffering through which Christ learned obedience to God the Father and that which we must also learn. It is the process of conforming one's life to the will of God, no matter how costly the sacrifice, just as the literal cross demonstrates of Christ. This is no easy task. In *De Scandalis*, Calvin likens this struggle to "waging war."[93] The expression to "wage war" in this context means to do battle internally and externally against those things which are contrary to the will of God. In particular it means to struggle against the internal desires of the flesh as well as to struggle "against all the assaults of spiritual

---

[91] Emphasis mine. Ibid.
[92] Emphasis mine. *Institutes* 3.8.1 (Battles, 702); *OS* 4, 161. The last part of the quote reads, "ut vere dici queat, non modo *perpetua cruce* exercitatum fuisse, quandiu terram incoluit: sed totam eius vitam nihil aliud fuisse quam *perpetuae crucis* speciem" (emphasis mine).
[93] *De Scandalis* (Fraser, 29–30); *OS* 2, 180.

enemies."[94] Through this conflict, God's grace will purify the Church and conform it to Christ. Thus, according to Calvin, "the ordained purpose of the Church," for as long as it is on earth, is to learn faithfulness and obedience to Christ through the sufferings and afflictions that the cross brings. In this way the Church mirrors Christ and becomes a revelation of the power and grace of God.

The suffering Church, then, not only indicates that it is the true Church of God by revealing God's spiritual power and grace, but, according to Calvin, is essential to God's "ordained purpose" for believers in this world. This is demonstrated by the connection Calvin makes between the contemptible and wretched appearance of the Church and its broken woundedness in this world with the same qualities in the life and death of Jesus Christ. Thus when the Church remains faithful in her suffering, like Christ, and in spite of her wretched appearance to the world, she shines with inner spiritual beauty in the sight of God. Finally, he calls this experience of the suffering Church what it means to "wage war under a perpetual cross." Calvin indicates that the corporate Christian life is always a struggle which believers must recognize as normative for a faithful Church in this world.

Persecution Reveals the Power of God in the Church

Divine and Human Reasons for the Suffering of the Church

Calvin's argument in *De Scandalis* makes a long but important digression. For several pages Calvin methodically outlines an historical overview of the Church's afflictions from the time of the Old Testament saints into the New Testament and continuing through Church history to his own day.[95] Calvin spends time on these details because he desires to show the repeated pattern that God's providence and power are revealed in times

---

[94] See *Institutes* 2.15.4 (Battles, 498); *OS* 3, 475–76. Calvin explains what he means by "waging war under the cross": "We said that we can perceive the force and usefulness of Christ's kingship only when we recognize it to be spiritual. This is clear enough from the fact that, while we must fight throughout life under the cross, our condition is harsh and wretched . . . For this reason we ought to know that the happiness promised us in Christ does not consist in outward advantages—such as being safe from all harm, and abounding with delights such as the flesh commonly longs after . . . Christ enriches his people with all things necessary for the eternal salvation of souls and fortifies them with courage to stand unconquerable against all the assaults of spiritual enemies. From this we infer that he rules—inwardly and outwardly—more for our sake than his."

[95] Fraser entitles this section of *Concerning Scandals* "God's Power Seen in the Church's Troubles." See *De Scandalis* (Fraser, 30–50); *OS* 2, 180–94.

when the Church undergoes affliction. Calvin proposes two reasons why "the Church's condition is very often calamitous and always unstable":[96]

> In the first place, the Lord is showing us in that [in the affliction of the Church] a clear example of his marvelous providence; and secondly, it provides a useful and indeed necessary exercise for putting our faith and our patience to the test. If the Church had been so established and equipped with aids of every kind that it glittered with its riches, it would be no different from any worldly power; and indeed, no one would doubt that it is ruled according to human standards if it had persisted to this very day in the accustomed manner. But when we see that its life has nevertheless endured for so many generations as if through innumerable deaths, we are bound to conclude that it was preserved by the providence of God.[97]

The reasons why the Church suffers affliction and instability according to Calvin are first, to provide a witness of God's providence, and, second, to put the faith and patience of the Church to the test. Calvin lingers on the first point. As in his exegesis of Isa 40:29–30, he explains that if the Church had a prosperous, wealthy, and easy history, observers would not be able to distinguish the Church as an institution from those worldly powers ruled according to human standards. But since the history of the Church is so full of affliction and suffering, Calvin concludes, its existence can only be accredited to the power and providence of God.[98] Calvin also had a pastoral reason for stressing this point. He knows that the Church needs encouragement in its time of persecution. He knows that if the Church can gain confidence in its suffering, it will also have a "fresh heart." He challenges his readers to search the Scriptures for themselves, so that they might learn from the struggles in the past—that "they might realize that the Church has always overcome by suffering." With this encouragement,

---

[96] *De Scandalis* (Fraser, 30); *OS* 2, 180.

[97] Ibid., (Fraser, 30–1); *OS* 2, 180–1.

[98] Calvin's thoughts here parallel what he says in his *Commentary on Isaiah* 40:29–30; namely, the fact that the Church continues to be perpetual even when it is afflicted to the point of near annihilation serves as a mark that the Church is of God and that it is supported by the grace and power of God and not by human strength. See *Commentary on Isaiah* 40:29–30 (Pringle, 237–39); *CO* 37, 28–29 and comments above concerning the same passage. Calvin finished writing his *Commentary on Isaiah* in the summer of 1550, the same year he published *Concerning Scandals*. See Parker, *Old Testament*, 25–26.

God's Spirit can "revive the godly" when they groan "under the severest hardships."[99]

To these two reasons, Calvin adds a third: the Church suffers affliction because of "men's constant revolts from God." Human sinfulness and rebellion have "interrupted the otherwise constant and unimpeded course of his grace."[100] Calvin argues this point starting with the book of Genesis. By the time eight generations had passed from Seth to the time of Noah, human wickedness was such that "the Church had been reduced to eight souls," only to have it reduced by a quarter by the next generation.[101] He demonstrates how this pattern repeats itself over and over again throughout the history of the Church. "After the descendants of Abraham were brought out of Egypt with wonderful power and crossed the Red Sea. . . who would not predict from auspices a perpetual state of blessedness?"[102] He laments that people fell in the desert because they "knew no limit to their sin, until they were destroyed. . . ." Even their children who entered the land knew no stability for six generations "because they were constantly disturbing it by their treacherous fickleness."[103] He describes the episodes of the nation of Israel's suffering for David's sin of taking a national census, the divisions and wars that occurred after Solomon's reign, the struggle of the Babylonian exile, and even the return to the land under Nehemiah. He places the blame for these problems squarely upon the Church at the time. The pattern unfolding in these stories is all too obvious:

> But unless we are reluctant to open our eyes we shall see that in the case of all those to whom God has ever revealed himself, it was only their own fault that when they placed their happiness in their own safety it was short-lived and slight; and we shall also see that they had nobody to blame but themselves for their own wretchedness.[104]

---

[99] *De Scandalis* (Fraser, 31); *OS* 2, 181.

[100] Ibid., (Fraser, 32). When Calvin calls human rebelliousness the "origin" of the Church's affliction, it is probably better to understand that Calvin means this to be the prime reason for the affliction and suffering of the Church. It could also be argued that the first two "reasons for affliction," presented above, are really more purposes of affliction or what God accomplishes through affliction (i.e. providing an example of God's providence and testing the faith of the Church), than reasons for affliction.

[101] Ibid.

[102] Ibid.; *OS* 2, 181–82.

[103] Ibid.; *OS* 2, 182.

[104] Ibid., (Fraser, 34–35); *OS* 2, 183.

As Calvin surveys biblical history, he sees the relationship between unfaithfulness and suffering come to light. The stories of Scripture act as a lens through which Calvin interprets and understands all of history, especially current events. He recounts how, in the early days of the reform movement, "thousands renounced the Pope and eagerly—so it seemed—came over to the side of the gospel."[105] However, he laments that numerous people came over to the side of the reform to be relieved of "superstitious practices," and to have "more freedom to abandon themselves to licentiousness" than to "acknowledge that the teaching of the gospel is truth!"[106] Thus, he concludes that the Church of his day had found itself in the miserable situation that it was in because of its own erroneous ways.

Examples of the Suffering Church Under the Cross

After Calvin establishes the origin of the Church's afflictions, he returns to his primary argument: "that God is known better as the preserver of his Church. . . [through the Church's miseries] . . . than if it had flourished peacefully and happily in the most favorable circumstances."[107] In other words, the miseries of the Church actually serve to reveal God's power and faithfulness. He substantiates this by relating how God preserved the Church from hopelessness and scandal from Seth to the Exodus.[108] He admits that he hardly mentioned a tenth of the stories of God's providence in preserving the Church. Yet the point he did not want his readers to miss is that "the more the Church has been crushed beneath the cross, the more clearly has the power of God shown itself in raising it up again."[109] For Calvin, there is a correlation between the degree of poverty and affliction suffered by the Church and the degree to which the Church reveals the power of God in its preservation. This point is nowhere illustrated more remarkably for Calvin than in the Jews' exile in Babylon:

> After the people had been carried away to Babylon *they were buried like a dead body in a tomb*. . . . they were torn in pieces and the parts scattered in all directions to prevent their coming together again. *There was no longer any worship, no solemn assemblies; in short, the*

---

[105] Ibid., (Fraser, 35); *OS* 2, 183–84.
[106] Ibid., (Fraser, 36); *OS* 2, 184.
[107] Ibid. Calvin's discussion of the history of the Church's suffering extends from *OS* 2, 184–94 (Fraser, 36–50).
[108] Ibid., (Fraser, 36–39); *OS* 2, 184–86.
[109] Ibid., (Fraser, 39–40); *OS* 2, 186–87.

> *name of the "Church" did not survive. . . .* Indeed, cruelty reached such a pitch that it was a capital offense to call upon God.[110]

When afflictions descend upon the Church, the effect is the same as in Christ's crucifixion: burial in a tomb. Suffering buries the faithful; Calvin uses this to mean that they are hidden from the eye. During the exile, none of the external symbols of faith existed for Israel: "There was no longer any worship, no solemn assemblies; in short, the name of the 'Church' did not survive." Just as a dead body loses all signs of life and disappears from sight by being buried in the ground, so it was with the Church during the Babylonian captivity. Nevertheless, Calvin reminds his audience that God brought Daniel and his friends out of slavery into positions of power so that they could help alleviate some of the suffering of the people. "This plainly happened so that it could be a lesson now—that whenever the Church seems to be utterly abandoned it is still the object of God's care."[111] Therefore though the Church may suffer extreme affliction, it will never be neglected by God.[112]

Calvin's reflections on the affliction of the Church in the New Testament are more brief than those of the Old Testament. In comparing the Testaments, however, Calvin draws the following conclusion: God's providential care for the Church during times of affliction are even more recognizable in the New Testament than in the Old.[113] After providing a number of examples, Calvin concludes:

> But in the midst of so many losses, which were not far short of ruinous, yet, the Church never ceased to expand more widely. And that really meant that it was triumphing under the ignominy of the cross. Moreover, anyone who will reflect upon all the circumstances with proper impartiality will acknowledge that among countless deaths there was a continuous sequence of many resurrections.[114]

---

[110] Emphasis mine. Ibid., (Fraser, 42); *OS* 2, 188.

[111] Ibid.

[112] Calvin's text continues to give example after example of how the Church was miserably afflicted and how God continued to preserve and protect it. As he has concluded several times before, he states: "those times give us far clearer evidence of the providence of God in protecting and saving the Church than if it had dwelt with magnificent and glorious triumphs concerning all the nations . . . nevertheless, by the extraordinary providence of God, the fact remains that in the midst of those tempestuous upheavals the Church firmly stood its ground." Ibid., (Fraser, 44); *OS* 2, 190.

[113] Ibid., (Fraser, 45); *OS* 2, 190.

[114] Ibid., (Fraser, 46); *OS* 2, 191.

The mere fact that the Church continued to thrive in the New Testament, something Israel under the Old Covenant never did, demonstrates in Calvin's mind that God's providential care of the Church is even more evident under the rule of Christ. He credits the fact that finally "under the rule of Christ," the Church is "triumphing under the ignominy of the cross"[115] to the reality of God's providence. In other words, Calvin sees that there is a change in how the Church can face suffering and affliction. This is the point he stresses regarding the Church waging war under the cross.

The True Church and Warfare Under the Cross

THE POVERTY AND SUFFERING OF THE TRUE CHURCH

Calvin's apology moves from relating the examples of God's providential care for the Church recorded in the Old and New Testaments to those examples in the history of the Church. Concerning the Roman Empire, Calvin argues that even when it was no longer pagan, the Church had problems with those who continued to persecute true and honest ministers of the Gospel. At this time, the Church possessed a dignity that surpassed that of everything else in the world yet "quite inconsistent with a spectacle of worldly dignity." This dignity which "far surpasses all the glories of the world" comes from the fact that the Church has survived persecution, tyrants, and heretics "with an unconquerable firmness of faith." There is dignity and glory in the preservation of the Church. Calvin is careful to note that this preservation is a result of passing along "the true doctrine of the faith."[116] This comment is probably a reference to the marks of the Church—that is, when the Word of God is rightly preached and heard, and the sacraments are administered according to Christ's institution.[117] Calvin regards the small number of godly people who remained faithful despite their suffering to be a testimony to God's glory and providential power.

This dignity which God lays upon the afflicted Church in Calvin's day, as in times before, is not the kind of dignity "that shines out to bring the heavenly kingdom of God before the eyes of men."[118] To humankind, Calvin points out, the Church's appearance looks much different:

---

[115] Ibid.
[116] Ibid., (Fraser, 47); *OS* 2, 191–92.
[117] *Institutes* 4.1.9 (Battles, 1023); *OS* 5, 13.
[118] *De Scandalis* (Fraser, 47); *OS* 2, 192.

> For when it has been overwhelmed, its enemies, with the title of the chief one himself, and equipped as if with booty, crush it under foot with both cruelty and pride. If anyone has ventured to offer even the slightest resistance to their ungodliness, they are formidable with sword, fire, and tortures of every kind, and leave hardly a place for the true Church in the whole earth.[119]

Calvin makes an important yet now familiar theological point. He calls the afflicted and persecuted Church the "true Church." This recalls his conclusions concerning Isaiah 40:30: that the grace of God is manifested in the afflicted Church by its perseverance and marks the Church as a true Church of God.[120]

Calvin's association between the ideas of the true Church and the Church that is poor and afflicted should not be used as a type of organizing principle that reinterprets the whole nature of Calvin's ecclesiology. In other words, this association should not be understood to mean that congregations *must* be poor and afflicted in order for them to be considered part of the true Church. Rather, this mark of the Church needs to be held in tension with what he wrote concerning the other marks of the Church (right preaching of the Word and a correct administration of the sacraments). A balanced interpretation would be as follows: the true Church of God becomes visible to the eye not only when it rightly preaches the word and administers the sacraments, *but also* when still doing these things it suffers poverty and affliction, even to the point of being extinguished and yet continues to flourish and manifest the grace and power of God to the world. Calvin indicates that when the Church does this, it participates in Christ's kingly office:

> But if it [the true Church] does find a few corners for itself, and it is now attacked with force of arms, now harassed by scoffers, and now tormented by threats and terrors, *it is displaying nothing less than that royal dignity of Christ* that is so greatly commended by the prophets. Certainly when the ungodly, with their threats and terrorizing and their furious raging, however, do not go so far that the Church of God does not stay firm and erect under the humiliation of the cross, why then do we not give great praise to the glory of God for preserving it so marvelously?[121]

---

[119] Ibid.

[120] CO 37, 28–29.

[121] Emphasis mine. *De Scandalis* (Fraser, 47–48); OS 2, 192.

The afflictions of the Church are indeed a mark of the true Church of God because they display nothing less *"than that royal dignity of Christ."* Calvin's theological consistency is demonstrated in his references to Christ's kingship amidst discussion of the suffering church. Just as Christ's poverty marked His kingship as spiritually authentic, such is the way of the Church. The tribulations of the Church are part of the humiliation of the cross in which the Church partakes. They are the way that the Church participates in Christ's kingship. Faithful persistence, enabled by God's grace, testifies to the reality of Christ's sovereign power. This grace of God preserves the church in midst of hardship to "stay firm and erect under the humiliation of the cross," and to ascribe glory and praise to God.[122]

The Critique of the Cross upon the Scandal of the Schmalkaldic War

For the remainder of this selection from his treatise, Calvin reflects on some of the scandalous events which concerned the Church in his day and its need to undergo the discipline of the cross. He marvels at the fact that over the previous thirty years, the Evangelical Church should have been "completely wiped out a hundred times" but instead had been preserved.[123] Reflecting on the most recent events,[124] he states:

> And now, although it breaks the hearts of many people that in less than two years it [the true Church] has been miserably torn in pieces, and its mangled parts are not very far from the lion's jaws, in the end the faithful will perceive that this took place according to God's very good purpose, so that the stretching out of his hand to deliver it might be all the more obvious. For we acknowledge that it is saved by him only when it has been snatched away from death.[125]

Calvin is aware of the severity of the afflictions endured by the Evangelical Church in France. He believes that the reason for their precarious situation was that the faithful will understand that their deliverance is by God's power alone. As indicated previously, this idea depends on Calvin's conviction that God's power alone sustains the perpetual nature of the Church. In this text, he stresses that God's hand in the Church's deliverance (and

---

[122] Ibid.
[123] Ibid., (Fraser, 48).
[124] See n. 130 below.
[125] *De Scandalis* (Fraser, 48); *OS* 2, 192.

thus in the Church's perpetuity) is most obvious when the Church is at the point of death.

Calvin offers one more reason why the Church suffered many afflictions in his day:

> Finally, yet another reason is to be added to this, that it is absolutely essential that our unruly spirit be tamed and subjugated by the discipline of the cross. We see that while the Church flourished with spiritual vigor in the midst of troubles, it has melted away when it has enjoyed peace too much. Today, when the Lord holds us in check with a tight and strict bridle, we see that everywhere nearly all are leading wanton lives. What would happen if they were given the chance to run riot without restriction? When the profession of the gospel held sway far and wide in Germany, and the forces were still complete of those who seemed disposed to support the good cause, and when, confident in this, they undertook that lamentable war, and everything turned out unfavorably. While people's spirits were raised to high hopes for our side, I said publicly on some occasions that more danger threatens us from our own victory than from that of our enemies, and that no disasters are to be feared so much as what I may call a highly triumphal gospel, which would transport us to a state of elation, and indeed today I still do not regret that statement. If the Lord had not been quick to resist their ungodly presumption, the disease would have become almost incurable in the course of time.[126]

Calvin understands that the afflictions and persecutions of the Evangelical Church resulted from God's discipline upon the Church. Calvin takes the depravity of the human heart seriously. He knows that the Church needs to be "tamed and subjugated by the discipline of the cross" because when the Church enjoys too much peace and prosperity, its spiritual life "melts away." Persecuted Evangelicals must not fear danger and disaster, but rather peace and success. A "highly triumphal gospel" is far more able to shipwreck one's faith than any kind of trial the Church may experience.[127]

Calvin does not explain what he means by the phrase "a highly triumphal gospel."[128] He does not use the phrase in the *Institutes* and leaves no clues to its meaning elsewhere in his writings. However, his reference to the "lamentable war" in Germany may provide some understanding

---

[126] Ibid.; *OS* 2, 192–93.

[127] Ibid.

[128] Ibid. The whole sentence reads: "Neque enim tam metuendas esse ullas clades, quam nimis triumphale, ut ita loquar, Evangelium, quod nos ad insolentiam efferret."

of its meaning. A footnote in the Barth-Niesel edition of *Opera Selecta*[129] suggests that this passage probably refers to the events of the Schmalkaldic War (1546–47).[130] If this is correct, the phrase a "highly triumphal gospel" most likely applies to those Protestants who were optimistic that they would defeat Charles V simply because they were Evangelicals and on the side of so-called truth. Calvin warns them in this text that "more danger threatens us from our own victory than from that of our enemies." The phrase "highly triumphal gospel" should probably be interpreted as a practical example of Luther's "theology of glory." A "theology of glory" relishes victory over one's political enemies. It seeks power and privilege through human structures. It is diametrically opposed to suffering and is unable to make sense of it theologically. Calvin sees the hydra that lurks behind this mask. He refuses to support the erroneous belief that just because people are on the side of the truth of the gospel, they will be exempt from defeat and suffering in this world—that is, exempt from bearing the cross. Calvin claims that he spoke out publicly against this "ungodly presumption" (possibly at the outset of the Schmalkaldic War). Even though "everything turned out unfavorably," he states that he does not regret what he said. In the end, it appears, Calvin sees this whole event as a major disgrace to the cause of the Reformation.[131]

The Schmalkaldic War was a scandal to the Protestant Church because of how it divided the Church. German Protestant rulers joined Catholic Charles V in his campaign against Protestant John Frederick, Duke of Saxony, and Philip of Hesse. Calvin was no doubt aware of how Maurice, cousin of John Frederick, had accepted a bribe from Charles V

---

[129] *OS* 2, 192 n. 2.

[130] The Schmalkaldic War was actually a number of skirmishes and truces that spanned the decade of 1546–55. Charles V had aligned most of Protestant Germany to war against two leading Protestant princes, the Elector John Frederick and Philip of Hesse under the justification that he was fighting because these princes breached the peace. Charles managed to bribe John Frederick's cousin, Maurice of Saxony, who was also a Protestant, to betray his cousin and seize Saxony while Frederick was away fighting in the South. Consequently, Charles defeated Frederick and Maurice was made ruler of Saxony. Philip surrendered not long afterward, and both princes were condemned to life in prison. In any case, Calvin saw the whole incident as a scandal to the cause of the Protestant reform. Especially since the defeat of the German Protestants was followed by a program of re-Catholicizing various Protestant cities in the years 1548–50. The city of Constance suffered a military conquest and was forced back into the Catholic Church. Catholic worship was reestablished in Strasbourg, and Bucer was exiled. Protestant worship remained in Strasbourg only after some negotiation.

[131] *De Scandalis* (Fraser, 48); *OS* 2, 192.

to betray John. That incident may be one of the several concerns fueling his exclamation:

> Again by this testing the Lord revealed what sort of character each one had. Haughtily they were all casting the gospel under a shadow. In many places the leading positions were filled by wicked hypocrites.... In one nation we see more impious and sacrilegious defections from Christ in the space of two years than the history of all times and people narrate.[132]

These people did not understand a basic fact of the Christian faith: the way of the cross is a way without compromise. They did not grasp the truth that in its essence following Christ necessarily includes the notion of suffering for what is right. In Calvin's opinion, most of the German nobility did that which was comfortable and politically expedient. They were not committed to the cause of the gospel or to the unity of the Church because this commitment would have entailed making personal sacrifices and suffering under a cross.

On the other hand, Calvin praises those from the ranks of the nobility who chose to defend the cause of the gospel. Most likely referring to the Protestant Prince John Frederick's betrayal, capture, and imprisonment Calvin writes:

> Indeed in others, it has been made plain how faith remains firm and unbroken when hearts are sustained by the power of the Spirit. The heroic magnanimity of the soul which the Lord made plain for all generations to see in one man, who was defeated and a captive, would never have been believed except from such an experience of the cross.[133]

Calvin sees that John's faithfulness in fighting for the cause of the reform and opposing to Charles V was sustained by the power of the Spirit. He also likens John's defeat and humiliation before Charles V to the experience of the cross, a cross that he willingly bore for the sake of the Gospel.

The events surrounding the Schmalkaldic War highlight the concepts he communicates in his treatise concerning the suffering Church. Most notably, he illustrates that the Church can expect to suffer and bear the cross of Christ in this age and that a triumphal gospel has no place next

---

[132] Ibid., (Fraser, 49); *OS* 2, 193.

[133] Ibid. See n. 1 in the Barth-Niesel edition of *Opera Selecta*. These editors contend that Calvin refers here to Duke John Frederick of Saxony's imprisonment. The Duke was imprisoned from 1547–52 (see n. 41 in Fraser, 49).

to the way of the cross. Furthermore, the Schmalkaldic War showed how God uses the threat of suffering to test and reveal the character of the Church. Will the Church choose the way of the gospel and thus the way of the cross? Will the Church choose what is best for its spiritual welfare? Or will the Church choose what is expedient for its own physical or political protection? Hardship and suffering show that true faith is resilient, it remains firm and unbroken in the face of adversity. As demonstrated by the life of Duke John Frederick of Saxony, such faithfulness is enabled by the power and providence of the Spirit. Finally, Calvin closes with a note of encouragement:

> Indeed, we ought always to hold this principle in our minds, that whenever the Church is temporarily oppressed, the very good Father, who exercises an extraordinary care of his own, will never allow it to be overwhelmed and disappear.[134]

Calvin's treatise *De Scandalis* holds one of his finest theological expositions on the nature of the poor and afflicted Church. In it, he defends the integrity of the deformed state of the Church, with his understanding of Christ's poverty as a mark of both His divine kingship and the authenticity of His spiritual kingdom. In fact, Calvin finds the suffering of the Church to be essential to its ordained purpose because the Church's task is "to wage war under the perpetual cross."[135] Calvin argues that the tribulations of the Church mark it as the true Church of God because they display nothing less than the royal dignity of Christ. Calvin uses this language because he finds Christ's royal dignity to be most evident when He went to the cross. Thus Calvin taught when the Church endures suffering, poverty, and hardships it is following Christ and His cross in its truest sense. This ecclesiology has no room for a triumphal gospel which teaches that believers will be free from poverty and affliction.

The final section of this chapter examines the ecclesiology of yet another of Calvin's theological treatises. This treatise is Calvin's "Address to King Francis" in the preface of the *Institutes*. Though it was written early in Calvin's life, it reveals a number of important perspectives on the nature of the Church. In particular, it expresses Calvin's theological understanding of the poverty and afflictions of French Evangelical Christians of his day in a manner consistent with what has been examined previously.

---

[134] *De Scandalis* (Fraser, 50); *OS* 2, 193.
[135] Ibid., (Fraser, 29–30); *OS* 2, 180.

The Nature of the Church in Light of Poverty and Affliction: An Examination of the Prefatory Address to King Francis I

Background and Purpose for the Prefatory Address

Calvin wrote the "Prefatory Address to King Francis I of France" in August of 1535, seven months before he published his first edition of the 1536 *Institutes*.[136] He indicates in the opening sentences of the "Address" that his initial purpose in writing the *Institutes* was catechetical, that is, solely to "transmit certain rudiments by which those who are touched with any zeal for religion might be shaped to true godliness."[137] Calvin had a concern for his French countrymen whom he knew "to be hungering and thirsting for Christ."[138] He acknowledges that after the work progressed, however, he saw the need to write an apology to Francis I, the King of France, to inform him about the kind of doctrine held by the persecuted French Evangelical Church.[139] His hope was that his effort would abate the persecution of the Church. He states: "It is sheer violence that bloody sentences are meted out against this doctrine without a hearing."[140] Calvin wished to provide that hearing for his French countrymen. Thus, he found a two-fold reason for writing the *Institutes*: First, to give instruction to the French Evangelical believers in their faith, and second, to make before the King a confession of the orthodoxy of the French Evangelical Church.[141]

---

[136] Calvin first published the *Institutes* in March 1536, but completed the "Address" to King Francis the previous year on August 23, 1535. See *Institutes* (Battles, 31, note 51) for further details on the erroneous August 1, 1536, dating of the "Address" in the Latin 1539 edition.

[137] *Institutes*, "Prefatory Address to King Francis" (Battles, 9); *OS* 3, 9; Calvin states that he wrote a clear and concise handbook of doctrine to instruct these people in "a good and right understanding of Holy Scripture." See *Institutes*, "Subject Matter of the Present Work" (Battles, 7); *OS* 3, 8.

[138] *Institutes* "Prefatory Address to King Francis" (Battles, 9); *OS* 3, 9.

[139] Calvin needed to write a defense for the French Evangelical Church against its enemies in the French court who considered the French Evangelicals to be Anabaptists who only wish to create an insurrection against the government. See Calvin's Preface to his *Commentary on Psalms* (Pringle, xxxv–xlix); *CO* 31, 13–36; and Willis, "Social Context," 133–53; for a more detailed analysis of the background of the "Preface". See also Ganoczy, *Calvin Théologien*, 184–92, for the historical background on the "Preface" as well as the Church in Calvin's 1536 *Institutes*.

[140] *Institutes*, "Prefatory Address to King Francis" (Battles, 10); *OS* 3, 10.

[141] Ibid., (Battles, 9); *OS* 3, 9. Ford Lewis Battles has a comprehensive study of the historical and literary background of the 1536 *Institutes*, and in particular, the historical and liter-

Though the *Institutes* had this two-fold objective, evidently the purpose of the Prefatory letter itself is primarily apologetic and meant to prepare the King to hear this confession.[142]

Calvin's Plea for the French Evangelical Church
KING FRANCIS' ORDAINED DUTY TO AID THE AFFLICTED CHURCH

In a paragraph of Battles' translation of Calvin's "Preface," entitled a "Plea for the Persecuted Evangelicals," the language of poverty and affliction plays a prominent role in Calvin's apology. He explains that he does not prepare his own personal defense but rather "the common cause of all believers. . . , a cause completely torn and trampled in your realm today, lying as it were utterly forlorn. . . ."[143] He continues:

> . . . certainly our cause lies afflicted. For the ungodly have so far prevailed that Christ's truth [*Christi veritas*], if not driven away, scattered and entirely destroyed, still lies hidden, buried and inglorious. Certainly, the poor little Church [*paupercula vero Ecclesia*] has either been wasted with cruel slaughter or banished into exile, or so overwhelmed by threats and fears that it dare not even open its mouth.[144]

Calvin connects the plight of the gospel in France with the plight of the Evangelical Church in France. The Evangelicals in France were in desperate straits, suffering everything from exile and imprisonment to slaughter. Calvin uses the diminutive form of *pauper* [*paupercula*] to indicate the great disdain the Evangelicals in France endured, adding *vero* [certainly] for further emphasis. However, a larger problem was at hand. Calvin tells the king that "Christ's truth," if not driven away, scattered, and destroyed, "lies hidden, buried and inglorious." By using the phrase *Christi veritas* (Christ's truth), he refers to the truth of the Gospel as it is embodied in the "pure preaching of God's Word and the lawful administration of the sacraments."[145] Clearly, then, due to the persecution of the Church, it could

---

ary background of Calvin's writing of the dedicatory letter to King Francis I. See Battles, introduction to Calvin, *Institutes 1536 Edition*, xvii–lix.

[142] See also Calvin's statement at the end of the prefatory letter; he states that he has "not tried to formulate a defense," but rather meant it as a vehicle "to dispose your mind to give a hearing to the actual presentation of our case." See *Institutes*, "Prefatory Address to King Francis" (Battles, 31); *OS* 3, 30:1–3.

[143] *Institutes*, "Plea for the Persecuted Evangelicals" (Battles, 11); *OS* 3, 11.

[144] Ibid.

[145] *Institutes*, "Prefatory Address to King Francis" (Battles, 24); *OS* 3, 11.

not worship God properly. Thus Calvin said that the gospel "lies hidden, buried and inglorious," in France. Alexandre Ganoczy sees Calvin's connection between the trampling of "truth of Christ" and that of the "poor little Church." However, he does not emphasize that the fate of the church is bound up with the proclamation of the gospel. He chooses instead to stress the way in which false theology veils the truth of Christ. [146] Though a false theology is indeed operative in the persecution of the Reformed Church in France, Calvin's juxtaposition of the fate of the Church with that of Christ strongly suggests that the truth of Christ lies buried (or invisible to the eye) when the Church is "so overwhelmed by threats and fears that it dare not even open its mouth." Calvin presents this charge to the King:

> It will be for you, most serene King, not to close your ears or your mind to such just defense, especially when a very great question is at stake: how God's glory may be kept safe on earth, how God's truth may retain its place of honor, how Christ's kingdom may be kept in good repair among us.[147]

Francis has the responsibility of preserving God's glory in their land, something which, in Calvin's opinion, now lies downtrodden in France. His charge seems to indicate that the "truth of Christ which lies buried and inglorious" is a reference to the pure preaching of God's Word and right administration of the sacraments in the worship of the Churches in France. In Calvin's theology, the only way that God's glory, truth, and kingdom might be proclaimed, lifted up, and made visible among the

---

[146] Concerning this passage Ganoczy writes: "What does Calvin mean by this 'poor little Church'? Is it a new Church opposed to the old? It is clear that there is a parallel between the fate inflicted upon the 'truth of Christ' and that of the 'poor little Church.' The first is 'hidden and buried as shameful,' and the second is 'destroyed,' 'pursued,' and 'overcome with threats and terror.' Although a false theology veils the truth of Christ, it does not at all follow that one truth is opposed to another truth. The same is true for the Church: because false brethren persecute the true sons of the Church, it does not follow that they are establishing themselves as one Church against another... For Calvin there can be only one Church, just as there can be only one truth." Ganoczy, *Young Calvin*, 100–1.

[147] *Institutes*, "Prefatory Address to King Francis" (Battles, 11); *OS* 3, 11. Calvin writes a similar comment in his "Reply to Sadolet": "But the most serious charge of all is that we have attempted to dismember the Bride of Christ... But I tell you that this wound, of which you falsely accuse us, is observed not dimly among yourselves–a wound not only of the Church, but of Christ himself, who is there beheld miserably rent. How can the Church adhere to the safety of Christ when the glory of his justice, and holiness, and wisdom is transferred elsewhere?" See *Calvin: Theological Treatises*, "Reply to Sadolet" (Reid, 255); *OS* 1, 488.

people is through the pure preaching of God's Word and the right administration of the sacraments in worship. After the manner of the Old Testament prophets, Calvin adds a warning to his charge:

> Worthy indeed is this matter for your hearing, worthy of your cognizance, worthy of your royal throne! Indeed, this consideration makes a true king: to recognize himself a minister of God in governing his kingdom. Now, that king who in ruling over his realm does not serve God's glory, exercises not kingly rule but a usurpation. Furthermore, he is deceived who looks for enduring prosperity in his kingdom when it is not ruled by God's scepter, that is, his Holy Word; for the heavenly oracle that proclaims that "where prophecy fails the people are scattered" cannot lie.[148]

Aside from the topic of the relationship between Church and state, one notes a few observations from this passage regarding the role of Francis' kingship which are significant for understanding Calvin's teachings regarding the suffering Church.

Calvin calls King Francis "a minister of God in governing his kingdom." He means that King Francis is responsible for creating favorable conditions for the true worship of God in his realm. If the king will not attend to this duty, his kingdom cannot be said to "serve God's glory" and will be considered "a usurpation." This is a strong statement in the light of the medieval belief that kings rule by divine right. For Calvin, a king's divine right depends upon whether the king fulfills his royal calling to foster the necessary conditions for the true worship of God. Because the "truth of Christ" in the kingdom of France "lies hidden, buried and inglorious," Calvin warns the King that if he does not act to address this situation, his kingdom cannot be considered to be "ruled by God's scepter, that is, his Holy Word," and that it will be in danger of divine judgment for ignoring the prophetic Word. Calvin's use of Prov 29:18, "Where prophecy fails the people are scattered," stresses this point. He warns that if Francis does not work to promote right worship in French Churches, not only will his monarchy fail to prosper, but his kingship and whole realm may be in danger of experiencing an affliction sent from the hand of God.[149]

THE POVERTY OF THE CHRISTIAN LIFE

Calvin understands well that King Francis I may not heed his admonition. After all, who is John Calvin when it comes to procuring an audience

---

[148] *Institutes*, "Prefatory Address to King Francis" (Battles, 11–12); *OS* 3, 11.
[149] Ibid.

with the King of France? Calvin anticipates this problem, writing, "And contempt for our lowliness ought not to dissuade you from this endeavor." Calvin is sensitive to his social location before the King:

> Indeed, we are quite aware of what mean and lowly little men we are [*quam pauperculi simus et abject*]. Before God, of course, we are miserable sinners; in men's eyes most despised—if you will, the off scouring and refuse of the world, or anything viler that can be named. Thus, before God nothing remains for us to boast of, save his mercy, whereby we have been received into hope of eternal salvation through no merit of our own; and before men nothing but our weakness, which even to admit by a nod is to them the greatest dishonor.[150]

Calvin does not miss the opportunity. He uses his low position before the King to illustrate humanity's spiritual position before God. This passage is full of the nouns and adjectives of poverty. He effectively uses the diminutive *pauperculi* both to communicate his own poverty and to denote all of the derision and contempt attributed to it. Just as he and those for whom he speaks appear to be "lowly little men" before the throne of France, so they are also "lowly little men" before the throne of God. In Calvin's mind, to realize that we are "lowly little men" is the only way that we can hope to receive "eternal salvation through no merit of our own." Calvin continues:

> For what is more consonant with faith than to recognize that we are naked of all virtue, in order, to be illumined by him? Lame, to be made straight by him? Weak, to be sustained by him? To take away from us all occasion for glorying, that he alone may stand forth gloriously and we glory in him.[151]

Calvin uses the language of poverty to make a defense of the nature of faith before the King. His point is simple. For us to imagine that we are anything more than needy paupers before God means that there remains in us some cause for boasting. But "take away from us all occasion for glorying," or take away all of the things of this world—what do we have in which to glory? Calvin illustrates the nature of faith: to stand naked, empty, enslaved, blind, lame, and weak before God, meaning that only God stands forth in glory and that we glory in him. Participation in the

---

[150] Ibid., (Battles, 12); *OS* 3, 11–12.
[151] Ibid., (Battles, 13); *OS* 3, 12–13.

kingdom of God requires that we stand before God empty-handed, as spiritually poor. This is the reality of faith.[152]

Calvin's concern in this passage is to target those teachers who believe that such affirmations of spiritual poverty and spiritual inability before God "subvert some blind light of nature, imaginary preparations, free will, and works that merit eternal salvation, and even with their supererogations." Calvin, however, perceives the true heart of the issue: "they cannot bear that the whole praise and glory of all goodness, virtue, righteousness, and wisdom should rest with God."[153]

> . . . to repose in certain expectation of salvation and in whom such treasures are hidden? Here they seize upon us, and cry out that such certainty of trust is not free from arrogance and presumption. But as we ought to presume all things of God; nor are we stripped of vain glory for any other reason than to learn to glory in the Lord.[154]

Humanity stands stripped of any spiritual merit or righteous ability before God. Calvin maintains that any position *other* than this is full of "arrogance and presumption." He exclaims:

> But our doctrine must tower unvanquished above all the glory and above all the might of the world, for it is not of us, but of the living God and his Christ whom the Father has appointed King to rule from sea to sea, and from the rivers even to the ends of the earth."[155]

The doctrine to which Calvin refers is the teaching that humanity comes to God utterly impoverished and dependent upon God's grace alone to be filled. It is the conviction concerning the poverty of humanity and the

---

[152] At the conclusion of his remarks on John 6:29, Calvin states: "Now faith brings nothing to God [*atqui fides nihil ad Deum affert*], but, on the contrary, places man before God as empty and poor [*vacuum et inopem*], that he may be filled with Christ and with his grace. It is, therefore, if we may be allowed the expression, a passive work, to which no reward can be paid, and it bestows on man no other righteousness than that which he receives from Christ" (*Commentary on John* 6:29 [Pringle, 245]; *CO* 47, 141). Calvin uses the language of poverty to delineate the nature of faith in the Christian life. The fact that faith places a person before God as "empty and poor," is theologically significant in the larger setting of Calvin's writings. See also Calvin's comments on Phil 3:9: "for while the law brings works, faith presents man before God as naked, that he may be clothed with the righteousness of Christ." *Commentary on Philippians* 3:9 (Pringle, 98); *CO* 52, 49.

[153] *Institutes*, "Prefatory Address to King Francis" (Battles, 13); *OS* 3, 13.

[154] Ibid.

[155] Ibid., (Battles, 12); *OS* 3, 12.

vast riches and power of God that "must tower unvanquished above all the glory and above all the might of the world." Calvin argues that any doctrine seeking men's glory, not God's, is not true. In fact, the test or "mark of true doctrine" is whether it may be "applied to any other purpose than to glorify the name of the one God."[156] Finally, Calvin's remark about Christ's kingship is strategic. No king tolerates a proud vassal, and Christ is no exception. If Christ led a life of poverty and affliction as a mark of His divine and spiritual kingship, surely those who claim to follow Christ must recognize their spiritual poverty and need for Christ's lordship over them. In other words, Calvin gives a subtle reminder to Francis I as to which King his own knee must bow.

In the text, Calvin returns to the issue that many have suffered greatly for the sake of such a reality, that is, for having "our hope set on the living God."[157] He describes the hardships Evangelicals in France are experiencing:

> For the sake of this hope some of us are shackled with irons, some beaten with rods, some led about as laughingstocks, some proscribed, some most savagely tortured, some forced to flee. All of us are oppressed by poverty, cursed with dire execrations, wounded by slanders, and treated in the most shameful ways.[158]

Though some have suffered severe persecution, Calvin argues that all Evangelicals are subject to physical deprivation and the curses, slander, and overall reproach of others. Thus the Evangelical Church not only maintains its spiritual poverty before God, but also has become despised, oppressed, and impoverished before all humanity. He places the blame for this situation upon priests "at whose nod and will the others are hostile toward us." These men "allow themselves and others to ignore, neglect, and despise the

---

[156] Ibid., (Battles, 17); *OS* 3, 16. Calvin makes this comment on the nature of true doctrine and its marks, in his discussion on the value of miracles. The text reads as follows: "When we hear that they [miracles] were appointed only to seal the truth, shall we employ them to confirm falsehoods? In the first place, it is right to investigate and examine that doctrine which, as the Evangelist says, is superior to miracles. Then, if it is approved, it may rightly be confirmed from miracles. Yet, if one does not tend to seek men's glory but God's, *this* is a mark of true doctrine [*Probae autem doctrinae, authore Christo, isthaec nota est*], as Christ says. Since Christ affirms *this* test of doctrine [*doctrinae probationem*], miracles are wrongly valued that are applied to any other purpose than to glorify the name of the one God." Emphasis mine.

[157] Ibid., (Battles, 14); *OS* 3, 13.

[158] Ibid.; *OS* 3, 13–14. Battles translates *alii proscribuntur* as "some proscribed." This could be better translated as "some deprived of property."

true religion, which has been handed down in the Scriptures"[159] and with contempt call it "'new' and 'of recent birth.'"[160] Yet this doctrine is far from recent birth. Calvin contends that because "it has lain long unknown and buried," this fact "is the fault of man's impiety."[161]

Calvin outlines numerous ways in which the Church buries true religion and true doctrine. In issue after issue, he cites that the Roman Church willfully obscures true religion by transgressing the limits set by its Fathers. For example, it transgresses the boundaries of the Fathers with excessive ceremonies,[162] the refusal to grant believers Christian freedom concerning issues such as diet, monks' living and working arrangements the use of images in worship,[163] use of the Eucharist, formulation of Church law, celibacy of clergy; it refuses to listen to Christ alone and claims that the authority of Scripture depends upon the judgment of the Church, its constant preoccupation with speculative theology, and its esteem for custom and human judgments over the eternal truth of God.[164] Though all of these issues are a great concern for Calvin, one error stands out as being the most fundamental of all. This error pertains to how the Roman Church understood the nature of the Church. Out of this error, all the others derive.

Roman Errors Concerning the Nature of the Church
THE MARKS BY WHICH THE TRUE CHURCH IS KNOWN

In the section which Battles entitles "Errors about the Nature of the Church," Calvin discusses the difference between the ecclesiology of the Evangelical Church and that of the Roman Church. Calvin is not willing to concede to his opponents "that the Church has been lifeless for some time or that we are now in conflict with it."[165] Calvin has two basic claims in this passage: first, that the Church shall exist as long as Christ reigns, and secondly that it shall exist because it is "sustained by his hand, defend-

---

[159] Ibid., (Battles, 14); *OS* 3, 14.
[160] Ibid., (Battles, 14–15).
[161] Ibid., (Battles, 16); *OS* 3, 15.
[162] This study will return to examine this topic in chapter 10.
[163] Good resources on the Reformer's views on images and icons in worship are Eire, *War against the Idols*; and Willis–Watkins, "Second Commandment."
[164] *Institutes*, "Prefatory Address to King Francis" (Battles, 19–23); *OS* 3, 18:15–23:23 passim.
[165] Ibid., (Battles, 24); *OS* 3, 23:23–25.

ed by his protection and is kept safe through his power."[166] Calvin argues that if believers consider this understanding of the Church in contrast to the Roman conception of the Church, they will "have no quarrel" with it.[167] It is important to note that Calvin's argument hinges on the way in which Christ's kingship influences the Church. Christ's reign sustains the Church, and her existence stands as evidence that Christ reigns as king. The balance of Calvin's analysis of the difference between the evangelical and Roman Catholic views of the Church must be understood in light of this point.

In order to assess the problem concerning the nature of Roman ecclesiology, Calvin first compares it with the evangelical perspective:

> But they stray very far from the truth when they do not recognize the Church unless they see it with their very eyes, and try to keep it within limits to which it cannot at all be confined. Our controversy turns on these hinges: first, they contend that the form of the Church is always apparent and observable. Secondly, they set this form in the See of the Roman Church and its hierarchy. We on the contrary, affirm that the Church can exist without any visible appearance, and that its appearance is not contained within that outward magnificence which they foolishly admire. Rather, it has quite another mark: namely, the pure preaching of God's Word and the lawful administration of the sacraments.[168]

According to Calvin, the basic error of Roman ecclesiology is that it confuses what is visible with what is invisible, the spiritual with the physical. It assumes that the marks of the Church reside in the pope and his prelates—institutional offices that are always observable.[169] Furthermore, it contends that the Church is recognized by its "outward magnificence." Such thinking is anathema to Calvin. This is the same error the Jews made concerning Christ's incarnation and crucifixion. The Jews had expected their king to display the outward magnificence and splendor of an earthly ruler. Instead, Christ came as a poor, ordinary peasant whose poverty demonstrated that His kingship was divine and that the kingdom He ruled was spiritual. Since the Church is the expression of Christ's kingdom on earth, it must also bear the signature of Christ's poverty and simplicity. Thus the

---

[166] Ibid.; *OS* 3, 23:25–28. This idea goes back to what Calvin called a mark of the Church in his exegesis of Isa 40:29–30.
[167] Ibid.; *OS* 3, 23:30–31.
[168] Ibid., (Battles, 24–25); *OS* 3, 23:34–24:6.
[169] Cf. Ganoczy, *Young Calvin*, 216–17.

marks of the Church for Calvin are not found in the magnificence of the Church, or in the grandiose manner of the pope and his prelates,[170] but instead in the restrained and spiritual activities of the preaching of God's Word and the correct administration of the sacraments. Though Calvin does not elaborate on this correlation in this passage, it is clear from the context of his thought that his understanding of Christ's kingship is the governing basis out of which his analysis stems.

An important clarification should be emphasized regarding Calvin's understanding of the visibility/invisibility of the Church. As stated above, Calvin's intent in his assertion that the Church may exist without any apparent or visible form is to affirm that the true form of the Church is found in spiritual, not physical realities.[171] This does not mean that he disparages the visible or institutional Church. Rather, this is why he calls the right preaching of the Word of God and the proper administration of the sacraments the "marks of the Church."[172] These are visible or physical marks by which the invisible or spiritual reality of the Church is made manifest to everyone.[173] It is the way a believer may determine that the

---

[170] Kingdon relates that Roman Catholic apologists assembled a considerable number of marks of the true Church to justify their theology and ecclesial structure. They pointed to their numerical superiority, material wealth, and the apostolic succession of their leaders to argue that God's providence had selected their institutions as God's own. Kingdon, "Peter Martyr Vermigli," 199.

[171] As a matter of background, it is important to understand a basic distinction in Calvin's ecclesiology. Calvin recognizes that Scripture oftentimes speaks about the Church in two different ways. Sometimes Scripture uses the term Church to refer to just the elect and the communion of saints throughout time "who are children of God by the grace of adoption and true members of Christ by sanctification of the Holy Spirit." Though this way of speaking about the Church is invisible to human eyes, it is visible to the eyes of God alone. Therefore, this way of speaking about the Church is often referred to by Calvin as the "invisible Church." Other times Scripture uses the term Church to refer to the "whole multitude of men spread over the earth, who profess to worship one God and Christ." Calvin states that it is the form of the Church that is "visible" that can be made known to humanity. However, Calvin admits that in the Church there are "mingled many hypocrites who have nothing of Christ but the name and outward appearance"; nonetheless "we are commanded to revere and keep communion" with it (*Institutes* 4.1.7 [Battles, 1021–22]; *OS* 5, 12). Calvin points out that the Church is known "by certain marks and tokens [*certis notis et quasi symbolis*]." We recognize the Church of God when the "Word of God purely preached and heard and the sacraments administered according to Christ's institution" (*Institutes* 4.1.8–9 [Battles, 1022–23]; *OS* 5, 12–13). See Niesel, *Theology of Calvin*, 191–92; and Neuser, "Calvin's Teaching," 79–95.

[172] Emphasis mine. *Institutes*, 4.1.8–9 (Battles, 1023); *OS* 5, 13:21–27.5

[173] In the *Institutes*, Calvin provides a further explanation his understanding of the visibility of the Church through its marks: "He has, moreover, set off by plainer marks [*notitiam*]

congregation with whom they worship is part of the true church of Christ. Hence, Calvin rejects the Roman notion that the Church is marked by "outward magnificence."[174] Outward splendor and magnificence are the tokens which come from an ecclesiology that deposits the form of the Church in something other than Christ proclaimed in word or sacrament. Therefore, Calvin argues that at times, the Church may exist "*nulla apparente forma.*" Calvin illustrates what he means:

> They rage if the Church cannot always be pointed to with the finger. But among the Jewish people how often was it so deformed that no semblance of it remained? What form do we think it displayed when Elijah complained that he alone was left? How long after Christ's coming was it hidden without form [*quandiu ab adventu Christi deformis latuit*]? How often has it since that time been so oppressed by wars, seditions, and heresies that it did not shine forth at all? If they had lived at that time, would they have believed that any Church existed? But Elijah heard that there still remained seven thousand men who had not bowed the knee before Baal. And we must not doubt that Christ had reigned on earth ever since he ascended into heaven. But if believers had then required some visible form, would they not have straightaway lost courage?[175]

Calvin's argument is straightforward. On numerous occasions throughout the history of the Church, the Church has been so "deformed," or "hidden without form," that no evidence of its existence remained. He particularly refers to Elijah in I Kings 19:10 and 14, where the prophet complains to God that he is the only one left who worships God. God's response to Elijah's complaint established for Calvin that even though there may be no visible indications of the Church's existence, the Church had not van-

---

the knowledge of his very body to us, knowing how necessary it is to our salvation. From this the face of the Church comes forth and becomes visible to our eyes [*emergit conspicua oculis nostris Ecclesiae facies*]. Whenever we see the Word of God purely preached and heard, and the sacraments administered according Christ's institution, there, it is not to be doubted, a Church of God exists" (*Institutes* 4.1.8–9 [Battles, 1023]; *OS* 5, 13, 21–27). Calvin's comments on the marks of the Church are based on the point that the Church is grounded as a spiritual reality and is therefore invisible to the eye. Only when the Word of God is rightly preached and heard, and only when the sacraments are correctly administered according to Christ's institution–only then does the nature of Church—which is invisible to the eye—become visible for all to see. See Hesselink, *Calvin's First Catechism*, 155–61 for a good discussion on the visible and invisible Church and the marks of the Church.

[174] *Institutes*, "Prefatory Address to King Francis" (Battles, 24); *OS* 3, 24:2–4. Calvin's understanding of the problem of pomp, magnificent decorations, and wealth in the Church will be examined in more detail below.

[175] Ibid., (Battles, 25); *OS* 3, 24:6–18.

ished from the earth. Thus, Calvin's point is demonstrated: the true nature and reality of the Church does not reside in what is seen—the papacy and prelates of the Church—but in what is unseen, the grace and power of God.[176] This invisible reality of the true Church is made visible by the marks of "the pure preaching of God's Word and the lawful administration of the sacraments,"[177] which occasionally are hidden and buried when the Church undergoes affliction or becomes disobedient.[178]

Calvin develops this teaching further. He contends that the marks of the Church are not always evident because God removes them from the Church when the Church persists in sin and disobedience:

> Yet what does the world today venerate in its horned bishops but to imagine those whom it sees presiding over renowned cities to be holy prelates of religion? Away, therefore, with such a foolish appraisement! Rather, since the Lord alone knows who are his, let us leave to him the fact that he sometimes removes from men's sight the external signs by which the Church is known. That is, I confess, a dreadful visitation of God upon the earth. But if man's impiety deserves it, why do we strive to oppose God's just vengeance? In such a way the Lord of old punished men's ingratitude. For, because they had refused to obey his truth and had extinguished his light, he allowed their blinded senses to be both deluded by foolish lies and plunged into profound darkness, so that no form of the true Church remained. Meanwhile, he preserved his own children from extinction, though they are scattered and hidden in the midst of these errors and darkness. And this is no marvel: for he knew how to preserve them in the confusion of Babylon, and in the flame of the fiery furnace.[179]

---

[176] See Calvin's statements in ibid., (Battles, 24); *OS* 3, 23:25–30 and 23:34–25:2.

[177] Ibid., (Battles, 24–25); *OS* 3, 24:5–6.

[178] Ganoczy writes: "For Calvin there can be only one Church, just as there can be only one truth. What he suggests here and states more precisely in the *Institutes* is that the true state or form of the Church does not consist in its external structure but in the faithful and Christ-centered life of the elect of God. Not all are elect, not all persons belong to the Church just because they are baptized and bear the name of Christian. Thus it is possible that the persecutors are outside the community of the elect, which for the moment, has been reduced to those who are ready to serve the Lord at any cost. The 'little Church' is then identified with the one and only Church of God. Like divine truth, it can be clouded over or ravaged for a time, but it can never cease to exist or be divided." Ganoczy, *The Young Calvin*, 101.

[179] *Institutes*, "Prefatory Address to King Francis" (Battles, 25–26); *OS* 3, 24: 5–6.

Calvin describes the condition of the visible Church during the Babylonian exile. At this time, the Church was in the midst of a very grave situation. Their disobedience of the truth of God extinguished God's light. Because of man's impiety and refusal to obey the truth, God "removes from men's sight the external signs by which the Church is known. . . ," and allows the people to be "both deluded by foolish lies and plunged into profound darkness so that *no form* of the true Church remains."[180] Calvin used strong language when he wrote that there is "*no form* of the true Church."[181] He means that the Church can no longer be identified by the human senses because the marks of the Church, or the things that reveal the true Church, are no longer present. Stated another way, the true Church has no visible form because the *form* of the true Church is identified by the pure preaching of God's Word and the lawful administration of the sacraments.[182] If the Church is not obedient to these mandates, it extinguishes God's light and is "plunged into profound darkness."

It is important to note what Calvin does not say here. He does not say that no true Church exists even if the marks of the true Church are not visibly observed. He does not say that everyone participating in this corrupted Church are outside the kingdom of God. Calvin knows that some members of the elect may lie hidden in this corrupt Church. He only says that this visible Church no longer bears the form (the marks) of the true Church. This distinction explains why he assures King Francis that the Lord knows and preserves God's children from extinction. Calvin speaks of two different crisis situations in which God preserves the faithful. The first situation has to do with spiritual crisis in the visible Church, such as the one Calvin claims is present in the Roman Church. He explains that God is able to "preserve His own children from extinction, though they are scattered and hidden in the midst of these errors and darkness." Thus, God is able to preserve a faithful remnant in spite of the fact that the Church which is visible to the eye does not bear the external signs by which the Church is known. The second situation is the crisis of a persecuted and afflicted Church, not unlike the situation of the

---

[180] Emphasis mine. Ibid.

[181] Emphasis mine. Though Calvin uses the phrase *Ecclesiae facies* to communicate the idea of the "form of the Church," the phrase is synonymous with Calvin's other expression *Ecclesiae formam* also translated "form of the Church." The fact that Calvin has shifted terms in this passage has no significance given the context of his argument. Compare the above use of *facies* with the following uses of *forma* (Ibid., [Battles, 24–25]; *OS* 3, 23:37–38, 24:1, 3, 4, 6–18).

[182] Ibid.; *OS* 3, 23:34–24:6.

persecuted French Evangelical Church in Calvin's day. He contends that God preserves the faithful remnant when God's justice visits the rebellious Church, as God did during the Babylonian exile, in order to purify and correct God's people. Calvin assures the King that God knows "how to preserve them in the confusion of Babylon, and in the flame of the fiery furnace."[183]

The Problem with the Roman Teaching that the Pope Embodies the Church

Calvin identifies what constitutes the nature of the true Church, comparing it to the Roman understanding, demonstrating from both Scripture and history the indefensibility of the Roman dogma. He shows the King the theological and spiritual problems that arise when the nature of the Church is perceived to be embodied in the institutional and physical dimensions of its existence, that is, in the papal office and its prelates:

> Now I shall point out how dangerous is their desire to have the form of the Church judged by some sort of vain pomp. This I shall sketch rather than explain at length lest I endlessly prolong my discourse. The pontiff of Rome, they say, who occupies the Apostolic See, and those who have been anointed and consecrated bishops by him, provided they are distinguished by miters and crosiers, represent the Church, and must be taken for the Church; therefore they cannot err. Why so? Because, they reply, they are pastors of the Church and have been consecrated by the Lord.[184]

It is reprehensible to Calvin not only that the Pontiff of Rome and the bishops of the Church represent the Church but also to conclude that they are without err simply because they are consecrated by the Lord.[185] Calvin probes this reasoning. Just because some are consecrated by God, this did not keep them from error within or outside their ecclesial offices. Did not the consecrated priest Aaron lead the people of Israel into idolatry and error by fashioning a calf? Did not the 400 prophets deceive Ahab appearing to represent the Lord? Was it not true that in those days there was only one who the king held in contempt named Micaiah, who spoke the truth? Were there not numerous prophets who bore "the

---

[183] Ibid., (Battles, 25–26); OS 3, 24:5–6.

[184] Ibid., (Battles, 26); OS 3, 25:7–14.

[185] Calvin adds in the above text: "provided they [the bishops and the Pope] are distinguished by miters and crosiers." The miter is that hat that the bishops and the pope wear and the crosier is the staff that they hold. Both items are considered marks or symbols of the Church and distinguish their office in the Church.

name and face of the Church," yet opposed Jeremiah? Did God not send Jeremiah alone to prophesy against these men? Finally, Calvin asks, "Was not such pomp manifested in that council where the priests, scribes, and Pharisees assembled to deliberate concerning the execution of Christ?" He exclaims, "Now let them go and cling to this outward mask—making all the prophets of God schismatics, Satan's ministers, conversely, the organs of the Holy Spirit!"[186]

Calvin's anger is justified. He cites example after example of those who appeared to speak for and lead the Church, but either fell into error or became Satan's ministers. He describes these men as those who bore the face of the Church only in the form of a mask.

As if the illustrations from Scripture are not convincing enough, Calvin refers to the incident in which Pope Eugenius IV was deposed by the Council of Basel in 1439 and replaced by Amadeus III (Pope Felix V). Since Pope Eugenius IV never relinquished his claim to the papacy, and indeed influenced Amadeus to abdicate ten years later, Calvin asks the question: "In what region or among what people do they think the Church resided after Eugenius . . . ?"[187] Calvin continues:

> For on what side will they bestow the name of the Church? Will they deny that the council was general, which lacked nothing of outward majesty, was solemnly convoked by two bulls, consecrated by the presiding legate of the Roman see . . . ? Will they admit that Eugenius and all his company, by whom they were consecrated, were schismatic? Let them therefore, either define the form of the Church in other terms, or we will adjudge them. . . . But if it had never been discovered before, they who under that fine title "Church" have for so long superciliously hawked themselves to the world, even though they have been deadly plagues upon the Church, can furnish us with abundant proof that the Church is not bound up with outward pomp.[188]

The Roman position on what constitutes the true form of the Church was seriously challenged by its own history. How can a consecrated pope be deposed if he were not in error? How can a whole council of consecrated bishops be ignored and also excommunicated by a deposed pope if popes and bishops are above error simply because they are recognized to be the marks of the true Church? How can there be two popes unless one is an

---

[186] Ibid.; *OS* 3, 25:14–33.
[187] Ibid.; *OS* 3, 25:34–26:1.
[188] Ibid., (Battles, 27); *OS* 3, 26:14–27.

impostor and unless there is error? Calvin challenges Rome to define the form of the Church another way, or accept that its definition of the form of the Church does not stand up to the test of its own history. Calvin has only one comment for this sort of display—"the Church is not bound up with outward pomp."[189]

Calvin enters into this discussion concerning the error of locating the form of the Church in the Papacy and its prelates and the marks of the true Church, in hopes that King Francis will become a protector of the Evangelical Church in France and be a force of reform in the existing Roman Church. His goal in the "Preface" is to better inform the King as to "how God's glory may be kept safe on earth, how God's truth may retain its place of honor and how Christ's kingdom may be kept in good repair among us."[190] Yet, Calvin is realistic. He knows that King Francis most likely will not be sympathetic to his concerns. At the end of the "Preface" he writes, "Your mind is now indeed turned away and estranged from us, even inflamed, I may add, against us."[191] Calvin reminds the King that if he chooses to listen to the whispers of their enemies, the French Evangelicals will not only be forbidden to speak for themselves but will be persecuted without mercy. The end will be that they will endure "imprisonings, scourgings, rackings, maimings, and burnings":[192]

> Then we will be reduced to the last extremity even as sheep destined for the slaughter. Yet this will happen that "in our patience we may possess our souls;" and may await the strong hand of the Lord, which will surely appear in due season, coming forth armed

---

[189] Ganoczy notes that Calvin could appear to be asserting principle of the "council over the pope" maintained by the conciliarism of John Major or others like him if it was not for the fact that Calvin mentions another famous council, the Sanhedrin that condemned Christ. Quoting Calvin, Ganoczy writes "'Did not such splendor shine forth in that council which the priests, scribes, and Pharisees called, to take counsel together about killing Christ?' This severe judgment concerning the 'external masks' of the councils seems to prove clearly that young Calvin was not influenced by the conciliarism of John Major or of anyone else." Ganoczy, *Young Calvin*, 216–17.

[190] *Institutes*, "Prefatory Address to King Francis" (Battles, 11); *OS* 3, 11.

[191] Ibid., (Battles, 31); *OS* 3, 30:3–4. Calvin was afraid that the revolutionary Anabaptist movement at Münster discredited the Reformation with the French monarchy. In June of 1535, the theocratic Anabaptist town of Münster, replete with polygamy and charismatic prophets, came to a bloody confrontation after a long siege where its inhabitants were slaughtered without mercy. Opponents of the reform movement regarded the innocent French Protestants as being synonymous with the Münster Anabaptists, asserting that evangelical doctrine was a threat to the state. See Balke, *Anabaptist Radicals*, 41–43; and Ozment, *Age of Reform*, 343.

[192] *Institutes*, "Prefatory Address to King Francis" (Battles, 31); *OS* 3, 30:10.

to deliver the poor from their affliction and also to punish their despisers, who now exult with such great assurance.[193]

Calvin knows that King Francis may fail to consider his concerns and those for whom he speaks. Yet he knows that God will not fail: he believes that the strong hand of the Lord will appear in due season. When God comes forth, Calvin assures the King, he will deliver the poor from their affliction and also punish their oppressors. It is as though the King is given a choice. Either he can be used by God to protect the Evangelical Church in France, or he can stand with those who despise the Church and receive divine punishment. Likewise, Calvin says believers have a choice to make. Though they are assured of ultimate deliverance, Calvin prepares them for the reality that they could be destined for a cross, or in his words, "reduced to the last extremity even as sheep destined for the slaughter."

Conclusion

Spiritual and physical poverty and suffering are closely related in Calvin's ecclesiology by way of his Christology. The troubled times in which Calvin wrote and ministered are well known. Evidence of an afflicted Church surrounded Calvin. Geneva swelled with French Protestant refugees. The evangelical congregations that Calvin pastored in Geneva and Strasbourg consisted of the poor, the afflicted, and the displaced. It is not surprising, then, to find the topic of the suffering Church arising periodically in his works. As this study of various passages has repeatedly demonstrated, Calvin saw the suffering and poverty of the church through the lens of Christ's life and death. Just as poverty and affliction mark Christ's kingship as divine and reveal that His kingdom is spiritual, so it is with the Church. Just as the majesty of Christ's kingship is most fully displayed in the midst of his poverty and afflictions on the cross, in Calvin's theology the suffering and persecution of the Church also participates in and reveals Christ's royal dignity. Thus because Calvin sees the Church as the expression of Christ's kingdom on earth, what is true of Christ's kingship must necessarily be true of the Church. The physical sufferings of the Church, then, act to reveal or disclose that which is spiritual, or that which is of God. This is demonstrated in Calvin's writings in the following three ways.

First, he believes the poverty and afflictions of the Church are the way in which God permits the Church to participate in the humiliation of Christ's cross. In essence, physical poverty cultivates spiritual poverty in

[193] Ibid., (Battles, 31); *OS* 3, 30:10–16.

the life of the Church. For Calvin, the cross represents the corruption of the "outward man," the loss of all external blessings such as health, wealth, honors, and friendships. When the Church engages in bearing the cross, its outward life is corrupted because it experiences physical afflictions and impoverishment. In such times, God works to restore the spiritual health or inward man of the Church. Calvin argues that the renovation of the inward man springs out of the decay of the outward man. Though the impoverishment and afflictions of the Church are visible for all to see, the renovation of the inward man, or the restoration of the Church's spiritual health, is invisible. Therefore the physical countenance of the Church can be deceiving. The impoverished and afflicted Church, no mater how frail, is not necessarily a dying Church. Calvin argues that what appears to be broken and wounded may in reality be vigorous and whole. Though the Church may appear to be in visible decay to the eye of the flesh, in reality it may be undergoing an invisible renovation by the work and judgment of God. Where the Church may appear to be impoverished and afflicted, this is fertile ground to develop the Church's spiritual beauty and splendor. Thus, Calvin states that if the stable and the cross are not offensive to believers, they should not also take offense at the poor condition of the Church.

Second, the experience of poverty and affliction, or the bearing of the cross, represents the way in which God conforms the Church to the image of Christ. Here again one notes the relationship between physical impoverishment and recognition of one's spiritual impoverishment. Just as the cross reveals a knowledge of God's righteousness and his judgments against sin, so also do the poverty and affliction of the Church. The sufferings of the Church reveal God's judgments and knowledge of his righteousness in that God uses them to awaken the Church from its sinful slumber, purge the Church of its wickedness, and purify its members. The afflictions of the Church are meant either to break the calloused hearts of the ungodly or to remove them from the congregation altogether. Yet to the godly, the cross brings renewal and resurrection. God uses poverty and suffering to discipline the elect and teach them obedience to Christ. This discipline stimulates spiritual growth and maturity as it prepares the elect for their future glory. Thus, through the experience of the cross, God raises up a faithful remnant that causes the visible Church to correspond more closely to the invisible and true Church of God.

Third, the poverty and afflictions of the Church magnify the power of God by displaying the royal dignity of Christ. Calvin contends that Christ's royal dignity was most fully displayed amidst the poverty and affliction of the cross. Thus, the more that the Church is crushed beneath the cross of suffering, the more God's power is revealed in raising it up again. God's power is displayed because poverty strips away all false assurances, leading the Church to rely solely upon a special dispensation of God's grace. This suggests that the poverty and afflictions of the Church, in Calvin's thought, have a sacramental dimension. When afflictions strip away all physical securities and false assurances, they draw the Church to rest alone upon God's strength and promises. In this way, the Church receives the grace of God. Dependency upon God's grace preserves the Church in the midst of its suffering and provides opportunity for it to ascribe glory to God. God's preservation of the Church in the midst of its afflictions marks the Church as true because it testifies to his power and grace. It demonstrates that the Church will exist as long as Christ reigns.

Calvin maintains that the Church can exist without any visible appearance because the vitality of the Church is not dependent upon what is seen, as in Roman ecclesiology, but rather upon what is unseen. This vitality is dependent upon the invisible grace and power of God. Therefore the experience of the cross plays a critical role in the life of the Church. It marks the true Church as such by driving the Church to depend upon God's grace, thus enabling it to display the royal dignity of Christ. Therefore Calvin teaches that when the Church endures suffering, poverty, and hardships, it follows Christ and participates in His cross. Calvin's ecclesiology has no room for a triumphal gospel which maintains believers will be protected from poverty and affliction. Instead, the true Church of God is constituted by those who follow Christ, and those who follow Christ will be led to the cross. Calvin maintains that being led to the cross is the ordained purpose of the Church while it remains in this world. Just as the afflictions of Christ displayed His royal dignity by marking His kingship as spiritual, so the poverty and afflictions of the Church display Christ's royal dignity by marking it as spiritual, thus revealing it to be the true Church of God.

10
Poverty and Wealth in Calvin's Ecclesiology

THE condition of the afflicted Church examined in chapter 9 comprises a significant part of Calvin's teaching concerning the role of poverty in his ecclesiology. Yet there is another side to this issue. A number of texts show Calvin's critique of luxury, display, pomp, and ceremony in the Church or the Church's use or abuse of its material resources. As it was demonstrated in chapter 9, informing Calvin's thought on these issues is a poor and afflicted Christ. Just as Christ's poverty (and simplicity) acts as an instrument of divine revelation, or as a means by which God chose to reveal to humanity the nature of true spirituality and godliness, so it is with the poverty and simplicity of the Church.

The notion that poverty acts to reveal that which is spiritual or mark that which is of God is supported in this chapter in a number of ways. Calvin delineates the nature of true spiritual worship as being simple and without magnificent pomp or display. Just as Christ came simply and without extravagant show, so the Church needs to proclaim the gospel in like manner. To subject the proclamation of the gospel to extravagant ceremony and display is to obscure the message and to effectively bury Christ. This informs the Church as to its responsibility with its resources. Because Christ is no longer physically present on earth, He is invisibly present with us in His power and grace. Thus, He ordained that worship not be attended by extravagance and pompous display but by ensuring that the physically poor receive what would otherwise be bestowed on Him.

Furthermore, Calvin maintains that the Church has the obligation to minister to the needs of the poor because in them, God places Christ before our eyes. To ignore this duty is paramount to committing sacrilege against the Son of God. Though charity toward the poor does not take the place of worship, Calvin teaches that charity is an outcome of worship, demonstrating the substance of believers' faith by their service to God. This chapter will examine what Calvin says concerning the wealth and poverty of the Church and how it influences its worship and its obligations toward the poor.

Much has been written on Calvin's social and economic thought and the ministry of the Genevan Church toward the poor.[1] Given the large amount of information in Calvin's writings on this topic, the focus of this chapter has to be narrowed considerably. This chapter will not engage the historical context of Geneva, except where relevant, but instead will focus attention upon Calvin's theological thought, which influenced the ministry and worship of the Genevan Church. Only a representative selection of texts will be used to outline Calvin's thought on this issue. This chapter will show how Calvin understands the nature of physical poverty and wealth in the Church from a biblical and theological perspective and how his ideas are consistent with the role of poverty in his Christology. This study seeks to understand how physical poverty or simplicity of life interfaces with Calvin's theology of spiritual poverty and the worship of the Church. It opens by visiting a topic that forms the backdrop of most of Calvin's dealings with physical poverty in his ecclesiology, namely, the dangers of ostentation in the Church.

The Peril of Pomp, Wealth, and Ceremony in the Church

Mary's Anointing of Jesus at Bethany: Matthew 26:10–12 & John 12:7–8

How the Church's misuse of its wealth contributed to the problem of physical poverty and to the degeneration of true worship was an issue of great concern for Calvin.[2] By the High Middle Ages, the affluence of

---

[1] See the Introduction to this study for studies on poor relief in Geneva.

[2] McKee shows how the importance of worship (*pietas*) to Calvin can be seen in the structure of the 1559 edition of the *Institutes*. She writes, "At the beginning of book one, Calvin treats directly the topic of piety, then the doctrine of Scripture . . . and thirdly, true and false worship, before proceeding to a discussion of the Trinity and the Nature of God. Thus the first chapters of the *Institutes* serve as a kind of prolegomenon to the whole of the reformer's "systematic" theology, demonstrating Calvin's conviction that there can be no speech about God—Theology—without actual reverent acknowledgement of God—worship—and no right worship or knowledge except according to God's revealed will." McKee, "Context, Contours, Contents," 175–76.

the Church was evident everywhere. The power and wealth of Rome rivaled that of any secular kingdom. Most bishops lived in palaces, enjoying the luxuries and power of princes. Monasteries were heavily laden with the wealth and estates of their benefactors. Cathedrals filled with painted furniture, ornate sculptures, tapestries, paintings, beautifully carved wood and stone, and embellishments of gold and silver dominated the landscape of every major city in Europe. Worship involved extravagant ceremony and ritual. Calvin recognized that behind all this display, there was a theology fostering it. Given this context, it is not surprising that Calvin uses his theology of a poor and afflicted Christ to ensconce his polemics against Rome and her ecclesiology.

According to Calvin, Mary's anointing of Jesus in Matt 26:10–12 and John 12:7–8 were favorite proof-texts for the legitimization of display in Roman worship. The first observation Calvin makes about this event is its incongruence with Christ's overall life and practice: Christ, "whose whole life was a rule and a pattern of temperance and frugality, now approves of immoderate expense," which appears to be "allied to luxury and superfluous indulgence." Calvin acknowledged, nevertheless, that Christ was pleased by Mary's actions. But Christ's affirmation was not given because "He wished that the same thing be done every day. . . ." For "Christ had had no desire for the use of the ointment." Rather, Calvin believed that Christ's anointing by Mary pleased Him because of the "circumstances in which it happened."[3] Calvin continued:

> Nor have we any reason to doubt that Mary was led by a secret movement of the Spirit to anoint Christ; as it is certain that, whenever the saints were called to any extraordinary performance [*extraordinarius vocatus*], they were led by an unusual movement, so as not to attempt anything without the guidance and authority of God. There was no precept in existence enjoining on Mary this anointing, nor was it necessary that a new law should be laid down for every single action; but as the heavenly calling is the only origin and principle of proper conduct, and as God rejects everything which men undertake at their own suggestion, Mary was directed by the inspiration of the Spirit, so that this duty, which she performed to Christ, was founded on assured confidence.[4]

By using the phrase *extraordinarius vocatus* [extraordinary performance] in this text, Calvin was able to explain a number of difficulties. He could

---

[3] *Commentary on Matthew* 26:10 (Pringle, 188); *CO* 45, 694.
[4] Ibid., (Pringle, 188–89); *CO* 45, 694–95.

uphold Christ's life-pattern of frugality and temperance because Mary's actions were part of a special or extraordinary situation. Mary's actions were not to be interpreted as a rule or example of piety in the Christian life. It was an *extraordinarius vocatus*, or an extraordinary act, in which she was secretly led by the Spirit to anoint Christ. Calvin is even clearer about this issue in his remarks on John 12:7:

> Christ, therefore, does not approve of it as an ordinary service [*ordinarium cultum*], or one which ought to be commonly used in the Church; for if He had intended that an office of this sort should be performed daily, He could have said something else instead of speaking of it as connected with His burial. God certainly does not approve of outward display. Nay, more, perceiving that the mind of man is too prone to carnal observances, He frequently enjoins us to be sober and moderate in the use of them. Those persons, therefore, are absurd interpreters, who infer from Christ's reply, that costly and magnificent worship is pleasing to God; for He rather excuses Mary on the ground that she rendered to Him an extraordinary service [*extraordinarium . . . officium*], which ought not to be regarded as a perpetual rule for the worship of God.[5]

Calvin makes a similar argument concerning Matt 26:11:

> For by saying that the poor will always be in the world, He distinguishes between the ordinary service [*cultum*], which ought to be maintained among believers, and the extraordinary service [*extraordinarius*], which ceased after His ascension to heaven. Do we wish to lay our money properly on true sacrifices? Let us bestow it on the poor, for Christ says that He is not with us, to be served by outward display.[6]

Both texts contrast "ordinary service" [*ordinarius* or *cultus*] and "extraordinary service" [*extraordinarius*] in worship. Calvin explicitly stated in his comments on the John text that Mary's act should not be interpreted as an ordinary service or something used in a common way in the Church. Since Jesus himself connected Mary's actions to His own burial, a one-time event, Calvin concludes that her extravagance is to be regarded as an "extraordinary service" of worship to Jesus Christ. The result? Mary's material display in worshipping Christ cannot be used as a standard rule for encouraging excessive display in the corporate worship of the Church. Calvin's reflections on Matt 26:11 use similar reasoning. He engaged the

---

[5] *Commentary on John* 12:7 (Pringle, 13); *CO* 47, 279.
[6] *Commentary on Matthew* 26:11 (Pringle, 190); *CO* 45, 695.

same distinction between ordinary and extraordinary service, but instead of emphasizing the nature of Mary's extraordinary service to Christ as he does in John 12:7, Calvin chooses to focus upon the nature of the ordinary service of worship in the Church. In his reasoning, the ascension of Christ demonstrates that there is no need for extravagance and therefore no need for an extraordinary service of worship. The task of the Church, then, is to practice its *ordinary service* of worship of Christ, which consists meeting the needs of the poor and not becoming preoccupied with *externis pompis*, or outward display.[7]

This is an important exegetical issue for Calvin. The Roman Church used such as Mary's anointing of Jesus to defend its ostentatious style of worship. Calvin has little patience for those who embrace this position.[8] He warned his readers that this passage "must be carefully weighed" so that "we may not fall into the error of contriving expensive modes of worshiping God, as the Papists do."[9] He believed that the Papists hold to this interpretation for this reason:

> . . . it said that Christ was pleased with being anointed by Mary, [and] they supposed that He took delight in incense, wax tapers, splendid decorations, and pompous exhibitions of that nature. Hence arises the great display which is to be found in their cer-

---

[7] McKee states that Calvin understands a two-fold aspect to worship that comes out of his understanding of the "third use" of the law. First is *pietas* or *officia pietas* which encompasses the duties of devotion, and worship of God as summed up in the first table of the law. The second is *caritas* or *officia caritas*, which include the duties or obligations of loving one's neighbor, and the acts of righteousness and justice as are given in the second table of the law. She writes: "The threads of these two primary expressions of faith are woven throughout Calvin's theology. They are particularly prominent in his exegetical works, evidence of the biblical source of the twofold structure. The tight connection between the service of God and the service of the neighbor is clear. Even when only one of the two is named in a particular biblical passage, for example, in prophetic pericopes attacking the sins of Israel against the poor, widows, and orphans, Calvin always mentions the other in his comment. The worship of God and the love of the neighbor are inextricably interwoven in the doxology of the Christian life" (181).

[8] In Calvin's *Commentary on John* 12:8 ([Pringle, 14–15]; *CO* 47, 279–80) he states, "We must observe what I have already pointed out, that a distinction is here drawn expressly between the extraordinary action of Mary [*extraordinarium Mariae*] and the daily service which is due to Christ. Those persons, therefore, are apes and not imitators, who are desirous to serve Christ by costly and splendid display [*pompis et sumptuoso apparatu*]; as if Christ approved of what was done once, and did not rather forbid that it should be done afterwards."

[9] *Commentary on Matthew* 26:11 (Pringle, 190); *CO* 45, 695.

> emonies; and they do not believe that they will worship God in a proper manner, if they are not immoderate in expense.[10]

Calvin refutes this misreading of the text by appealing to the theological implications of Christ's ascension. Because Christ ascended, said Calvin, He is not served by outward display: "He is present with us by power and spiritual grace; but He is not visibly with us, so as to receive from us earthly honor."[11] According to Calvin, because Christ is no longer "visibly" present with us, the worship of the Church should not be attended by splendid decorations or pompous exhibitions. Instead, Christ's "spiritual" presence by His power and grace necessitates a completely different approach. The physical resources of the Church should rather be used for the benefit of the poor, as a part of Christian worship, as Calvin articulates, the "alms, by which the wants of the poor are relieved, are sacrifices acceptable and of sweet savor, to God, and that any other kind of expense in the worship of God is improperly bestowed."[12] Calvin's conclusions from Matt 26:11 echo this:

> In short, this passage teaches us that, though the Lord commands us to dedicate to Him ourselves and all our property, yet, with respect to Himself, He demands no worship but that which is spiritual, and which is attended by no expense, but rather desires us to bestow on the poor what superstition foolishly expends on the worship of God.[13]

For Calvin, the worship of God is a spiritual event. This means that worship ought to be characterized by restraint with regard to outward display and that any extravagant expense in the worship of God is bestowed in error. The resources of the Church should be directed to relieve the

---

[10] Ibid.

[11] Ibid. That God is Spirit and is spiritually and invisibly present with the Church is the conviction that stands behind Calvin's position that sought to correct the abuse of images in worship. See Willis-Watkins, "Second Commandment," 1–80.

[12] *Commentary on John* 12:8 (Pringle, 15); *CO* 47, 280. Zwingli uses this passage to argue against the use of images in worship. Speaking concerning John 12:8 in his *Commentary on True and False Religion*, Zwingli asserts "For as soon as human reason says, 'thou shalt set up this statue in honor of God or of some Saint,' faith certainly contradicts declaring that all the moneys you expend for the honor of the Lord ought to be converted to the use of the poor." See Zwingli, "[29] Statues and Images," *Commentary*, 331. Calvin, on the other hand, does not specifically target images, but all inordinate and immoderate expenses that are improperly bestowed in worship.

[13] *Commentary on Matthew* 26:11 (Pringle, 190); *CO* 45, 696.

needs of the poor; any other kind of worship, Calvin argues, is foolish and full of superstition.

The central thought running through Calvin's comments on these texts is the spiritual nature of the Church's worship. The theological implication of the ascension, that Christ is no longer physically present on earth, but rather present in His power and grace, had both an aesthetic and an ethical consequence for Calvin. Because Christ cannot personally receive such lavish gifts as He did from Mary, proper worship must be characterized by spiritual, not material, expressions. Therefore Calvin rejects Rome's use of splendid decorations and pompous exhibitions for this reason: proper worship of Christ needs to be attended by no expense. For Calvin, worship should use a simple aesthetic for an ethical reason—this allows the Church's physical resources to be bestowed upon the poor.

The Problem of Pomp and Ceremony in Worship

The word *pompa* is Calvin's favorite term to describe the nature of Roman worship and ceremony. *Pompa* is a transliteration of the Greek word πομπη, literally meaning a solemn procession or a parade. Its Latin use, however, assumed the additional connotation of display, show, and ostentation.[14] Calvin often employs the term *pompa* to characterize Roman ceremony in worship and the ostentation of the Church. In his exegesis of 2 Cor 10:2, he uses the phrase "outward pomp" [*externa pompa*] to define the biblical term "flesh."[15] Addressing Matt 24:2, he joins the term "*pompa*" to the vanity of human senses, luxury, and the pursuit of pleasure.[16] Calvin finds no spiritual value in magnificent ceremony and pomp in Christian worship. He contends that anyone who is "greatly puffed up with worldly wisdom is marvelously captivated by ceremonial spectacles." According to Calvin, deeper investigation into "the rule of piety" shows that "empty pomp" serves "no usefulness" but only "delude[s] the eyes of the spectators . . . [and has] no other use than to benumb the people rather than to teach them."[17]

Calvin's rejection of the elaborate ceremony of Roman Church goes beyond its affront to his sense of piety. His rejection of pomp and pageantry in worship is actually rooted in his Christology. Calvin declared that the use of pomp and ceremony in worship caused the Church to revert to

---

[14] See Lewis, *Elementary Latin Dictionary*, 623.
[15] *Commentary on 2 Corinthians* 10:2 (Pringle, 320); *CO* 50, 114.
[16] *Commentary on Matthew* 24:2 (Pringle, 117); *CO* 45, 649.
[17] *Institutes* 4.10.12 (Battles, 1190); *OS* 5, 174.

the practices of Judaism—the system that preceded the revelation of the gospel of Jesus Christ. In 4.10.14 of the *Institutes*, Calvin writes:

> What shall I say of ceremonies which, with Christ half buried, cause us to return to Jewish symbols? "Our Lord Christ," says Augustine, "has bound the fellowship of the new people together with sacraments, very few in number, very excellent meaning, very easy to observe." How far from this simplicity is that multitude and variety of rites, with which we see the Church entangled today, cannot be fully told.[18]

Not only does pomp and ceremony confine the Church to the use of Jewish symbols, but more alarmingly, they bury Christ! In his *Short Treatise on the Lord's Supper*, Calvin levels a similar criticism: Such "ceremonies borrowed from the Jews [go] beyond the simplicity which the apostles left us [and do not] expound the doctrine [of the Supper] but rather bury it as if the Supper were a kind of magical trick."[19] Clearly, Calvin is concerned with the effects of elaborate ceremony and the embellishment of Roman worship. It leads the church towards superstition and Judaism, while it conceals from the worshipers the simple message of the gospel.

Calvin anticipates the following question: Why would God institute elaborate ceremony, symbolism, and splendorous display in the worship of the Old Covenant if, in the New Covenant, it would be discouraged as something that buried Christ and hindered the gospel? Calvin affirms that the worship of the Old Testament by necessity "took place with much ornament and ceremony," explaining that "the whole was suited to instruct and excite the people to piety."[20] He also observes that the ceremonies used by the Jews are "far from being similar to those now used, which serve no end but the amusement of the people without any advantage."[21] Calvin continues:

> For as He had not then granted such clarity of doctrine, He desired that this people be more exercised in symbols, to compensate them for what they lacked in another direction. But since Jesus Christ was manifested in the flesh, doctrine has been so much the more clarified, and the symbols have been diminished. Since then we have the body, we should relinquish the shadows. For if we are to

---

[18] *Institutes* 4.10.14 (Battles 1191–92); *OS* 5, 175.
[19] *Calvin: Theological Treatises*, "Short Treatise on the Holy Supper" (Reid, 163); *CO* 5, 457.
[20] Ibid., *CO* 5, 455.
[21] Ibid.

return to ceremonies which are abolished, we should repair the veil of the temple, which Jesus Christ rent by his death, and should thus obscure the clarity of the Gospel. Thus we see that such a multitude of ceremonies in the mass is a kind of Judaism, manifestly contrary to Christianity.[22]

While ceremony assisted the people of God in times when they lacked clarity of doctrine, Calvin teaches that such ceremony in his day acts to obscure the clarity of the gospel now that Jesus Christ has been manifested in the flesh. Calvin's reason for rejecting the multitude of ceremonies in the mass is primarily because of the way in which Christ functions as God's definitive revelation. The incarnation of Christ makes the message of the gospel clear. To turn back to the ceremony and symbols of the Old Covenant is to cling to the shadows instead of to the body of Christ itself. In Calvin's words, it is "a kind of Judaism, manifestly contrary to Christianity."[23] Such worship practices not only attempt to repair the veil rent at Christ's death but also overturn an order instituted and sanctioned by Christ.[24]

The Nature of True Worship

Does Calvin's position mean that he rejects the use of *all* ceremony or symbol in Christian worship? He anticipated this question:

> Shall no ceremonies then (you will ask) be given to the ignorant to help them in their inexperience? I do not say that. For I feel that this kind of help is very useful to them. *I only contend that the means used ought to show Christ, not to hide Him.* Therefore, God has given us a few ceremonies, not at all irksome, *to show Christ present.* To the Jews more were given as images *of Christ absent.* He was absent, I say, not in power, but in the means by which

---

[22] Ibid.; *CO* 5, 455–56. Calvin writes: "Ceremonies we have in great measure abolished; but we were compelled to do so, partly because by their multitude they had degenerated into a kind of Judaism, partly because they had filled the minds of the people with superstition and could not possibly remain without greatly obstructing the piety they should have promoted." See *Calvin: Theological Treatises*, "Reply to Sadolet" (Reid, 232); *OS* 1, 467.

[23] *Calvin: Theological Treatises*, "Short Treatise on the Holy Supper," (Reid, 162); *CO* 5, 456. Calvin writes, "But the new worshipers differ from the old in that under Moses the spiritual worship as God was figured and so to speak, enwrapped in many ceremonies; but now that these are abolished, He is worshiped more simply. Accordingly, he who confuses this difference is overturning an order instituted and sanctioned by Christ" (*Institutes* 4.10.14 [Battles, 1192]; *OS* 5, 175).

[24] *Institutes* 4.10.14 (Battles, 1192); *OS* 5, 175.

He might be made known. Accordingly, to keep that means, it is necessary to keep fewness in number, ease in observance, dignity in representation, which also includes clarity.[25]

Calvin's concern is for Reformed worship to maintain its focus, namely, to reveal Christ's presence. Worship is a spiritual event and Calvin understands the power of ceremony and symbol either to facilitate true spiritual worship by showing Christ present or hide Him. Calvin expresses pastoral concern for the unlearned in his congregation and states that he is not opposed to ceremony in and of itself. He allows space for aesthetics to provide the church with "dignity in [the] representation" of its worship. However, He lays down boundaries. He understands that aesthetics may either encourage or hinder the church's encounter with Christ. Proper decorum in worship means that the aesthetic form must never draw attention to itself, but rather should lead one straight to Christ. Calvin judges the aesthetics of ceremony in worship by one criteria only: does it hide Christ, or does it reveal His presence? Does it obscure or bury the gospel, or does it aid in its proclamation?[26]

Calvin offers some ways in which Christian worship may be judged to have a true decorum:

> As a consequence, we shall not say that decorum exists where there is nothing but vain pleasure. We see such an example in the theatrical props that the Papists use in their sacred rites, where nothing appears but the mask of useless elegance and fruitless extravagance. But decorum for us will be something so fitted to the reverence of the sacred mysteries that it may be a suitable exercise for devotion, or at least will serve as an appropriate adornment of the act. And this should not be fruitless but should indicate to believers with how great modesty, piety, and reverence they ought to treat sacred things. Now, ceremonies, to be exercises of piety, ought to lead us straight to Christ.[27]

Calvin does not wish to do away with all ceremony and adornment in worship, but he teaches that they should characterize modesty, piety, and

---

[25] *Institutes* 4.10.14 (Battles, 1192); *OS* 5, 176. In the same text, Calvin states: "I reply, that we are not unmindful of what is owed to the infirmity of the brethren; but we object, on the contrary, that this is not the way to take care of the weak—to overwhelm them with great heaps of ceremonies."

[26] Speaking of ceremonies, Calvin writes: "Still we have retained those which seemed sufficient for the circumstances of the times." See *Calvin: Theological Treatises*, "Reply to Sadolet" (Reid, 232); *OS* 1, 467.

[27] *Institutes* 4.10.29 (Battles, 1206–7); OS 5, 191.

reverence. Most importantly, they should foster a piety that leads a people to Christ. Anything else, in Calvin's opinion, can be considered "vain pleasure," a "mask of useless elegance," or "theatrical props."

Though Calvin states that he is not against ceremonies which exercise people in piety, one must recall that the ceremonies he has in mind are primarily the Lord's Supper and baptism. When Calvin wrote in the *Institutes* that "God has given us a few ceremonies . . . to show Christ present,"[28] he is referring to the sacraments. For Calvin, the Lord's Supper and baptism recall the way in which Christ was and is present with His Church. Both ceremonies use humble, simple, common elements such as bread, wine, and water. Calvin reflects on the connection between the Word of God incarnate and the word of God proclaimed in the sacraments when he pondered Gabriel's words in Luke 2:12, "And this shall be a sign to you":

> This method of proceeding, which might appear, to the view of men, absurd and almost ridiculous, the Lord pursues toward us every day. Sending down to us from heaven the word of the Gospel, he enjoins us to embrace Christ crucified, and holds out to us signs in earthly and fading elements, which raise us to the glory of a blessed immortality. Having promised to us spiritual righteousness, he places before our eyes a little water: by a small portion of bread and wine, he seals the eternal life of the soul. But if the stable gave no offence whatever to the shepherds, so as to prevent them from going to Christ to obtain salvation, or from yielding to his authority, while he was yet a child; no sign, however mean in itself, ought to hide his glory from our view, or prevent us from offering him lowly adoration, now that he has ascended to heaven, and sits at the right hand of the Father.[29]

The Word of God incarnate in the Christ child and the word of God proclaimed through "a little water [and] by a small portion of bread and wine" have much in common. Both have a simplicity in appearance and a sense of absurdity and ridiculousness. Both appear mean in themselves and have the ability to hide God's glory from our view. But truly the incarnation and sacraments are endowed with the presence of God, the power to "raise us up to the glory of a blessed state." Calvin sees the instruments of revelation God chose in both cases correspond to a theology of the cross which

---

[28] Ibid., 4.10.14 (Battles, 1192); *OS* 5, 176. Calvin also states: "I reply, that we are not unmindful of what is owed to the infirmity of the brethren; but we object, on the contrary, that this is not the way to take care of the weak—to overwhelm them with great heaps of ceremonies" (*Institutes* 4.10.14 [Battles, 1192]; *OS* 5, 176).

[29] *Commentary on Luke* 2:12 (Pringle, 118); *CO* 45, 75–76.

offensively presents itself as a foolish affront to a theology of glory. These are the ceremonies appropriate for true Christian worship, symbols which express the character of God's revelation in Christ. One finds Calvin's conclusion to the matter in the *Institutes* to be fitting: "It is certain that all ceremonies are corrupt and harmful unless through them men are led to Christ."[30]

Calvin's critique of elaborate ceremony and pomp in the Church is consistent with his understanding that the true nature of the Church is invisible. As previously noted, when Calvin speaks of the Church's nature as being primarily invisible, he meant that the true nature of the Church consists in what is spiritual and not in what is carnal. Thus, the symbols and customs of the Church must also reflect this distinction. Only when the Word of God is rightly preached and heard and the sacraments are correctly administered according to Christ's institution does the spiritual nature of the invisible Church become visible. This is why Calvin calls the right preaching of the Word of God and the proper administration of the sacraments the marks of the Church and also the reason for his outcry against pompous displays of elaborate ceremony in the Church. Performed in the Church, they obscure the gospel, and therefore bury the revelation of Christ. These practices captivate the carnal senses of people and hinder their ability to perceive the invisible reality before them. However, when worship is conducted free of flamboyance and magnificent display, and the Word is rightly preached and the sacraments are administered in simplicity, then the gospel is revealed and Christ is made known.

The idea that Christian worship needs to be simple and unadorned so as to clearly communicate the gospel of Jesus Christ informed Calvin's understanding of the role the concept of poverty played in his ecclesiology. In his critique of Roman worship practices, Calvin joins together the ideas of simplicity in worship and the clarity of the revelation of Christ in the gospel. He shows that this association should characterize the whole of Christian worship as an exercise of piety which is void of external pomp, extravagant excesses, and worldly splendor. The connection between the simplicity of worship and clarity of the revelation of Christ in the gospel in turn informs Calvin's ecclesiology as to the nature of the true splendor of the Church.

---

[30] *Institutes* 4.10.15 (Battles 1193); *OS* 5, 177.

The True Splendor of the Church: Isaiah 49:18

Calvin's conviction that the nature of Christian worship needs to be simple and unadorned so as not to obscure the message of the gospel is fundamental to his understanding of the true ornament and splendor of the Church. Commenting on Isa 49:18,[31] he identified the "true ornament of the Church . . . [to be] a great number of children, who are brought to her by faith and guided by the Spirit of God." Calvin declares, "This is the true splendor; this is the glory of the Church, which must be filthy and ugly, ragged, and mangled, if she have not these ornaments."[32] In the same section, he compares this understanding of the true splendor of the Church to Roman worship practices:

> Hence we see how well the Papists understand what is the true manner in which the Church ought to be adorned; for their whole attention is given to painted tables, to statues, to fine buildings, to gold, precious stones, and costly garments; that is, they give their whole attention to puppets, like children. But the true dignity of the Church is internal, so far as it consists of the gifts of the Holy Spirit, and of progressive faith and piety. Hence it follows, that she is richly provided with her ornaments, when the people, joined together by faith, are gathered into her bosom, to worship God in a proper manner.[33]

In Calvin's theology, the true manner in which the Church ought to be adorned concerns spiritual reality and not what is carnal. The proper adornments of the Church pertain to whether many children are being brought to faith in God by the power if the Spirit and whether the people of God are worshiping God in a proper manner, consistent with the gifts of the Spirit and not simply with costly furnishings.

Calvin's argument is established on the idea that the nature of the Church is grounded in what is invisible and spiritual, not on what is physical or carnal. This means that the Church becomes manifest in the world via its marks when it engages in true worship of God. Therefore, Calvin has little patience for the obsession with "painted tables, statues, fine buildings, gold, precious stones, and costly garments" in the practice of Roman worship. Such priorities not only demonstrate how little

---

[31] "Lift up your eyes round about and see; they all gather, they come to you. As I live says the Lord, you shall put them all on as an ornament, you shall bind them on as a bride does" (*RSV*).
[32] *Commentary on Isaiah* 49:18 (Pringle, 34); *CO* 37, 207.
[33] *Commentary on Isaiah* 49:18 (Pringle, 34); *CO* 37, 207.

the Papists understand the true splendor of the Church, but they are also another manifestation of the fact that "they contend that the form of the Church is always apparent and observable."[34] Because the Roman Church has an ecclesiology which asserts that the form of the Church is always apparent and observable and because the form of the Church is embodied in the Papacy and the Church's hierarchy, it follows that these offices represent the heavenly glory and splendor of the Church. The result of such doctrine is for the Church to be endowed with magnificent buildings, lavish garments, and splendorous adornments. On the contrary, if a person maintains that the form of the Church is invisible and spiritual and that the Church may only become visible through the simple ceremonies of the sacraments (that is, the marks of the Church), then the valued ornaments of the Church will not be those of earthly treasures but instead of a "people, joined together by faith, [who] are gathered into her bosom, to worship God in a proper manner."[35]

In summary, Calvin's Christology influenced his ecclesiology concerning the nature of the Church's material existence and how this directs the spiritual worship of the Church. He believes that proper worship of Christ is evidenced by what is spiritual, not by what is physical. Thus, Calvin rejects the outward display of Roman worship for its pompous and extravagant exhibitions. He regards pomp and most ceremony to have no redeeming value in Christian worship. They serve only to captivate people's superstitions and carnal senses. Calvin rejects the excesses of ornamentation and ritual in the Church because they turn the people of God back to Jewish symbols and thereby obscure the Gospel. Costly displays such as Mary's anointing of Jesus' feet are no longer appropriate because Christ is not physically present with His Church, but instead, is present spiritually through His grace and power. God is worshiped in spirit and in truth which has nothing to do with inordinate embellishment. Thus, true worship, according to Calvin, is marked by simplicity. It employs the simple elements found in the waters of baptism and the wine and bread of the Lord's Supper. These elements reveal the presence of Christ within His Church and do not hide Him under heaps of elaborate ceremony and pomp. The true splendor of the Church, then, lies not in its physical beauty and costly furnishings but in the spiritual ornaments of its many children who follow the guidance of the Holy Spirit and who worship God in a proper manner.

---

[34] *Institutes*, "Prefatory Address to King Francis" (Battles, 24–25); *OS* 3, 23:34–24:6.
[35] *Commentary on Isaiah* 49:18 (Pringle, 34); *CO* 37, 207.

The consequence of an ecclesiology which teaches that the form of the Church is always apparent and observable is two fold: first, it means that the resources of the Church will be used for costly furnishings and magnificent buildings in order to display the heavenly glory and the splendor befitting Christ's kingdom on earth; second, it means that the needs of the poor will be neglected. The following section will examine Calvin's arguments against this abuse of wealth in the Church. Looking particularly at the abuse of ecclesial resources perpetrated by those in the ministry, Calvin uses examples from the Fathers to show the error of this practice and the necessity for the Church to attend to the needs of the destitute.

The Pomp of the Church and the Plundering of the Poor

Poverty and the Abuse of Church Property

THE ANCIENT CHURCH'S MINISTRY TO THE POOR

In the *Institutes*, Calvin outlines how the Church had distributed its resources to the poor early in its history. He explains that at first, the administration of the Church's wealth was a "free and voluntary" exercise because the "bishops and deacons were faithful of their own free will, and integrity of conscience and innocence of life stood in place of laws."[36] Then, because of greed and mismanagement, the Church sought to establish canons that "divided the income of the Church into four parts: one for clergy, another for the poor, a third for the repair of Churches and other buildings, a fourth for the poor, both foreign and indigenous."[37] Calvin writes that there were some other canons which assigned the final part to the bishop. These monies allocated to the bishop were not meant to be his private income, but according to the writer Gelasius, were rather to be bestowed "upon prisoners and wayfarers."[38] Calvin supports this argument with a quote from Gregory:

> It is the custom of the apostolic see to command the bishop, once ordained, to divide into four portions all the revenue that comes in: that is, one for the bishop and his household, for hospitality,

---

[36] *Institutes* 4.4.7 (Battles, 1074); *OS* 5, 63.

[37] Ibid., (Battles, 1074–75); *OS* 5, 63–64; Bucer also states, "In former times, a fourth part of all the assets of the churches which came from the property or the gifts and offerings of the faithful was set aside for the poor." Bucer, *De Regno Christi*, 310; See *Corpus Iuris Canonici* II, c. XII, 9 as quoted in Bucer, *De Regino Christi*, 310.

[38] *Institutes* 4.4.7 (Battles, 1075); *OS* 5, 64.

and maintenance; another for the clergy; a third for the poor; and a fourth for the repair of churches.[39]

Calvin draws the following conclusion:

> Therefore, the bishop was not allowed to take anything for his own use, except what was sufficient for moderate and frugal food and clothing. If anyone began to go to excess, either in luxury, or ostentation and pomp, he was reprimanded at once by his colleagues; if he did not obey, he was deprived of his office.[40]

Calvin cites the practices of the early Church Fathers to demonstrate the integrity with which they administered the resources of the Church and the kind of discipline that all were expected to uphold. The office of bishop was not to be a place for private gain. It was meant to meet the needs of the Church—especially the poor. Pomp, luxury, and excess were repudiated for a simple, frugal life.

Calvin argues that even though over the years the Church continued to grow more wealthy, the value of moderation was kept intact, and money was regularly distributed to the poor whenever a need arose. In fact, when famine gripped Jerusalem and the surrounding area, Cyril sold the vessels and vestments of the Church and spent the money to relieve the needs of the poor. When famine seized Persia, Acacius, Bishop of Amida, stated, "Our God needs neither plates nor cups, for He neither eats nor drinks." Bishop Acacius then melted down the sacred vessels "to obtain both food and the price of ransom for the pitiable folk." Calvin also recalls how Jerome criticized "the excessive splendor of churches" and praised Exuperius, Bishop of Toulouse, "who carried the Lord's body in a wicker basket and His blood in a glass vessel, but suffered no poor man to hunger."[41] Calvin also appealed to Bishop Ambrose, who gave the following statement when he was confronted by the Arians for using the sacred vessels in order to ransom prisoners:

> He who sent out the apostles without gold also gathers churches without gold. The Church has gold not to keep but to pay out, and to relieve distress. What need to keep what helps not? Or are we ignorant of how much gold and silver the Assyrians carted off from the Temple of the Lord? Would it not be better for the priest to melt it to sustain the poor, if other aid is lacking, than for a sac-

---

[39] Ibid. Battles notes that Calvin takes this passage from a letter by Gregory I.
[40] Ibid.
[41] Ibid.

rilegious enemy to bear it away? Will not the Lord say, 'Why have you allowed so many needy to die of hunger? Surely you had gold with which to minister sustenance. Why were so many prisoners carried off and not ransomed? Why were so many killed by the enemy? It were better for you to preserve vessels of living men than of metals.' To these you cannot give a reply, for what would you say? I was afraid lest the temple of God lack ornament.' He would reply: 'The sacraments do not require gold, nor do those things please with gold that are not bought with gold. The ornament of the sacraments is the ransom of prisoners.'"[42]

Calvin argues that the early Church Fathers had a clear understanding of how the resources of the Church were to be used. Though many of the Church buildings by that time had become ornate places of worship, the bishops did not hesitate to strip them of their adornment and treasures in order to help the poor. Quoting Ambrose again, Calvin concludes, "'Whatever, then the Church had was for the support of the needy.' Likewise, 'The bishop had nothing that did not belong to the poor.'"[43]

The Roman Church's Neglect of the Poor

The way in which the Roman Church handled the needs of the poor in Calvin's day was much different than in the day of the Fathers. He laments that "all these ancient customs which we have set forth here have not only been disturbed but completely erased and hidden."[44] Calvin contends that the whole purpose of the diaconate, which is to care for the poor, has been disregarded. The bishops and presbyters have seized the greater part of the distribution for themselves and have grown rich. They ignore the fact that half of Church revenue rightfully belongs to the poor. Calvin contends that even the revenues assigned to building maintenance "ought to be made available to the poor in time of need."[45] He states, "So far are they from taking due care of living temples that they would rather let many thousands of the poor die of hunger than break the smallest cup or cruet to relieve their need."[46] Calvin held nothing back in his judgment against the depravity of these Church leaders:

---

[42] *Institutes* 4.4.8 (Battles, 1076); *OS* 5, 65. Battles's note says that this quote came from Ambrose, *On the Duties of the Clergy*, II.xxviii.
[43] Ibid.
[44] Ibid., 4.5.16 (Battles, 1098); *OS* 5, 86.
[45] Ibid.; *OS* 5, 87.
[46] Ibid., (Battles, 1100); *OS* 5, 88.

> If they had one spark of the fear of God in their hearts, I ask, would they bear the thought that all they eat and all they wear comes from theft—nay, from sacrilege? . . . Let them answer me briefly whether the diaconate is license to steal and rob. If they deny this, they will be also compelled to admit that they have no diaconate left, inasmuch as the entire administration of the church property has plainly turned into sacrilegious plundering.[47]

In a lengthy passage, Calvin proves that the wealth of the Church and its leaders is evidence enough that the diaconate has been ravaged and its resources desecrated. This violation means that the poor are plundered. Calvin says that any sense "of that early frugality" among the leaders of the Church, that is, any "honest moderation," is rejected. No amount of wealth, endowments, or benefices are "able to satisfy the voraciousness of the priests." While they "spare themselves," these priests prey on people's superstitions "to apply what should have been distributed to the poor, to the constructing churches, erecting statues, buying vessels, and providing vestments." Calvin thunders, "Thus are daily alms consumed in this abyss."[48]

Calvin believes the plight of the poor to be directly related to the opulent wealth of the Church. More specifically, he believes that the persistence of poverty is a result of a defunct diaconate, a diaconate which, because of avarice, are looted by Church officials in order to grow rich.[49] The daily alms for the poor are consumed by costly church buildings, ornamented vessels, and vestments for the clergy which demonstrate a blatant disregard for any rule of moderation or frugality. Yet behind all such error in ecclesial practice lurks error in doctrine. According to Calvin, Roman teachers affirm "that the dignity of the Church is decently sustained by this magnificence"; furthermore, they claimed that this is the only way "those prophecies [will be] fulfilled with which the ancient prophets describe the splendor of Christ's kingdom, when that kingly magnificence is beheld in the priestly order."[50] Calvin responds that even a Jew would rebuke such stupidity. Such teachers

---

[47] Ibid., 4.5.16 (Battles, 1098–99); *OS* 5, 87.

[48] Ibid., 4.5.18 (Battles, 1100–1101); *OS* 5, 88–89.

[49] Calvin also writes, "my sole intention was to show that the lawful order of the diaconate has long since been removed from their midst, so that they may no longer boast of this title to the commendation of their Church." See ibid., 4.5.19 (Battles, 1102); *OS* 5, 90.

[50] Ibid., 4.5.17 (Battles, 1099); *OS* 5, 87.

transferred to flesh and the world the things spiritually spoken of Christ's spiritual kingdom. For we know that the prophets sketched for us under the image of earthly things God's heavenly glory, which ought to shine in the Church. For the Church never abounded less with these blessings which their words express than under the apostles; and yet all admit that the force of Christ's kingdom flourished most at that time.[51]

The doctrinal error which justifies the Roman practice of ecclesial extravagance is rooted in a faulty Christology. Rome taught that such wealth is necessary to depict Christ's heavenly kingdom on earth. Calvin finds this thinking preposterous. Obviously such teachers are ignorant of the humility of Christ's incarnation into impoverished and afflicted human flesh—things that point to the spiritual nature of His kingdom. Instead, Roman doctrine has reversed the symbolic significance of the incarnation and "transferred to flesh and the world the things spiritually spoken of Christ's spiritual kingdom."[52] To infer from the example of Christ that the Church needs to be adorned with extravagant wealth and ornaments is to deny that the splendor of the Church resides in Christ's invisible grace and power, the way it did at the time of the apostles.

The source of this reasoning resides in the Roman assumption that the form of the Church is always apparent and observable and is identified with the hierarchy of the Church. It is demonstrated above that Calvin refutes this idea in his "Prefatory Letter to King Francis I." He argues just the opposite—that the form of the Church is not always visible. Rather, the nature of the Church is invisible and spiritual becoming visible only when the Word of God is rightly preached and the sacraments are correctly administered. Thus, he contends that Christ's kingdom was most evident in the Apostolic Church during a time which, materially speaking, was the most austere of all Church periods.

It is evident that this issue is of utmost important to Calvin. His critique of Roman worship and neglect of the poor show just one more way that the Word and worship of God was corrupted by the vanity of men. Calvin reasons that the greed, wealth, and splendor of the Roman Church are directly related to its neglect of the poor. The Church justified its excesses and its neglect of the poor using an interpretation of the prophets that confused the spiritual kingdom of Christ with that of the earthly realm. In Calvin's estimation, Roman ecclesiology has not grasped

[51] Ibid.
[52] Ibid.

the gravity of the cross and instead became enamored with the foolish embellishment of worship to the neglect of its responsibility to the poor. This ecclesiology is a far cry from the view of the Church that the Fathers embraced. This brings Calvin to examine another issue, the neglected ideal of poverty, better understood as simplicity, and its relationship to the ministry.

Poverty, Simplicity, and the Ministry
Calvin's Challenge to the Clergy

Calvin's ecclesiology includes two aspects to the issue of poverty and wealth. As shown above, Calvin believes that the abuse of Church wealth fosters involuntary poverty through an impotent diaconate. This section discusses another aspect of the poverty and wealth issue in the Church of Calvin's day: how the excesses of the clergy and their abuses of Church wealth measured up to the Church's historic poverty ideal or the virtue of simplicity for those in ministry. Calvin gives an apt analysis of the problem:

> Was it fitting that they whose life ought to have been a singular example of frugality, modesty, continence and humility should rival the magnificence of princes in number of retainers, splendor of buildings, elegance of apparel, and banquets? And how much did this disagree with the office of those whom God's eternal and inviolable decree forbids to be seekers of filthy lucre, and bids be content with simple fare—not only to lay hands on villages and castles, but to carry off vast provinces, finally to seize whole kingdoms! If they despise the Word of God, what will they reply to those ancient decrees of synods, which establish that the bishop should have a little house not far from his church, with inexpensive fare and furnishings? What will they reply to that statement of the Synod of Aquileia, where poverty is proclaimed glorious in the priests of the Lord? For perhaps they will repudiate as too rigorous the command laid upon Nepotianus by Jerome, that poor men and strangers, and with them Christ as guest, should frequent his little table. But they will be ashamed to disavow what Jerome adds immediately: that the glory of the bishop is to provide for the poor; the disgrace of all priests, to seek after their own riches.[53]

The picture Calvin describes is one which finds the clergy adrift from the original poverty ideal of frugality, modesty, and humility. Instead of exemplifying a life of frugality and poverty proscribed by the early decrees,

---

[53] Ibid., 4.5.19 (Battles, 1101–2); OS 5, 89.

the clergy in Calvin's day was beset with avarice and an insatiable appetite for more wealth. He uses the Fathers as the standard against which he measures the Church's disobedience on this matter. Regarding the Synod of Aquileia, Calvin articulates the theological reasoning behind the joyful, frugal, and simple lives of these ancients:

> But how priests at that time did not abound in superfluous possessions is sufficiently declared by that one statement of the Synod of Aquileia, presided over by Ambrose: "Glorious is poverty in the priests of the Lord." Surely the bishops then had some riches with which they could have rendered conspicuous honor to the Church, if they had thought these the true ornaments of the Church. But since they knew nothing to be more contrary to the pastoral office than to glow with pride in the delicacies of the table, splendor of apparel, a great retinue of servants and magnificent palaces, they followed and cultivated humility and modesty [*humilitas ac modestia*], indeed that very poverty [*imo paupertas ipsam*] which Christ consecrated among His ministers.[54]

Three statements in this text are important to Calvin's argument and to this study. The first is that the priests "did not abound in superfluous possessions." This is another way of saying that in the days of the Fathers, priests led frugal, simple, humble lives. The second reveals that bishops had some resources available to them but did not use them in a conspicuous manner. Calvin, in part, credits their disdain for extravagance to their belief that such practice does not adorn the Church. The third item of significance is the most important theological statement in the text: "They followed and cultivated humility and modesty, indeed that very poverty which Christ consecrated among his ministers."[55]

On the grounds of his Christology, Calvin rejects the cupidity of the Roman priesthood. According to Calvin, authentic poverty, which Christ consecrated, has both an inward and outward dimension to it. He defines *imo paupertas ipsam* [indeed that very poverty] by the previous phrase *humilitas ac modestia* [humility and modesty]. When Calvin uses the term "humility," he evidently means an inner and contrite attitude of the heart that recognizes itself as spiritually bankrupt before God. This attitude of contrition before God manifests itself externally by being in proper relationship with other people as well as with physical things. True poverty is demonstrated visibly through modesty, otherwise known in Calvin's writ-

---

[54] Ibid., 4.5.17 (Battles, 1100); *OS* 5, 88.
[55] Ibid.

ings as "simplicity." Thus, the poverty that Christ consecrated in His life and for His ministers is a spiritual posture before God which bears the mark of Christ's life in the external form of modesty. It is a condition intended to portray the spiritual nature of Christ's kingdom in the leaders of the Church.

Calvin recognizes that by Christ's own example, His poverty consecrated a simple and modest lifestyle for those who minister in the Church. Furthermore, Calvin believes that the ancient Fathers of the Church authentically imitated Christ in the kind of simple, frugal, and humble lives that they lived. Calvin's remarks suggest that he supports the practice of a form of voluntary poverty among ministers that is different from the stylized poverty ideal that emerged in the Middle Ages with monks, hermits, and friars. This restrained form of voluntary poverty was put into practice by Calvin and other ministers who served the city of Geneva. It was characterized by the simple, frugal, and humble lives they lived in an effort to imitate Christ and His example. The details of this aspect of Calvin's lifestyle are revealed in his treatise, *Reply to Sadolet*. It shows that Calvin not only held to his convictions doctrinally but that he also put them into practice after the example he believed Christ Himself consecrated.

Calvin's Reply to Sadolet: An Apostolic Model of the Church

Calvin's *Reply to Sadolet* is one of the few writings in which Calvin speaks at some length about the kind of simplicity and modesty of life to which he and other reformed pastors adhere. In March of 1539, almost a year after the city of Geneva banished Calvin and Farel, Cardinal Sadolet (b. 1477–d. 1547) wrote the city of Geneva a letter to lure them away from the Reform and solicit them to come back into fellowship with the Roman Church. One of the ways in which Sadolet attempted to accomplish this task was to discredit the ministers of Geneva by accusing them of personal ambition and avarice.[56] Because no one in Geneva felt capable of responding to Sadolet, the letter was forwarded to Calvin in Strasbourg. Though much of Calvin's *Reply to Sadolet* is worthy of close study, Calvin's response to these particular attacks are of special significance for understanding that

[56] Calvin writes: "Accordingly you allege that we had no other end in view than to gratify our avarice and ambition. Since then your device has been to cast some stain upon us, in order that the minds of your readers be preoccupied with hatred and might give us no credit, I shall briefly reply to that objection before proceeding to other matters." *Calvin: Theological Treatises*, "Reply to Sadolet" (Reid, 225); *OS* 1, 460. See "Sadolet's letter to the Genevans," in Olin, *Reformation Debate*, 45; *OS* 1, 453.

Calvin placed moral authority in the humility and modest lives of those in the ministry.[57]

Calvin directly responds to Sadolet's charge that the ministers of Geneva are guilty of avarice and personal ambition. He specifically asks Sadolet what honors, power, riches, or dignities fell to their lot. He argues that not only is there "no trace of the ambition with which you charge us"[58] but also that the ministers worked hard to purge their Church of such snares. Calvin writes:

> ... with a clear voice we denounced as thief any bishop who, out of ecclesial revenue, appropriated more to his own use than was necessary for a frugal and sober subsistence; when we protested that the Church was exposed to a deadly poison, so long as pastors were loaded with such affluence that they might ultimately sink under it; when we declared it inexpedient that these revenues should fall into their possession; finally; when we counseled that as much should be distributed to ministers as might suffice for a frugal life befitting their order without luxurious superabundance, and that the rest should be dispensed according to the practice of the ancient Church . . . was this to capture any of these for ourselves, or was it not rather voluntarily to shake ourselves free of them?'. . . . But if these things are so plainly and generally known that not one iota can be denied, with what face can you proceed to reproach us with aspiring to extraordinary wealth and power, especially in the presence of men to whom none of these things are unknown?[59]

Calvin and the other ministers exhibited no evidence of avarice or personal ambition. Instead, he said the standard to which the Reform held their ministers required far more discipline than what was evidenced by Roman practice. Calvin contends that a bishop should only be granted what is necessary for a frugal and sober subsistence and that the revenues distributed to ministers "might suffice for a frugal life befitting their order without luxurious superabundance." Though Calvin states above that the remainder of the revenues should be "dispensed according to the practice of the ancient Church," it is clear from this text that the Genevan ministry's handling of revenue as a whole is based upon the example given in the ancient Church.

[57] See Ganoczy, *Calvin Théolgien de L'Église et du Ministère*, 300–67; for background on Calvin's understanding of the ministry and office of pastor.
[58] *Calvin: Theological Treatises*, "Reply to Sadolet" (Reid, 226); *OS* 1, 461.
[59] Ibid., (Reid, 226–27); *OS* 1, 462.

The form and practice of the ancient Church are very important to Calvin.[60] Sadolet charged against the ministers of Geneva that the tradition of the last fifteen hundred years of the Church has been "torn up and destroyed" by their "rashness."[61] In response, Calvin accuses Sadolet of disguising the fact that

> ... not only that our agreement with antiquity is far closer than yours, but that all we have attempted has been to renew the ancient form of the Church which, at first distorted and stained by illiterate men of indifferent character, was afterwards criminally mangled and almost destroyed by the Roman pontiff and his faction. I shall not press you so closely as to call you back to that form [of the Church] which the apostles instituted, though in it we have *the only model of a true Church*, and whosoever deviates from it in the smallest degree is in error.[62]

Calvin did not hold the Genevan ministers responsible for the neglect of fifteen hundred years of Church tradition, but rather, that a large segment of Church tradition had neglected the model of the "true Church" instituted by the apostles. The model of the "true Church" of antiquity is a critical component of Calvin's ecclesiology. Calvin regards the outward appearance of the Church with great seriousness; he argues that the "true Church" may be visibly recognized by its conformity to the simplicity and frugality of its apostolic ideal. Calvin does not theologically elevate simplicity and frugality to a level of a "mark" of the Church. But his writings reveal that in his ecclesiology, simplicity among the ministers of the church is a witness to the fact that the Word of God is being rightly preached and heard. Just as faithfulness in times of persecution is a way in which the invisible Church becomes identifiable as true, so it is with simplicity manifested in the lives of its clergy.

---

[60] See Ganoczy, *Calvin Théologien*, 261–97 and 371–81, for background on Calvin's understanding of ministry in the ancient Church and that of the first century.

[61] *Calvin: Theological Treatises*, "Reply to Sadolet" (Reid, 231); *OS* 1, 466. Sadolet asks Geneva if they would rather believe and follow the Catholic Church which has for more than thirteen hundred years been approved "with general consent," or would they rather believe and follow the "innovations introduced within these twenty-five years, by crafty or, as they think themselves, acute men ..." See "Sadolet's letter to the Genevans," in Olin, *Reformation Debate*, 40–41, 45; *OS* 1, 450. See also page 45 for further accusations of Sadolet against the leaders of the reform in Geneva (*OS* 1, 453).

[62] Emphasis mine. *Calvin: Theological Treatises*, "Reply to Sadolet" (Reid, 231); *OS* 1, 466.

Toward the end of his letter, Calvin returns once more to address Sadolet's accusations that the Genevan pastors are guilty of avarice and ambition.[63] In this passage Calvin makes sport of Sadolet's claims and exposed them as ridiculous. Most importantly, he shows how the pastors of Geneva do indeed model simplicity with integrity in their lives. Contemplating the testimony of those who were acquainted with the Genevan pastors, he writes:

> I would yet ask what could make you think of accusing us of avarice? Do you think the Reformers were so dull as not to perceive from the very outset that they were entering on a course most adverse to money and advantage? When they charged you with greed, did they not see that they were necessarily binding themselves to temperance and frugality, if they were not to become ridiculous even to children? When they showed that the method of correcting that greed was to relieve pastors of their excessive wealth, in order that they might care more for the Church, did they not spontaneously shut against themselves the road to wealth? For what riches now remained to which they might aspire? What? Would not the shortest road to riches and honor have been to have done business with you at the very first on the terms offered? How much would your pontiff then have paid to many for their silence? How much would he pay even today? If they are actuated by the least avarice, why do they cut off all hope of improving their fortune and prefer to be thus perpetually poor, rather than enrich themselves without great difficulty and in a moment?[64]

Calvin eloquently silenced Sadolet's accusations regarding the question of avarice. Yet more importantly for this study, Calvin's words reveal much about the Genevan pastors' adherence to the ancient canons in their ministries and their attempts to exemplify the only model of the true Church demonstrated by the ancient Church. Calvin and the Genevan pastors voluntarily bound themselves to temperance and frugality to guard against greed. These ministers sought to "relieve pastors of their excessive wealth" so that they would be certain to care for the welfare of the Church: they preferred "to be thus perpetually poor."[65] Therefore, Calvin can state with confidence:

---

[63] See "Sadolet's letter to the Genevans," in Olin, *Reformation Debate*, 45; *OS* 1, 453.
[64] *Calvin: Theological Treatises*, "Reply to Sadolet" (Reid, 254); *OS* 1, 487.
[65] Ibid.

> But if you think that our intention must be judged by the result, it will be found that we aimed only at promoting the kingdom of Christ by our poverty and insignificance [*quam ut nostra tenuitate atque humilitate regni Christi amplitudo promoveretur*]. So far are we from having abused His sacred name for the purposes of avarice.[66]

Calvin understands the significance of Christ's poverty for the kingdom. He recognizes how a life of *tenuitate atque humilitate* [smallness and humility] authenticates and reveals the spiritual message of the Gospel and promotes the kingdom of Christ. Calvin claims that because this is the lifestyle he and the Genevan ministers have followed, accusations such as Sadolet's appear ridiculous.

Calvin's Christology shapes his ecclesiology concerning the lifestyle appropriate for clergy. Calvin's letter to Sadolet asserts that the poverty which Christ consecrated among His ministers and that which is expressed in the ancient synods and canons needs to be revisited upon the Church and its leaders in the form of a disciplined life. The form of poverty that Calvin supports for those in ministry is a form of poverty exemplified and consecrated by Christ, a form that is characterized by a modest simplicity of life evidenced by humility and frugality. This simplicity also means that a bishop or pastor should be given enough pay to meet his and his family's needs. This prevented the ministry from attracting the kind of people who wish to gain personally by it, drawing instead those who would faithfully care for the Church's needs.

Just as Calvin's understanding of Christ's poverty shapes his ecclesiology concerning the need for simplicity in worship in the adornments of the physical structure and in the lifestyle of the Church's ministers, so it informs the Church on its response towards the poor. Calvin's comments on Matt 25:31–46 examine the place of charity in the spiritual worship of the Church and, in particular, the place of the physically poor in the kingdom of God and their role in the worship and life of the community of faith.

---

[66] Ibid., (Reid, 227); *OS* 1, 462.

Ministry to the Poor and the Spiritual Worship of the Church

Physical Poverty and the Kingdom of God: Matthew 25:31–46

THE NATURE OF THE FLOCK

Calvin's remarks on the judgment of the sheep and the goats of Matt 25:31–46 are notable because of his placement of the poor in relationship to the Kingdom of God. He recognizes that the purpose of the passage is to encourage believers in holy and upright conduct through the contemplation of the heavenly life with the eyes of faith.[67] That is, if believers can receive a glimpse of the final judgment and see that their actions toward the poor really matter, then they will be more inclined toward conduct that is holy and upright. With this objective in mind, Calvin considers the judge described in verse 31—Jesus Christ. Christ "will come in His glory; because, while He dwelt in this world as a mortal man, He appeared in the despised form of a servant," Calvin writes. He is aware of the dramatic contrast between Christ's earthly life among the disciples and His state of glorification with the Father. Christ "did not appear for the purpose of immediately setting up His kingdom" and at present "He has not . . . erected before the eyes of men that throne from which His divine majesty will be far more displayed." But in that day of judgment, Christ will "assume the title of King" and will display His glory "before the eyes of men" when He sits down to be "the Judge of the whole world."[68]

In the first part of verse 32, Christ has assembled the nations before Him for judgment; Calvin interprets the image of a shepherd separating His flock in the second part of the verse as a reference to the Church. Calvin explains, "When our Lord said that the separation of the sheep from the goats is delayed till that day, He meant that the wicked are now mixed with the holy, so that they live together "*in eodem grege Dei*" [in the same flock of God]."[69] The phrase "*in eodem grege Dei*" is a description of the visible Church for Calvin. He suggests that the image "appears to be borrowed from Ezek 34:18, where the Lord complains of the fierceness of the goats, which attacks with their horns the poor sheep, and destroy the pastures, and pollute the water; and where the Lord expressly declares that He will take vengeance."[70]

---
[67] *Commentary on Matthew* 25:31 (Pringle, 174); *CO* 45, 685.
[68] Ibid., (Pringle, 174–75); *CO* 45, 686.
[69] Ibid., 25:32 (Pringle, 176); *CO* 45, 686.
[70] Ibid.

Calvin's advice to the miserable sheep is as follows: first, they should not consider that their condition is too difficult because they must at present live with the goats; and second, they must be careful not to become "infected by the contagion of their vices"; third, they must recall that their effort in maintaining a holy and innocent life is not in vain, but that "the difference will one day appear."[71] Calvin assures them of the promised kingdom to strengthen their hope in the midst of being weakened by afflictions.[72]

> For though the life of the godly be nothing else than a sad and wretched banishment, so that the earth scarcely bears them; though they groan under hard poverty, and reproaches, and other afflictions; yet, that they may with fortitude and cheerfulness surmount these obstacles, the Lord declares that a "kingdom" is elsewhere "prepared for them."[73]

Calvin's assumption that Christ's image of the sheep and goats is borrowed from Ezek 34:18 has a great bearing on his interpretation of this text. As stated above, he believed the image of the sheep and goats to represent the visible Church, "the same flock of God."[74] He says that the judgment pictured in Matt 25:33–34 is not the Great White Throne Judgment of Rev 20:11–15, in which all people are assembled before Christ; instead, Calvin sees this judgment to be a judgment of the visible Church. Because he believes that Christ uses the text of Ezek 34:18 in His teaching, Calvin employs this passage as an interpretive key. Thus, he associates the sheep with the godly and the goats with the ungodly in the Church. He also associates the sheep with those who are poor, oppressed, and afflicted. Furthermore, he sees the goats not only as the ungodly but also as those who actively persecute and afflict the poor sheep, as they do in Ezek 34:18. Unfortunately, Calvin died before he completed his lectures on Ezekiel so that his full thoughts on this text are not known.[75] Yet what is clear is that

---

[71] Ibid.

[72] Ibid., 25:34 (Pringle, 177); *CO* 45, 687.

[73] Ibid.

[74] Ibid., 25:32 (Pringle, 176); *CO* 45, 686.

[75] Due to Calvin's illness and death in 1564, his *Ezekiel Lectures/Commentary* ended at chapter 20. Parker says that Calvin did preach through Ezekiel weekday mornings from Nov. 21, 1552–Feb. 21, 1554 and that there are 174 Ezekiel manuscript sermons in four volumes sitting in the *Bibliothèque Publique*, Geneva. However, sermons on Ezek 16–22 are lost, and the rest of Ezek 1–15 & 23–48 have not yet been printed in *Supplementa Calviniana*, a series committed to publishing the rest of Calvin's unpublished sermons. Calvin's sermons on Ezekiel were originally planned for volume IX and X. See Parker,

he interprets the scene of the sheep and goats before the throne of Christ as the judgment of the visible Church. Furthermore, the sheep are not only holy ones, but they are also poor, oppressed, and afflicted.

Using Ezek 34:18 to bring insight into the character of the sheep of Matt 25 and their relationship to the goats fits well with Calvin's overall understanding of the poor in his ecclesiology. When speaking of the visible Church, Calvin maintains in this text that those who are physically poor and afflicted are also those who are holy and declared by Christ's judgment to be the true Church. It is to these godly ones that the kingdom of Christ is promised. This argument is important for Calvin's instruction to the Church concerning proper treatment of the poor and the role of charity in the worship of the Church.

The Role of Charity toward the Poor in Worship

In exegeting Matt 25:35–36,[76] Calvin focuses almost exclusively on the corrupt interpretations of others. Against the Papists, he argues that this text does not teach that eternal life is a result of one's good works:

> We do not deny that a reward is promised to good works, but maintain that it is a reward of grace, because it depends on adoption. . . . We must therefore hold these two principles first, that believers are called to the possession of the kingdom of heaven, so far as relates to good works, not because they deserve them through the righteousness of works, or because their own minds prompted them to obtain that righteousness, but because God justifies those whom He previously elected. Secondly, although by the guidance of the Spirit they aim at the practice of righteousness, yet as they never fulfill the law of God, no reward is due to them, but the term "reward" is applied to that which is bestowed by grace.[77]

Calvin places Christ's words into a proper theological context. The passage does not teach that good works are meritorious for salvation as the Papists believe. Rather, God bestows a reward on those He elects and justifies by grace. Calvin wants to make sure that his readers do not assume the text teaches that salvation is merited by charity toward the poor.[78]

Oracles of God, 160–64; and *Calvin's Preaching*, 179, 197.

[76] Matt 25:35–36 reads: "For I was hungry and you gave me food, I was thirsty and you gave me drink, I was a stranger and you welcomed me, I was naked and you clothed me, I was sick and you visited me, I was in prison and you came to me" (*RSV*).

[77] Ibid., 25:35 (Pringle, 178–79); *CO* 45, 688.

[78] Biéler points out all reform theology taught that the gift of the rich to the poor is a gift

Calvin is careful to place charitable works toward the poor in relationship to other good works in the Christian life. He contends that Christ provides an example of what it means to live a holy and pious life and therefore mentions only a few duties of charity. He argues that Christ actually commends all duties of charity to the believer, not only the feeding of the hungry:

> For to comfort mourners, to relieve those who are unjustly oppressed, to aid simple-minded men by advice, to deliver wretched persons from the jaws of wolves, are deeds of mercy not less worthy of commendation than to clothe the naked or to feed the hungry.[79]

In spite of the value of charity in the Christian life, Calvin wants to be certain that his readers understand that good works do not take precedence over the corporate worship of God. "If a man were to take no thought of God, and were only to be beneficent toward men, such compassion would be of no avail to him for appeasing God." In Calvin's thought, there is an order to the worship of God. Good works are a result of what happens when the Church gathers to worship. Calvin is concerned about fanatics who "under the pretext of this passage withdraw from hearing the Word, and from observing the Holy Supper, and from other spiritual exercises; for with equal plausibility might they set aside faith, and bearing the cross, and prayer, and chastity." This is not acceptable to Calvin, who says that "the worship of God is more important than charity toward men, and in like manner, faith and supplication are more valuable than alms."[80]

Calvin's distinction between the worship of God and works of charity is rooted in his understanding of the law. The first table of the law commands the worship of God alone [*fides*]. The second table commands love [*caritas*] toward one's neighbor. In Calvin's thought, the first table [*fides*] always takes precedence over the second table [*caritas*], and the second table is derivative from and subordinate to the first: "*caritas* flows from *fides*, the love of neighbor is the fruit of forgiveness and justification."[81] Because

---

of out of their graciousness to God and that this kind of gift derives from faith which has no meritorious value for salvation for the giver. Biéler, *Pensée Économique*, 325. See also *Commentary on Luke* 11:37–40 ([Pringle, 160–62]; *CO* 45, 392–93) for Calvin's comments on for the place of alms in true spiritual worship.

[79] *Commentary on Matthew* 25:35 (Pringle, 179–80); *CO* 45, 688–689.

[80] Ibid., (Pringle, 179).

[81] McKee, *Calvin on the Diaconate*, 255 n. 91; Graham, *Constructive Revolutionary*, 74–75. McKee also states that in Calvin's thought, "*Caritas* is not the simple equivalent of the English 'charity'—far from it! The bare statement that *caritas* is the sum of the second table

the worship of God is a spiritual exercise, Calvin recognizes that the best demonstration of the authenticity of one's worship is works of charity.[82] Also because works of charity flow from the worship of God, Calvin is careful not to diminish the importance of charitable works. "Christ had good reason for bringing forward those evidences of true righteousness which are more obvious."[83] Calvin writes:

> Accordingly, Christ does not make the chief part of righteousness to consist in alms, but, by means of what may be called more evident signs [*signis notioribus*], shows what it is to live a holy and righteous life; as unquestionably believers not only profess with the mouth, but prove by actual performances, that they serve God.[84]

Charitable works toward the poor are *signis notioribus* [evident or well-known signs] that demonstrate believers' not only say that they professes faith in Christ but display by their actions that they serve God. Calvin concludes:

> But while Christ, in recommending to us the exercise of charity [*caritatem*], does not exclude those duties which belong to the worship of God, He reminds His disciples that it will be an authentic evidence of a holy life, if they practice charity [*caritate exerceant*], agreeably to those words of the prophet, "I choose mercy, and not sacrifice," (Hosea 6:6;) the import of which is, that hypocrites, while they are avaricious, and cruel, and deceitful, and extortionists, and haughty, still counterfeit holiness by an imposing array of ceremonies.[85]

While reminding his readers that Christ's teaching does not exclude the importance and priority of worship for the believer [*fides*], Calvin juxtaposes two contrasting ideals. He places works of charity toward the poor against the imposing array of ceremonies in the Roman Church. Furthermore, he calls this imposing array of ceremonies a counterfeit holiness. Calvin not only sees that the magnificent worship and excesses of the Church contribute to the problem of poverty in the community at large but also identifies such pomp and ceremony as false holiness. This difference helps to explain why he emphatically maintains that pomp and ceremony in worship con-

---

is filled out by comments which situate it vis-à-vis other things or qualities... Caritas is the fruit of faith that justifies, the evidence of repentance and regeneration" (242).

[82] McKee, *Calvin on the Diaconate*, 257.
[83] *Commentary on Matthew* 25:35 (Pringle, 179); *CO* 45, 688–89.
[84] Ibid., (Pringle, 180); *CO* 45, 688.
[85] Ibid., 25:37 (Pringle, 180); *CO* 45, 689.

ceal the simple message of the Gospel and bury Christ. If an imposing array of ceremonies display a counterfeit holiness, then simplicity in worship takes on added significance. Simplicity not only keeps the gospel free from spiritual obstacles but also models the nature of true holiness. True holiness is free of hypocrisy, avarice, cruelty, deceit, extortion, and pride. Behavior that participates in a grand array of ceremony runs counter to a true life of holiness, which is evidenced by true works of charity, such as supplying the needs of the poor.[86]

The Identification of the Poor with Christ

Calvin assures his readers that a life of true holiness, characterized by being generous to the poor, will not be overlooked by Christ.

> God will one day repay with usury what we bestow on the poor. The administration which Christ here expresses is intended to instruct us to rise above the apprehension of our flesh, whenever afflicted brethren ask our confidence and aid, that the appearance of a despised man may not hinder us from treating him with kindness.[87]

Becoming holy, according to Calvin, means that we are generous to fellow believers in need regardless of our own personal feelings. It means that we rise above appearances and treat the despised with kindness. Calvin finds a good textual and theological reason for exhorting his readers to such acts of charity emerging from this passage. In verse 40, Christ states, "Truly, I say to you, as you did it to one of the least of these my brethren, you did it to me."[88]

> As Christ has just now told us, by a figure, that our senses do not yet comprehend how highly He values deeds of charity, so now He openly declares, that He will reckon as done to Himself whatever we have bestowed on His people. We must be prodigiously sluggish, if compassion is not drawn from our bowels by this statement, that Christ is either neglected or honored in the person of those who need our assistance. So then, whenever we are reluctant to assist the poor, let us place before our eyes the Son of God, to

---

[86] McKee makes the observation that hypocrites can fake worship through the use of ceremonies but that works of love stand as "stern proof for or against the integrity of the worship of the worshiper" (*Calvin on the Diaconate*, 257).

[87] *Commentary on Matthew* 25:37 (Pringle, 180); *CO* 45, 689.

[88] (RSV); Calvin's Latin translation reads: "Amen dico vobis, quatenus fecistis uni de his fratribus meis minimis, mihi fecistis."

whom it would be base sacrilege [*immane sacrilegium*] to refuse anything.[89]

Deeds of charity are extremely important in the Church. Calvin insists that rendering charity to the poor is regarded by Christ as being offered to Himself. In the poor, Christ is placed before the eyes of Church. To underscore this point, Calvin explains what truly happens when the poor are neglected: that is, not to assist the needy is tantamount to committing sacrilege against the Son of God.[90] He specifically uses the word *sacrilegium*, a word that means to rob that which is holy or to treat something as profane that is considered sacred or holy. This is strong language. It assumes that the poor have a particular spiritual role in the Church. If to supply the needs of the poor is to minister to Christ, then what Calvin suggests is that the poor have a sacramental role in the community of faith. They provide the Church with a unique opportunity to minister directly to Christ Himself because, in the poor, "Christ is either neglected or honored."[91] Nevertheless, Calvin does make a significant qualification concerning the poor in this text. He does not interpret "to the least of my brethren" to refer indiscriminately to all who are indigent. Calvin asserts:

> Believers only [*Solos autem fideles*] are expressly recommended to our notice; not that He bids us altogether despise others, but because the more nearly a man approaches to God, he ought to be the more highly esteemed by us; for though there is a common tie that binds all the children of Adam, there is a still more sacred union among the children of God. So then, as those who belong to the household of faith ought to be preferred to strangers, Christ makes special mention of them. And though His design was to encourage those whose wealth and resources are abundant to relieve the poverty of brethren [*fratrum inopiam*], yet it affords no ordinary consolation to the poor and distressed, that, though shame and contempt follow them in the eyes of the world, yet the Son of

---

[89] *Commentary on Matthew* 25:40 (Pringle, 181); *CO* 45, 689.

[90] Both Cyprian and Clement maintained that Christ resided in the poor and despised. Clement went so far as to say that hidden within the poor "dwells the Father, and His Son, who died for us and rose with us." See Clement, "Rich Man's Salvation," par. 33 (Butterworth, 341); *PG* 9, 640. And Cyprian, *Treatises*, "On Works and Almsgiving," chap. 23 (Deferrari, 250); *PL* 4, 643. See also Biéler, *Pensée Économique*, 328.

[91] *Commentary on Matthew* 25:40 (Pringle, 181); *CO* 45, 689. See also McKee, *Calvin on the Diaconate*, 245.

God holds them as dear as His own members. And certainly, by calling them "brethren," He confers on them inestimable honor.[92]

Calvin reads Christ's reference to "the least of my brethren" as pertaining specifically to those who are needy within the Church. The determining word for Calvin is "brethren." He chooses to interpret Christ's use of *fratres* as describing the "more sacred union among the children of God" as opposed to the "common tie that binds all the children of Adam." Matthew's wording could allow a more universal interpretation of the phrase. Had Calvin chosen a broader interpretation of Matthew's words, he would have interpreted Christ's brotherhood with all humanity from the standpoint of His incarnation. This perspective would call all who are hungry, thirsty, naked, and in prison Christ's brethren. Probably because he read this text with Ezek 34:18 in mind, Calvin chose a more selective reading of the text and does not apply this to the Christian's responsibility toward the impoverished Turk or Jew of his day. His only intention with this point is to establish that God does not intend for believers to despise these people.[93]

Calvin's comments may be interpreted in two ways. First, they could be seen as a typical example of Calvin's exegetical faithfulness to the text, given Christ's use of the wording "my brethren." In support of this view, one could argue that Calvin's narrow interpretation does not mean that in his wider theology he overlooks the necessity for believers to perform acts of charity towards those outside the Church. In reference to Luke 10:30, he acknowledges that believers are bound to show acts of love to all people.[94] This observation is also stressed by Biéler.[95] Biéler uses universal

---

[92] *Commentary on Matthew* 25:40 (Pringle, 181); *CO* 45, 689–90.

[93] In chapter 1 of this study, it was pointed out that the position that only believers are to be the recipients of the charity of the Church can be found among numerous Fathers, some of the earliest being Justin Martyr and Tertullian. See Winslow, "Poverty and Riches," 325–26. This teaching is also found in Clement's writings (see "Rich Man's Salvation," par. 30 [Butterworth, 333]; *PG* 9, 633) and in Cyprian's writings (see *Treatises*, "On Works and Almsgiving," chap. 23 [Deferrari, 250]; *PL* 4, 643). Calvin may be following the lead of the Fathers on this point.

[94] "Christ might have stated simply, that the word neighbor extends indiscriminately to every man, because the whole human race is united by a sacred bond of fellowship . . . the Lord purposely declares that all are neighbors, that the very relationship may produce mutual love. To make any person our neighbor, therefore, it is enough that he be a man; for it is not in our power to blot out our common nature" (*Commentary on Luke* 10:30 [Pringle, 61]; *CO* 45, 613); Cf. *Commentary on Matthew* 5:43 (Pringle, 303–4); *CO* 45, 187; *Institutes* 2.8.55 (Battles, 418–19); *OS* 3, 346–48; See McKee, *Calvin on the Diaconate*, 243, note 55.

[95] See Biéler, *Pensée Économique*, 326–35.

language to express Calvin's understanding of the poor and their social role.⁹⁶ However, in the Matthew text, Calvin stresses though believers do indeed have a natural bond with all humanity, requiring them to show acts of love towards all people, there is an even stronger bond tying members of the Church together. He believes that Christ teaches a distinction in relationship when He calls the poor in the Church "brethren . . . , [and] confers on them inestimable honor." When Calvin uses the word *brothers* in this text, he does not refer to a believer's solidarity with all humanity, but rather he exhorts the wealthy within the Church to care for their poor brothers in the faith.

The second possible interpretation is more critical of Calvin. Some might see Calvin's exegesis as influenced by his sixteenth century provincialism, which prevents him from seeing the way the text participates in the gospel's call to missions in service to the unbeliever. In Calvin's defense, however, it must be recognized that he understood the term "brethren" to apply to the whole visible Church. This means that everyone in the city of Geneva would be considered as "brethren" because there was no separation between Church and state, and neither was there a choice of religions. Religious pluralism was not an option in the sixteenth century as the persecution of the French Huguenots demonstrate. Given the social realities of Calvin's world, his interpretation would have included most everyone in the city.

Calvin's Christology indeed shapes his ecclesiology with regard to the response of the Church toward the poor. Through the poor, God places Christ before the eyes of the Church and expects the Church to serve them as they would Christ Himself. To ignore this duty is equal to committing sacrilege against the Son of God. This, however, does not mean that charity towards the poor takes the place of corporate worship. Rather, chari-

---

⁹⁶ Biéler states, that "God momentarily grants to the pauper less goods than to his neighbor so that the former gives to the poor man what he provisionally holds on the part of God." Then Biéler adds, "This social interdependence specifically expresses the deep spiritual solidarity that unites human kind" (my translation); See Biéler, *Pensée Économique*, 326. Biéler's statement needs to be qualified. Though there is indeed a spiritual solidarity between believers and all humanity, there is still a special and closer bond that exists within the community of faith. Calvin upholds solidarity between believers and unbelievers on the grounds that there is a solidarity, which results from our common nature (see note 96). Yet in this passage he demonstrates that Christ's call to minister to the poor within the Church is a result of the special bonds the poor and rich share in Christ. See Biéler, *Pensée Économique*, 338. McKee writes, "Calvin insists that though obviously love to the faithful takes precedence, *caritas* must nonetheless also extend to the limits of humanity" (*Calvin on the Diaconate*, 244).

table works are a result of worship because they demonstrate that believers are able to prove their profession of faith in Christ is authentic by their acts of service to God. Calvin's sermon on Deut 15:11–15 expands these ideas and reveals more of his understanding of the particular place and role of the poor in the worship of the Church.

The Church and the Poor: Calvin's Sermon on Deuteronomy *15:11–15*

Background

On Wednesday, October 30, 1555, Calvin preached his *Sermon on Deuteronomy* 15: 11–15.[97] Hans Scholl calls this sermon "Calvin's whole social message in germ," which "focuses like a burning-glass what Calvin had to say to his congregation and his age on the question of the Church and poverty."[98] Calvin's sermon on verses 11–15 was his third sermon from chapter fifteen. The two preceding sermons also have something to do with poverty. His first sermon on verses 1–6 focuses on the wealthy Israelite's obligation to forgive the debts of the poor by discharging them every seven years.[99] His second sermon, on verses 7–10, continues along the same line, calling on the believer to lend freely to the poor and to have compassion upon them, even if they cannot repay the sum borrowed.[100] Calvin's third sermon on Deut 15, which examines verses 11–15, has two parts. The first half addresses the question of the Church's response to the impoverished among them as a matter of worship.[101] His comments in this half pertain only to verse 11, which reads: "For the poor will never cease out of the land; therefore I command you, You shall open wide your hand to your brother, to the needy and to the poor, in the land" (*RSV*). The second part of his discourse is concerned with verses 12–15, pertaining to the treatment of Hebrew slaves in Israel.[102] When Calvin's homily moves from verse 11 to verse 12, he switches topics as well. He leaves behind the subject of the Church's responsibility toward the poor as a matter of worship, shifting to focus upon the cultural laws surrounding Hebrew slaves and the details of their manumission.

---

[97] *Sermon on Deuteronomy* 15:11–15; *CO* 27, 336–49.
[98] Scholl, "Church and the Poor," 243.
[99] *Sermon on Deuteronomy* 15:1–6; *CO* 27, 313–25.
[100] *Sermon on Deuteronomy* 15:7–10; *CO* 27, 325–36.
[101] See *Sermon on Deuteronomy* 15:11–15; *CO* 27, 336–42.
[102] See *Sermon on Deuteronomy* 15:11–15; *CO* 27, 342–49.

This study will not address the second half of Calvin's sermon concerning 12–15 because the topic of slavery, though important, falls outside of the present focus of Calvin's theological understanding of poverty and its impact on the worship of the Church. Also, Calvin's previous two sermons on the poor and usury, including the forgiveness of the poor's debts, will not be discussed. These remarks pertain to the area of Calvin's social ethics and his economic thought, a topic which is already well researched in Calvin studies.[103] However, because Calvin's remarks on Deut 15:11 offer a concise theological rationale for a social ministry toward the poor and its relationship to the worship of the Church, this sermon, along with some related texts, will bring a fitting conclusion to this theological study on poverty in Calvin's thought and particularly for his ecclesiology. One final reason remains as to why Calvin's preaching on Deut 15:11 is valuable. Though Calvin wrote a *Harmony of Exodus, Leviticus, Numbers, and Deuteronomy*, his comments on Deut 15:11 in the *Harmony* are not as extensive as those in his sermon on the same text. Calvin's *Sermon on Deuteronomy* 15:11, therefore, serves as a unique window into Calvin's thought concerning the Church's relationship and responsibility to the physically poor.

Reasons for Physical Poverty

Calvin's Sermon opens with a brief discussion regarding the laws God makes concerning activities necessary for people to practice daily. Calvin states, "And this is why our Lord says in this text that it is not without cause that he speaks of providing for the poor."[104] Calvin observes that Deut 15:11 prophesies: "For the poor will never cease out of the land. . . ."[105] The continuing presence of poverty brings him to question its causes in the world. Though he recognizes that God "is rich enough to supply all men's needs,"[106] he reckons:

> This was spoken in order to help us to understand that God will test our charity. . . . Why does God permit men to be poor down here, but only to give us occasion to do good? Therefore, let us not

[103] See Biéler, *Pensée Économique*, for the most comprehensive study on this topic.
[104] My translation. *Sermon on Deuteronomy* 15:11–15; *CO* 27, 336–37; "Et voila pourquoy en ce passage nostre Seigneur dit: que ce n'est point sans cause qu'il parle de subvenir aux povres."
[105] *RSV*.
[106] My translation. *Sermon on Deuteronomy* 15:11–15; *CO* 27, 337; "car il est assez riche pour fournir à chacun tout ce qui luy seroit besoin."

attribute it to fortune when we see one man rich and another one poor; but let us understand that God disposes things in this way, and that it is not without reason. It is true that our eyes do not always see why God enriches one, and leaves another in his poverty, we cannot discern with certainty the cause of these things. And in this manner, God will have us cast our eyes down to the end that we should give Him the honor of governing men at His will, and according to His own counsel which is incomprehensible to us.[107]

According to Calvin, neither fortune nor chance is involved in the distribution of material resources throughout the world. Rather, God "disposes things in this way." God permits the poor to be such while choosing another to enrich. Yet this unequal distribution of wealth is not without reason. Though Calvin admits that no person can penetrate the full counsel of God's providential decisions,[108] he does propose that this inequity occurs as God's test of our charity. Calvin explains his meaning:

> ... in general we have to remember what I have already touched upon: which is, that God unequally distributes the goods of this world so as to probe the will of men, that in this way He conducts an examination. So that if a man is rich, one can better judge what kind [of rich man] he is. Because he has opportunity to harm, he can bring injury to his enemies. But if he abstains from doing evil, if he exerts no cruelty against his neighbors, if he exercises self-control without desiring more than what God gives to him: it is a sign of honesty, which would not be known if such occasions had not made present to him. Again, if a man is liberal with the things he has, and is determined to do good to those who have need of his help, and does not promote himself in pride, nor in pomp; but always behaves soberly: this is a good test.[109]

---

[107] My translation. *Sermon on Deuteronomy* 15:11–25; *CO* 27, 337–38; "Notamment ceci a esté prononcé, afin que nous sachions que Dieu veut esprouver nostre charité ... Pourquoy donc est-ce que Dieu permet que il y ait des povres ici bas, sinon d'autant qu'il nous veut donner occasion de bien faire? Ainsi n'attribuons point à fortune, quand nous voyons que l'un sera riche, et l'autre povre: mais cognoissons que Dieu le dispose ainsi, et que ce n'est point sans raison. Il est vray que tousiours nous ne verrons point à l'oeil pourquoy Dieu aura enrichi l'un, et qu'il aura laissé l'autre en sa povreté: nous ne pourrons pas avoir discretion certaine de cela: et ainsi Dieu veut que nous baissions les yeux souvent afin de luy faire cest honneur, qu'il gouverne les hommes à sa volonté, et selon son conseil qui nous est incomprehensible."

[108] Hans Scholl comments on this passage in Calvin's sermon: "the poor man in the world points to the mystery of God, which man must not approach too near with explanations and theories" (Scholl, "Church and the Poor," 244).

[109] My translation. *Sermon on Deuteronomy* 15:11–15; *CO* 27, 338; "... en général nous

Wealth comes to people as a divine test because wealth provides an opportunity for people to do harm or good. Calvin maintains that people's use of their wealth brings to light the true spiritual condition of their hearts. Concerning Calvin's conviction on this matter, Biéler adds that material goods are instruments that measure the practicality of a believer's faith and that test the heart. The consecration of wealth to the needy is a sign of authentic faith. In this way, God uses the poor to reveal the spiritual character of those within the Church. Both Calvin and Biéler understand that believers must be taught that the way they manage with their material life directly influences their spiritual life. That is, believers' acts involving their material possessions manifest their spirituality, and specifically, the way that they use money is a direct and tangible expression of their faith.[110]

Calvin recognizes a particular significance for the poor and the rich in the way God chooses to distribute wealth.[111] He does not simply target the rich person but finds that the inequity of wealth put the poor to the test as well:

> If another man being poor patiently takes whatever it pleased God to send him, and additionally does not solicit any fraud nor malice, no matter how much he suffers, or how hard his condition may be: this is also a good and useful examination. Therefore, let it be noted that there are the poor and rich in this world, because God has so ordained it this way, and that this comes from His providence and yet, it is necessary for us to firmly hold that there will never be lack of poor people.[112]

---

avons à retenir ce que i'ay touché: c'est que Dieu distribue ainsi inegalement les biens caduques de ce monde, afin de sonder quel est le courage des hommes: que voila un examen qu'il fait. Que si un homme est riche, on peut mieux iuger quel il est: car il a des moyens de nuire, et pourroit apporter du dommage à ses ennemis: mais s'il s'abstient de mal faire, s'il n'exerce nulle cruauté contre ses prochains, s'il se tient en sa mesure, sans appeter plus que Dieu ne luy a donné: voila un signe de sa preudhommie, qui n'eust point esté cogneue quand les occasions ne s'y fussent point presentees. Et puis, si un homme est liberal quand il a dequoy, qu'il tasche de bien faire à ceux qui ont faute de son aide, qu'il ne s'esleve point en orgueil, ni en pompe, mais qu'il chemine tousiours sobrement: voila une bonne espreuve."

[110] Biéler, *Pensée Économique*, 314–16: "C'est donc à l'attitude du chrétien à l'égard des biens matériels que se juge sa vie spirituelle. Le comportement de l'homme envers l'argent est l'expression tangible de sa foi veritable," 316.

[111] Scholl makes a similar but not as broad observation. He states: "Calvin sees a certain meaning of the question of poverty in the fact that God here takes the poor and rich into his own school." "Church and the Poor," 244.

[112] My translation. *Sermon on Deuteronomy* 15:11–15; CO 27, 338: "Si l'autre estant povre prend en patience ce qu'il plaist à Dieu de luy envoyer, et cependant qu'il ne soit

Just as the condition of a rich man's heart is judged according to how he uses his wealth, God also judges the poor man according to how he receives his poverty. Just as the righteous rich man should be honest in his business and generous with his wealth, so the righteous poor man is called to not solicit any fraud or malice but instead to endure patiently the suffering God has ordained for him. The presence of poverty in the Church probes both ends: it not only reveals the spiritual fitness of the wealthy but also the spirituality of the poor themselves. For Calvin, this pattern is indicative of the nature of Christ and His kingdom. Just as the poverty of Christ proclaims the spiritual nature of His kingship, so the presence of poverty in the Church reveals the spiritual nature and character of the Church.

One also observes in the above passage that Calvin uses statements such as "God has so ordained it this way" and "this comes from His providence" to explain why some people are poor and others rich.[113] Calvin believes that a person's socioeconomic status is divinely given. Other than stating that poverty and wealth are divine tests, Calvin does not speculate any further as to the reasons why God would enrich one and impoverish another. In Calvin's mind, these reasons are known only to God. He only concludes that "God disposes things in this way . . . [and] not without reason."[114]

The Role of the Poor in the Worship of the Church

After declaring that wealth or poverty are divine tests meant to reveal the character of an individual's heart, Calvin turns his attention to the role of the poor in Christian worship. Here, he focuses upon the Lord's command in Deut 15:11: "You shall open wide your hand to your brother, to the needy and to the poor, in the land".[115] Calvin provides an interpretation of this charge:

> . . . as if it had been said, that God shows us to our faces how and by what means He wants to be served by us, that is, in giving homage to Him with the goods which He has abundantly given to us;

---

point solicité à fraude, ni à aucune malice, combien qu"il [sic] souffre, et que sa condition soit dure: voila aussi un bon examen et utile. Ainsi donc notons, que quand il y a des povres et des riches en ce monde, que Dieu l'ordonne ainsi, et que cela vient de sa providence: et cependant il nous faut tenir pour resolu, que iamais il n'y aura faute de povres."

[113] My translation. Ibid.: "que Dieu l'ordonne ainsi, et que cela vient de sa providence."
[114] Ibid.; *CO* 27, 337.
[115] (*RSV*); see *Sermon on Deuteronomy* 15:11–15; *CO* 27, 338.

for indeed, He sends us the poor to be as those who receive in His place. And although the alms gift is given to mortal creatures, so it is that God accepts and acknowledges this, and reckons it in His account as if the things which we give to a poor person were placed into His own hands. It is true that for God, it is not alms gift that we make, but rather it is the homage of the goods which He has given to us, and for which we are indebted to Him. Yet, there is also this, that besides what He accepts from us, the recognition that we give Him for the good that He does for us, it is as if the mercy which we show to our brethren, was addressed to Him.[116]

As stated earlier, in Calvin's mind the poor possess a special role in the eyes of God and in the community of faith. God designates the poor as the appropriate vessels to receive alms-gifts by the Church as part of its worship.[117] Though God has no need for our alms, God provides this as means for the faithful to express homage and loyalty by bestowing alms upon the poor. When alms are given to the poor, God not only affirms and accepts the act but also "reckons it in His account as if the things which we give to a poor person were placed into His own hands."[118] According to Calvin, the poor are God's representatives on earth ordained to be served as part of the worship of the people of God.[119]

---

[116] My translation. Ibid.: ". . . comme s'il estoit dit, que Dieu nous monstre à l'oeil en quoy il veut estre servi de nous, et par quel moyen: c'est que nous luy facions hommage des biens qu'il nous a eslargis en abondance: voire, car il nous envoye les povres comme ses receveurs. Et combien que l'aumosne s'adresse à des creatures mortelles, si est-ce que Dieu accepte et advouë cela, et le met en ses contes, comme si nous luy avions mis entre les mains ce que nous donnons à un povre. Il est vray, quant à Dieu, que ce n'est point une aumosne que nous luy fasons: mais c'est l'hommage du bien qu'il nous a donné, et duquel nous luy sommes tenus: mais tant y a encores qu'outre ce qu'il accepte de nous la recognoissance que nous luy faisons des biens qu'il nous fait, que c'est autant comme si la misericorde dont nous usons envers nos freres, s'adressoit à luy."

[117] In his *Commentary on I Timothy* 6:19 he writes: "It is true that God accepts as given to himself everything that is bestowed on the poor." (Pringle, 172); *CO* 52, 334.

[118] My translation. *Sermon on Deuteronomy* 15:11–15; *CO* 27, 339–38: ". . . et le met en ses contes, comme si nous luy avions mis entre les mains ce que nous donnons à un povre."

[119] A contemporary liturgist Richard Paquier claims that benevolence in the Reformed tradition was not rooted in its life of worship and that this is why it became autonomous and secularized. McKee rightly responds to this assertion by asking whether Paquier's "criticism of Reformed worship is valid for the sixteenth century, especially for John Calvin." It is the conclusion of this author that the criticism of Paquier on the relevance of benevolence to the life of Reformed worship in the sixteenth century or in the theology of Calvin does not apply. See Paquier, *Traité de Liturgique*, 10; as quoted in McKee, *Calvin on the Diaconate*, 25.

Since the poor have the role of God's representatives on earth in the worship of God, it is not surprising to find Calvin expressing serious consequences for those who neglect to show them mercy:

> And here is why it is said, that the one who has shut his ears to the cry of the poor, shall cry himself and God will not hear. On the contrary, if we are compassionate (moved with pity) and, having heard the destitution of the poor, are moved to help them, God also will have pity and bestow compassion upon us to rescue us in our time of need. This is why in this passage Moses particularly says that God ordained that we should have an open hand to the poor who dwell among us, he says. For God offers them to us so that we shall have no excuse and say "I do not know to whom I should do good." Since our Lord gives us the means, we must not seek a subterfuge (we must no longer seek excuses), for we shall still remain guilty, if [because] we have not used the occasion that was offered to us.[120]

If to give to the poor is to offer worship to God, then to disregard the needs of the poor is to neglect the worship of God. Calvin's exegesis of Matt 25:31–46 calls the neglect of the poor *sacrilegium*.[121] One now sees why this offense is so profound. Christ offers Himself to the Church through the poor. To neglect ministering to the poor is to neglect a critical aspect of the worship of Christ. This teaching explains why God will not hear the prayers and respond to the needs of those who do not extend mercy to the poor. "God ordained that we should have an open hand to the poor . . . [and] God offers them to us so that we shall have no excuse."[122] God is offended by the those who neglect the needs of the poor because God offers them to the Church as a way to worship Him.

---

[120] My translation. *Sermon on Deuteronomy* 15:11–15; *CO* 27, 338–39: "Et voila pourquoy il est dit, que celuy qui aura fermé son aureille au cri du povre, qu'il criera à son tour, et Dieu ne l'excaucera point. A l'opposite, si nous sommes pitoyables, et qu'oyant les indigences des povres nous soyons esmeus à les aider: que Dieu usera aussi de pitié, et de compassion envers nous pour secourir au besoin. Voila donc pourquoy notamment Moyse en ce passage dit: que Dieu ordonne qu'on ait la main ouverte: voire, aux povres (dit-il) qui habitent entre nous: car Dieu nous les offre, afin que nous n'ayons nulle excuse, disant: Ie ne say à qui bien faire. Puis que nostre Seigneur nous donne le moyen, il ne faut plus cercher subterfuge: car nous demeurerons tousiours coulpables, quand nous n'aurons point usé de l'occasion qui nous estoit offerte."

[121] *Commentary on Matthew* 25:40 (Pringle, 181); *CO* 45, 689.

[122] My translation. *Sermon on Deuteronomy* 15:11 15; *CO* 27, 338–39: ". . . que Dieu ordonne qu'on ait la main ouverte: voire, aux povres (dit-il) qui habitent entre nous: car Dieu nous les offre, afin que nous n'ayons nulle excuse, disant. . . ."

Because worship is the central concern of this text, Calvin directs his hearers to Matt 26 and John 12 where Christ quotes from the first part of Deut 15:11 to provide an interpretation of Mary's anointing:

> Our Lord Jesus Christ goes further in saying that He will not always be with us, but that the poor will be. For in approving this act which was done for His honor, inasmuch as the precious ointment seemed superfluous when His Lord had already anointed Him, He said, "It is well for this time." But from this point on He sent His disciples to the poor, and why? It was as if He said, that the ordinary service [*service ordinaire*] that He receives, either for His own person, or for the person of God His Father, is not that one should bring to Him the precious things of this world: for He has no need of them, but He wills that we give to the poor that which we would offer to Him. And let us note here, as I have already touched on, that our Lord accepts the alms that we give to the poor as sacrifices. Let us not mistakenly think therefore, to offer to Him, as though He receives anything from our hands: but rather He sends us back to do good to those that have need of our aid.[123]

Calvin uses Christ's interpretation of Deut 15:11 in Matt 26 to demonstrate that Mary's extraordinary anointing of Christ was indeed an act of worship. However, Mary's act, according to Calvin, was not a normative example of what Calvin calls the "ordinary service" of worship which Christ requires. An example of an act of "ordinary service" of worship is to bestow alms on the poor. Since God needs no earthly things, "He wills that we give to the poor that which we would offer to Him."[124]

The idea that God is not benefited by material gifts is central to two of Calvin's arguments in his remarks on Deut 15:11. First, as demonstrated above, this concept supports the teaching that the poor are God's ordained

---

[123] My translation. Ibid.; *CO* 27, 339: "Nostre Seigneur Iesus Christ passe encores plus outre, en disant qu'il ne sera pas tousiours avec nous, et que les povres y seront: car en approuvant cest acte qui avoit esté fait pour honneur, d'autant que l'onction precieuse avoit semblé superflue, quand son chef luy avoit esté oinct, il dit: Et bien, pour ce coup: mais doresenavant il renvoye ses disiples aux povres. Et pourquoy? Comme s'il disoit, que ce n'est point un service ordinaire qu'il demande, ni pour sa personne, ni pour celle de Dieu son Pere, qu'on luy apporte choses precieuses de ce monde: car il n'en a point besoin: mais il veut qu'on employe envers les povres ce qu'on luy voudroit offrir. Et en cela notons bien (comme i'ay desia touché) que nostre Seigneur accepte les aumosnes que nous ferons aux povres, comme sacrifices. Ne nous abusons point donc à luy offrir, comme s'il recevoit rien de nos mains: mais plustost il nous renvoye à bien faire à ceux qui ont faute de nostre aide."

[124] My translation. Ibid.: ". . . il veut qu'on employe envers les povres ce qu'on luy voudroit offrir."

representatives on earth, indeed Christ placed before our eyes. The poor, therefore, are meant to receive the material gifts which the community of faith renders to God as part of their service of worship to Christ. Second, this teaching furnishes Calvin with grounds for arguing against the wealth and the magnificent display of the Roman Church. In conclusion, McKee offers a critique of the place of costly ceremony in the Church and sets this against the needs of the poor and the proper worship of the Church in Calvin's theology:

> Almsgiving is the proper expression of giving to God in ordinary service or worship. Costly ceremonies are not regular Christian worship. They were appropriate to certain conditions before Christ's advent or exceptionally for His person, but now His person is represented by the poor. Therefore, almsgiving . . . are the Christian sacrifices of sweet odor on the altar of the poor.[125]

A Critique of the Wealth and Pomp of the Church

The monetary waste of the Roman Church was intolerable for Calvin. He attributes its behavior to an erroneous interpretation of Scripture which in turn fosters a fallacious understanding of Christian worship. Calvin declares:

> Now if this lesson had been properly remembered, the poor world would not have wasted its labor and money on some foolish pomps, as one sees in the Papacy, where they use many lights, and many other petty trifles. And why is this? Oh, it seems that God takes pleasure in paintings, in tapestry, and in such jests. Behold, what wholly occupies the poor world! and in the mean time, the poor are robbed and forgotten.[126]

The lesson to which Calvin refers is Christ's affirmation of the extraordinary service of worship demonstrated in Mary's extravagant anointing. As discussed previously, Calvin understands this event as a singular exception to what is otherwise called the ordinary service of worship of the Church,

---

[125] McKee, *John Calvin on the Diaconate and Liturgical Almsgiving*, 244. See also Calvin's *Sermon on Deuteronomy* 15:11–15; CO 27, 342.

[126] My translation. *Sermon on Deuteronomy* 15:11–15; *CO 27*, 339: "Or si ceste leçon eust esté bien retenue, le povre monde n'eust point ainsi perdu sa peine et son argent en folles pompes, comme on voit en la Papauté qu'on usera de beaucoup de luminaires, on aura des menus fatras beaucoup. Et comment? O! il semble que Dieu prenne plaisir en peinture, en tapisserie, en ces badinages. Et voila où le povre monde s'occupe du tout: et cependant les povres sont destituez et mis en oubli."

that is, the giving of alms to the poor. The Roman Church interpreted this event to mean that Christ approved of using extravagant materials for the Church's ordinary service of worship. Calvin uses hyperbole to show the absurdity of God being benefited or taking "pleasure in paintings, in tapestry, and in such jests."[127] If the Roman Church had correctly understood this text, he reasoned, then the magnificent adornments in worship would be greatly diminished and a tremendous waste of ecclesial resources avoided. Most importantly, if this text were understood properly, the needs of the poor would not be neglected. Calvin regards the excessive expenditures of the Church on physical ornamentation as nothing short of despising an essential aspect of the Church's worship of Christ, that is, providing for the poor. The belief that display and magnificence in Christian worship somehow pleases God not only betrays a misunderstanding of God's character and the nature of Christian worship, but it also brings disastrous consequences upon the poor. Error in doctrine always begets error in practice.

After reflecting upon the disastrous social implications of Roman worship practices concerning the plight of the poor, Calvin returns to pondering the reason for poverty in the world. He applies his thoughts to his hearers:

> On the contrary, our Lord Jesus declares that this is the kind of situation that God will use to test whether we desire to honor Him. For, as we have said, He could well have made it that all men would be rich. But He sends us poor people in order to give us the opportunity to demonstrate if we have any desire to show to whom we are indebted to for our goods. So let us be advised to apply these to a usage He approves of. Therefore, if we have any such desire, the opportunity is offered to us, and is never lacking. Here is in sum what we must remember from this passage.[128]

Because God is capable of making all people rich, the presence of the poor is indeed a divine test to see how the people of God shall choose to wor-

---

[127] My translation. Ibid.; *CO* 27, 339: "O! il semble que Dieu prenne plaisir en peinture, en tapisserie, en ces badinages."

[128] My translation. Ibid.: "Au contraire, nostre Seigneur Isus declaire que c'est là où Dieu veut essayer si nous aurons affection de l'honorer: car il pourroit bien faire que tous seroyent riches (comme nous avons déclairé) mais il nous envoye des povres, afin que nous ayons matiere de nous employer, si nous avons quelque affection de monstrer de qui nous tenons les biens, et que nous advisions de les appliquer en usage qui luy soit approuvè. Si donc nous avons un tel desir: l'occasion nous est offerte, et ne nous deffaut iamais. Voila en somme ce que nous avons à retenir de ce passage."

ship God. Will they spend their resources on expensive ornamentation for worship, or will they reveal to the world to whom they are indebted for all that they have by faithfully providing for the needs of the poor? The poor indeed reveal the spiritual character of the Church and reveal the character of both the Church and people's hearts. This is a test that Calvin exhorts his congregation in Geneva not to fail.

An Examination of Begging

The Problem of Begging

Calvin perceives that his exposition of Deut 15:11 raises a number of important practical questions for his community. One of those considerations dealt with the pervasive and preponderant problem of begging. Calvin recognizes that, at first glance, everything he said about the poor being placed in the world by the divine ordination of God to test the Church and its quality of worship seems to conflict with the text which reads that "there shall be no beggars in the land."[129] Calvin concludes that the solution to this conflict is simple. It is possible to have the poor dwelling in the land and to not have begging.[130] Calvin presents his rationale as to why, according to nature, begging is "against public order and honorableness":[131]

> For people do not know to whom to give; if they (that is, if people or anyone) go about shouting from door to door, people cannot discern whether there is a real need or not, and loudest ones will carry off that by which the poor should be fed and sustained. And then when they go about begging in this manner, this supports deceivers, for the greatest tricks that one can imagine will be found in

---

[129] Ibid.: "At first glance it certainly seems that this does not agree with what we have already seen, that there should be no *beggars* in the land" (my translation and emphasis). [Or il semble bien de prime face que ceci ne s'accorde point à ce que desia nous avons veu: Qu'il n'y doit point avoir de povres mendiens en la terre.]

[130] Ibid.: "But the solution is very easy, because it is quite possible for there to be poor people, and yet that mendicant life (as they call it) is taken away" (my translation). [Mais la solution est bien aisee: pource qu'il se pourra bien faire qu'il y ait des povres, et cependant que la mendicite, qu'on dit, soit ostee.]

[131] Ibid.; *CO* 27, 339–40: "Truly, this must be a great shame for people that profess God, that there are beggars among them. That in itself is against public order and honorableness. Even if we did not have the Commandment of our God; let us consider, the question according to nature, what may happen when begging is permitted" (my translation). [Et de faict, ce doit estre grand' honte à un peuple qui se renomme de Dieu, qu'il y ait des mendiens: pource que cela mesmes est contre l'ordre et honnesteté publique. Encores que nous n'eussions point le commandement de nostre Dieu: regardons selon nature: quand on souffrira qu'il y ait des mendiens, que cela peut apporter.]

these con-men that go about begging. And the one who becomes accustomed to such delinquent behavior will finally become thief. And then, even if there are not other misfortunes; yet we see how these that are accustomed to beg are unable to perform any kind of work, so that they never learn to do good, but are always idle and strolling about. Thus you see how begging, even according to the order of nature, is always to be condemned as it is, for it brings nothing but vice and corruption, and it is certain that in the end everything will be in confusion where begging is permitted and endured.[132]

Calvin offers three reasons why giving to beggars ought to be rejected as a method of poverty relief. First, it is too difficult for the average person to discern to whom it is appropriate to give. Calvin describes a familiar medieval sight of professional beggars going about the street making a conspicuous display of their indigence by shouting from door to door. This introduces his second reason for supporting a ban on begging: giving alms to people who carry on in this way does more harm than good to society. Giving to beggars condones the practice of deceit. In Calvin's mind, these people are thieves, willing to go to any length to persuade others to sustain them while the truly indigent are neglected. Third, tolerating begging brings about nothing good. Those who beg never learn to work or contribute to society in a positive way. Where begging is permitted, Calvin argues, the practice will only lead to confusion and result finally in sin and corruption. Begging presents a great temptation for the poor, exacerbated by their need to survive. To permit begging means that the poor will surely fail the divine test. If this occurs, Christ will not be honored, nor will righteousness be advanced in the kingdom. For these reasons, Calvin sees the logic of Scripture's prohibition.

---

[132] My translation. Ibid.; *CO* 27, 340: ". . . si on va ainsi crier par les huis et par les portes, on ne peut pas discerner s'il y a nécessité ou non, et les plus grands criars emporteront ce dont les povres devroyent estre nourris et substantez. Et puis quand on vient ainsi mendier, c'est pour entretenir des trompeurs: car les plus grandes ruses qu'on pourroit imaginer se trouveront en ces conquins qui vont ainsi mendier. Et cependant celuy qui aura esté ainsi accoquiné, il deviendra larron à la fin. Et puis encores qu'il n'y eust autre mal, si voit-on que ceux qui sont ainsi accoustumez à mendier ne peuvent faire un mestier: tellement que iamais ils ne se peuvent appliquer à bien faire, ce sont tousiours des fayneans, et des frians. Voila comme la mendicité, selon l'ordre de nature mesmes, sera tousiours à condamner, comme elle est: car elle n'apporte que vice et corruption, et faut en la fin que tout soit confus où elle sera soufferte, et enduree."

Calvin offers an alternative to begging that is more socially and spiritually beneficial for the poor and the community at large. The method he advances is best described as informed giving.[133] Calvin states:

> But we have God's commandment, which is an even higher authority, when it says that we must not have beggars among us, but that the necessity of this must be warded off by support for those in need, according to the best of one's discernment, and according to the means available. So it is then that these two passages are not at all contrary. For when He says that there will always be poor people, well, this is (as we have touched on) so that the rich may have occasion to make sacrifices to God, just as He asks from them, to provide for those in need with the things that they have in their hands. And let this be done with discretion, i.e. let there be as much as possible and investigation into those who are in need. But, however, that one should give without discretion (discernment), or that also people might be permitted to beg in the streets and by the doors, this is a shameful thing and against all good order, and it brings nothing but confusion, and it supports for the worse all those to whom one gives such license, as we have already demonstrated.[134]

---

[133] In *De Regno Christi*, Bucer wrote the following problems associated with uninformed giving or begging. Several of these reflect Calvin's arguments and concerns as well: "For when each person wishes to distribute his own alms for himself, there is violated, first of all the institution of the Holy Spirit and the legitimate communion of saints. Secondly, alms due to the least of Christ's brethren, and therefore to Christ Himself, are more often given to the unworthy than to the worthy. Nor can every single individual know and investigate each of the poor who happen to encounter him; for those who are least worthy are much better instructed at begging, indeed, extorting, the alms which should be dispensed to the poor alone. Furthermore, when everyone gives alms by his own hand, it is with great difficulty that he will exclude from his heart a desire for the appreciation and praise of men; and when he receives this empty reward from men, a real and sure one is not to be expected from God. Finally, since it is obvious that those who voluntarily give themselves over to beggary are men prone to every crime, what else do those people who foster them do but sustain and support very harmful pests of society." See Bucer, *De Regno Christi*, 257–58. In these arguments, Bucer and Calvin summarize the main ideas that pertained to organized poor relief during the Reformation. See Holl, *Cultural Significance*, 91, 99–100.

[134] My translation. *Sermon on Deuteronomy* 15:11–15; *CO* 27, 340: "Mais nous avons le commandement de Dieu, qui est encores par dessus, quand il dit que nous ne devons point avoir de mendiens entre nous, et qu'on doit prevenir ceste necessité-la, subvenant à ceux qui ont faute, selon qu'on en pourra iuger, et selon que la faculté aussi y sera. Voila donc comme ces deux passages ne sont point repugnans. Car quand il dit qu'il y aura tousiours des povres: et bien; c'est (comme nous avons touché) afin que les riches ayent occasion de faire sacrifices à Dieu tels qu'il les demande, que de ce qu'ils ont entre mains ils advisent d'en subvenir à ceux qui en ont faute: voire, et que cela se face par discretion, c'est à dire

There seems to be a question with Calvin's opening statement in this text. Calvin remarks, "But we have God's commandment, which is an even higher authority, when it says that we must not have beggars among us. . . ."[135] In an earlier part of this sermon, Calvin states what seems to be another idea: "Truly, this must be a great shame for people that profess God, that there are beggars among them. That in itself is against public order and honorableness. Even if we did not have the Commandment of our God; let us consider, the question according to nature, what may happen when begging is permitted."[136] Since there is no statement in Scripture which specifically outlaws the practice of begging *per se*, it is best to understand Calvin's statement as an observation of this fact. This would also explain why he provides a detailed argument from nature to explain why begging should not be tolerated.

In his *Harmony* concerning Deut 15:4 and 7, Calvin reveals more of the exegesis behind his thoughts.[137] Throughout this text, Calvin consistently translates the Hebrew term *'ebyôn* into the Latin term *mendicus*.[138] The term *'ebyôn* conveys a sense of want and destitution, characteristic of a beggar, a needy or a very poor person.[139] He describes two popular ways of interpreting verse 4. Some claim that the text refers to a prohibition against begging; therefore, they translate it to read, "Nevertheless let

---

qu'on s'enquiere tant qu'il sera possible de ceux qui ont necessité. Mais cependant qu'on donne sans iuger, et qu'aussi il soit permis d'aller mendier par les rues et par les portes, c'est une chose villaine et contre toute bonne police: et cela n'apporte que confusion, et mesmes on nourrit au mal tous ceux ausquels on donne une telle licence, comme desia nous avons monstré."

[135] My translation. Ibid.: "Mais nous avons le commandement de Dieu, qui est encores par dessus, quand il dit que nous ne devons point avoir de mendiens entre nous . . ."

[136] My translation. Ibid.; *CO* 27, 339–40: "Et de faict, ce doit estre grand' honte à un peuple qui se renomme de Dieu, qu'il y ait des mendiens: pource que cela mesmes est contre l'ordre et honnesteté publique. Encores que nous n'eussions point le commandement de nostre Dieu: regardons selon nature: quand on souffrira qu'il y ait des mendiens, que cela peut apporter."

[137] *Commentary on Deuteronomy* 15:4–7 (Pringle, 155–58); *CO* 24, 698–99.

[138] See Calvin's translation of the text in *Commentary on Deuteronomy* 15:4, 7, 9 and twice in verse 11 (Pringle, 153); *CO* 24, 697.

[139] The term *'ebyôn* occurs 61 times in the Hebrew Old Testament. Calvin translates this term with the Latin word *mendicus* or *mendico* only 5 times with all 5 of those occurrences found in his translation of Deut 15:4–11 in his *Harmony*. See *Commentary on Deuteronomy* 15:4–11 (Pringle, 159–62); *CO* 24, 696–97. He uses the Latin term *mendicus* one other time in his Old Testament translations, and that occurrence is in Ps 109:10, to translate the Hebrew word *shâêl*, which generally means "to ask or inquire" (Pringle, 274); *CO* 32, 148. See Brown, Driver and Briggs, *Hebrew and English*, 981–82; see also the entry for "*'ebhyôn*" in Botterweck, *TDOT*, 1:27–41; and also Wevers, *Concordance*, 49 m.

there be no beggar among you."¹⁴⁰ This interpretation says that it is the responsibility of the brethren to assist the poor so that they might not be overcome by their distress. Others understand the verse as a promise that there will be no beggars among the people if they are faithful in keeping the Law because God promises to bless them. Though he acknowledges the acceptability of these interpretations, he presents his particular understanding which is based on the grammar of the text. Calvin posits that the translation of the words *ephes ci* at the beginning of the verse would be better translated as "unless because" [*nisi quod*] so that the phrase might be read parenthetically and understood to say, "Whenever there should be any poor among your brethren, an opportunity of doing them good is presented to you. Therefore the poverty of your brethren is to be relieved by you, in order that God may bless you."¹⁴¹ Yet Calvin understands the phrase *ephes ci*, [*nisi quod*], in a more exclusive or emphatic way. He interprets the entire phrase to mean: "On no account let there be a beggar." Calvin is insistent that the responsibility for the abolition of begging falls not upon the poor but instead upon the community at large. He writes, "howsoever it may be, do not permit by *your* fault there should be any beggar [*mendicum*] among you; for He would put an end to all vain excuses, and as necessity arose, would have them disposed to give assistance, lest the poor should sink under the pressure of want and distress."¹⁴²

Calvin recognized that there is an implicit command against begging in the text of Deut 15:4, which he uses in his sermon on Deut 15:11. God commanded Israel to provide for the needs of the poor through the community. Calvin reasons that if nature shows begging to be an unhealthy practice, then the command of God to meet the needs of the poor must

---

¹⁴⁰ "Verumtamen non sit apud te mendicus . . ." *Commentary on Deuteronomy* 15:4 (Pringle, 155); *CO* 24, 698. In Calvin's comments on verse 11 he gives a further critique of this idea. Calvin writes: "The notion of those is far fetched who suppose that there would be always poor men [*pauperes*] among them, because they would not keep the law, and consequently the land would be barren on account of their unrighteousness. I admit that this is true; but God does not here ascribe it to their sins that there would always be some beggars [*mendici*] among them, but only reminds them that there would never be wanting matter for their generosity, because He would prove what was in their hearts by setting the poor [*pauperibus*] before them. Ibid., 15:11 (Pringle, 158); *CO* 24, 699.

¹⁴¹ Ibid., 15:4 (Pringle, 156); *CO* 24, 698.

¹⁴² Emphasis mine. Ibid., 15:3 (Pringle, 156). Calvin makes a similar observation in his *Commentary on Deuteronomy* 15:7: "The same word *ebyon*, is used, which we have seen just above, verse 4; nor is there any contradiction when He had before forbidden to exist among His people; for the object of the prohibition was, that if any were reduced to beggary, they should not be cast out and forsaken . . . He explains the mode of preventing this . . . that the hands of the rich should be open to assist them" (Pringle, 157); *CO* 24, 699.

imply meeting those needs before they become so acute that the person is forced to beg. This reasoning allows him to argue that the giving of funds to beggars is not supported by the text. Instead, it is a command for the people of God to take care of the indigent in order to abolish the practice of begging.

Another important distinction which Calvin highlights is the differentiation between being poor and being a beggar: the former does not necessitate the latter. Because the practice of begging by the poor has a history which reached back into the millennia, with the rise of the mendicant movement in the twelfth century these two concepts became all the more entangled and confusing for those living in the Middle Ages. What Calvin wishes to demonstrate is that even though begging is indeed a hazard to society and thus should not be permitted, this realization does not release the rich from their responsibility to share their abundance with the poor. Calvin cites an old and familiar idea to his hearers: the poor are a divine opportunity for the rich "to make sacrifices to God just as He demands it from them, by providing for these that have need."[143]

In Calvin's ecclesiology, the poor are chosen to represent God upon the earth. God designates the poor to receive a significant portion of the gifts and offerings of the Church. Calvin realizes that forbidding begging puts an even greater responsibility on the Church to fulfill its role in serving the poor. Although in the economy of the sixteenth century the poor were vulnerable and dependant on the benevolence of the rich, Calvin's remarks suggest that in the spiritual economy of the kingdom of God, the rich have a far greater need for the poor. It is only through the poor that the generosity of the rich may become an appropriate spiritual sacrifice to God that exemplifies a righteous and obedient life. Hans Scholl makes a similar insight in his study:

> According to Calvin's message, that is, to his exegetical insights, it is clear that the rich man needs the poor man more than the latter needs him. God in His miraculous power can and will care for the poor man. The rich man, however, ... lives in an ultimate sense according to faith, only through the poor. Only in and through the poor man can he really come to be. "And that is why it is said that

---

[143] See original text above. *CO* 27, 340; In another passage on right sacrifices found in Calvin's *Commentary on Philippians* 4:18, he writes "For the altars, on which sacrifices from our resources ought to be presented, are the poor [*pauperes*], and the servants of Christ [*servi Christi*]" (Pringle, 128); *CO* 52, 66.

he who shuts his ears to the cry of the poor will cry in his turn and God will not answer him."[144]

In Calvin's ecclesiology, the poor serve in the important spiritual role of authenticating the worship of the Church. Through a ministry of service to the poor, the people of God manifest their faith. How the people of God minister to the poor reveals to all the quality of their spiritual lives and their devotion to Christ. Likewise, Calvin maintains that the degree to which the people of God minister to the poor is the same measure with which God will show faithfulness to them.

Calvin provides some practical advice recommending how the Church can care for the poor, fulfill its spiritual obligation, and end the problem of begging. He is not speaking exclusively of the rich in this context but about all who have enough to survive and can sacrifice something for another. Calvin exhorts his congregation:

> It remains now to practice this doctrine, and in the first place, according to how urgent the needs are, we must understand that God urges us more than ever to do good, and there is reason to strive thus when there is any famine or scarcity. Then, each one ought to subtract from their own table (or means for supplying their table) rather than permit others to lack and themselves living in excess (with a laden table). And in lieu of the fact that many take opportunity to pinch when they see a costly year, when it seems to them that this is the time to catch the best prey, may we understand that our Lord then summons us and shows us that if we ever have the desire to do Him homage with the goods that He has put in our hands, He wants them employed there at that time. Here is one item.[145]

To care for the poor requires personal sacrifice. The responsibility of generosity to those less fortunate does not lessen in the lean times. During fam-

---

[144] Scholl, "Church and the Poor," 245. Scholl's quote came from Calvin's *Sermon on Deuteronomy* 15:11; *CO* 27, 338.

[145] My translation. *Sermon on Deuteronomy* 15:11; *CO* 27, 340–41: "Il reste maintenant de prattiquer ceste doctrine. Et en premier lieu, selon que les nesessitez seront urgentes, cognoissons que Dieu nous sollicite plus que iamais à bien faire, et que c'est la raison de s'efforcer, quand il y a quelque famine, quelque cherté: alors chacun doit plustost retrancher ses morceaux, que de souffrir que les autres ayent indigence, et qu'on vive ainsi en gourmandant. Et au lieu que beaucoup prennent occasion à serrer, quand ils voyent une annee chere, qu'il leur semble que c'est pour attrapper meilleure proye: que nous cognoissions qu'alors nostre Seigneur nous adiourne, et nous monstre, que si iamais nous avons eu affection de lui faire hommage de biens qu'il nous a mis entre les mains, qu'il veut qu'adonc l'on s'y employe. Voila pour un item."

ine or inflation, believers must not hoard food in order to sell it at a greater profit, and thereby exploit the poor, or keep all for themselves and live in excess. Calvin regards both of these actions as unacceptable. Instead, believers are to share their resources with the poor by subtracting from their own means; this is the only way that believers can honor the Lord with what God has put into their hands. Calvin offers some counsel:

> And when we see a lot of poor people in need, let us understand that our Lord is alerting us, as if He wakes us up so that we do not remain asleep, and when we have not thought of our duty enough, then our Lord comes to remind us of what He had commanded us, and if we are not too slack (or lazy) He must remind us; let each of us consider the measure that is given to him and his abilities and let him busy himself in that way. This is what we have to note in the first place.[146]

Calvin wants his congregation to see the poor with eyes that are sensitive to the spiritual economy of God's kingdom. He earnestly believes that God uses the necessity of the poor to waken the Church from spiritual slumber. Believers are commanded to give to the poor according to their ability. Thus the indigence of the poor not only authenticates the worship of the Church and exercises the faith of believers but also spiritually awakens the Church.

The Need for Social Reform

Because begging is not an option for the poor in the Church, Calvin turns to address the issue of the beggar's social reform. As a preface to his second practical point, Calvin explains why begging is detrimental to community life, describing the profile of the stereotypical beggar:

> And then for the second point let us seek to keep proper order, so that this shame and baseness of begging is not among us. And why? Because this will only feed a wicked parasite. It will not even profit those who receive, because it will make them delinquent, and they will be rogues and idle persons, as has already been demonstrated. And finally, they take pleasure in their begging and like

---

[146] My translation. Ibid.; *CO* 27, 341: "Et quand nous verrons beaucoup de povres en necessité, cognoissons que nostre Seigneur nous advertit, que c'est autant comme s'il nous esveilloit pour ne point estre endormis: et quand nous a'avons point assez pensé à nostre devoir, qu'alors nostre Seigneur vient nous reduire en memoire ce qu'il nous avoit commandé, et que si nous ne sommes par trop lasches, qu'il nous faut esverruer: qu'un chacun regarde la mesure qui luy est donnee, la faculté de son pouvoir, et qu'il s'employe là. C'est donc ce que nous avons à noter en premier lieu."

their bag better, and will never change it for a certain guaranteed income. And experience demonstrates this too well. They progress from rogues to thieves; it has to come out that way. And nevertheless let this whole thing be removed, unless we want to provoke knowingly the wrath of God, and always cause things to become worse.[147]

At the core of the problem of begging is a serious spiritual problem. Beggars ultimately do not beg in order to relieve their poverty but because they enjoy the activity and do not intend to be productive with their lives. Beggars are motivated by greed, covetousness, and idleness, wishing only to live off the resources of others. The community that permits begging, therefore, invites social disorder. According to Calvin, by permitting the practice of begging, a city cultivates thieves and sanctions idleness. The only remedy for this situation is to forbid the practice altogether.

Calvin echoes the frustration and anxiety of his times. By the sixteenth century, cities were desperate to find solutions to the problem of poverty. No doubt one of the practices to which Calvin refers in this statement is the outlawing of begging without providing any other means to care for the poor to meet their needs. As early as two centuries before Calvin preached this sermon, governments all over Europe began to take harsh measures to control the numbers of beggars. In England, the indigent were issued passes. Beggars caught on a road without a pass were branded. Similar legislation was passed by the French parliament in Paris. Many towns in Europe forbade a beggar to stay more than one night "on pain of death by hanging."[148] These examples indicate attitudes of open hostility and distrust of the beggar in the later Middle Ages—attitudes which Calvin's own writings confirm. Mollat's words substantiate Calvin's suspicions:

---

[147] My translation. Ibid.; *CO* 27, 341: "Et puis pour le second, que nous advisions d'avoir ordre et police, tellement que ceste vergongne et turpitude ne soit point au milieu de nous, qu'on mendie. Et pourquoy? Car ce ne sera que nourrir une meschante vermine: qu'on ne sera que nourrir une meschante vermine: qu'on ne fera point mesmes le profit de ceux à qui on donnera: car on les accoquine, ils s'accagnardent, comme desia nous avons monstré: et en la fin ils se plaisent en leur mendicité, et aiment mieux leur sac, et ne le changeroyent point à une rente certaine: et l'experience le monstre par trop: et de coquins ils deviennent larrons, qu'il faut en la fin en venir là. Et pourtant que tout cela soit osté, si nous ne voulons à nostre escient provoquer l'ire de Dieu, et faire que tousiours les choses iront en empirant."

[148] Mollat, *Poor in the Middle Ages*, 291.

It is but a short step from mistrust to fear, from suspicion to accusation. People were afraid not so much of the beggar's indigence as of his idleness, his rootlessness, and his anonymity. They no longer knew with whom they were dealing.[149]

Calvin's remarks are amazing. Even though he has a contempt for beggars common among many of the sixteenth century, he is careful not to transfer these feelings to those who are legitimately poor. Instead, he urges generosity toward the less fortunate. Calvin exhorts:

> But be that as it may, let us see that the poor are maintained, because to forbid their begging and nevertheless not to give any alms is as much as to cuts the throats of those that are suffering scarcity. But it is necessary so to provide for the poor and to remedy the need there, that those beggars whom one sees plainly that there is no piety in them, those ought to be rebuked, for they only ask to eat up the bread of others and to rob from those who are destitute what one would have given them. This I say in sum is what we have to remember.[150]

Calvin once again makes an important distinction. He contrasts the activities of giving alms to the poor with maintaining the practice of begging. The poor should be treated with charity until their needs are remedied. The beggar, however, should not only be refused those alms reserved for the poor but also denied pity. What the beggar needs most is to be reformed. Yet if begging is forbidden and at the same time a community fails to provide alms for the poor, "this as much as cuts the throat of these that are in scarcity," Calvin declares.[151] The answer to this problem is for alms to be distributed in a way other than begging.

Calvin does not spend an inordinate amount of time considering the practical details of how poor relief is administrated in Geneva. A sermon

---

[149] Mollat, *Poor in the Middle Ages*, 251. See chapter 3 of this study for more extensive comments on this topic.

[150] My translation. *Sermon on Deuteronomy* 15:11; *CO* 27, 341: "Mais quoy qu'il en soit, advisons que les povres soyent substantez: car qui defendra de mendier, et cependant qu'on ne face nulle aumosne: c'est comme coupper la gorge à ceux qui sont en disette. Mais il faut tellement pourvoir à la pauvreté et y remedier, que ceux qui sont mendiens, et qu'on voit à l'oeil qu'il n'y a point de pitié en eux, que ceux-la soyent reprins: car ils ne demandent qu'à manger la substance d'autruy, et desrobent à ceux qui sont indigens ce qu'on leur devroit donner. Voila (di-ie) en somme ce que nous avons à retenir."

[151] My translation. Ibid.; *CO* 27, 341: ". . . c'est comme coupper la gorge à ceux qui sont en disette."

was probably not the appropriate setting for such directives to the Church. He does, however, reflect on the following rhetorical question:

> How is that done? In the first place, the hospitals (the poor relief institutions) should provide well for such need. For what a shame it is if the goods are dedicated to God and the poor but nevertheless are applied to other uses. This is not robbery, rather this is sacrilege. Therefore, let them be used as He says, and not hold back household goods for one's self that should be used for God, and for those whom He presents to us. And each one also in his own place, as he recognizes special needs there, let him try to provide for them, let him look where there is lack and indigence, and let him remedy it. When this is done, then begging will be removed as it should be, and let them not make a simple prohibition which says that no one may beg anymore while the poor remain there destitute, dying of hunger and thirst.[152]

Calvin affirms the hospital as the best institution for administrating poverty relief. By mentioning the hospital, he makes an indirect reference concerning the tasks of deacons in Geneva. In the autumn of 1541, Calvin drafted a treatise called the "Ecclesiastical Ordinances." In it, he outlined "four orders of offices instituted by our Lord for the government of His Church": pastors, doctors, elders and deacons.[153] In the passage in which

---

[152] My translation. Ibid.; *CO* 27, 341–42: "Et comment cela se fera-il? Qu'en premier lieu les hospitaux doyvent bien fournir à telle necessité: car quelle honte sera-ce, que le bien soit dedié à Dieu, et aux povres, et cependant qu'il soit appliqué à autre usage? ce n'est point larrecin, mais c'est un sacrilege. Ainsi, que cela s'employe comme il dit, et qu'on ne face point des bons mesnagers, reservant à ie ne say quel usage ce qui doit estre employé à Dieu, et à ceux qu'il nous presente: et qu'un chacun aussi en son endroit, selon qu'il cognoist les necessitez speciales, qu'il tasche d'y subvenir: qu'il regarde là où il y aura faute et indigence, et qu'il y remedie. Quand donc cela se fera: alors la mendicité sera ostee, comme elle doit: et non pas qu'on face une simple defense, pour dire qu'on ne mendie plus, et cependant que les povres demeurent là desnuez, et que ils meurent de faim, et de soif."

[153] See *Calvin: Theological Treatises*, "Ecclesiastical Ordinances" (Reid, 58); *CO* 10a, 15–16. McKee states that the Genevan hospital or welfare system had been reorganized in 1535, before Calvin arrived in Geneva, and that this reorganization followed a widespread pattern of social reform in the sixteenth century. She notes that Calvin's "Ecclesiastical Ordinances" are often interpreted as "an *ex post facto* consecration, or possibly an attempt to resacralize or re-establish ecclesiastical control over a lay institution." Yet given the historical evidence for Calvin's exegesis of Rom 12:8, she claims that Calvin's diaconate is not "socially induced eisegesis" and that there are theological factors for why Calvin interpreted the two kinds of deacons as "*procureur* and *hospitalier*." According to Calvin's understanding of Rom 12:8, the office of deacon had two functions: the responsibility of giving or administrating aid, and the performance of acts of mercy in the care of the sick and poor. Both these functions were embodied in the separate tasks of the "*procureur* and *hospitalier*."

he discusses the responsibilities of deacons, he names two types: first, the "procurators [who] receive, dispense and hold goods for the poor, not only daily alms, but also possessions, rents and pensions"; second, the "*hospitaller*." These *hospitallers* "tend and care for the sick and administer allowances to the poor."[154] In the "Ecclesiastical Ordinances," Calvin identifies these poor whom the *hospitallers* serve. They are "the sick and the old people unable to work, widowed women, orphaned children and other poor creatures."[155] He also recognizes that others within the city who are poor, or possibly unable to help themselves (probably old, sick, or handicapped) are the responsibility of the *hospitallers* as well.[156] This description of the poor in the "Ecclesiastical Ordinances" is probably a good indication to whom Calvin refers when he distinguishes the poor from the beggar in his *Sermon on Deuteronomy* 15:11. It is interesting to note that at the end of his comments on deacons in the "Ordinances," Calvin states the need "to discourage mendicancy . . . [and that there should be] one of our officials at the entrance of the churches to remove from the place those who loiter." Furthermore, he says that the "Overseers of Tens are to take care that the total prohibition of begging be well observed."[157]

The "Ecclesiastical Ordinances," written fourteen years earlier, confirm what Calvin said about the poor and the beggar in his *Sermon on Deuteronomy* 15:11. Calvin knew that the best way to remove begging from the streets of Geneva was not simply by outlawing it (so that "in the mean time, the poor reside there destitute, and they die of hunger and thirst");[158] but instead by charting a devoted diaconate to faithfully look after the poor according to each person's particular needs, trying to relieve whatever indigence there may be. When the diaconate acts responsibly with the gifts and alms devoted to God, putting them to proper use in ministering to the poor, and not employing them in sacrilegious ways such as giving them to beggars or buying expensive ornaments for church

---

See *Calvin on the Diaconate*, 127–28, 196–200.

[154] *Calvin: Theological Treatises*, "Ecclesiastical Ordinances" (Reid, 64); *CO* 10, 23. Jeannine Olson, in her chapter "Ideology and Origins of the *Bourse Française*: John Calvin," provides an outline of the social history of the two types of deacons in Geneva—"the procurators and the *hospitalers*." *Calvin and Social Welfare*, 29–36.

[155] *Calvin: Theological Treatises*, "Ecclesiastical Ordinances" (Reid, 65); *CO* 10, 23–24.

[156] Ibid.; *CO* 10, 24.

[157] Ibid., (Reid, 66); *CO* 10, 25.

[158] *Sermon on Deuteronomy* 15:11–15; *CO* 27, 342.

buildings, it is then that God is honored, the poor are cared for, and begging will cease.¹⁵⁹

The Social and Spiritual Relationship between the Rich and the Poor

Calvin offers a final theologically significant observation in his discourse on Deut 15:11. He notes the kinds of pronouns used in the biblical text:

> And indeed, it is not without cause that our Lord says here, "Your poor your indigent which are in your land." He could well have said: "the poor and the indigent," but He uses other language. "Your poor" He says. It is as "if a man is poor, people disdains him, and each turns his back to him." And why is that? Oh, it seems to the rich that the poor should not approach them at all, and they would almost want to have the world divided; if it were not that they want to be served by the poor, they would be contented never to see them. Now on the contrary, in order to destroy such presumption and pride, our Lord says, "And who are you who despise your brother in this way? He is your poor, your indigent." He addresses our own flesh. Thus let us weigh well the words which the Holy Spirit has used, in order that no pride may prevent us from having compassion on those who are thus joined to us.¹⁶⁰

Calvin cut through the social presumptions of his day to make this insightful remark. The language of Deuteronomy deliberately uses the possessive pronoun "your" not the definite article *the*, in order to personalize the poor within the Church. Calvin applies this insight to the contempt of the rich toward the poor in his day: "they would almost want to have the world divided; if it were not that they want to be served by the poor, they would be contented never to see them." With the exception of having

---

¹⁵⁹ Ibid. See Elsie McKee's work, *John Calvin on the Diaconate and Liturgical Almsgiving*, for a complete discussion of Calvin's practical and exegetical theology of the diaconate.

¹⁶⁰ My translation. *Sermon on Deuteronomy* 15:11–15; *CO* 27, 342: "Et de faict, ce n'est point sans cause que nostre Seigneur dit ici: Ton povre, ton indigent qui sera en ta terre. Il pouvoit bien dire: Le povre et l'indigent: mais il use d'un autre langage: Ton povre, dit-il. Comme s'il disoit: Si un homme est povre, on le desdaigne, chacun luy tourne le dos: et pourquoy cela? O il semble aux riches que les povres ne doivent point approcher d'eux, et voudroyent quasi avoir un monde divisé: si ce n'estoit qu'ils veulent estre servis des povres, ils seroyent contens de iamais n'en voir. Or à l'opposite, nostre Seigneur, pour abatre une telle presomption et fierté, dit: Et qui es-tu qui mesprises ainsi ton frere? c'est ton povre, ton indigent. Il s'adresse à nostre propre chair. Ainsi poisons bien les mots dont le sainct Esprit a usé: afin que nul orgueil ne nous empesche d'avoir compassion de ceux qui sont ainsi conioints à nous."

servants, the rich preferred to live a segregated life, living on large estates, removed from the ills and unsightly afflictions of the poor. Calvin observes that instead of showing compassion and generosity, the rich ignore the poor and loathe them. Calvin calls his congregation back to the point of the text: "'And who are you who despise *your* brother in this way? He is *your* poor, *your* indigent.' He addresses *our own* flesh."[161]

Calvin recognizes that a major obstacle in relieving the needs of the poor is not resources but "presumption and pride." Pride impedes the flow of compassion. It is also antithetical to the true humility of spirit necessary for spiritual growth in the Christian life. Thus it is not surprising that the pride of the rich keeps the poor at arm's length and seeks to depersonalize them. The Lord's words, however, do quite the opposite. Calvin finds that the language of Deut 15:11 personalizes the poor, calling them "our own flesh":

> Let us note that they are our own poor people, that is to say that our Lord offers to us those who have this lack, as if He said, I want to make such intercourse that the rich are mixed among the poor, and that they meet together so as to communicate with each other, let the poor receive and the rich give, and let me be honored by both the one and the other, when the rich person has the means to do good, and the poor person recognizes that it is for my name's sake that he is nourished, and let both of them bless me. This is why Moses has spoken about the poor and indigent in this way, that he demonstrates to (shows) the rich that this is addressed to them, and that they must have a community, not to be [social] equals, but to provide for the destitution of those that God thus offers to them.[162]

Calvin knows that the only way to break the pride and presumption of the rich toward the poor was to end the segregation of the rich from the poor.

---

[161] Emphasis mine. Ibid. Rolf Kramer in *Umgang mit der Armut* draws attention to this point. See page 34.

[162] My translation. *Sermon on Deuteronomy* 15:11–15; CO 27, 342: "Et notons qu'ils sont nos povres, c'est à dire, que ceux qui ont ainsi faute, nostre Seigneur nous les offre: comme s'il disoit: Ie veux faire une telle discussion, que le riche soit meslé parmi le povre, et qu'ils se rencontrent ainsi, afin de communiquer ensemble: et que le povre reçoyve, et que le riche donne, et que ie soye honoré se l'un et de l'autre, quand le riche aura dequoy pour bien faire, et que le povre recognoistra que c'est à mon nom qu'il est nourri, et que tous les deux me benissent. Voila pourquoy Moyse a parlé des povres et indigens en telle sorte, qu'il monstre aux riches, que c'est à eux que ceci s'adresse: et qu'ils doivent avoir une communauté, non point pour estre esgaux: mais pour subvenir à l'indigence de ceux que Dieu leur offre ainsi."

The rich need to be "mixed among the poor and that they meet together so as to communicate with each other, let the poor receive and the rich give."[163] Fellowship will only happen if the rich agree to associate with the poor and truly live in community with them. Ultimately community is only possible if the rich and poor see their relationship to one another as being part of their relationship to Christ. If the rich give to the poor as giving to the Lord, and if the poor receive as if they received from the Lord able to recognize "that it is for my [Christ's] name's sake that he is nourished," then God will be honored.[164] It is only when the worship of Christ is the focus of the relationship between the rich and poor that the spiritual economy of the kingdom is in proper balance. It is precisely then that both the spiritual needs of the rich and the physical needs of the poor are met. When pride is purged from the hearts of the rich, and when the rich and poor alike see one another from the perspective of Christ, then God will be honored and the worship of the Church will be spiritually acceptable.

In closing, Calvin's *Sermon on Deuteronomy* 15:11 offers a clear theological rationale for a social ministry to the poor and its impact on the worship of the Church. Although it is not always explicit, Calvin's Christology does govern his understanding of the role of the poor in the worship of the Church and how the poor are to be served. Calvin is concerned that his congregation understand that the place of the poor in the community life and worship of the Church derives from their role in the kingdom of God. They are ordained by God to receive the physical gifts of the Church as part of its ordinary service of worship. The presence of the impoverished is a divine test meant to reveal the quality of the spiritual life of the Church, especially that of the rich. According to Calvin, ministry to the poor authenticates the spiritual worship of the Church. To spend ecclesial resources on extravagant buildings, furnishings, vestments, and expensive ceremonies is nothing short of sacrilege, because with such priorities, the resources of the Church cannot furnish the needs of the poor. To neglect their needs is to neglect a spiritual ministry to Christ Himself. Thus Calvin's Christology judges the pride of the rich when they seek a life segregated from the ills of the poor. In Calvin's ecclesiology, the poor and

---

[163] Ibid.: Calvin makes a point in his *Commentary on Deuteronomy* 15:11: "For (as I have observed above) this is why the rich [*dives*] and poor [*pauper*] meet together, and the Lord is maker of them all; because otherwise the duties of charity would not be observed unless they put them to exercise by assisting each other." See *Commentary on Deuteronomy* 15:11 (Pringle, 158); *CO* 24, 699–700.

[164] My translation. *Sermon on Deuteronomy* 15:11–15; *CO* 27, 342: ". . . que c'est à mon nom qu'il est nourri, . . ."

the rich are joined together in their mutual worship of Christ in order to manifest the spiritual economy of the kingdom.

Conclusion

By the sixteenth century, the affluence of the Church was evident everywhere. The landholdings and power of the Church extended to every corner of Western Europe. Monasteries became laden with the wealth and estates of their benefactors. The skyline of every major city in Europe was dominated by cathedrals filled with painted furniture, ornate sculptures, lavish tapestries, expensive paintings, and embellishments of gold and silver. By Calvin's day, the ruling ministers of the Church lived like aristocracy who acquired all the trappings of the social elite. Most bishops resided in homes that resembled palaces and enjoyed the indulgence of servants and the privileges, luxuries, and power of princes. All this grandeur lay in stark contrast to the squalid realities of the poor and indigent. According to Calvin, the Church appeared to be more concerned with its elaborate ceremonies and magnificent displays of wealth than in going about its business of ministering to the needs of the poor.

The fundamental problem, according to Calvin, was an inadequate understanding of worship. According to Calvin, a proper understanding of worship is illumined only by a proper understanding of Christ and the Church. This chapter has examined a selection of Calvin's writings to uncover his understanding of poverty, wealth, pomp, and simplicity and how these affect his theology of worship. The thesis which this chapter has argued is that Calvin makes a theological connection between the role of poverty in his Christology and the role of poverty in his ecclesiology, which guides his theology of worship. Just as Christ's poverty and simplicity acted to reveal spiritual reality, or mark that which is truly of God, so it is with the poverty and simplicity of the Church. Calvin's teaching of a poor and afflicted Christ fueled his criticism against the deficiencies of Roman ecclesiology that contribute to the degeneration of true spiritual worship. This chapter has demonstrated this conclusion in several ways.

First, Calvin believes that true spiritual worship ought to be characterized by simplicity and a lack of expense. Calvin reasons from his Christology. True spiritual worship must be simple outwardly because Christ is no longer physically present. Christ is present with His Church spiritually, through His power and grace; therefore, the worship of the Church ought to reflect Christ's spiritual presence through its simplicity. Furthermore, true spiritual worship must be simple because elaborate pomp and ceremony obscure the message of the Gospel and bury Christ. Calvin argues that pomp and extravagant ceremony consign the Church to a time before the coming of the gospel in Jesus Christ, that is, back to the time of Judaism where people lacked the clarity of doctrine found in Christ. Because elaborate ceremonies turn the Church toward the symbols of the Old Covenant, they cling to what Calvin calls the "shadows of the Gospel." These shadows reveal Christ absent, thus act to obscure the spiritual presence of Christ. Calvin claims that is only when the Church is free of extravagant pageantry and proclaims the gospel in a simple manner can the spiritual nature of Christ's power and grace be properly revealed through its worship.

Second, Calvin firmly maintains that the true adornment of the Church does not consist of painted furniture, ornate sculptures, lavish tapestries, and embellishments of gold and silver. Rather, the true adornment of the Church resides in its many children who are brought to faith by the power of the Spirit. Because Rome held that the marks of the Church are always apparent and observable and embodied in the Church hierarchy, the extravagant wealth of the Church is needed to display the glory of Christ's heavenly kingdom on earth. According to Calvin, this reasoning demonstrates gross error. Such logic transfers to the flesh what is spiritually spoken of Christ's kingdom. Christ's incarnation into afflicted and impoverished human flesh testifies to the spiritual nature of His kingdom and grounds the Church in the invisible and spiritual power and grace of Christ. Because the true nature of the Church is grounded in what is invisible, the true splendor of the Church does not rest in what is seen but in what is unseen. In the same way, Christ's splendor was spiritual and did not rest on what was seen. Instead, the glory of both the Church and Christ remains hidden from those who do not possess the eyes of faith.

Calvin does not wish to do away with all ceremony and adornment in worship. He strove to bring a corrective to the Church so that the ornaments and ceremonies befitting Christian worship would be characterized by modesty, piety, and reverence, acting to reveal Christ and not conceal Him. The two most important ceremonies in the Church, the sacraments of the Lord's Supper and baptism, use the simple and unadorned elements of water, bread, and wine. Because of their simplicity, Calvin argued, these elements do not act to obscure the gospel but instead reveal the invisible presence of Christ and His spiritual power and grace.

Third, since the adornment of the Church does not reside in the acquisition of superfluous possessions, Calvin calls ministers to imitate the poverty Christ exemplified. This poverty is described by Calvin as a life of humility and modesty. He reasoned that a minister should be granted only what is necessary for a frugal and simple subsistence according to the practice of the ancient Church. Yet this recommendation of poverty is more than just a way of dealing with the material world. It is a spiritual posture as well. The poverty exemplified by Christ was also a poverty of spirit that ministers of the gospel are to possess before God. It is a poverty that determines how ministers are to relate to others and affects their acquisition and use of their possessions. Finally, the poverty exemplified by Christ was something that He consecrated to cultivate humility and modesty among His ministers in order to reveal that His kingdom is not of this world.

Fourth, Calvin teaches that the result of true spiritual worship is a life of holiness. The person who is holy is the one who assists brethren in need. Calvin argues that the imposing array of ceremonies in the Roman Church run counter to a true life of holiness. Elaborate ceremonies not only confuse the things of the spirit with the things of the flesh, but they also consume resources that should be bestowed upon the poor, the act of true spiritual worship. Worship that is simple does not make this error. Calvin asserts that God will not overlook acts of true holiness confirmed by generosity to the poor.

Fifth, Calvin claims that God has ordained the poor to be served as part of the spiritual worship of the Church. In the treatment of the poor, Christ regards Himself as neglected or honored. When alms are given to the poor, Christ accepts them as given to Himself. Because Christ presents the Church with the opportunity to minister physically to Himself by way of the poor, then not to assist the needy, according to Calvin, is to commit sacrilege against the Son of God. The poor, then, come as a divine test, to awaken the Church spiritually. How the poor are treated reveals the spiritual character of the Church and authenticates its worship. This point finds that there is meaning in the way that God distributes wealth. Poverty is God's tool to probe the hearts of the rich and poor and to confirm true holiness. The poor, on the other hand, are not to resort to fraud, but are required to trust in God to meet their needs. The rich are obligated to consecrate their wealth to God and to oblige the poor as an act that validates their faith.

The poor, then, fill a special role in the kingdom, and therefore are essential to the worship of the Church. In the midst of poverty, God reveals the spiritual fitness of the rich and the poor, and determines whether the worship of the Church is acceptable. Only when the spiritual economy of the kingdom is in proper balance are the physical needs of the poor met.

Summary and Conclusion

THIS study was undertaken to explore the role of the concept of poverty in John Calvin's theology. To set Calvin's historical and theological context, Part One looks at the way in which the Church Fathers, the Church of the Middle Ages, and the Reformers theologically understood and articulated the spiritual implications of poverty and affliction. These chapters demonstrate two important points: first, that no singular interpretation of poverty dominates the history of the Church; and second, that the diverse range of ideas regarding poverty and affliction throughout the history of the Church directly relates to the Church's openness to reform and level of authentic spirituality. The diverse range of theological ideas about poverty was also determined by two factors: the use of Scripture to bring about spiritual reform and the place of the Church in the social, cultural, and economic setting of its day.

Chapter 2 examines the ideas of four Church Fathers regarding poverty: Clement of Alexandria, Cyprian, Chrysostom, and Augustine. It demonstrates that in spite of their differing situations and approaches to the issue of poverty, they have some common perspectives that also surface in the writings of Calvin. First, Clement of Alexandria, Cyprian, Chrysostom, and Augustine share a rejection of radical asceticism and embrace the idea that a person's property is a gift from God meant to be used to meet the needs of the poor. They teach that all wealth belongs to God and what belongs to God also belongs to the poor. Therefore, believers must be generous to the needy because not to do so is stealing what belongs to God. Second, these Church Fathers also agree that poverty and wealth themselves do not determine the quality of the Christian life for a believer. They merely provide opportunities that reveal the spiritual condition of one's heart by how a person responds to his or her circumstances.

Chapter 3 traces out the cultural and religious views concerning the way poverty and the poor were valued in the Middle Ages. The importance of this brief study is to show that the medieval religious and cultural understanding of poverty was far from static and to discuss the factors involved in the development of beliefs that Calvin and the Reformers either refuted or tried to reconstruct in their theology.

The first issue the medieval Church struggled to define concerned the poverty of Christ and His apostles and how this should be manifested in the Church and lived out in the Christian life. This was provoked by ecclesial tensions concerning the question of what role the physical world (or physical poverty) should play in the cultivation of spiritual poverty. The Benedictines, Franciscans, Pope John XXII, and the later heretical groups differed concerning their understandings of biblical poverty in the light of their particular social and historical circumstances. The result was a highly varied and relative notion of the relationship between physical poverty (voluntary or involuntary) and spiritual poverty.

The second issue that the medieval Church struggled to determine was the theological place of the poor in the kingdom of God. Since the time of the Church Fathers, the Church taught as part of the doctrine of sanctification that the poor were favored by God and that God promised to hear their prayers and vindicate injustices committed against them. Yet what began in the writings of the Church Fathers as an articulation of the promises of God to the poor living the Christian life ultimately came to buttress the merit system of salvation in the Middle Ages. It was up to Luther and the Reformers to purge the doctrine of merit from the doctrine of justification while properly upholding the spiritual position of the poor in the kingdom of God.

The third question that plagued the medieval Church was how to relate poverty to spiritual renewal in the Church or society at large. Depending upon historical circumstances, many in the Church effectively joined spiritual poverty to a life of physical poverty, whether voluntary or involuntary, to bring about spiritual change or renewal in the Church or the greater society. For example, the Benedictines interpret biblical poverty as humility and countered the abuse of power and violence in feudal society; the Franciscans interpret biblical poverty as physical poverty and challenged the sin of avarice in the new money economy. Similarly, when the Church resisted the call to integrate a form of moderation or simplicity into its lifestyle as an expression of its understanding of spiritual poverty, or when it accepted a completely spiritualized interpretation of biblical poverty, its spiritual vitality and openness to reform fell into decline. This pattern can also be witnessed in the decline of the Benedictines and the Franciscans as a force of reform in the Church, as well as in the rise of the heretical movement in the later Middle Ages.

Poverty is a topic more widely associated with the Middle Ages than with the Protestant Church or the Reformation. Yet along with the doctrine of salvation, the Reformers re-thought the biblical notion of poverty and the position of the poor in the kingdom of Christ and the Church. Chapter 4 of this study demonstrates that though the Reformers were united in their objection to monastic vows of poverty and the Roman understanding of poverty that supported the merit system of salvation, they vary in their theological understanding of poverty and its implications for the Church. For Luther, the poor are the evangelical faithful in the Church, those who hunger after God and desire to be filled with God's Word. In his theology of the cross, Luther calls the poor *Christians under the cross*. Luther's approach of spiritualizing poverty was an effective tool in combating the doctrinal errors of Rome. Nevertheless, his interpretation of the poor in Scripture was emptied of its socio-economic force, leaving Luther no biblical grounds to respond to the impoverished situation of the German peasants.

Unlike Luther, Zwingli uses the full socio-economic force of the poor in Scripture to judge the extravagant worship practices of the Roman Church, and in particular, to attack of the use of images in worship. He argues that Christ ordains the poor as the true images of God to receive the material honor of the Church. His view dignifies the poor while it keeps the worship of God free of extravagance. Calvin is clearly the beneficiary of Zwingli's thoughts on worship and the poor.

Melanchthon approaches the topic of poverty from the perspective of its influence on the Christian life. For Melanchthon, the most important question for the believer is not what to do with poverty or wealth in a believer's life, but rather concerns remaining obedient to the gospel. Melanchthon contends that if believers are concerned with obedience to the gospel, they will be patient in affliction and poverty, and generous in abundance and wealth. A Church that is obedient to the gospel will also relinquish its wealth and property if keeping these possessions compromises the message or the faithfulness of the Church to the gospel. Furthermore, Melanchthon recognizes that when believers learn humility and obedience to the gospel through adversity, they are instructed in their sinfulness and strengthened in their faith. Affliction and poverty, according to Melanchthon, are part of what it means to follow Christ and remain obedient to the gospel.

Even though Bucer's approach to poverty is more practically oriented than the approaches of Luther, Zwingli, and Melanchthon, his theological understanding of poverty is anchored by his Christology and understanding of the Church. Bucer calls the sufferings of believers the "cross of Christ." The poverty and afflictions of Christ are something in which believers participate, giving spiritual significance to their hardships. Thus, ministering to those in need is regarded by Bucer as giving to Christ himself. This association gives the poor a special role to play in the Church. Bucer considers ministering to Christ through the poor to be an act of corporate worship—not a practice to be left up to the judgment and generosity of individuals but an intentional ministry of the Church.

Chapter 5 examines Calvin's understanding of the right use of this world. It demonstrates that Calvin's ecclesiology guides both his critique of monasticism and his view of stewardship. Though Calvin's statements on monasticism do not carry the vitriolic tone of Luther's, his rejection of religious poverty is as absolute. Calvin compares the institution of monasticism of his day with the monasticism of antiquity. He accuses the former of introducing a "double Christianity" into the Church and thereby causing schism in the body of Christ. Calvin accuses these monks of breaking the communion of the Church embodied in the sacraments by setting up their own altars and teaching a second baptism, things that their predecessors of antiquity would not have done. In addition, their ascetic practices produced attitudes of pride and self-righteousness rather than the humility that characterizes spiritual poverty and acts of service toward the needy.

Calvin rejects asceticism not only because he believes creation is a good gift from God but also because he saw that such lifestyle binds people's consciences beyond the requirements of the Word. Because vows of poverty place obligations upon people not found in the Word, Calvin argues that they run the risk of creating a "self-made religion," a true threat to both the Christian life and the Church. Instead, Calvin embraces an ethic of moderation which is expressed in an aesthetic of simplicity. This frees the conscience to use the things of this world without guilt. It enables the believer to bestow their material blessings upon the needs of others while it protects the believer from "wanton intemperance." In addition, this chapter shows that Calvin's perspective on stewardship is rooted in his ecclesiology, and more specifically, his theology of worship. Alms received as part of the Church's worship meet the needs of the poor; this is a generous response of the Church in gratitude to God for its material blessings. These alms, distributed through the ministry of the Genevan diaconate, fed the hungry, housed refugees, and cared for the orphan and the sick. All of this testifies to the effectiveness of Calvin's pastoral leadership and the extent to which his teachings impacted the reform and the social ministry of the Church in Geneva.

Summary and Conclusion 351

As a second-generation Reformer, Calvin had the benefit of reading the works of Luther, Zwingli, Melanchthon, and Bucer. He, too, rethought the biblical notion of poverty and the position that the poor had in the kingdom of Christ and the Church. Part Two of this study examines Calvin's understanding of poverty in light of his Christology, doctrine of the Christian life, and ecclesiology. It demonstrates that Calvin's thought on poverty is not only integrated into his understanding of these doctrines, but also that it is a decisive factor in each of these areas and is clearly exhibited in each one. In other words, the poverty and affliction of Christ is laid upon the Christian life as well as the life of the Church. Therefore, in Calvin's thought, poverty functions as a theological motif guided by his Christology.

An examination of the way Calvin understands poverty and impoverishment in conjunction with his Christology reveals the fundamentals of his convictions on this topic. Chapter 7 demonstrates that for Calvin, the poverty of Christ was an elected aspect of his incarnation, meant to serve a specific purpose: to reveal the divine nature of his kingship and mark the spiritual character of his kingdom. Wherever Calvin speaks about Christ's physical poverty and impoverishment or his lack of pomp, wealth, and display, he also discusses the nature of Christ's kingship or kingdom. Christ's poverty and impoverishment stand as visible proof that Christ is King of Israel. He is their Redeemer-King and Deliverer from sin, ruling from a cross and suffering an ignominious death. Therefore, Calvin's understanding of Christ's poverty and his interpretation of the atonement go hand in hand. Through his work as Redeemer, God consecrated poverty in Christ as a revelatory instrument by which God chooses to disclose to humanity the nature of true spirituality, godliness, and poverty of spirit. Knowledge of this consecration not only removes the offensiveness of Christ's poverty but also removes the offensive aspect of the poverty of all poor while it provides a sacred status for them in the divine economy of the kingdom. Finally, Calvin teaches that the sufferings of Christ are imprinted on the entire kingdom, leaving their mark upon the nature of the Christian life and the Church.

Wherever Calvin's Christological beliefs on poverty intersect his theology of the Christian life, the language of the cross emerges. Chapter 8 demonstrates that Calvin's doctrine of the Christian life was influenced by Christ's suffering when he discusses what it means for the believer to bear the cross. Cross bearing, in Calvin's thought, is a theological description for the way poverty and affliction benefit a believer's spirituality. It pertains to the manner in which a believer endures the experiences of hardship.

The experience of poverty and affliction for the Christian is consecrated in the life and death of Christ in such a way that these experiences are now essential instruments of divine grace and blessing. Believers can experience God's grace in the midst of their troubles because poverty challenges the kind of self-confidence which hinders self doubt and humility. This revelation of a true knowledge of self allows the Holy Spirit to work, driving believers to flee to Christ where they can receive aid for their ailing consciences in the grace of his cross. When this communion with Christ and experience of his grace occurs, the impoverishment of believers takes on a sacramental dimension because it presents opportunities for a knowledge of God's glory to be revealed. Calvin regarded this outcome as the prime reason for bearing the cross. Poverty and afflictions in the lives of believers serve the kingdom of Christ by the way they manifest a knowledge of God's glory. When people willingly bear the cross they act by faith, demonstrating that they have grasped Christ and his grace which gives spiritual value to their hardships. Poverty and afflictions, then, serve as God's self-revealing instruments. If a person undergoing the hardship willingly bears the burden of the cross, then the Holy Spirit can conform such a person to Christ's example, revealing a knowledge of God's glory, and thus their impoverishment becomes an instrument of divine grace and blessing.

Chapter 9 demonstrates that Calvin makes a theological connection between the poverty and affliction of Christ and the suffering experienced by the Church. The Church is the expression of Christ's kingdom on earth; therefore, what is true for Christ's kingship is carried over to the Church. The trials of the Church are the way God enables the Church to participate in the humiliation of Christ's cross. The impoverishment of bearing the cross awakens the people of God to their sin and reveals the judgments of God. This awakening results in spiritual purification and a renewal of the spiritual lives of those within the Church, which in turn brings the Church to testify to the power of God. The more that the Church is crushed beneath the cross of afflictions, the more God's power is revealed in raising it up again. God's power is revealed because poverty and afflictions strip away all false assurances and bring believers to rest alone in the grace of God's strength and promises. This dependence upon God's grace preserves the Church in the midst of its suffering and marks the Church as true because it testifies to the power and grace of God. This preservation of the Church not only demonstrates that God wills the Church to continue as long as Christ reigns, but it also magnifies the power of God by displaying the royal dignity of Christ crucified because it displays the faithfulness of the Church amidst the poverty and affliction of the cross. Therefore, the experience of the cross plays a critical role in the life of the Church. The true Church of God is made of those who follow Christ. All those who follow Christ will be led to a cross. Calvin maintains that being led to the cross is the ordained purpose of the Church while it remains in this world. Just as the afflictions of Christ display his royal dignity by marking his kingship as spiritual and coming from God, so the poverty of the Church displays Christ's royal dignity by marking its nature as spiritual, thus revealing it to be the true Church of God.

Chapter 10 examines Calvin's understanding of poverty, wealth, pomp, and simplicity and how these affect his theology of worship. This chapter maintains that the poverty and simplicity of Calvin's Christology are carried into his ecclesiology by the way they inform and guide his understanding of worship. Just as Christ's poverty and simplicity acted to reveal the spiritual nature of his kingship, or marked that he was from God, so it is with the poverty and simplicity of the Church. When Calvin asserts that worship in the Church needs to be simple, he means that worship must be devoid of pomp, lacking in display of wealth and magnificent ceremony. True spiritual worship needs to be simple because Christ is no longer physically present. Since Christ is now present with his Church only spiritually, the worship of the Church should reflect this through its simplicity. Calvin argues that extravagant pomp and show transfer to the flesh what is spiritually spoken about Christ's kingdom and consign the Church to a time before the revelation of the gospel in Jesus Christ, that is, back to the time of Judaism when God's people were without a knowledge of God the Redeemer in Christ. For Calvin, elaborate pomp and ceremony obscure the clear message of the gospel and bury Christ by turning the Church toward the symbols of the Old Covenant—symbols that represent Christ absent and do not bear witness to his presence. Calvin argues that it is only when the Church is free of extravagant pomp and elaborate ceremony and proclaims the gospel in a simple manner does it properly reveal the spiritual power and grace of Christ in its worship.

This chapter also demonstrates that Calvin's opposition to elaborate worship is also related to his concern for the poor. He instructs that the resources of the Church be spent not on magnificent worship but instead on the needs of the poor. Because Christ is no longer physically present on earth, he has ordained that the poor receive what would otherwise be bestowed on him. According to Calvin, decorations and ceremonies which consume the resources that should be bestowed on the poor as a proper display of true worship are really bestowed in error. God places the Son of God before the Church through the poor. In the poor and needy, Christ regards himself as neglected or honored. Thus to ignore the needs of the poor is tantamount to committing sacrilege against the Son of God. The presence of the poor in the Church, for Calvin, comes as a divine test to probe the hearts of believers and authenticate the worship of the Church.

Calvin's understanding of poverty is indeed directed and guided by his Christology. At the core of his theology of poverty, as it is expressed in his doctrine of the Christian life and the Church, stands a poor and afflicted Christ—a King who reigns over his spiritual kingdom from the affliction of the cross. Thus, Calvin did not discard what many might perceive to be an historic Catholic doctrine. Instead, he wove his Christological understanding of poverty throughout his theology in order to guide the Church in its proper worship of God and its reform.

Bibliography

Primary Sources

Aquinas, St. Thomas. *Summa Theologiae.* Vol 53. Translated by Samuel Parsons and Manuel Pinheiro. New York: McGraw-Hill, 1971.

Augustine. *Commentary on the Lord's Sermon on the Mount with Seventeen Related Sermons.* Fathers of the Church 11. Translated by Denis J. Kavanagh. New York: Fathers of the Church Inc., 1951.

———. *Letters: 131–164.* Fathers of the Church 20. Translated by Sister Wilfrid Parsons. New York: Fathers of the Church, 1953.

———. *Commentary on the Lord's Sermon on the Mount with Seventeen Related Sermons.* Fathers of the Church 11. Translated by Dennis J. Kavanaugh. New York: Fathers of the Church, 1951.

———. *Confessions.* Fathers of the Church 21. Translated by Vernon J. Bourke. New York: Fathers of the Church, 1953.

Bucer, Martin. "*De Regno Christi.*" In *Melanchthon and Bucer.* Translated by Wilhelm Pauck. Edited by Paul Larkin. The Library of Christian Classics. Philadelphia: Westminster, 1969.

———. *De Regno Christi.* Martini Bvceri Opera Latina 15b. Edited by François Wendel. Paris: Presses Universitaires de France, 1955.

———. *Du Royaume de Jesus Christ.* Martini Bvceri Opera Latina 15a. Edited by François Wendel. Paris: Presses Universitaires de France, 1954.

Calvin, John. *Opera Quae Supersunt Omnia, Corpus Reformatorum.* Edited by Guilelmus Baum, Eduardus Cunitz, and Eduardus Reuss. Brunsvigae: Wiegandt & Appelhans, 1863–1900.

———. *Opera Selecta.* Edited by Petrus Barth, Guilelmus Niesel et.al. Monachii in Aedibus: Kaiser, 1926–1952.

———. *Calvin: Theological Treatises.* Translated with introduction and notes by J.K.S. Reid. Philadelphia: Westminster, 1954.

———. *Calvin's Commentaries.* 22 vols. Translated by William Pringle. Calvin Translation Society, 1843; Reprint, Grand Rapids: Baker, 1989.

———. *Concerning Scandals* [*De Scandalis*]. Translated by John W. Fraser. Grand Rapids: Eerdmans, 1978.

———. *Calvin's Ecclesiastical Advice.* Translated by Mary Beaty and Benjamin W. Farley. Louisville: Westminster John Knox, 1991.

———. *Golden Booklet of the True Christian Life.* Translated by Henry J. Van Andel. Grand Rapids: Baker, 1952.

———. *Institutes of the Christian Religion.* The Library of Christian Classics 20-21. Translated by Ford Lewis Battles. Edited by John T. McNeill. Philadelphia: Westminster, 1960.

———. *Institutes of the Christian Religion 1536 Edition.* Translated and Annotated by Ford Lewis Battles. Grand Rapids: Eerdmans, 1975.

———. *Sermons from Job.* Translated by Leroy Nixon. Grand Rapids: Eerdmans, 1952.

———. *The Deity of Christ and Other Sermons by John Calvin.* Translated by Leroy Nixon. Grand Rapids: Eerdmans, 1950.

———. *Treatises against the Anabaptists and against the Libertines.* Translated and edited by Benjamin Wirt Farley. Grand Rapids: Baker, 1982.

Chrysostom, John. *On Wealth and Poverty.* Translated and introduced by Catharine P. Roth. Crestwood, New York: St. Vladimir's Seminary, 1984.

Clement of Alexandria. "The Rich Man's Salvation." In *Clement of Alexandria*, translated by G.W. Butterworth, 265–367. Loeb Classical Library 92. New York: Putnam, 1919.

Cyprian. *Treatises.* Translated and edited by Roy J. Deferrari. Fathers of the Church 36. New York: Fathers of the Church, 1959.

Luther, Martin. *D.Martin Luthers Werke.* Weimar: Böhlaus, 1883–1957.

———. *Luther's Works.* Edited by Jaroslav Pelikan, Helmut T. Lehmann et.al. Philadelphia: Fortress; St. Louis: Concordia, 1955–86

———. "The Heidelberg Disputation." In *Luther: Early Theological Works.* Edited and translated by James Atkinson. Philadelphia: Westminster, 1962.

Melanchthon, Philip. *Loci Communes 1543.* Translated by J. A. O. Preus. St. Louis: Concordia, 1992.

———. *Loci Communes Theologici.* Vol. 19, *The Library of Christian Classics: Melanchthon and Bucer.* Translated by Lowell J. Satre. Edited by Wilhelm Pauck. Philadelphia: Westminster, 1969.

Migne, J.-P. *Patrologiae cursus completus: Series graeca.* 162 vols. Paris: Migne, 1857–1866.

———. *Patrologiae cursus completus: Series latina.* 221 vols. Paris: Migne, 1844–1864.

Origen. *Contra Celsum.* Translated with an introduction and notes by Henry Chadwick. Cambridge: Cambridge University Press, 1953.

Zwingli, Huldreich. *Commentary on True and False Religion.* Edited by Samuel Macauley Jackson and Clarence Nevin Heller. Durham, NC: Labyrinth, 1981.

———. *Huldreich Zwinglis Sämtliche Werke.* Vol. 3, *Corpus Reformatorum.* Vol. 90. Zürich: Theologisher Verlag, 1982.

———. *Huldreich Zwingli's Werke: Der Deutschen Schriften.* Vol. 1. Edited by Melchior Schuler and Joh. Schultheß. Zürich: ben Friedrich Schultheß, 1828.

———. *Huldrych Zwingli Writings: The Defense of the Reformed Faith.* Vol. 1. Translated by E. J. Furcha. Allison Park, PA: Pickwick, 1984.

———. *Huldrych Zwingli Writings: In Search of True Religion: Reformation, Pastoral and Eucharistic Writings.* Vol. 2. Translated by H. Wayne Pipkin. Allison Park, PA: Pickwick, 1984.

Secondary Sources

Aland, Kurt. *Four Reformers: Luther Melanchthon, Calvin, Zwingli.* Translated by James L. Schaaf. Minneapolis: Augsburg, 1979.

Alves, Abel Athouguia. "The Christian Social Organism and Social Welfare: The Case of Vives, Calvin, and Loyola." *Sixteenth Century Journal* 20 (1989) 3–22.
Anderson, Marvin. "John Calvin: Biblical Preacher (1539–1564)." *Scottish Journal of Theology* 42 (1989) 167–81.
Armstrong, Brian G. "Response to Calvin's Conversion to Teachableness." In *Calvin and Christian Ethics: Papers Presented at the Fifth Colloquium on Calvin Studies*, edited by Peter DeKlerk, 79–82. Grand Rapids: Calvin Studies Society, 1988.
———. "The Nature and Structure of Calvin's Thought According to the Institutes: Another Look." In *John Calvin's Institutes: His Opus Magnum: Proceedings of the Second South African Congress for Calvin Research*, edited by B. J. Van der Walt, 55–81. Potchefstroom, South Africa: Potchefstroom University for Christian Higher Education, 1986.
———. "The Nature of French Protestantism." In *Calvin—France—South Africa: Papers Read at the Third South African Congress on Calvin Research Stellenbosch, 26–29 July 1988*, edited by A.D. Pont, 25–40. Pretoria: Kital, 1990.
Aubert, Jean-Marie. "Pauvres. Paureté: III Théologie." In *Catholicisme Hier Aujourd'hui Demain*. 10: 985–1001. Paris: Letouzey et Ané, 1985.
Augustijn, Cornelius. "Bucer's Ecclesiology in the Colloquies with the Catholics, 1540–41." In *Martin Bucer: Reforming the Church and Community*, edited by D. F. Wright, 107–21. Cambridge: Cambridge University Press, 1994.
Auksi, Peter. *Christian Plain Style: The Evolution of a Spiritual Ideal*. Montreal: McGill-Queen's University Press, 1995.
Avis, Paul D. L. *The Church in the Theology of the Reformers*. Atlanta: John Knox, 1981.
———. "The True Church in Reformational Theology." *Scottish Journal of Theology* 30 (1977) 319–45.
Backus, Irena. "Church, Communion and Community in Bucer's Commentary on the Gospel of John." In *Martin Bucer: Reforming the Church and Community*, edited by D. F. Wright, 61–71. Cambridge: Cambridge University Press, 1994.
Balke, Willem. *Calvin and the Anabaptist Radicals*. Translated by William Heynen. Grand Rapids: Eerdmans, 1981.
Bahmann, Manfred K. "Calvin's Controversy with Certain 'Half-Papists.'" *Hartford Quarterly* 5 (1965) 27–41.
Baker, J. Wayne. "Christian Discipline and the Early Reformed Tradition: Bullinger and Calvin." In *Calviniana: Ideas and Influences of John Calvin*, edited by Robert V. Schnucker, 107–119. Kirksville, MO: Sixteenth Century Essays and Studies, 1988.
Baron, Hans. "Franciscan Poverty and the Civic Wealth as Factors in the Rise of Humanistic Thought." *Speculum* 13 (1938) 1–37.
Bandstra, Andrew J. "Law and Gospel in Calvin and in Paul." In *Exploring the Heritage of John Calvin*, edited by David E. Holwerda, 11–39. Grand Rapids: Baker, 1976.
Barnard, P. Mordaunt, editor. *A Homily of Clement of Alexandria entitled Who is the Rich Man that is Saved?* London: Society for Promoting Christian Knowledge, 1901
Baron, Hans. "Franciscan Poverty and Civic Wealth as Factors in the Rise of Humanistic Thought." *Speculum* 13 (1938) 1–37.
Barth, Peter and Dora Scheuner. Introductory note to *Concerning Scandals*, by John Calvin. Translated by John W. Fraser. Grand Rapids: Eerdmans, 1978.
Battles, Ford Lewis. "Against Luxury and License in Geneva: A Forgotten Fragment of Calvin." *Interpretation* 19 (1965) 182–202. Reprinted in *Articles on Calvin and Calvinism*. Vol. 3, *Calvin's Work in Geneva*, edited by Richard Gamble, 198–218. New York: Garland, 1992.

———, editor and translator. *The Piety of John Calvin: An Anthology Illustrative of the Spirituality of the Reformer of Geneva*. Pittsburgh: Pittsburgh Theological Seminary, 1973.

———. "Calculus Fidei." In *Calvinus Ecclesiae Doctor*, edited by W. H. Neuser, 85–105. Kampen: Kok, 1980.

———. Introduction and indexes to *Institutes of the Christian Religion*, by John Calvin. The Library of Christian Classics 20–21. Edited by John T. McNeill. Philadelphia: Westminster, 1960.

———. "Notes on John Calvin, Justitia and the Old Testament Law." In *Intergerini Parietis Septvm (Eph. 2:14): Essays Presented to Markus Barth on His Sixty-fifth Birthday*, edited by Dikran Y. Hadidian, 23–37. Pittsburgh: Pickwick, 1981.

Benestad, J. Brian. "Chrysostom on Wealth and Poverty." *Diakonia* 24 (1991) 201–10.

Benoît, Jean-Daniel. *Calvin Directeur D' Ames Contribution A L' Histoire De La Piété Réformeé*. Strasbourg: Editions Oberlin Strasbourg, 1947.

———. *Calvin in His Letters: A Study of Calvin's Pastoral Counseling, Mainly from His Letters*. Translated by Richard Haig. Oxford: Sutton Courtena, 1991.

———. "Calvin the Letter Writer." In *John Calvin: A Collection of Distinguished Essays*, edited by G. E. Duffield, 67–101. Grand Rapids: Eerdmans, 1966.

———. "Pastoral Care of the Prophet." In *John Calvin Contemporary Prophet*, edited by Jacob T. Hoogstra, 51–67. Philadelphia: Presbyterian and Reformed Publishing, 1959.

Bergvall, Åke. "Reason in Luther, Calvin and the Sidney." *Sixteenth Century Journal* 23 (1992) 115–27.

Berkouwer, G. C. *Calvin and the Church*. Reprinted from *Free University Quarterly* 6.4 (1959) 247–52.

———. "Calvin and Rome." In *John Calvin Contemporary Prophet*, edited by Jacob T. Hoogstra, 185–96. Philadelphia: Presbyterian and Reformed Publishing, 1959.

Biéler, André. "Calvin and Capitalism." *Reformed and Presbyterian World* 26 (1960) 151–58.

———. *La Pensée Économique et Sociale de Calvin*. Geneva: Libraire de l'Université Georg, 1961.

———. *The Social Humanism of Calvin*. Translated by Paul T. Fuhrmann. Richmond: John Knox, 1964.

Bienvenu, Jean-Marc. "Préhistoire du Franciscanisme: Aspects pré-franciscains de l'érémitisme et de la prédication itinérante dans la France de l' Ouest, fin XIe et début XIIes." In *Poverty in the Middle Ages*, edited by David Flood, 27–36. Franziskanische Forschungen 27. Werl: Deitrich-Coelde, 1975.

Biller, Peter. "*Thesaurus Absconditus*: The Hidden Treasure of the Waldensians." In *The Church and Wealth*. Vol. 24, *Papers Read at the 1986 Summer Meeting and the 1987 Winter Meeting of the Ecclesiastical History Society*, edited by W. J. Sheils and Diana Wood, 139–60. Oxford: Blackwell, 1987.

Biot, François. *The Rise of Protestant Monasticism*. Translated by W. J. Kerrigan. Baltimore: Helicon, 1963.

Blockmans, Wim. "Circumscribing the Concept of Poverty." In *Aspects of Poverty in Early Modern Europe*, edited by Thomas Riis, 39–45. Stuttgart: Klett-Cotta, 1981.

Bolton, Brenda M. "The Poverty of the Humiliati." In *Poverty in the Middle Ages*, edited by David Flood, 52–59. Franziskanische Forschungen 27. Werl: Deitrich-Coelde, 1975.

———. "*Paupertas Christi*: Old Wealth and New Poverty in the Twelfth Century." In *Renaissance and Renewal in Christian History: Papers Read at the Fifteenth Summer Meeting and the Sixteenth Winter Meeting of the Ecclesiastical History Society*, edited by Derek Baker, 95–104. Studies in Church History 14. Oxford: Blackwell, 1977.

Bosl, Karl. *Armut Christi: Ideal der Mönche und Ketzer, Ideologie der Aufsteigenden Gesellschaftsschichten vom 11. bis zum 13 Jahrhundert*. Munich: Verlag der Bayerischen Akademie der Wissenschaften, 1981.

Botterweck, G. Johannes and Helmer Riggren, editors. *Theological Dictionary of the Old Testament*. Vol. 1. Translated by John T. Willis. Grand Rapids: Eerdmans, 1974.

Bouwsma, William J. "Calvin and the Renaissance Crises of Knowing." *Calvin Theological Journal* 17 (1982) 190–211.

———. "Humanism: The Spirituality of the Renaissance Humanism." In *Christian Spirituality: High Middle Ages and Reformation*, edited by Jill Raitt, 236–51. World Spirituality 17. New York: Crossroad, 1987.

———. *John Calvin: A Sixteenth Century Portrait*. New York: Oxford University Press, 1988.

———. "The Two Faces of Humanism: Stoicism and Augustianism in Renaissance Thought." In *Itinerarium Italicum: The Profile of the Italian Renaissance in the Mirror of Its European Transformations. Dedicated to Paul Oscar Kristeller on the Occasion of His 70th Birthday*, edited by Heiko Oberman and Thomas A. Brady Jr., 3–60. Studies in Medieval and Reformation Thought 14. Leiden: Brill, 1975.

Brady, Thomas A. "'You hate us Priests:' Anticlericalism, Communalism, and the Control of Women at Strasbourg in the Age of the Reformation." In *Anticlericalism in Late Medieval and Early Modern Europe*, edited by Peter A. Dykema and Heiko A. Oberman, 167–207. Studies in Medieval and Reformation Thought 51. Leiden: Brill, 1993.

Brändle, Rudolf. "Jean Chrysostome-L'Importance de Matth. 25:31–46 pour son Éthique." *Vigilae Christianae* 31 (1971) 47–52.

Breen, Quirinus. *Christianity and Humanism: Studies in the History of Ideas*. Grand Rapids: Eerdmans, 1968.

———. *John Calvin: A Study in French Humanism*. Hamden, CT: Archon, 1968.

Bromiley, Geoffrey W. "The Reformers and the Humanity of Christ." In *Perspectives on Christology*, edited by Maruerite Shuster and Richard Muller, 79–104. Grand Rapids: Zondervan, 1991.

Brown, F., S. R. Driver, and C. A. Briggs. *A Hebrew and English Lexicon of the Old Testament*. Oxford: Claredon Press, n.d.

Brummel, Bonnie Lee. "Luther and the Biblical Language of Poverty." *Ecumenical Review* 32 (1980) 40–58.

———. "Luther on Poverty and the Poor: A Study of Luther's Exegetical Understanding and Use of the Biblical Language of Poverty and the Poor." PhD diss., Columbia University, 1979.

Brümmer, Vincent. "Calvin, Bernard and the Freedom of the Will." *Religious Studies* 30 (1994) 437–55.

Bulman, James M. "The Place of Knowledge in Calvin's View of Faith." *Review and Expositor* 50 (1953) 323–29.

Burr, David. *Olivi and Franciscan Poverty: The Origins of the Usus Pauper Controversy*. Philadelphia: University of Pennsylvania Press, 1989.

———. "Poverty as a Constituent Element in Olivi's Thought." In *Poverty in the Middle Ages*, edited by David Flood, 71–78. Franziskanische Forschungen 27. Werl: Deitrich-Coelde, 1975.

Burrell, Sidney A. "Calvinism, Capitalism and the Middle Classes: Some Afterthoughts on an Old Problem." *Journal of Modern History* 32 (1960) 129–41. Reprinted in *Articles on Calvin and Calvinism*. Vol. 11, *Calvin's Thought on Economic and Social Issues and the Relationship of the Church and State*, edited by Richard Gamble, 171–84. New York: Garland, 1992.

Büsser, Fritz. "Bullinger as Calvin's Model in Biblical Exposition: An Examination of Calvin's Preface to the Epistle to the Romans." In *In Honor of John Calvin, 1509–64: Papers from the 1986 International Calvin Symposium McGill University*, edited by E. J. Furcha, 64–95. ARC Supplement. Montreal: Faculty of Religious Stuides, McGill University, 1987.

———."Elements of Zwingli's Thought in Calvin's Institutes." In *In Honor of John Calvin, 1509–1564: Papers from the 1986 International Calvin Symposium McGill University*, edited by E. J. Furcha, 1–27. ARC Supplement. Montreal: Faculty of Religious Studies, McGill University, 1987.

———. "The Zurich Theology in Calvin's Institutes." In *John Calvin's Institutes: John Calvin's Institutes: His Opus Magnum: Proceedings of the Second South African Congress for Calvin Research*, edited by B. J. Van der Walt, 133–47. Potchefstroom, South Africa: Potchefstroom University for Christian Higher Education, 1986.

Butin, Philip W. "John Calvin's Humanist Image of Popular Late–Medieval Worship." *Calvin Theological Journal* 29 (1994) 419–31.

Cadier, Jean. "Sadolet et Calvin." *Revue d'Histoire et de Philosophie Religieuses* 45 (1965) 79–92.

Campenhausen, Hans von. *The Fathers of the Greek Church*. Translated by Stanley Godman. New York: Pantheon, 1959.

Chadwick, Henry. "The Ascetic Ideal in the History of the Church." In *Monks, Hermits and the Ascetic Tradition: Papers Read at the 1984 Summer Meeting and the 1985 Winter Meeting of the Ecclesiastical History Society*, edited by W. J. Sheils, 1–23. Studies in Church History, 22. Oxford: Blackwell, 1985.

Chiappa, Paola Vismara. *Il Tema Della Povertà Nella Predicazione di Sant' Agostino*. Milano: A. Giuffre, 1975.

Chrisman, Miriam U. "Urban Poor in the Sixteenth Century: The Case of Strasbourg." In *Social Groups and Religious Ideas in the Sixteenth Century*, edited by Miriam Usher Chrisman and Otto Gründler, 59–67. Kalamazoo: Medieval Institute, Western Michigan University, 1978.

Christophe, Paul. *Les Pauvres et la Pauvreté: Ire Partie des Origines au XVe Siècle*. Paris: Desclée, 1985.

———. *Les Pauvres et la Pauvreté: IIe Partie du XVIe Siècle à nos jours*. Paris: Desclée, 1987.

Clark, Dorothy. "Erasmus and Zwingli's On the True and False Religion." In *Prophet Pastor Protestant*, edited by E. J. Furcha and H. Wayne Pipkin. Pittsburgh Theological Monography Series 11. Allison Park, PA: Pickwick, 1984.

Cocks, Nancy L. "Metaphors and Models in John Calvin's *Institutes of the Christian Religion*: A Feminist Critique." PhD diss., Toronto School of Theology, 1989.

Cohn, Norman. *The Pursuit of the Millennium*. Fairlawn, NJ: Essential, 1957.

Campenhausen, Hans von. *The Fathers of the Greek Church*. Translated by Stanley Godman. New York: Pantheon, 1959.

Compier, Don H. "The Independent Pupil: Calvin's Transformation of Erasmus' Theological Hermeneutics." *Westminster Theological Journal* 54 (1992) 217–33.

Constantelos, Demetrios J. *Poverty, Society and Philanthropy in the Late Medieval Greek World.* New York: Aristide D. Caratzas, 1992.

Cooper, David J. C. "The Theology of Image in Eastern Orthodoxy and John Calvin." *Scottish Journal of Theology* 35 (1982) 219–41.

Coulie, Bernard. *Les Richesses dans L'Oeuvre de Saint Grégoire de Nazianze: Étude Littéraire et Historique.* Louvain-la-Neuve: Universite Catholique de Louvain, Institut Orientaliste, 1985.

Countryman, L. William. *The Rich Christian in the Church of the Early Empire: Contradictions and Accommodations.* Texts and Studies in Religion 7. New York: Mellen, 1980.

Courvoiser, Jaques. "Bucer et Calvin." In *Calvin à Strasbourg 1538–1541*, 37–66. Strasbourg: Fides, 1938.

Davis, Natalie Zemon. "Poor Relief, Humanism, and Heresy: The Case of Lyon" In *Studies in Medieval and Renaissance History*, edited by William M. Bowsky, 217–69. Lincoln: University of Nebraska Press, 1968.

Deferrari, Roy J. Introduction to *Treatises*, by Cyprian. New York: Fathers of the Church, 1959.

Dent, C. M. "The Anabaptists." In *The Study of Spirituality*, edited by C. Jones, G. Wainwright, and E. Yarnold, 350–54. New York: Oxford University Press, 1986.

———. "Zwingli." In *The Study of Spirituality*, edited by C. Jones, G. Wainwright, and E. Yarnold, 346–49. New York: Oxford University Press, 1986.

Douglass, Jane Dempsey. "Calvin's Relation to Social and Economic Change." *Church and Society* 74 (1984) 75–81; Reprinted in *Articles on Calvin and Calvinism.* Vol. 11, *Calvin's Thought on Economic and Social Issues and the Relationship of the Church and State*, edited by Richard Gamble, 127–33. New York: Garland, 1992.

Dowey, Edward A. *The Knowledge of God in Calvin's Theology.* New York: Columbia University Press, 1952.

Duby, Georges. "Les Pauvres des Campagnes dans l' Occident Médiéval jusqu' au XIIIe siècle." *Revue D' Histoire de l' 'Église de France* 52 (1966) 25–32.

Edwards, Charles E., ed. *Devotions and Prayers of John Calvin.* Grand Rapids: Baker, 1954.

Eire, Carlos M. N. "Antisacerdotalism and the Young Calvin." In *Anticlericalism in Late Medieval and Early Modern Europe*, edited by Peter A. Dykema and Heiko A. Oberman, 583–603. Studies in Medieval and Reformation Thought 51. Quellen und Forschungen zur Reformationsgeschichte 46. Leiden: Brill, 1993.

———. "True Piety Begets True Confession: John Calvin's Attack on Idolatry." In *Calvin Studies IV: Papers Presented at a Colloquium on Calvin Studies at Davidson College and Davidson College Presbyterian Church*, edited by John H. Leith and W. Stacy Johnson, 105–133. Davidson, NC: Davidson College, 1988.

———. *War against the Idols: The Reformation of Worship from Erasmus to Calvin.* Cambridge: Cambridge University Press, 1986.

Engel, Mary Potter. "Calvin and the Jews: A Textual Puzzle." *Princeton Seminary Bulletin* 11 (1990) 106–23. Supplementary Issue.

Engem, John van. "Late Medieval Anticlericalism: The Case of the New Devout." In *Anticlericalism in Late Medieval and Early Modern Europe*, edited by Peter A. Dykema and Heiko A. Oberman, 19–52. Studies in Medieval and Reformation Thought 51. Leiden: Brill, 1993.

Eßer, Kajetan. "Die Armutsauffassung des hl. Franziskus." In *Poverty in the Middle Ages*, edited by David Flood, 60–70. Franziskanische Forschungen 27. Werl: Deitrich-Coelde, 1975.

Erbe, Michael. *Francois Bauduin (1520–1573) Biographie eines Humanisten*. Germany: Güttersloher Verlagshaus Mohn, 1978.

Farley, Ben W. "The Theology of Calvin's Tract Against the Libertines." In *Calvin Studies I*, edited by Leith and Raynal, 16–28. Richmond: Union Theological Seminary, 1982. Reprinted in *Articles on Calvin and Calvinism*. Vol. 5, *Calvin's Opponents*, edited by Richard Gamble, 206–18. New York: Garland, 1992

Farris, Allan L. "Calvin's Letter to Luther." *Canadian Journal of Theology* 10 (1964) 124–31.

Fenger, Anne-Lene. "Armut: A. Biblisch-historisch." *Neues Handbuch Theologischer Grundbegriffe*, edited by Peter Eicher, 1:66–77. Munich: Kösel, 1991.

Flood, David. "Armut und Erneuerung im Franziskanerorden. Zur Geschichte des Gentile von Spoleto." In *Poverty in the Middle Ages*, edited by David Flood, 79–83. Franziskanische Forschungen 27. Werl: Deitrich-Coelde, 1975.

―――. "Armut: VI Mittelalter." In *Theologische Realenzyklopädie*: 88–98. Berlin: de Gruyter, 1979., 88–98.

Forde, Gerhard O. *On Being a Theologian of the Cross: Reflections on Luther's Heidelberg Disputation, 1518*. Grand Rapids: Eerdmans, 1997.

Fowler, Stuart. "The Persistent Dualism in Calvin's Thought." In *Our Reformational Tradition*, edited by T. Van der Walt, 339–52. Potchefstroom, South Africa: Potchefstroom University for Christian Higher Education, 1984.

Foxgrover, David. "The Humanity of Christ: Within Proper Limits." In *Calviniana: Ideas and Influences of John Calvin*, edited by Robert V. Schnucker, 93–105. Kirksville, MO: Sixteenth Century Essays and Studies, 1988.

Frye, Roland M. "Calvin's Theological Use of Figurative Language." In *Calvin Studies IV: Papers Presented at a Colloquium on Calvin Studies at Davidson College and Davidson College Presbyterian Church*, edited by John H. Leith and W. Stacy Johnson, 73–94. Davidson, NC: Davidson College,1988.

Fuller, Ross. *The Brotherhood of the Common Life and its Influence*. Albany: State University of New York Press, 1995.

Gagg, Robert. "Calvins Brief an Sadolet als Warnung an uns Protestanten." *Reformatio* 16 (1977) 76–79.

Gamble, Richard C. "Brevitas et Facilitas: Toward an Understanding of Calvin's Hermeneutic." *Westminster Theological Journal* 47 (1985) 1–17.

―――. "Calvin's Theological Method: The Case of Caroli." In *Calvin: Erbe und Auftrag*, edited by Willem van't Spijker, 130–37. Kampen: Kok Pharos, 1991.

―――. "Current Trends in Calvin Research, 1982–1990." In *Calvinus Sacrae Scripturae Professor: Calvin as a Confessor of Holy Scripture*, edited by Wilhelm H. Neuser, 91–112. Grand Rapids: Eerdmans, 1994.

―――. "Exposition and Method in Calvin." *Westminster Theological Journal* 49 (1987) 153–65.

Ganoczy, Alexandre. "Calvin avait-il Conscience de Réformer L'Église?" *Revue d'Histoire et de Philosophie Religieuses* 118 (1986) 161–77.

―――. *Calvin Théolgien de L'Église et du Ministère*. Paris: Cerf, 1964.

―――. *Calvins handschriftliche Annotationen zu Chrystostom; ein Beitrag zur Hermeneutik Calvins*. Wiesbaden: Steiner, 1981.

———. *Ecclesia Ministrans: Dienende Kirche und Kirchlicher Dienst bei Calvin.* Ökumenische Forschungen. Ekklesiologische Abteilung 3. Freiburg: Herder, 1968.
———. "Ist Calvin der 'Vater des Kapitalismus'?" *Reformatio* 23 (1974) 416–25.
———. *The Young Calvin.* Translated by David Foxgrover and Wade Provo. Philadelphia: Westminster, 1987.
George, Timothy. "John Calvin and Menno Simons: Reformation Perspectives on the Kingdom of God." In *Calviniana: Ideas and Influences of John Calvin,* edited by Robert V. Schnucker, 195–214. Kirksville, MO: Sixteenth Century Essays and Studies, 1988.
Gilbreath, W. J. S. "Martin Luther and John Calvin on Property." *Evangelical Review of Theology* 11 (1989) 218–28.
Gingerich, Barbara Nelson. "Property and the Gospel: Two Reformation Perspectives." *Mennonite Quarterly Review* 59 (1985) 248–67.
Gisel, Pierre. *Le Christ De Calvin.* Paris: Desclée, 1990.
Gleason, E. G. "Baudouin, François (Baldwin)." *New Catholic Encyclopedia* 2:170. New York: Catholic University of America, 1967.
Goodloe IV, James C. "The Body in Calvin's Theology." In *Calvin Studies V: Papers Presented at a Colloquium on Calvin Studies at Davidson College and Davidson College Presbyterian Church,* edited by John H. Leith, 103–17. Davidson, NC: Davidson College, 1990.
Graham, W. Fred. *The Constructive Revolutionary: John Calvin and His Socio-Economic Impact.* Richmond, VA: John Knox, 1971.
Graus, Frantisek. "The Church and its Critics in Time of Crises." In *Anticlericalism in Late Medieval and Early Modern Europe,* edited by Peter A. Dykema and Heiko A. Oberman, 65–81. Studies in Medieval and Reformation Thought 51. Leiden: Brill, 1993.
Greef, Wulfert de. *The Writings of John Calvin: An Introductory Guide.* Translated by Lyle D. Bierma. Grand Rapids: Baker, 1993.
Greschat, Martin. "The Relation between Church and Civil Community in Bucer's Reforming Work." In *Martin Bucer: Reforming the Church and Community,* edited by D. F. Wright, 17–31. Cambridge: Cambridge University Press, 1994.
Gribomont, Jean. "Monasticism and Asceticism: Eastern Christianity." In *Christian Spirituality,* edited by Bernard McGinn and John Meyendorff, 89–112. World Spirituality 16. New York: Crossroad, 1985.
Grosclaude, Charles. *Exposition et Critique l'Ecclésiologie de Calvin.* Geneva: Kündig, 1896.
Gründler, Otto. "Devotio Moderna." In *Christian Spirituality: High Middle Ages and Reformation,* edited by Jill Raitt, 176–93. World Spirituality 17. New York: Crossroad, 1987.
Hall, Basil. "Martin Bucer in England." In *Martin Bucer: Reforming the Church and Community,* edited by D. F. Wright, 144–60. Cambridge: Cambridge University Press, 1994.
Hammann, Gottfried. "Ecclesiological Motifs behind the Creation of the 'Christlichen Gemeinschaften." In *Martin Bucer: Reforming the Church and Community,* edited by D. F. Wright, 129–43. Cambridge: Cambridge University Press, 1994.
Harkness, Georgia. *John Calvin: The Man and His Ethics.* New York: Holt, 1931.
Hazlett, Ian. "Calvin's Latin Preface to His Proposed French Edition of Chrysostom's Homilies: Translation and Commentary." In *Humanism and Reform in Europe,*

England and Scotland, 1400–1643: Essays in Honour of James K. Cameron, edited by James Kirk, 129–50. Cambridge: Blackwell, 1991.

———. "Eucharistic Communion: Impulses and Directions in Martin Bucer's Thought." In *Martin Bucer: Reforming the Church and Community*, edited by D. F. Wright, 72–82. Cambridge: Cambridge University Press, 1994.

Heller, Henry. *The Conquest of Poverty: The Calvinist Revolt in the Sixteenth Century*. Studies in Medieval and Reformation Thought 35. Leiden: Brill, 1986.

Helleman, Adrian. "The Contribution of John Calvin to an Ecumenical Dialogue on Papal Primacy." *One in Christ* 30 (1994) 328–43.

Hellmann, A. Wayne. "The Mendicants: The Spirituality of the Dominicans." In *Christian Spirituality: High Middle Ages and Reformation*, edited by Jill Raitt, 31–62. World Spirituality 17. New York: Crossroad, 1987.

Helm, Paul. "Calvin and Bernard on Freedom and Necessity: A Reply to Brümmer." *Religious Studies* 30 (1994) 457–65.

Henderson, R. W. "Sixteenth Century Community Benevolence: An Attempt to Resacralize the Secular." *Church History* 38 (1969) 421–28.

Hengel, Martin. *Property and Riches in the Early Church: Aspects of a Social History of Early Christianity*. Translated by John Bowden. Philadelphia: Fortress, 1973.

Hesselink, I. John. *Calvin's First Catechism: A Commentary*. Louisville: Westminster John Knox, 1997.

———. "Christ, the Law, and the Christian: An Unexplored Aspect of the Third Use of the Law in Calvin's Theology." In *Readings in Calvin's Theology*, edited by Donald McKim, 179–91. 1984. Reprint, Eugene, OR: Wipf & Stock, 1998.

———. "Governed and Guided by the Spirit—A Key Issue in Calvin's Doctrine of the Holy Spirit." In *Calvin Studies V: Papers Presented at a Colloquium on Calvin Studies at Davidson College and Davidson College Presbyterian Church*, edited by John H. Leith, 29–40. Davidson, NC: Davidson College, 1990.

———. "Law and Gospel or Gospel and Law? Calvin's Understanding of the Relationship." In *Calviniana: Ideas and Influences of John Calvin*, edited by Robert V. Schnucker, 13–32. Kirksville, MO: Sixteenth Century Essays and Studies, 1988.

Hickman, James T. "The Friendship of Melanchthon and Calvin." *Westminster Theological Journal* 38 (1976) 152–65.

Higman, Francis M. *The Style of John Calvin in His French Polemical Treatises*. Oxford: Oxford University Press, 1967.

Hillerdal, Gunnar. "Armut: 16.–20. Jahrhundert (ethisch.)" In *Theologische Realenzyklopädie* 4:98–121. Berlin: de Gruyter, 1979.

Hobbs, Gerald. "Martin Bucer and the Englishing of the Psalms: Pseudonymity in the Service of the Early English Protestant Piety." In *Martin Bucer: Reforming the Church and Community*, edited by D. F. Wright, 161–75. Cambridge: Cambridge University Press, 1994.

Hoitenga, Dewey. "Faith and Reason in Calvin's Doctrine of the Knowledge of God." In *Rationality in the Calvinian Tradition*, edited by Hendrik Hart, Johan van der Hoeven, and Nicholas Wolterstorff, 17–39. Christian Studies Today. Lanham, MD: University Press of America, 1983.

Holl, Karl. *The Cultural Significance of the Reformation*. Translated by Karl and Barbara Hertz and John H. Lichtblau. New York: Meridian, 1959.

Holler, Z. N. "Calvin's Exegesis of the Sermon on the Mount." In *Calvin Studies V: Papers Presented at a Colloquium on Calvin Studies at Davidson College and Davidson College*

Presbyterian Church, edited by John H. Leith, 5–20. Davidson, NC: Davidson College, 1990.
Hopf, Constantin. *Martin Bucer and the English Reformation*. Oxford: Blackwell, 1946.
Hordern, Richard. "Luther's Attitude Towards Poverty: Theology and Social Reform." In *Festschrift: A Tribute to Dr. William Hordern*, edited by Walter Freitag, 94–108. Saskatoon: University of Saskatchewan, 1985.
Hughes, Philip E. *The Register of the Company of Pastors of Geneva in the Time of Calvin*. Grand Rapids: Eerdmans, 1966.
Innes, William C. *Social Concern in Calvin's Geneva*. Pittsburgh Theological Monograph Series 7. Allison Park, PA: Pickwick, 1983.
Izard, Camille. "Jean Calvin à l'Écoute de Saint Bernard." *Etudes Théologiques et Religieuses* 67 (1992) 19–41.
Jackson, Samuel Macauley. *Huldreich Zwingli: The Reformer of Germany Switzerland, 1484–1531*. Heroes of the Reformation 5. London: Putnam, 1901.
Jaeger, Werner. *Humanism and Theology*. Aquinas Lecture 1943. Milwaukee: Marquette University Press, 1943.
Jansen, John Frederick. *Calvin's Doctrine of the Work of Christ*. London: James Clarke, 1956.
———. "Calvin on a Fixed Form of Worship—A Note in Textual Criticism." *Scottish Journal of Theology* 15 (1962) 282–87.
Johnson, Merwyn S. "Calvin's Handling of the Third Use of the Law and its Problems." In *Calviniana: Ideas and Influences of John Calvin*, edited by Robert V. Schnucker, 33–50. Kirksville, MO: Sixteenth Century Essays and Studies, 1988.
Kaiser, Christopher B. "Calvin's Understanding of Aristotelian Natural Philosophy: Its Extent and Possible Origins." In *Calviniana: Ideas and Influences of John Calvin*, edited by Robert V. Schnucker, 77–92. Kirksville, MO: Sixteenth Century Essays and Studies, 1988.
Kannengiesser, Charles. "The Spiritual Message of the Great Fathers." In *Christian Spirituality:Origins to the Twelfth Century*, edited by Bernard McGinn and John Meyendorff, 61–88. World Spirituality 16. New York: Crossroad, 1985.
Keesecker, William F. "The Law in Calvin's Ethics." In *Calvin and Christian Ethics: Papers Presented at the Fifth Colloquium on Calvin and Calvin Studies*, edited by Peter DeKlerk, 19–49. Grand Rapids: Calvin Studies Society, 1987.
Kempff, D. *A Bibliography of Calviniana: 1959–1974*. Studies in Medieval and Reformation Thought 15. Leiden: Brill, 1975.
Kennedy, Kevin Dixon. *Union with Christ and the Extent of the Atonement in Calvin*. Studies in Biblical Literature. New York: Lang, 2002.
Kingdon, Robert M. "Anticlericalism in the Registers of the Geneva Consistory 1542–1564." In *Anticlericalism in Late Medieval and Early Modern Europe*, edited by Peter A. Dykema and Heiko A. Oberman, 617–23. Studies in Medieval and Reformation Thought 51. Leiden: Brill, 1993.
———. "Calvinism and Social Welfare." *Calvin Theological Journal* 17 (1982) 212–30; Reprinted in *Articles on Calvin and Calvinism*. Vol. 3, *Calvin's Work in Geneva*, edited by Richard Gamble, 74–92. New York: Garland, 1992.
———. "Calvin's Ideas About the Diaconate: Social or Theological in Origin?" In *Piety, Politics and Ethics: Reformation Studies in Honor of George Wolfgang Forell*, edited by Carter Lindberg, 3:119–38. Kirksville, MO: The Sixteenth Century Journal, 1984. Reprinted in *Articles on Calvin and Calvinism*. Vol. 10, *Calvin's Ecclesiology: Sacraments and Deacons*, edited by Richard Gamble, 265–78. New York: Garland, 1992.

———. *Geneva and the Coming of the Wars of Religion in France 1555–1563.* Geneva: Droz, 1956.

———. "Peter Martyr Vermigli and the Marks of the True Church." In *Continuity and Discontinuity in Church History: Essays Presented to George Huntston Williams on the Occasion of His 65th Birthday,* edited by F. Forrester Church and Timothy George, 198–214. Studies in the History of Christian Thought 19. Leiden: Brill, 1979.

———. "Social Welfare in Calvin's Geneva." *American Historical Review* 76 (1971) 50–69. Reprinted in *Articles on Calvin and Calvinism.* Vol. 3, *Calvin's Work in Geneva,* edited by Richard Gamble, 22–42. New York: Garland, 1992.

———. "The Deacons of the Reformed Church in Calvin's Geneva." In *His Church and Society in Reformation Europe,* 81–90. London: Variorum Reprints, 1985. Reprinted in *Articles on Calvin and Calvinism.* Vol. 10, *Calvin's Ecclesiology: Sacraments and Deacons,* edited by Richard Gamble, 255–64. New York: Garland, 1992.

———. "Was the Protestant Reformation a Revolution? The Case of Geneva." In *Church, Society and Politics: Papers Read at the Thirteenth Summer Meeting and the Fourteenth Winter Meeting of the Ecclesiastical History Society,* edited by Derek Baker, 203–22. Studies in Church History 12. Oxford: Blackwell, 1975.

Kittelson, James. "Martin Bucer and the Ministry of the Church." In *Martin Bucer: Reforming the Church and Community,* edited by D. F. Wright, 83–94. Cambridge: Cambridge University Press, 1994.

Klassen, Peter James. *The Economics of Anabaptism, 1525–1560.* Studies in European History 3. London: Mouton, 1964.

Kolfhaus, W. *Christusgemeinschaft bei Johannes Calvin.* Neukirchen: Moers, 1939.

———. *Vom Christlichen Leben nach Johannes Calvin.* Neukirchen: Moers, 1949.

Kooi, Cornelius van der. "Within Proper Limits: Basic Features of John Calvin's Theological Epistemology." *Calvin Theological Journal* 29 (1994) 364–87.

Kramer, Rolf. *Umgang mit der Armut: Eine Sozialethische Analyse.* Berlin: Duncker & Humblot, 1990.

Kraye, Jill. "Moral Philosophy." In *The Cambridge History of Renaissance Philosophy,* edited by Charles B. Schmitt, 364–70.

Kristeller, Paul Oskar. "Humanism." In *The Cambridge History of Renaissance Philosophy,* edited by Charles B. Schmitt, 113–37. Cambridge: Cambridge University Press, 1988.

———. *Renaissance Concepts of Man and Other Essays.* New York: Harper and Row, 1972.

Lambert, Malcolm D. *Franciscan Poverty: The Doctrine of the Absolute Poverty of Christ and the Apostles in the Franciscan Order, 1210–1323.* London: SPCK, 1961.

———. *Medieval Heresy: Popular Movements from Bogomil to Hus.* New York: Holmes & Meier, 1976.

Lane, A. N. S. "Bernard of Clairvaux: A Forerunner of John Calvin?" In *Bernardus Magister,* edited by John R. Sommerfeldt. Spencer, MA: Cistercian Publications, 1992.

———. "Calvin's Sources of St. Bernard." *Archiv für Reformationsgeschichte* 67 (1976) 253–83.

———. "The City of God: Church and State in Geneva." In *God and Caesar,* 42–53. London: British Evangelical Council, 1973. Reprinted in *Articles on Calvin and Calvinism.* Vol. 10, *Calvin's Ecclesiology: Sacraments and Deacons,* edited by Richard Gamble, 140–51. New York: Garland, 1992.

Lane, Frank Peter. "Poverty and Poor Relief in the German Church Orders of Johann Bugenhagen, 1485–1558." PhD diss., Ohio State University, 1973.

Lazareth, William H. *Luther on the Christian Home.* Philadelphia: Muhlenberg, 1960.
LeClercq, Jean, François Vanderbroucke, and Louis Bouyer. *The Spirituality of the Middle Ages.* Translated by The Benedictines of Holme Eden Abbey, Carlisle. London: Burns and Oates, 1968.
LeClercq, Jean. "Aux Origines Bibliques Du Vocabulaire de la Pauvrete." In *Études sur l'Histoire de la Pauvreté: Moyen Age—XVIe siècle*, edited by Michel Mollat, 1: 35–43. Paris: Publications de la Sorbonne, 1974.
———. "Les Controverses sur la Pauvrete du Christ." In *Études sur l'Histoire de la Pauvreté: Moyen Age—XVIe siècle*, edited by Michel Mollat, 1:46–56. Paris: Publications de la Sorbonne, 1974.
———. "Monasticism and Asceticism: Western Christianity." In *Christian Spirituality: Origins to the Twelfth Century*, edited by Bernard McGinn and John Meyendorff, 113–31. World Spirituality 16. New York: Crossroads, 1985.
Leff, Gordon. "Heresy and the Decline of the Medieval Church." In *Religious Dissent in the Middle Ages*, edited by Jeffrey B. Russell, 99–114. New York: Wiley & Sons, 1971.
———. *Heresy in the Later Middle Ages: The Relation of Heterodoxy to Dissent c.1250–c.1450.* 2 vols. Manchester: Manchester University Press; New York: Barnes and Noble, 1967.
Leith, John H. *John Calvin's Doctrine of the Christian Life.* Louisville: Westminster John Knox, 1989.
Leithart, Peter J. "Stoic Elements in Calvin's Doctrine of the Christian Life: Part I: Original Corruption, Natural Law, and the Order of the Soul." *Westminster Theological Journal* 55 (1993) 31–54.
Lewis, Charlton T. *A Latin Dictionary.* Oxford: Clarendon, 1980.
Lindberg, Carter. *Beyond Charity: Reformation Initiatives for the Poor.* Minneapolis: Fortress, 1993.
———. "Luther on Property and Poverty." *Lutherjahrbuch* 57:251–53. Göttingen: Vandenhoeck & Ruprecht, 1990.
———. "Reformation Initiatives for Social Welfare: Luther's Influence at Leisnig." In *The Annual of the Society of Christian Ethics*, edited by D. M. Yeager, 79–99. Washington: Georgetown University Press, 1987.
———. "'There Should be no Beggars Among Christians': Karlstadt, Luther, and the Origins of Protestant Poor Relief." *Church History* 46 (1977) 313–34.
———. "Through a Glass Darkly: A History of the Church's Vision of the Poor and Poverty." *Ecumenical Review* 33 (1981) 37–52.
Linder, Robert D. "Calvinism and Humanism: The First Generation." *Church History* 44 (1975) 167–81.
Littell, Franklin H. "New Light on Butzer's Significance." In *Reformational Studies: Essays in Honor of Roland H. Bainton*, edited by Franklin H. Littell, 145–67. Richmond: John Knox, 1962.
———. "What Calvin Learned at Strassburg." In *The Heritage of John Calvin: Heritage Hall Lectures 1960–1970*, edited by John H. Bratt, 74–86. Grand Rapids: Eerdmans, 1973.
Little, A. G. *Studies in English Franciscan History.* Manchester: Manchester University Press, 1917.
Little, Lester K. "Evangelical Poverty, the New Money Economy and Violence." In *Poverty in the Middle Ages*, edited by David Flood, 11–26. Franziskanische Forschungen 27. Werl: Deitrich-Coelde, 1975.

———. L'Utilite Sociale de la Pauveté Volontairé." In *Études sur l'Histoire de la Pauvreté: Moyen Age—XVIe siècle*, edited by Michel Mollat, 1: 747–59. Paris: Publications de la Sorbonne, 1974.

———. "Pride Goes before Avarice: Social Change and the Vices in Latin Christendom." *American Historical Review* 76 (1971) 16–49.

———. *Religious Poverty and the Profit Economy in Medieval Europe*. Ithaca, NY: Cornell University Press, 1978.

Locher, Gottfried W. *Die Theologie Huldrych Zwinglis im Lichte seiner Christologie*. Studien zur Dogmengeschichte und systematische Theologie 1. Zürich: Attinger, 1952.

———. "The Theology of Exile: Faith and the Fate of the Refugee." In *Social Groups and Religious Ideas in the Sixteenth Century*, edited by Miriam Usher Chrisman and Otto Gründler, 85–92. Studies in Medieval Culture 13. Kalamazoo: The Medieval Institute Western Michigan University, 1978.

Loewenich, Walther von. *Luthers Theologia Crucis*, 4th edition. Munich: Kaiser, 1954.

———. *Luther's Theology of the Cross*. Translated by Herbert J. A. Bouman. Minneapolis: Augsburg, 1976.

Louth, Andrew. "Augustine." In *The Study of Spirituality*, edited by C. Jones, G. Wainwright, and E. Yarnold, 134–45. New York: Oxford University Press, 1986.

Lynch, Joseph H. *The Medieval Church: A Brief History*. New York: Longman, 1992.

Mackenzie, Ross. "The Reformed Tradition and the Papacy." *Journal of Ecumenical Studies* 13 (1976) 359–67.

Mangrum, Bryan D., and Giuseppe Scavizzi. *A Reformational Debate: Karlstadt Emser, and Eck on Sacred Images: Three Treatises in Translation*. Renaissance and Reformation Texts in Translation 5. Ottowa: Dovehouse, 1991.

Manteuffel, Tadeusz. *Naissance d'une Hérésie: les adeptes de la pauvreté volontaire au moyen âge*. Civilisation et sociétés 6. Paris: Mouton, 1970.

Marcel, Pierre. "The Humility of the Prophet." In *John Calvin Contemporary Prophet*, edited by Jacob T. Hoogstra, 21–38. Philadelphia: Presbyterian and Reformed Publishing, 1959.

Margolin, Jean-Claude. *Humanism in Europe at the Time of the Renaissance*. Translated by John L. Farthing. Durham: Labyrinth, 1989.

———. "La Notion de Dignité Humanaine selon Erasme de Rotterdam." In *Humanism and Reform in Europe, England and Scotland, 1400–1643: Essays in Honour of James K. Cameron*, edited by James Kirk, 37–56. Cambridge: Blackwell, 1991.

Marié, C. P. "Calvin, God and Humanism." In *Our Reformed Tradition*, edited by T. Van der Walt, 353–65. South Africa: Potchefstroom University for Christian Higher Education, 1984.

Maruyama, Tadataka. "Simple Lifestyle from the Perspective of Church History." In *Lifestyle in the Eighties: An Evangelical Commitment to Simple Lifestyle*, edited by Ronald J. Sider, 138–56. Exeter: Paternoster, 1982.

———. *The Ecclesiology of Theodore Beza: The Reform of the True Church*. Geneva: Librairie Droz, 1978.

Matheson, Peter. "Martin Bucer and the Old Church." In *Martin Bucer: Reforming the Church and Community*, edited by D. F. Wright, 5–16. Cambridge: Cambridge University Press, 1994.

McConica, James. "Northern Humanists Before the Reform." In *The Study of Spirituality*, edited by C. Jones, G. Wainwright, and E. Yarnold, 338–41. New York: Oxford University Press, 1986.

McDonnel, Kilian. *John Calvin, the Church and Eucharist*. Princeton: Princeton University Press, 1967.
McDonnell, Kilian. "The Ecclesiology of John Calvin and Vatican II." *Religion in Life* 36 (1967) 542–56.
McElrath, Hugh T. "Some Reformation Resources for Worship from John Calvin and His Circle." *Review and Expositor* 86 (1989) 65–75.
McFarlane, K. B. "Wyclif's Career." In *Religious Dissent in the Middle Ages*, edited by Jeffrey B. Russel, 114–22. Major Issues in History. New York: Wiley, 1971.
McGrath, Alister E. *A Life of John Calvin: A Study in the Shaping of Western Culture*. Oxford: Blackwell, 1990.
———. *Luther's Theology of the Cross: Martin Luther's Theological Breakthrough*. Oxford: Blackwell, 1985.
———. *Reformation Thought: An Introduction*. Cambridge: Blackwell, 1993.
———. *The Intellectual Origins of the European Reformation*. Cambridge: Blackwell, 1987.
McIndoe, John H. "John Calvin: Preface to the Homilies of Chrysostom." *The Hartford Quarterly* 5 (1965) 19–26.
McKee, Elsie Anne. "Calvin's 1536 Institutes: The Church's Book." In *Calvin Studies III: Papers Presented at a Colloquium on Calvin Studies at Davidson College and Davidson College Presbyterian Church*, edited by John H. Leith, 33–38. Davidson, NC: Davidson College, 1986.
———. "Context, Contours, Contents: Towards a Description of the Classical Reformed Teaching on Worship." *The Princeton Seminary Bulletin* 16 (1995) 172–201.
———. "Exegesis, Theology and Development in Calvin's *Institutio*: A Methodological Suggestion." In *Probing the Reformed Tradition: Historical Studies in Honor of Edward A. Dowey Jr.*, edited by Elsie Anne McKee and Brian Armstrong, 154–74. Louisville: Westminster John Knox, 1989.
———. *John Calvin on the Diaconate and Liturgical Almsgiving*. Geneva: Librairie Droz, 1984.
McLelland, Joseph C. "Renaissance In Theology: Calvin's 1536 *Institutio*—Fresh Start or False?" In *In Honor of John Calvin, 1509–1564: Papers from the 1986 International Calvin Symposium McGill University*, edited by E. J. Furcha, 154–74. Montreal: McGill University, 1987.
McNeill, John T. "John Calvin: Doctor Ecclesiae," In *The Heritage of John Calvin: Heritage Hall Lectures 1960–1970*, edited by John H. Bratt, 9–22. Grand Rapids: Eerdmans, 1973. Reprinted in *Articles on Calvin and Calvinism*. Vol. 10, *Calvin's Ecclesiology: Sacraments and Deacons*, edited by Richard Gamble, 109–18. New York: Garland, 1992.
———. "The Church in Sixteenth-Century Reformed Theology." *Journal of Religion* 22 (1942) 251–69. Reprinted in *Articles on Calvin and Calvinism*. Vol. 10, *Calvin's Ecclesiology: Sacraments and Deacons*, edited by Richard Gamble, 17–35. New York: Garland, 1992.
Meijering, E.P. *Calvin wider die Neugierdie: ein Beitrag zum Vergleich zwischen reformatorischen und patristischem Denken*. Nieuwkoop: De Graaf, 1980.
Melia, Pius. *The Origin, Persecutions, and Doctrines of the Waldenses*. London: Toovey, 1870.
Meredith, Anthony. "Clement of Alexandria." In *The Study of Spirituality*, edited by Cheslyn Jones, Geoffrey Wainwright, and Edward Yarnold, 112–15. New York: Oxford University Press, 1986.

Millet, Olivier. *Calvin et la Dynamique de la Parole: Etude de Rhétorique Réformée*. Paris: Champion, 1992.
Milner, Benjamin Charles. *Calvin's Doctrine of the Church*. Studies in the History of Christian Thought 5. Leiden: Brill, 1970.
Minnema, Theodore. "Calvin's Interpretation of Human Suffering." In *Exploring the Heritage of John Calvin*, edited by David E. Holwerda, 140–62. Grand Rapids: Baker, 1976.
Mollat, Michel. "En guise de Préface: Les Problèmes de la Pauvretè." In *Études sur l'Histoire de la Pauvreté: Moyen Age—XVIe siècle*, edited by Michel Mollat, 1:11–30. Paris: Publications de la Sorbonne, 1974.

———. "Hospitalité et assistance au début du XIIIe siècle." In *Poverty in the Middle Ages*, edited by David Flood, 37–51. Franziskanische Forschungen 27. Werl: Deitrich-Coelde, 1975.

———. "La Notion de la Pauvreté au Moyen Age: Position de Problèmes." *Revue D' Histoire de l' Église de France*, 52 (1966) 5–23.

———. "Pauvreté Chrétienne: III Moyen âge." *Dictionaire de Spiritualité: Ascétique et Mystique Doctrine et Histoire*, 12:648–58. Paris: Beauchesne, 1984.

———. "Poverty and the Service of the Poor in the History of the Church." In *The Poor and the Church*, edited by Norbert Greinacher and Alois Müller, 46–55. New York: Seabury, 1977.

———. *The Poor in the Middle Ages: An Essay in Social History*. Translated by Arthur Goldhammer. New Haven: Yale University Press, 1986.

———. "The Poor in the Middle Ages: The Experience of a Research Project." In *Aspects of Poverty in Early Modern Europe*, edited by Thomas Riis, 29–37. Stuttgart: Klett-Cotta, 1981.

———. "The Poverty of Francis: A Christian and Social Option." In *Francis of Assisi Today*, edited by Christian Duquoc and Casiano Floristán, 23–29. Concilium 149. New York: Seabury, 1981.
Moorman, John R. H. "The Franciscans." In *The Study of Spirituality*, edited by C. Jones, G. Wainwright, and E. Yarnold, 301–8. New York: Oxford University Press, 1986.
Morel, Maxine B. "Jacques Lefevre d'Etaples." *Iliff Review* 42 (1985) 43–48.
Mulhern, Philip F. *Dedicated Poverty: Its History and Theology*. New York: Alba House, 1972.
Müller, Gerhard. "Protestant Veneration of Mary: Luther's Interpretation of the Magnificat." In *Humanism and Reform in Europe, England and Scotland, 1400–1643: Essays in Honour of James K. Cameron*, edited by James Kirk, 99–111. Oxford: Blackwell, 1991.
Muller, Richard A. "The Hermeneutic of Promise and Fulfillment in Calvin's Exegesis of the Old Testament Prophecies of the Kingdom." In *The Bible in the Sixteenth Century*, edited by David C. Steinmetz, 68–82. Durham: Duke University Press, 1990.
Murray, Alexander. "Religion Among the Poor in the Thirteenth-Century France: The Testimony of Humbert de Romans." *Traditio* 30 (1974) 285–324.
Murray, Robert. "The Features of the Earliest Christian Asceticism." In *Christian Spirituality: Essays in Honour of Gordon Rupp*, edited by Peter Brooks, 63–77. London: SCM, 1975.
Nelson, Benjamin. *The Idea of Usury: From Tribal Brotherhood to Universal Otherhood*. Chicago: University of Chicago Press, 1969.
Nestingen, James Arne. "Challenges and Responses in the Reformation." *Interpretation* 46 (1992) 250–60.

Neuser, Wilhelm. "Calvin and the Refugees." In *Calvin—France—South Africa: Papers Read at the Third South African Congress on Calvin Research Stellenbosh, 26–29 July 1988*, edited by A.D. Pont, 1–10. Pretoria: Kital, 1990.

———. "Calvin's Conversion to Teachableness." In *Calvin and Christian Ethics: Papers Presented at the Fifth Colloquium on Calvin Studies*, edited by Peter DeKlerk, 57–77. Grand Rapids: Calvin Studies Society, 1987.

———. "Calvin's Teaching on the *notae fidelium*: An Unnoticed Part of the *Institutio* 4.1.8." In *Probing the Reformed Tradition: Historical Studies in Honor of Edward A. Dowey Jr.*, edited by Elsie Anne McKee and Brian G. Armstrong, 79–95. Louisville: Westminster John Knox, 1989.

Niesel, Wilhelm. *The Theology of John Calvin*. Translated by Harold Knight. London: Lutterworth, 1956.

Nobel, T. A. "Our Knowledge of God According to John Calvin." *Evangelical Quarterly* 54 (1982) 2–13.

Nottingham, William Jesse. "The Social Ethics of Martin Bucer." PhD diss., Columbia University, 1962.

Oberman, Heiko A. "Europa Afflicta: The Reformation of the Refugees." *Archiv für Reformationsgeschichte* 83 (1992) 91–111.

———. "Initia Calvini: The Matrix of Calvin's Reformation." In *Calvinus Sacrae Scripturae Professor*, edited by Wilhelm H. Neuser. Grand Rapids: Eerdmans, 1994.

———. *The Dawn of the Reformation: Essays in Late Medieval and Early Reformation Thought*. Grand Rapids: Eerdmans, 1992.

———. "The Pursuit of Happiness: Calvin between Humanism and Reformation." In *Humanity and Divinity in Renaissance and Reformation: Essays in Honor of Charles Trinkaus*, edited by John O'Mally, Thomas M. Izbicki and Gerald Christianson, 251–83. Studies in the History of Christianity. Leiden: Brill, 1993.

O'Brien, George. *An Essay on the Economic Effects of the Reformation*. Westminster: The Newman Bookshop, 1944.

Old, Huges Oliphant. "John Calvin and the Prophetic Criticism of Worship." In *Calvin Studies III: Papers Presented at a Colloquium on Calvin Studies at Davidson College and Davidson College Presbyterian Church*, edited by John H. Leith, 73–87. Davidson, NC: Davidson College, 1986.

———. *The Patristic Roots of Reformed Worship*. Zürcher Beiträge zur Reformationsgeschichte 5. Zürich: Theologischer Verlag, 1975.

Olin, John C, ed. *A Reformation Debate: John Calvin and Jacopo Sadoleto*. Grand Rapids: Baker, 1966.

Olson, Jeannine. "Calvin and the Diaconate." Liturgy 2 (1982) 78–83; Reprinted in *Articles on Calvin and Calvinism*. Vol. 10, *Calvin's Ecclesiology: Sacraments and Deacons*, edited by Richard Gamble, 242–47. New York: Garland, 1992.

———. "Calvin as Pastor-Administrator During the Reformation in Geneva." *Pacific Theological Review* 14 (1981) 10–17. Reprinted in *Articles on Calvin and Calvinism*. Vol. 3, *Calvin's Work in Geneva*, edited by Richard Gamble, 2–10. New York: Garland, 1992.

———. "Reformation and Revolution in Calvin's Geneva." *Halcyon* (1985) 93–103. Reprinted in *Articles on Calvin and Calvinism*. Vol. 3, *Calvin's Work in Geneva*, edited by Richard Gamble, 11–21. New York: Garland, 1992.

———. *Calvin and Social Welfare: Deacons and the Bourse Française*. Selinsgrove: Susquehanna University Press, 1989.

———. "The Bourse Française: Deacons and Social Welfare in Calvin's Geneva." *Pacific Theological Review* (1982) 18–24; Reprinted in Articles on *Calvin and Calvinism*. Vol. 10, *Calvin's Ecclesiology: Sacraments and Deacons*, edited by Richard Gamble, 248–54. New York: Garland, 1992.

Ozment, Steven. *The Age of Reform (1250–1550): An Intellectual and Religious History of Late Medieval and Reformational Europe*. New Haven: Yale University Press, 1980.

Paquier, Richard. *Traité de Liturgique*. Paris: Delachaux & Niestlé, 1954.

Parker, Charles H. "French Calvinist's as the Children of Israel: An Old Testament Self Consciousness in Jean Crespin's Histoire des Martyrs before the Wars of Religion." *Sixteenth Century Journal* 24 (1993) 227–48.

Parker, T. H. L. *Calvin's New Testament Commentaries*. Louisville: Westminster John Knox, 1993.

———. *Calvin's Old Testament Commentaries*. Louisville: Westminster John Knox, 1993.

———. *Calvin's Preaching*. Louisville: Westminster John Knox: 1992.

———. "Calvin the Biblical Expositor." *Churchman* 78 (1964) 23–31.

———. "Calvin the Exegete: Change and Development." In *Calvinus Ecclesiae Doctor*, edited by W. H. Neuser, 33–46. Kampen: Kok, 1980.

———. *Portrait of Calvin*. Philadelphia: Westminster, 1954.

———, editor and translator. *Sermons on Isaiah's Prophecy of the Death and Passion of Christ by John Calvin*. London : James Clarke, 1956.

———. *Supplementa Calviniana: An Account of the Manuscripts of Calvin's Sermons Now in Course of Preparation*. London: Tyndale, 1962.

———. *The Doctrine of the Knowledge of God*. Edinburgh: Oliver and Boyd, 1952.

———. *The Oracles of God: An Introduction to the Preaching of John Calvin*. London: Lutterworth, 1947.

———. "The Sources of the Text of Calvin's New Testament." *Zeitschrift für Kirchengeschichte* 73 (1962) 272–98.

Partee, Charles. "Calvin Calvinism, and Rationality." In *Rationality in the Calvin Tradition*, edited by Hendrik Hart, Johan van der Hoeven, and Nicholas Wolterstorff, 1–15. London: University Press of America, 1983.

———. "The Revitalization of the Concept of 'The Christian Philosophy' in Renaissance Humanism." *Christian Scholars Review* 3 (1973) 360–69.

Pasztor, Janos. "Calvin and the Renewal of the Worship of the Church." *Reformed World* 40 (1988) 910–17.

Pater, Calvin Augustine. "Calvin, the Jews and the Judaic Legacy." In *In Honor of John Calvin, 1509–64: Papers from the 1986 International Calvin Symposium McGill University*, edited by E. J. Furcha, 256–95. ARC Supplement 3. Montreal: McGill University, 1987.

Paul, J. "Les Franciscains et la Pauvreté aux XIIIe et XIVe Siècles." *Revue d'Histoire de l'Église de France* 52 (1966) 3–37.

Payton, James R. "Calvin and the Legitimation of Icons: His Treatment of the Seventh Ecumenical Council." *Archive für Reformationsgeschichte* 84 (1993) 222–41.

———. "History as Rhetorical Weapon: Christian Humanism in Calvin's Reply to Sadoleto, 1539." In *In Honor of John Calvin, 1509–64: Papers from the 1986 International Calvin Symposium McGill University*, edited by E. J. Furcha, 96–132. ARC Supplement 3. Montreal: McGill University, 1987.

Paulsell, William O. "The Use of Bernard of Clairvaux in Reformation Preaching." In *Erudition at God's Service: Studies in Medieval Cistercian History*, edited by John R. Sommerfeldt, 327–38. Kalamazoo, MI: Cistercian, 1987.

Pelkonen, J. Peter. "The Teaching of John Calvin on the Nature and Function of the Conscience." *The Lutheran Quarterly* 21 (1969) 74–88.
Perrot, Alain. *Le Visage Humain de Jean Calvin*. Geneva: Labor et Fides, 1986.
Peterson, Robert A. *Calvin's Doctrine of Atonement*. Phillipsburg, NJ: Presbyterian and Reformed Publishing, 1963.
Pipkin, H. Wayne. "The Nature and Development of the Zwinglian Reformation to August 1524." PhD diss., Hartford Seminary Foundation, 1968.
Potgieter, P. C. "The Providence of God in Calvin's Correspondence." In *Calvin: Erbe und Auftrag Festschrift für Wilhelm Heinrich Neuser um 65. Geburtstag*, edited by Willem Van't Spijker, 85–94. Kampen: Kok Pharos, 1991.
Potter, G. R., and M. Greengrass. *John Calvin*. New York: St. Martin's, 1983.
Potter, Mary Lane. "The 'Whole Office of the Law' in the Theology of John Calvin." *Journal of Law and Religion* 3 (1985) 117–39.
Praamama, L. *Calvijn*. Wageningen: Zomer en Keuning, 1953.
Puckett, David L. *John Calvin's Exegesis of the Old Testament*. Columbia Series in Reformed Theology. Louisville: Westminster John Knox, 1995.
Pullan, Brian. *Poverty and Charity: Europe, Italy, Venice, 1400–1700*. Brookfield, VT: Variorum, 1994.
———. *Rich and Poor in Renaissance Venice: The Social Institutions of a Catholic State to 1620*. Cambridge: Harvard University Press, 1971.
Quasten, Johannes. *Patrology*. Vol. 2. Westminster, MD: Newman, 1960.
Quere, France, and Gauthier Adalbert Hamman, eds. *Riches et Pauvres dans l'Église Ancienne*. Paris: Bernard Grasset, 1962.
Raitt, Jill. "Calvin's Use of Bernard of Clairvaux." *Archiv für Reformationsgeschichte* 72 (1981) 98–121.
Ramsey, Boniface. "Christian Attitudes to Poverty and Wealth." In *Early Christianity: Origins and Evolution to A.D. 600*, edited by Ian Hazlett, 256–65. London: SPCK, 1991.
Rapp, Francis. "Les Mendiants et la Société Strasbourgeoise à la fin du Moyenâge." In *Poverty in the Middle Ages*, edited by David Flood, 84–102. Franziskanische Forschungen 27. Werl: Deitrich-Coelde, 1975.
Reed, Antony C. "Melanchthon's 1521 Loci Communes: The First Protestant Apology." *Churchman* 85 (1971) 191–204.
Reid, W. Stanford. "Bernard of Clairvaux in the Thought of John Calvin." *Westminster Theological Journal* 41 (1978) 127–45.
———. "John Calvin, Early Critic of Capitalism (1) An Alternative Interpretation." *The Reformed Theological Review* 43 (1984) 74–78. Reprinted in *Articles on Calvin and Calvinism*. Vol. 11, *Calvin's Thought on Economic and Social Issues and the Relationship of the Church and State*, edited by Richard Gamble, 158–70. New York: Garland, 1992.
———. "Jean Calvin: The Father of Capitalism?" *Themelios* 8 (1983) 19–25. Reprinted in *Articles on Calvin and Calvinism*. Vol. 11, *Calvin's Thought on Economic and Social Issues and the Relationship of the Church and State*, edited by Richard Gamble, 199–206. New York: Garland, 1992.
Richard, Lucien. "John Calvin and the Role of the Church in the Spiritual Life." *Journal of Ecumenical Studies* 11 (1974) 477–500.
———. *The Spirituality of John Calvin*. Atlanta: John Knox, 1974.

Riis, Thomas. "Poverty and Urban Development in Early Modern Europe (15th–18th/19th Centuries) A General View." In *Aspects of Poverty in Early Modern Europe*, edited by Thomas Riis, 1–28. Stuttgart: Klett-Cotta, 1981.

Roth, Catharine P. Introduction to *On Wealth and Poverty*, by John Chrysostom. Crestwood, NY: St. Vladimir's Seminary, 1984.

Rott, Jean. "The Strasbourg Kirchenpfleger and Parish Discipline: Theory and Practice." In *Martin Bucer: Reforming Church and Community*, edited by D. F. Wright, 122–28. Cambridge: Cambridge University Press, 1994.

Rupp, Gordon. "The Spirituality of Luther and Calvin." In *Christian Spiritual Theology*, edited by Noel J. Ryan, 205–22. Melbourne: Dove, 1976.

Russel, S. H. "Calvin and the Messianic Interpretation of the Psalms." *Scottish Journal of Theology* 21 (1968) 37–47.

Ryan, John A. "Poverty." In *The Catholic Encyclopedia*. Vol. 12, 324–30. New York: Appleton, 1911.

Schaff, Philip. *The Creeds of Christendom: With a History and Critical Notes.* Vols. 1 and 3. New York: Harper and Brothers, 1877.

Scholl, Hans. *Calvinus Catholicus: Die Kaatholische Calvinforschung im 20. Jahrhundert.* Freiburg: Herder, 1974.

———. "The Church and the Poor in the Reformed Tradition." *The Ecumenical Review* 32 (1980) 236–56.

Schreiner, Susan E. "'Through a Mirror Dimly:' Calvin's Sermons on Job." *Calvin Theological Journal* 21 (1986) 175–93.

Schulze, Lud. *Calvin and 'Social Ethics': His Views on Property, Interest and Usury.* Pretoria: Kital, 1985.

———. "Calvin on Interest and Property—Some Aspects of His Socio-Economic View." In *Our Reformed Tradition*, edited by T. Van der Walt, 217–30. South Africa: Potchefstroom University for Christian Higher Education, 1984. Reprinted in *Articles on Calvin and Calvinism*. Vol. 11. *Calvin's Thought on Economic and Social Issues and the Relationship of the Church and State*, edited by Richard Gamble, 185–98. New York: Garland, 1992.

Schwöbel, Christoph. "The Creature of the Word: Recovering the Ecclesiology of the Reformers." In *On Being the Church: Essays on the Christian Community*, edited by Colin E. Gunton and Daniel W. Hardy, 110–55. Edinburg: T. & T. Clark, 1989.

Scribner, Bob. "Anticlericalism and the Cities." In *Anticlericalism in Late Medieval and Early Modern Europe*, edited by Peter A. Dykema and Heiko A. Oberman, 147–66. Studies in Medieval and Reformation Thought 51. Studies in Medieval and Reformation Thought. Leiden: Brill, 1993.

Seebass, Gottfried. "Calvin's Latin Preface to His Proposed French Edition of Chrysostom's Homilies: Translation and Commentary." In *Humanism and Reform in Europe, England and Scotland, 1400–1643: Essays in Honour of James K. Cameron*, edited by James Kirk, 113-50. Oxford: Blackwell, 1991.

Senarclens, Jacques de. *De la Vraie Eglise, Selon Jean Calvin.* Geneva: Éditions Labor et Fides, 1965.

Shewring, Walter. *Rich and Poor in Christian Tradition: Writings of Many Centuries Chosen, Translated and Introduced.* London: Burns, Oates & Washbourne, 1948.

Singer, C. Greg. "Calvin and the Social Order." In *John Calvin Contemporary Prophet*, edited by Jacob T. Hoogstra, 227–42. Philadelphia: Presbyterian and Reformed Publishing, 1959. Reprinted in *Articles on Calvin and Calvinism.* Vol. 11, *Articles on Calvin and*

Calvinism Calvin's Thought on Economic and Social Issues and the Relationship of the Church and State, edited by Richard Gamble, 143–57. New York: Garland, 1992.

Simpson, H. W. "Pietas in the Institutes of Calvin." In *Our Reformed Tradition*, edited by T. Van der Walt, 179–91. South Africa: Potchefstroom University for Christian Higher Education, 1984.

Smits, Luchesius. *Saint Augustine dans L'Oeuvre de Jean Calvin*. 2 vols. Assen: Van Gorcum, 1957.

Spalding, James C. "Discipline as a Mark of the True Church in its Sixteenth Century Lutheran Context." In *Piety, Politics and Ethics: Reformation Studies in Honor of George Wolfgang Forell*, edited by Carter Lindberg, 3:119–38. Kirksville: Sixteenth Century Journal, 1984.

Spearritt, Placid. "Benedict." In *The Study of Spirituality*, edited by C. Jones, G. Wainwright, and E. Yarnold, 148–56. New York: Oxford University Press, 1986.

Spijker, Willem van't. "Bucer's Influence on Calvin: Church and Community." In *Martin Bucer: Reforming Church and Community*, edited by D. F. Wright, 32–44. New York: Cambridge University Press, 1994.

———. "Bucer und Calvin." In *Martin Bucer and Sixteenth Century Europe*, edited by Christian Krieger and Marc Lienhard, 460–70. Studies in Medieval and Reformation Thought 53. Leiden: Brill, 1993.

———. "The Influence of Bucer on Calvin as becomes Evident from the *Institutes*." In *John Calvin's Institutes: His Opus Magnum: Proceedings of the Second South African Congress for Calvin Research*, edited by B. J. Van der Walt, 106–32. Potchefstroom, South Africa: Potchefstroom University for Christian Higher Education, 1986.

———. "The Influence of Luther on Calvin According to the *Institutes*." In *John Calvin's Institutes: His Opus Magnum: Proceedings of the Second South African Congress for Calvin Research*, edited by B. J. Van der Walt, 83–105. Potchefstroom, South Africa: Potchefstroom University for Christian Higher Education, 1986.

Spitz, Lewis W. *The Reformation: Material or Spiritual?* Problems in European Civilization. Boston: Heath, 1962.

———. *The Protestant Reformation*. Needham Heights, MA: Ginn, 1990.

Spinka, Matthew. "John Hus." In *Religious Dissent in the Middle Ages*, edited by Jeffrey Russell, 123–24. Major Issues in History. New York: Wiley & Sons, 1971.

Stahr, John S. "The Ethics of Calvinism." In *Essays on the Life and Work of John: In Commemoration of the Four Hundredth Anniversary of His Birth*, 85–100. Philadelphia: Reformed Church, 1909.

Stauffenegger, R. "Réforme, Richesse, et Pauvreté." *Revue D'Histoire de l'Église de France* 52 (1966) 47–58.

Steenkamp, J. J. "A Review of the Concept of Progress in Calvin's Institutes." In *Calvin: Erbe und Auftrag: Festschrift für Wilhelm Heinrich Neuser zum 65. Geburtstag*, edited by Willem van't Spijker, 69–76. Kampen: Kok Pharos, 1991.

Steinbicker, Carl R. *Poor Relief in the Sixteenth Century*. Washington, D. C.: Catholic University of America, 1937.

Steinmetz, David C. "Calvin and the Monastic Ideal." In *Anticlericalism in Late Medieval and Early Modern Europe*, edited by Peter A. Dykema and Heiko A. Oberman, 605–16. Studies in Medieval and Reformation Thought 51. Leiden: Brill, 1993.

———. "Calvin and the Patristic Exegesis of Paul." In *The Bible in the Sixteenth Century*, edited by David C. Steinmetz, 100–118. Duke Monographs in Medieval and Renaissance Studies 11. Durham: Duke University Press, 1990.

———. "The Reformation and the Ten Commandments." *Interpretation* 43 (1989) 256–66.
Stephens, Peter. "The Church in Bucer's Commentaries on the Epistle to the Ephesians." In *Martin Bucer: Reforming the Church and Community*, edited by D. F. Wright, 45–60. Cambridge: Cambridge University Press, 1994.
Stephens, W. P. *The Theology of Huldrych Zwingli*. Oxford: Claredon, 1986.
Stoker, H. G. "Calvin and Ethics." In *John Calvin Contemporary Prophet*, edited by Jacob T. Hoogstra, 127–48. Philadelphia: Presbyterian and Reformed Publishing, 1959.
Stone, Ronald H. "The Reformed Economic Ethics of John Calvin." In *Reformed Faith and Economics*, edited by Robert L. Stivers, 33–48. Lanham, MD: University Press of America, 1989.
Strand, Kenneth A. "John Calvin and the Brethren of Common Life." *Andrews University Seminary Studies* 13 (1975) 67–78. Reprinted in *Articles on Calvin and Calvinism*. Vol. 5, *Calvin's Opponents*, edited by Richard Gamble, 133–44. New York: Garland, 1992.
———. "John Calvin and the Brethren of Common Life: The Role of Strassburg." *Andrews University Seminary Studies* 15 (1977) 43–56. Reprinted in *Articles on Calvin and Calvinism*. Vol 5, *Calvin's Early Writings and Ministry*, edited by Richard Gamble, 193–206. New York: Garland, 1992.
Stroup, George W. "The Relevance of the Munus Triplex for Reformed Theology and Ministry." *Austin Seminary Bulletin: Faculty Edition* 98 (1983) 22–32.
Swanepoel, J. "Calvin as a Letter-Writer." In *Our Reformed Tradition*, edited by T. Van der Walt, 279–99. South Africa: Potchefstroom University for Christian Higher Education, 1984.
Tamburello, Dennise E. *Union with Christ: John Calvin and the Mysticism of St. Bernard*. Louisville: Westminster John Knox, 1994.
Tavard, George H. "Apostolic Life and Church Reform." In *Christian Spirituality: High Middle Ages and Reformation*, edited by Jill Raitt, 1–11. World Spirituality 17. New York: Crossroad, 1987.
Templin, J. Alton. "The Individual and Society in the Thought of John Calvin." *Calvin Theological Journal* 23 (1989) 161–77. Reprinted in *Articles on Calvin and Calvinism*. Vol. 3, *Calvin's Work in Geneva*, edited by Richard Gamble, 57–73. New York: Garland, 1992.
Tierney, Brian. *Medieval Poor Law: A Sketch of Canonical Theory and Its Application in England*. Berkeley: University of California Press, 1959.
Thouzellier, Christine. "Heresie et Pauvrete a la Fin du XIIe et au Debut du XIIIe Siecle." In *Études sur l'Histoire de la Pauvreté: Moyen Age—XVIe siècle*, edited by Michel Mollat, 1:371–88. Paris: Publications de la Sorbonne, 1974.
Todd, William Newton. "The Function of the Patristic Writings in the Thought of John Calvin." PhD diss., New York: Union Theological Seminary, 1964.
Tonkin, John. *The Church and the Secular Order in Reformation Thought*. New York: Columbia University Press, 1971.
Torrance, Thomas F. "Calvin and the Knowledge of God." *Christian Century* (May 27, 1964) 696–99.
———. *Calvin's Doctrine of Man*. Grand Rapids: Eerdmans, 1957.
———. "Knowledge of God and Speech about Him to John Calvin." *Revue d'Histoire et de Philosophie Religieuses* 44 (1964) 402–22.
———. *The Hermeneutics of John Calvin*. Monograph Supplements to the Scottish Journal of Theology. Edinburgh: Scottish Academic Press, 1988.

———, editor. *Tracts and Treatises on the Reformation of the Church by John Calvin.* Translated by Henry Beveridge. (Reprinted from 1844 ed.) Grand Rapids: Eerdmans, 1944.

———. "The Reformation and Economic Change." In *Capitalism and the Reformation,* edited by M. J. Kitch, 24–36. New York: Barnes & Noble, 1967.

Tripp, D. H. "Calvin." In *The Study of Spirituality,* edited by C. Jones, G. Wainwright, and E. Yarnold, 354–56. New York: Oxford University Press, 1986.

———. "Luther." In *The Study of Spirituality,* edited by C. Jones, G. Wainwright, and E. Yarnold, 343–46. New York: Oxford University Press, 1986.

Tugwell, Simon. "The Dominicans." In *The Study of Spirituality,* edited by C. Jones, G. Wainwright, and E. Yarnold, 296–300. New York: Oxford University Press, 1986.

———. "The Mendicants: The Spirituality of the Dominicans." In *Christian Spirituality: High Middle Ages and Reformation,* edited by Jill Raitt, 15–31. World Spirituality 17. New York: Crossroad, 1987.

Tylenda, Joseph H. "Calvin's First Reformed Sermon? Nicholas Cop's Discourse—1 November 1533." *Westminster Theological Journal* 38 (1976) 300–18.

———. "Calvin's Understanding of the Communication of Properties." *Westminster Theological Journal* 38 (1975) 54–65.

Vasey, Vincent R. *The Social Ideas in the Works of St. Ambrose: A Study on De Nabuthe.* Studia Ephemeridis Augustinianum 17. Rome: Institutum Patristicum Augustinianum, 1982.

Venter, W. "Calvin and Economics According to the Institutes." In *John Calvin's Institutes: His Opus Magnum: Proceedings of the Second South African Congress for Calvin Research,* edited by B. J. Van der Walt, 266–325. Potchefstroom, South Africa: Potchefstroom University for Christian Higher Education, 1986.

Verhey, Allen D. "Calvin's Treatise Against the Libertines." *Calvin Theological Journal* 15 (1980) 16–28. Reprinted in *Articles on Calvin and Calvinism.* Vol. 5, *Calvin's Opponents,* edited by Richard Gamble, 220–50. New York: Garland, 1992.

Violante, Cinzio. "The Pauvrete dans les Heresies du Xie Siecle en Occident." In *Études sur l'Histoire de la Pauvreté: Moyen Age—XVIe siècle,* edited by Michel Mollat, 1:347–69. Paris: Publications de la Sorbonne, 1974.

Vos, Arvin. "Calvin: The Theology of a Christian Humanist." In *Christianity and the Classics,* edited by Wendy E. Helleman, 109–18. New York: University Press of America, 1990.

Vos, Louis A. "Calvin and the Christian Self-Image: God's Workmanship, A Wretched Worm or a New Creature?" In *Exploring the Heritage of John Calvin,* edited by David E. Holwerda, 76–109. Grand Rapids: Baker, 1976.

Walchenbach, John Robert. "John Calvin as Biblical Commentator: An Investigation into Calvin's Use of John Chrysostom as an Exegetical Tutor." PhD diss., University of Pittsburgh, 1974.

Walker, G. S. M. "Calvin and the Church." In *Readings in Calvin's Theology,* edited by Donald K. McKim, 212–30. Grand Rapids: Baker, 1984. Reprinted in *Articles on Calvin and Calvinism.* Vol. 10, *Calvin's Ecclesiology: Sacraments and Deacons,* edited by Richard Gamble, 120–38. New York: Garland, 1992.

Wallace, Ronald S. *Calvin, Geneva and the Reformation: A Study of Calvin as Social Worker, Churchman, Pastor, and Theologian.* Grand Rapids: Baker, 1988.

———. *Calvin's Doctrine of the Christian Life.* Grand Rapids: Eerdmans, 1959.

Walt, A. G. P. van der. "Calvin on Preaching." In *John Calvin's Institutes: His Opus Magnum: Proceedings of the Second South African Congress for Calvin Research,* edited by B. J.

Van der Walt, 326–41. Potchefstroom, South Africa: Potchefstroom University for Christian Higher Education, 1986.

———. "John Calvin and the Reformation of Preaching." In *Our Reformed Tradition*, edited by T. Van der Walt, 192–202. South Africa: Potchefstroom University for Christian Higher Education, 1984.

Walt, J. L. van der. "John Calvin as a Person: A Few Arresting Aspects of His Life and Work." In *Our Reformed Tradition*, edited by T. Van der Walt, 155–75. South Africa: Potchefstroom University for Christian Higher Education, 1984.

Walton, R. C. "The Visible Church: A Mixed Body or a Gathered Church of Visible Saints, John Calvin and William Ames." In *Calvin: Erbe und Auftrag: Festschrift für Wilhelm Heinrich Neuser zum 65. Geburtstag*, edited by Willem van't Spijker, 168–78. Kampen: Kok Pharos, 1991.

Wandel, Lee Palmer. *Always Among Us: Images of the Poor in Zwingli's Zurich*. New York: Cambridge University Press, 1990.

Weaver, Rebecca H. "Wealth and Poverty in the Early Church." *Interpretation* 41 (1987) 368–81.

Wendel, François. *Calvin: The Origins and Development of His Religious Thought*. Translated by Philip Mairet. New York: Harper & Row, 1963.

Wevers, Robert F. *A Concordance to Calvin's Institutio 1559 Based on the Critical Text of Petrus Barth and Guilelmus Niesel*. Vols. 1–6. Grand Rapids: Digamma, 1992.

———. *Institutes of Christian Religion of John Calvin 1539 Text and Concordance*. vols.1–4. Grand Rapids: Meeter Center for Calvin Studies at Calvin College and Seminary, 1988.

Wilcox, Peter. "'The Restoration of the Church' in Calvin's 'Commentaries in Isaiah the Prophet.'" *Archiv für Reformationsgeschichte* 85 (1994) 68–96.

Willis-Watkins, David. *Calvin's Catholic Christology: The Function of the So-Called Extra Calvinisticum in Calvin's Theology*. Studies in Medieval and Reformation Thoughts. Leiden: Brill, 1960.

———. "Calvin's Prophetic Reinterpretation of Kingship." In *Probing the Reformed Tradition: Historical Studies in Honor of Edward A. Dowey Jr.* edited by Elsie Anne McKee and Brian G. Armstrong, 116–34. Louisville: Westminster John Knox, 1989.

———. "Persuasion in Calvin's Theology: Implications for His Ethics." In *Calvin and Christian Ethics*, edited by Peter DeKlerk, 83–94. Grand Rapids: Calvin Studies Society, 1987.

———. "The Second Commandment and Church Reform: The Colloquy of St. Germain-en Laye, 1562." *Studies in Reformed Theology and History* 2, no. 2 (1994) 1–80.

———. "The Unio Mystica and the Assurance of Faith According to Calvin." In *Calvin: Erbe und Aftrag*, edited by Willem van't Spijker, 77–84. Kampen: Kok Pharos, 1991.

———. "The Social Context of the 1536 Edition of Calvin's Institutes." In *In Honor of John Calvin, 1509–64: Papers from the 1986 International Calvin Symposium McGill University*, edited by E. J. Furcha, 133–53. ARC Supplement 3. Montreal: McGill University, 1987.

Winecoff, David K. "Calvin's Doctrine of Mortification." *Presbyterion* 13 (1987) 85–101.

Winslow, Donald F. "Poverty and Riches: An Embarrassment for the Early Church." In *Studia Patristica.*, vol. 18, pt. 2, edited by Elizabeth A. Livingstone, 317–28. Kalamazoo, MI: Cistercian, 1989.

Witters, D. Willibrord. "Pauvres et Pauvrete dans les Coutumiers, Monastiques du Moyen Age." In *Études sur l'Histoire de la Pauvreté: Moyen Age—XVIe Siècle*, edited by Michel Mollat, 1:177–215. Paris: Publications de la Sorbonne, 1974.

Wolter, Maurus. *The Principles of Monasticism*. Translated by Bernard A. Sause. St.Louis: B. Herder, 1962.

Woudstra, Marten Hendrik. "John Calvin's Concern for the Poor." *Outlook* 33 (1983) 8–10.

Wright, David. "Infant Baptism and the Christian Community in Bucer." In *Martin Bucer: Reforming the Church and Community*, edited by D. F. Wright, 95–106. Cambridge: Cambridge University Press, 1994.

Wyk, J. H. van. "Calvin on the Christian Life." In *Our Reformed Tradition*, edited by T. Van der Walt, 231–278. South Africa: Potchefstroom University for Christian Higher Education, 1984.

Wyneken, Karl H. "Calvin and Anabaptism." *Concordia Theological Monthly* 36 (1965) 18–29; Reprinted in *Articles on Calvin and Calvinism*. Vol 5. *Calvin's Opponents*, edited by Richard Gamble, 2–13. New York: Garland, 1992.

Young, Frances M. "John Chrysostom on First and Second Corinthians." In *Studia Patristica XVIII*, edited by Elizabeth A. Livingstone, 1:349 52. Kalamazoo, MI: Cistercian, 1985.

Yule, George. "Luther and the Ascetic Life." In *Monks, Hermits and the Ascetic Tradition: Papers Read at the 1984 Summer Meeting and the 1985 Winter Meeting of the Ecclesiastical History Society*, edited by W. J. Sheils, 229–39. Studies in Church History 22. Oxford: Blackwell, 1985.

———. "The Church in the Theology of the Reformers." *Journal of Ecclesiastical History* 34 (1983) 591–603.

Zimmermann, Gunter. "Die Vereinigung mit Gott und das Reich Christi nach Calvins 'Institutio.'" *Zwingliana* 18 (1990) 193–212.

———. "Geschöpflichkeit und Selbster-Kenntnis nach Johannes Calvin." *Evangelische Theologie* 48 (1988) 127–45.

Zimmerman, Jacquelyn A. K. "The Christian Life in Luther and Calvin." *Lutheran Quaterly* 16 (1964) 222–30.

www.ingramcontent.com/pod-product-compliance
Lightning Source LLC
Chambersburg PA
CBHW052139300426
44115CB00011B/1447